Mary Lonergan

Fodor's EXPLORING

BRITAIN

FODOR'S TRAVEL PUBLICATIONS

NEW YORK • TORONTO • LONDON • SYDNEY • AUCKLAND

WWW.FODORS.COM

Important Note

Time inevitably brings change, so always confirm prices, travel facts, and other perishable information when it matters. Although Fodor's cannot accept responsibility for errors, you can use this guide in the confidence that we have taken every care to ensure its accuracy.

Copyright © Automobile Association Developments Ltd. 1994, 1996, 1998, 2000, 2002

Ordnance Survey® This product contains mapping data licensed from Ordnance Survey® with the permission of the Controller of Her Majesty's Stationery Office. © Crown copyright 2002. All rights reserved. License number 399221.

All rights reserved under International and Pan-American Copyright conventions. Published in the United States by Fodor's Travel Publications, a unit of Fodors LLC, a subsidiary of Random House, Inc., and simultaneously in Canada by Random House of Canada Limited, Toronto. Distributed by Random House, Inc., New York. No maps, illustrations, or other portions of this book may be reproduced in any form without written permission from the publishers.

Published in the United States by Fodor's Travel Publications.
Published in the United Kingdom by AA Publishing.

Fodor's is a registered trademark of Random House, Inc.

ISBN 0-676-90175-1
Fifth edition

Fodor's Exploring Britain

Authors: **Tim Locke, Richard Cavendish, Barnaby Rogerson**
Accommodations and restaurants revised by:
Elizabeth Carter
Revision Verifier: **Tim Locke**
Cartography: **The Automobile Association**
Cover Design: **Tigist Getachew, Fabrizio La Rocca**
Front Cover Silhouette: **Catherine Karnow**

Special Sales

Fodor's Travel Publications are available at special discounts for bulk purchases (100 copies or more) for sales promotions or premiums. Special editions, including personalized covers, excerpts of existing guides, and corporate imprints can be created in large quantities for special needs. For more information, contact your local bookseller or write to Special Marketing, Fodor's Travel Publications, 280 Park Avenue, New York, NY 10017. Inquiries from Canada should be directed to your local Canadian bookseller or sent to Random House of Canada Ltd., Marketing Department, 2775 Matheson Blvd. East, Mississauga, Ontario L4W 4P7.

Printed and bound in Italy by Printer Trento srl
10 9 8 7 6 5 4 3 2 1

How to use this book

ORGANIZATION

Britain Is, Britain Was
Discusses aspects of life and culture in contemporary Britain and explores significant periods in its history.

A–Z
Breaks down the country into regional chapters, and covers places to visit, including walks and drives. Within this section fall the Focus On articles, which consider a variety of subjects in greater detail.

Travel Facts
Contains the strictly practical information vital for a successful trip.

Accommodations and Restaurants
Lists recommended establishments throughout Britain, giving a brief summary of their attractions.

ABOUT THE RATINGS
Most places described in this book have been given a separate rating. These are as follows:

▶▶▶   **Do not miss**

▶▶   **Highly recommended**

▶   **Worth seeing**

MAPS
To make each particular location easier to find, every main entry in this book has a map reference to the right of its name. This comprises a number, followed by a letter, followed by another number, such as 176B3. The first number (176) refers to the page on which the map can be found, the letter (B) and the second number (3) pinpoint the square in which the main entry is located. The maps on the inside front cover and inside back cover are referred to as IFC and IBC respectively.

Contents

How to use this book 4

Contents pages 5–7

My Britain 8

BRITAIN IS 9–22
Variety 10
Government 11
The British people 12–13
The economy 14
The pub 15
Gardens 16–17
Events 18–19
The industrial past today 20–21
The semidetached house 22

BRITAIN WAS 23–41
People and the landscape 24–25
Castles and manors 26–27
Churches and monasteries 28–29
Domestic architecture 30–31
Kings and queens 32–33
A maritime nation 34–35
Writers and places 36–37
Landscape artists 38–39
The Industrial Revolution 40–41

A–Z

London 42–59
Walks
Covent Garden, Royal London, and
Westminster 52–53
Along the South Bank to Tower
Hill 53

The West Country 60–85
Focus On
The north Cornish coast 68–69
The south Cornish coast 70–71
English place-names 81
Walks
West Country walks 64
Bath 66
Drive
Thomas Hardy country 76

6

Southern England 86–109
  Focus On
  Seaside resorts 94–95
  Houses of the Weald 102–103
  Walks
  Southern England walks 92
  Drive
  The Weald 106–107

The Heart of England 110–133
  Focus On
  The Cotswolds 118–120
  Ironbridge Gorge 123
  The canal system 128–129
  Walk
  Oxford walk 127
  Drive
  The Cotswolds 121

Eastern England 134–149
  Focus On
  The north Norfolk coast 142
  Preserving the landscape
    144–145
  East Anglian artists 149
  Walk
  Cambridge walk 139
  Drive
  Constable country 148

Wales 150–171
  Focus On
  The Valleys 156
  Welsh culture and politics
    160–161
  Walks
  Wales walks 158
  Drive
  Snowdonia National Park 170

Northwest England 172–189
  Focus On
  The Lake District 178–179
  Revitalizing the cities 184–185
  Port Sunlight 188
  Walks
  Northwest England walks 175
  Drive
  The Lakes 180–181

Northeast England 190–209
  Focus On
  The Brontës 198
  Walks
  Northeast England walks 193
  York city highlights 205
  Drive
  The Yorkshire Dales 207

Southern Scotland 210–233
  Focus On
  Clans and tartans 233
  Walks
  Southern Scotland walks 214
  Edinburgh walk 225
  Drive
  The (Scottish) Borders 217

Northern Scotland 234–262
  Focus On
  Bonnie Prince Charlie 246
  Highland land use 262
  Walks
  Northern Scotland walks 238
  Drives
  Loch Ness and the Black Isle 243
  Oban and Argyll 249

TRAVEL FACTS 263–274

ACCOMMODATIONS AND RESTAURANTS 275–284

Index 285–288

Acknowledgments 288

Maps and plans
Regions and 3-star sights IFC
London 42–43
London walks 52
The West Country 60–61
Bath walk 66
Thomas Hardy country drive 76
Southern England 86–87
The Weald drive 106
The Heart of England 110–111
The Cotswolds drive 121

Oxford walk 127
Eastern England 134–135
Cambridge walk 139
Constable country drive 148
Wales 150–151
Snowdonia drive 170
Northwest England 172
Lake District drive 180–181
Northeast England 190–191
York city highlights 205
Yorkshire Dales drive 207
Southern Scotland 210–211
The (Scottish) Borders drive 217
Edinburgh walk 224–225
Northern Scotland 234–235
Loch Ness and the Black Isle
drive 243
Relief map of Britain IBC

7

Tim Locke has contributed to _Boston and New England_, _Thailand_ and _Germany_ in the Fodor _Exploring_ series, as well as to other guides on Britain. Richard Cavendish—who wrote most of the Britain Is, Britain Was and Focus On features—has written numerous books on Britain. Travel writer Barnaby Rogerson, the author of _Exploring Britain_'s Scottish chapters, has contributed to a number of other books on Scotland.

My Britain

From my house in Sussex I can look upon Lewes Castle, an administrative headquarters set up in Norman times. The town's main thoroughfare slopes down between numerous Georgianized half-timbered buildings, past the White Hart Hotel—where Tom Paine held meetings in the 18th century—to family-run Harvey's brewery, little changed in over a hundred years. A short walk away are the sheep-grazed slopes of the South Downs, dotted with ancient remains. On one slope is the site of the Battle of Lewes, where in 1264 Simon de Montfort defeated Henry III, forcing him to grant rights that paved the way for parliamentary democracy.

I find this sense of continuum an impressive aspect of Britain: its landscapes, both rural and urban, pockmarked with historical incident. I sometimes wonder what else would strike me about Britain if I had never seen it before. I imagine being confronted with a series of cameos: a sheep auction in Mid Wales, with cloth caps and ruddy Celtic faces in abundance; the landscapes of East Anglia, where the quality of light imparts subtle differences each time a view is encountered; a county cricket match at the spa town of Tunbridge Wells; or the hypnotic patter of a dealer at London's Brick Lane market.

Britain, as much as any other corner of the earth, has been much traveled in and much written about. This book is our selection of the most rewarding places in the kingdom. It doesn't include every city or attraction, but aims to be a balance between the well known and the less obvious.

It constantly surprises me that, in an age ever tending toward standardization, so many aspects of Britain have survived intact: its communities, its lifestyles, its idiosyncracies. The pressure to change is still there, but there has been a realization that we need our heritage as a point of reference to tell us who we are. It would take a great deal to erode that national persona.

Tim Locke

Britain

9

►►► **ABBREVIATIONS USED**

N.T. = *National Trust*
(see page 102)

E.H. = *English Heritage*
(see page 124)

Cadw = *Welsh Historic Monuments Commission (see page 167)*

H.S. = *Historic Scotland (see page 124)*

N.T.S. = *National Trust for Scotland (see page 102)*

Britain is by no means a uniform entity: the more you travel around this compact island, the more there is for you to see and enjoy. Within the boundaries of its 88 sq miles Britain shows an astonishingly rich variety of landscape, architecture, climate, regional accents and cuisine, cultural traditions, social make-up and economic activity.

10

Britain constantly reminds us that it is an island. Once a mighty naval power and the center of a huge empire, it still has a rich heritage of its past, and plenty of unmistakably British hallmarks. The Industrial Revolution began here, as did punk rock, railways and soccer and it's only in this country that you will find the quintessentially British village *fête* complete with striped tents and bring-and-buy stalls, the seaside pleasure pier, the pub, the English stately home in its landscaped park, Scottish haggis, Welsh cakes and leafy suburbs dotted with Tudor-style semi-detached houses and the odd fish and chip shop. British contributions to world culture include an incomparable and all-embracing literary output, from Shakespeare to Winnie-the-Pooh.

THE DIVERSITY Many newcomers to Britain are surprised by how quickly the urban scene gives way to beautiful rural landscapes. Factors include the compactness of many urban centers, restrictive zoning laws, and the constant variations in the natural environment: low-level arable fens, rolling hedgerow-lined pastures, craggy dales, blustery moorland, post-glacial mountain scenery, rugged cliffs, and shingle shores. This in turn has given rise to numerous types of local architecture: sometimes the bedrock itself supplies the building material, as can be seen in the Cotswolds, Cornwall, rural Wales, the Scottish Highlands, and the Pennines, while elsewhere wood and/or bricks predominate.

Progress has inevitably eroded some of the finer distinctions in various locales (high-tech agriculture today blankets vast tracts of farmland, and chain stores dominate small towns' main shopping streets), but in spite of this, much has either been carefully preserved or has survived. Regional accents, for instance, continue to thrive: a well-trained ear can distinguish from which side of the Pennines, part of Scotland, or even district of London the speaker comes.

Britain's greatest assets for visitors include its sense of history and variety, all of which are packed into one accessible island where the driving distances are never too long between distinctively different landscapes and cultures. The curious explorer will be well served.

Market day (this one is Norwich)— a colorful experience in every way

The British system of government is that of parliamentary democracy, based on principles of common law. Led by its prime minister (since 1997 Tony Blair, of the Labour party), the country is a "constitutional monarchy," although there is no written constitution, since it has evolved over the centuries. Queen Elizabeth II gives royal assent to Acts of Parliament, but this is really a mere formality. Universal male suffrage in Britain dates only from 1918, and women did not get the vote until as recently as 1928.

> ❏ "Let not England forget her precedence of teaching other nations how to live."
> —John Milton (1644) ❏

The British Isles are the two islands of Britain and Ireland. Britain, or Great Britain, is used to refer to England, Wales and Scotland together. Wales was conquered by England in the 13th century. The King of Scots succeeded the English throne in 1603, and the political union of England and Scotland dates from 1707.

The United Kingdom is England, Wales, Scotland and Northern Ireland, the latter being the six counties of Ulster (predominantly Protestant) that refused to join the rest of Ireland when it broke away from Britain in 1921. Scotland, Wales and Northern Ireland are ruled, like England, from London but in 1999 certain powers were devolved to Scotland and Wales, with the Scottish Parliament in Edinburgh and the Welsh Assembly in Cardiff.

THE SEAT OF POWER The head of state is officially the Queen. Much of the ceremony of British life revolves round **the monarchy**, dating from a time when the monarch ruled the country. Today, power rests with the democratically elected government answerable to **parliament** and to the **House of Commons**, the chief legislative body. The unelected **House of Lords** is the secondary chamber. Britain's relationship with the European Union, however and the consequences for British sovereignty and parliament are under debate.

> ❏ "Great Britain has lost an empire and has not yet found a role."
> —Dean Acheson (1962) ❏

11

Class distinctions are still important in British life. They involve the most acutely discriminating judgements—concerning people's houses and furnishings, clothes, cars, jobs, education, manners, and personal tastes. The simplest clue to someone's class is usually gained by listening to their accent—as George Bernard Shaw once remarked, an Englishman cannot open his mouth without making some other Englishman despise him.

The population of Great Britain numbers over 58 million. A small and densely populated country, it would fit neatly inside the American state of Oregon, which has a population of only 3 million. Or, keeping the comparison within Europe, the country has about the same number of people as France, in an area less than half the size.

12

EARLY ANCESTRY The British are a nation of mongrels, principally a mixture of Germanic and Celtic strains. The original "English," or Anglo-Saxons, came across the North Sea in their dragon-prowed

longships from northwest Germany and southern Denmark some 1,500 years ago. They subjugated most of the native Celtic people on the island, whom they dismissively called Welsh, meaning "foreigners."

More Germanic invaders came from Denmark and Norway in the Viking Age. Then the famous Norman Conquest of England in 1066 eventually gave all areas of the British Isles a new and initially French-speaking ruling class. From the 16th to the 18th centuries, thousands of French Protestants, known as Huguenots, came to England to escape the religious persecution of Europe. The 19th century brought substantial Irish immigration to Britain and an influx of Jewish families fleeing from persecution in Russia and Eastern Europe. After World War II fresh waves of immigrants came from the West Indies, the Indian subcontinent, Cyprus and many other countries of the former British Empire that now form part of the Commonwealth association of nations.

ETHNIC AND RELIGIOUS MIX Despite the presence of many ethnic and religious minorities, statistics show that more than 80 percent of the U.K. population is still classified as English, about 10 percent as Scottish, 2.5 percent as Irish and 2 percent as Welsh. Britain is 95 percent white, with West Indians, Indians, and Pakistanis now numbering about 1 percent each. There are also tiny percentages of Bangladeshis and Chinese. Of the ethnic minority population, close to 50 percent is British by birth.

The population is overwhelmingly Christian, or thinks of itself that way. More than 85 percent of the British people regard themselves as Christians, but less than one person in five goes regularly to church or chapel. The Muslim population is about 2 percent and those practicing the Jewish faith total 1 percent.

Male and female members of the population are nearing equality in numbers. In the 20th century the birth rate increased slowly; during the 1970s population fell for a time.

❏ Arthur Koestler, a notable foreign writer who lived in Britain for many years, described the average Englishman as an attractive hybrid between an ostrich and a lion: keeping his head in the sand for as long as possible, but, when forced to confront reality, capable of heroic deeds. ❏

A NATIONAL CHARACTER? Whether there is anything that can be called a British national character is open to question. The Scots, the Welsh, and the Irish have retained their separate identities despite (or because of) English domination. Even in England itself, people from London, Yorkshire, Lancashire, the Northeast, the West Country, and other areas cherish their regional identities.

Class distinctions are being steadily eroded, but certain national traits live on: reserve, politeness, a sense of fair play, a genius for compromise and a gift for understatement to name but five. Voluntary work plays a major role in the everyday life of many people, with thousands of charity stores, civic societies, women's institutes, and fund-raising ventures spread across the country. The affection for gardens, dogs, and horses is nationally ingrained. Although they love the countryside, most of them do not actually live in it; walking or hiking in the countryside is by far their most popular activity. They love sports and taught the rest of the world orga-nized games, such as soccer and cricket.

Perhaps the most fundamental trait that all the British have in common is an ironic sense of humor which allows them to make fun of themselves with good grace.

If anything causes the British more complaint, anxiety and frustration than the weather, it is the economy. In the Victorian Age, Britain was the most powerful industrial nation on earth, with a mighty economy based on coal, iron, and steel, heavy machinery, textiles, shipbuilding and foreign trade. Queen Victoria ruled the largest empire in history. This commanding position has since been lost and with it the self-confidence of that era.

14

The British economy today is based on private enterprise; in the 1980s many of the nationalized industries were restored to private ownership. Heavy industry has declined while the service sector has grown. Britain used to import raw materials for its factories. Now it is a net importer of manufactured goods from countries that make them better and cheaper. The fishing industry has shrunk after over-fishing led to EU and government restrictions. Inflation, high in the 1970–1980s, is now under control.

❏ The change that has come over Britain can be observed in the mining valleys of South Wales, where King Coal once raised his grimy sceptre above teeming pits and slag heaps. Today not a nugget of coal is mined in the Rhondda Valley and the valleys are being extensively "greened." ❏

TRADE AND RESOURCES A strong financial sector brings in more wealth from overseas. Less food is imported today and more grown at home, but only 2 percent of the population is employed in agriculture. In 1973, Britain joined the European Union (EU), which accounts for more than half of its trade, but did not join the European Monetary Union when the Euro was launched as the European currency in 1999. That year, the trade gap reached a new record with the strength of sterling and a collapse in demand from countries hit by the global economic crisis.

The U.K. was the sixth richest country in the world in 1950, while in 1980 it was only the 22nd richest. All the same, in the 1990s, with two-thirds of British households owning their homes and two-thirds owning cars, Britons had a higher standard of living than ever before.

The Bank of England, at the heart of the City of London

Pubs are much more than places in which to drink. They are enclaves of laughter and gossip, arenas for playing games and havens of sympathy in times of trouble. A good pub has its own distinctive atmosphere, complete with its own resident cast of characters.

> ❏ "When you have lost your inns drown your empty selves, for you will have lost the last of England."—Hilaire Belloc (1870–1953) ❏

Some pubs are dedicated to thoughtful imbibing and peaceful conversation, others to deafening taped music and clattering slot machines. There are venerable half-timbered Tudor hostelries, leaning at an angle and apparently held up as much by the strength of the ale on tap as they are by their massive black timbers. There are broad-fronted Georgian coaching inns, glittering Victorian "gin palaces," and dubious little backstreet taverns. There are pubs with romantic tales to tell of smugglers and highwaymen, rose-wreathed pubs idyllically set by rivers and canals, lobster-potted inns gazing over picturesque fishing harbors and patronized by sailing enthusiasts, while grim-faced pubs accustomed to wind and weather and perched high on remote moors are frequented by hikers in thick boots and waterproof jackets.

THEN AND NOW The neighborhood pub of today is descended from the local alehouse of Anglo-Saxon and medieval England, an ordinary house whose occupants brewed and sold ale. In the 12th and 13th centuries inns began to open up, providing overnight accommodations for travelers. In recent years, the traditional pub has found a new identity: serving food—"pub grub"—has become more important

There are town pubs, village pubs, country pubs…and boaty pubs

and there has been a comeback of "real ale," meaning old-fashioned beer, once threatened with extinction by the big commercial brewers. Most pubs have become less aggressively masculine, and women can feel quite comfortable in them.

WHAT'S IN A NAME? Pubs have picture-signs hanging above their doors, illustrating their names—a custom dating from days when few people could read. Some names are derived from heraldry, like the White Hart and the Red Lion. Others are named for royalty, as in the Crown or the King's Head. Other names reflect country life—the Plough or the Fox and Hounds. There are New Inns that are centuries old, and there are strange and enigmatic names: the Pig and Whistle, the Cat and Fiddle. All are part of the richness and variety that keep the British pub a vital institution.

Gardens and gardening are often seen as a national passion. Opportunities for self-expression and creativity can be found in the tiniest cottage garden or on the grandest estate. This selected list of gardens that are open to the public gives you an idea of the scope and diversity of the nation's "backyards."

16

The British garden dates from Roman times, when every upwardly mobile villa owner aspired to have an atrium with a small garden. Monastic gardens were merely practical affairs for growing food or cultivating herbs and plants for dyes or for medicinal purposes. With the first great houses of the 16th century came the first true pleasure gardens, with their "knots" of herbs and flowers. In the next century the aristocratic classes toured France and Italy and saw the formal creations of Le Nôtre; topiary and water parterres were the rage.

The classical 18th century age of English landscaping rejected formality in favor of the naturalistic contrivances of Lancelot "Capability" Brown and others, who designed green expanses fringed by woodlands, interrupted by lakes, and punctuated by classical follies. Victorian times saw formal rockeries, ferneries, roseries, and other horticultural extravaganzas back in fashion.

Meanwhile the working classes tended small plots in allotment gardens where they grew their own vegetables and middle-class suburban villas sported lawns and herbaceous borders. In their back gardens, people found a private haven from the outside world.

THE WEST COUNTRY Subtropical species thrive in the gardens of **Tresco Abbey**, on the Isles of Scilly. On the mainland of Cornwall **Glendurgan** (N.T.), **Penjerrick**, and **Trebah** are neighbouring subtropical havens; **Trelissick** (N.T.) is noted for rhododendrons and azaleas with color all year round; paths wind down to the waterside with glimpses of Pendennis Castle. At **Trewithen**

magnolias, rhododendrons, and rare shrubs surround a Georgian mansion, while the **Lost Gardens of Heligan** is Europe's largest garden restoration project, begun in 1991 in a neglected Victorian estate. In Wiltshire, **Stourhead** (N.T.) is a splendid example of traditional 18th-century landscaping.

SOUTHERN ENGLAND AND LONDON
Kew Gardens in London is the king of all botanic gardens. The collection of rare specimens from all over the world owes much to the 19th-century botanist Sir Joseph Banks. Don't miss the elegant Palm House and the Princess of Wales Conservatory. **Wisley Garden**, Surrey, was set up in 1904 as experimental gardens for the

Stourhead in Wiltshire, the quintessential landscaped garden

Late spring at Sissinghurst

Royal Horticultural Society: it has many scarce species and an excellent garden center. **Winkworth Arboretum** (N.T.), Surrey, is a great tree collection, splendid for spring and autumn colors. Sussex gardens to head for are **Sheffield Park** (N.T.), with azaleas and rhododendrons backed by a lake, **Nymans Garden** (N.T.), full of romantic vistas, **Wakehurst Place** (N.T.), an outpost of the Royal Botanic Gardens at Kew and of interest year-round and **Great Dixter**, the manor house garden of the gardening writer David Lloyd. In Kent the gardens of **Hever Castle** are strongly Italian in feel, and those of **Scotney Castle** (N.T.) are of the picturesque-romantic style in a lake and island setting. **Sissinghurst Garden** (N.T.) is the wonderful 1930s creation of Harold Nicholson and Vita Sackville-West.

THE HEART OF ENGLAND Barnsley House, **Hidcote Manor** (N.T.), **Kiftsgate Court**, **Miserden Park**, **Painswick Rococo Garden,** and **Westonbirt Arboretum** are all in the Cotswolds, each offering something different (see panels, pages 118 and 120). **Rousham House**, Oxfordshire, is an example of an 18th-century romantic rural idyll by William Kent.

WALES Powis Castle (N.T.) in Powys is set amid fine 18th-century terraces.

In Conwy, **Bodnant Garden** (N.T.) is based on five Italianate terraces with the mountains of Snowdonia as a beautiful backdrop.

NORTHERN ENGLAND Chatsworth in Derbyshire is a masterly marriage of parkland, landscaped by Lancelot "Capability" Brown and gardens full of surprises that owe much to Joseph Paxton, head gardener from 1827 and later designer of Crystal Palace. **Studley Royal** (N.T.), North Yorkshire, is an ultra-romantic creation around Fountains Abbey.

SCOTLAND Culzean Country Park (N.T.S.), in South Ayrshire, is landscaped park and woodland. At **Edzell Castle** (N.T.S.), in Stirling, is a 17th-century "pleasaunce", while **Branklyn** (N.T.S.), near Perth, is a modest-sized, amazingly stocked suburban garden. **Crathes Castle**, in Aberdeenshire, is enchanting and innovative. In the wilds of the Highlands, **Inverewe** (N.T.S.) is a spectacular oasis.

❑ The National Gardens Scheme is an umbrella organization for gardens throughout Britain. Included are many private gardens whose owners open them to the public just one or two days a year. See the booklet *Gardens of England and Wales.* ❑

The national calendar of events ranges from the local customs of Mayday dancing and Shrove Tuesday pancake racing to the royal pageantry of Trooping the Colour and the great sports events held at the Millennium Stadium, Royal Ascot, and Lord's Cricket Ground. Local tourist information offices have details of what's on where and when.

PAGEANTRY AND SPECTACLE

Trooping the Colour, the celebration of the Queen's official birthday, takes place in June in Horse Guards' Parade in central London and shows off the best of royal pageantry. The Lord Mayor's Show in November features the new mayor of the City of London in procession in a golden coach.

Other annual spectacles include the Chelsea Flower Show (May, London), Cruft's Dog Show (March, Birmingham) and the International Air Show (September, even-numbered years, Farnborough, Hampshire).

The Randwick Wap, a Cotswolds mayoral swearing-in

ARTS FESTIVALS

The major arts festival of the year is the Edinburgh Festival in August/September; other sites include Bath, Brighton, and Glasgow, plus Gloucester, Herefordshire, or Worcestershire for the Three Choirs Festival (see page 117) and Llangollen for the International Eisteddfod in Wales (see page 163). The Promenade Concerts ("Proms") at London's Royal Albert Hall take place from July to September, with classical music, old and new, being performed.

SPORTS

Professional soccer matches are held every Saturday between August and April; the FA (Football Association) Cup Final in May is the big match. The cricket season lasts from April to September. Reserve tickets for Test matches well ahead; there is rarely a problem getting to see a four-day or one-day county game. The Wimbledon Lawn Tennis Championships are held in London late June to early July. As for horse racing, the Grand National is a notoriously tough steeplechase run at Aintree near Liverpool in April and the ultra-fashionable Royal Ascot takes place in June. Regattas are rowed at Henley and Fowey and a round-the-island yacht race takes place at Cowes on the Isle of Wight. In March the University Boat Race (Oxford versus Cambridge) is rowed on the Thames in west London.

Numerous traditional sports get an annual revival: variants of medieval football are played in the streets of St. Columb Major in Cornwall and Ashbourne in Derbyshire, while Cumberland wrestling takes place in the Lake District. In Scotland the summer Highland Games at Braemar and elsewhere feature caber-tossing, mountain races, and bagpipe bands.

SHOWS AND FÊTES

County shows have an agricultural emphasis, with livestock and horticultural competitions attracting the nearby farming communities, but also include sport and entertainment.

Village *fêtes* (fairs) are in many ways miniature versions of these, with tombolas (raffles), cake competitions, produce, bric-à-brac stalls and maybe sheepdog trials—essential for anyone wanting to see the real rural Britain.

FOLK AND RELIGIOUS CUSTOMS

The only nationally celebrated event unique to this country is Guy Fawkes Night, on November 5, when fireworks are set off and effigies of Guy Fawkes, the anarchist caught attempting to blow up the Houses of Parliament in 1605, are burned on the top of big bonfires.

Locally, an amazing variety of folk customs are celebrated. Some of the oldest owe their origins to Mayday fertility rites, including maypole dancing around the country and, in Cornwall, the Furry Dance in Helston and the 'Obby 'Oss Festival at Padstow. Elsewhere, you can take your pick from such oddities as oyster-blessing at Whitstable (Kent), a pancake (crêpe) race at Olney (Buckinghamshire), or face pulling through a horsecollar at Egremont (Cumbria). Church customs include rush-bearing (dating from times when churches needed rushes to cover earthen floors) and, in the Peak District, well-dressing, when wells are decorated with pictures made of flowers.

The 'Obby 'Oss Festival, Padstow

19

The Industrial Revolution began in Britain, in a phenomenal burst of innovation in the late 18th and 19th centuries. In the new millennium, even as Britain's heavy industrial base continues to decline, museums that explore this aspect of the national heritage are a boom industry—and you don't have to be a fan of rusty sprockets and cogwheels to appreciate and learn from them.

Listed here is a selection of the best museums to visit. You can also see evocative reminders of Britain's industrial past—though they haven't been turned into museums as such—in the textile mill towns of West Yorkshire, the valleys of South Wales, the factory villages of Port Sunlight and Saltaire, and numerous abandoned mining landscapes such as the tin mines of Cornwall and the lead mines of Swaledale. Many of the sites and museums mentioned below are described more fully in the A–Z section of the book.

THE WEST COUNTRY Coldharbour Mill at Cullompton in Devon is an old wool mill that recalls the heyday of the Devon wool industry; the processes of carding, drafting, and spinning are shown and there are some fine old machines. At **Wheal Martyn**, St. Austell, Cornwall's still-surviving china clay industry is explained, with a tour around an abandoned site and a view of the moonscape of working pits nearby.

SOUTHERN ENGLAND At **Amberley Museum**, West Sussex, visitors see craftsmen at work in a former chalk pit and lime works. The **Royal Naval Base** in Chatham, Kent, is the world's largest Georgian dockyard. At Hove in East Sussex, the **British Engineerium** evokes the age of steam power, within a Victorian water pumping station.

THE HEART OF ENGLAND The **Black Country Living Museum**, Dudley (West Midlands), is a skillful reconstruction of an industrial Black Country community of yesteryear, with a colliery, redbrick cottages, a canal where you can try "legging" along the tunnel in the time-honored fashion. The **Ironbridge Gorge Museum** (in Shropshire), considered the birthplace of the Industrial Revolution, is the undoubted star of Britain's many distinguished industrial museums.

WALES Visit the **Big Pit Museum**, Blaenavon, Torfaen, to get the full experience of going down into a coal mine in the heart of the Welsh valleys. **Sygun Copper Mine** in Beddgelert, Gwynedd and **Llechwedd Slate Caverns** in Blaenau Ffestiniog, Gwynedd, offer imaginatively conceived tours of the old mines, and the **Welsh Slate Museum**, Llanberis, is an evocative semi-abandoned slate quarry. **The Museum of the Welsh Woollen Industry**, at Drefach Felindre in western Wales, has fabric-making

The Museum of Iron at Ironbridge Gorge, a World Heritage Site

20

The Black Country Museum

demonstrations, factory trails, and bygone tools and machinery; you can even try your hand at spinning.

NORTHWEST ENGLAND Cromford Mill, in Cromford, Derbyshire, is an exciting monument to Richard Arkwright on the site of his first water-powered cotton mill. In the Potteries area (around Stoke-on-Trent), the **Royal Doulton**, **Wedgwood**, and **Spode** factories are open to visitors. The **Gladstone Pottery Museum** is the last surviving 19th-century pottery in the Stoke area, and now has excellent working displays. At Etruria, atmospherically placed between two canals, the **Etruria Industrial Museum** occupies the steam-powered mill where flint was crushed for use in the ceramics industry. The **Paradise Silk Mill and Museum** in Macclesfield, Cheshire, gives the story of the town's heyday when anyone who was anyone wore Macclesfield silk buttons. **Quarry Bank Mill**, Styal, Cheshire, is an excellent restoration of an 18th-century water-powered cotton mill in a fine verdant setting. Authentically clanking old machines can be seen and heard, at the **Helmshore Textile Museums**, in the heartland of the former Lancashire cotton-making country. At **Stott Park Bobbin Mill** in Finsthwaite, Cumbria, former mill workers explain the process of one of the last bobbin mills to be operational in England; it functioned from 1835 until as recently as 1971.

NORTHEAST ENGLAND West Yorkshire has a rich heritage of textile manufacturing. Some of its mills have now become tourist attractions, such as **Armley Mills** in Leeds and the **Bradford Industrial Museum**. The **North of England Open Air Museum**, Beamish, Co Durham, is a clever evocation of the early 1900s.

SOUTHERN SCOTLAND New Lanark Mills at Lanark, South Lanarkshire, is a remarkably well-preserved factory village with working machinery, a period store and house, and craft workshops; the village has a dramatic setting near waterfalls. At Newtongrange, Midlothian, the **Scottish Mining Museum** has a fine working steam engine used for winding. Ambitious displays cover the lives of the miners, and some of the colliery buildings can be visited.

Gladstone Pottery Museum

Although it is often taken for granted, the "semi" is a major component of British cityscapes. Rapidly and cheaply built during the 1930s, semidetached houses were laid out in neat rows, avenues and crescents. Within two decades a large part of Britain's countryside had given way to suburbanization. The semi may never have been chic, but over the years it has adapted well for modern living, and is still going strong today.

22

Mention the word suburbia in Britain and it is the semi that springs first to mind. The length and breadth of the country, pairs of mirror-image houses under a single roof line the roads that lead into every major town. At first glance, each semi is identical, but closer inspection will reveal certain marks of individuality. For an Englishman's home is his castle, and none more so than his semi.

RISE OF THE SEMI Terraced houses, similar to the American row house, had been the dominant feature of 19th-century popular housing in England and Wales (Scottish cities specialized more in tenements); inexpensive and quick to build, the terrace provided housing for the artisan classes. Wealthier folk aspired to semidetached or detached (separate) properties.

The semidetached was a feature of the urban scene in Victorian and Edwardian times, but it was in the 1930s Depression years that it really came into its own. Labor was low-cost and plentiful, cheap materials readily available. Speculative builders were creating new subdivisions in the verdant fringes of major cities, and improved rail and road links made commuting more feasible. Advertisements promised a rural idyll.

THE BUILDING BOOM With this boom came the mass-produced semi: a square plan, a common pitched roof, one party wall, a front and back garden, often a garage built onto one side. Since only a modest down payment was needed, the semi was available to virtually anyone with a reasonable income. Rustic and fanciful flourishes were added to the basic design: leaded windows, gables sporting Tudor-style half-timbering, tile-covered walls, stained-glass windows, sunrise motifs. Interior plans varied little: three or four bedrooms and a bathroom, a living room, and a small kitchen (in the new labor-saving age of convenience foods, after all, who needed a big kitchen?). "Three-piece suites" (a sofa for the children, an armchair for each parent) in the living room exemplified traditional solidity.

The semi has shown itself readily adaptable to modern living, with new porches and extra rooms over the garage being frequent alterations.

A typical semi, in Basingstoke

England's "green and pleasant land" is not a natural phenomenon, but the product of 200 generations of hard work. To oversimplify matters, imagine Britain's underlying geology as dividing the country into a highland zone in the north and west, including Scotland, the Pennines, the Lake District, and Wales and a lowland zone in the south and east. No matter what the geology, however, hardly any part of the landscape is unaltered by human hand.

The first people to make a mark on the landscape were the mesolithic people, nomadic hunters who burned forests and cleared large areas of land in order to gather herds of wild animals together. This lifestyle gradually became more settled over the years as neolithic peoples introduced crops, farming, and domesticated animals. In order to make the necessary cropland and pasture for their cattle, sheep, and pigs, they made permanent clearings, creating landscapes that were not unlike those we see today, although the actual use of the land was substantially different. Generally, small groups lived in hamlets of a few huts surrounded by an earth bank or a wooden palisade (a tall fence), with fields outside. These were the forerunners of subsequent centuries of village life.

A well-preserved Roman road on Wheeldale in the North York Moors

❏ The stone axes with which neolithic farmers cleared the land were far more effective implements than is generally realised. Experiments indicate that one man working alone could have cleared a half acre a week. ❏

THE EARLIEST COMMUNITIES Over many centuries, villages grew up where there was fertile soil and an adequate water supply. The "typical" English village of houses clustered around a village green and duck pond is only one of several types (in Wales and Scotland the green is not a common feature). Other villages are stretched out along a road or have more than one center or sprawl about in a congenial muddle.

Each village was a service center for the surrounding countryside, providing a church, a drinking house, craftsmen, a market for produce. The more successful ones usually had some geographical advantage—they were situated at a ford or an important road junction, for instance—and they grew into towns. Other towns were founded by landowners looking for profit.

TRACKS AND ROADS The earliest roads were created by farmers and their livestock and many of today's country lanes, lying deep between high banks, may be thousands of years old. Trade also had its part to play and a network of prehistoric "high roads" can still be traced.

24

❑ Britain's human history stretches back over a vast period of time to the arrival of manlike beings over 300,000 years ago. It is conventionally divided into the periods shown here, but the dates should be taken only as extremely rough approximations.

Period	Dates	Outstanding example
Paleolithic (Old Stone Age)	500,000–8,300 BC	
Mesolithic (Middle Stone Age)	8,300–4,500 BC	
Neolithic (New Stone Age)	4,500–2,300 BC	Belas Knap tomb
Bronze Age	2,300–700 BC	Stonehenge
Iron Age	from 750 BC	Maiden Castle hill fort
Roman	AD 43–410	Roman Baths, Bath

Oak woodlands near Butts Lawn in Hampshire's ancient New Forest

The Romans introduced the first centrally planned road network—dig a few feet beneath a long, straight stretch of today's highway and you'll find Roman road. The Roman network sufficed until a new era of road building began in the 1700s.

❑ "The great charm…of English scenery is the moral feeling that seems to pervade it. It is associated in the mind with ideas of order, of quiet, of sober well-established principles, hoary usage and reverend custom. Everything seems to be the growth of ages of reverend and peaceful existence."
—Washington Irving (1820) ❑

FOREST AND WOODLANDS As well as clearing forest for agriculture, neolithic people managed woodlands very successfully. Coppicing is a good example: the tree is cut down to ground level so that several shoots grow up to replace the lost one. Over several years this produces a crop of poles of just the right size for whatever use the woodsman decides upon. And coppiced trees live on almost indefinitely so long as coppicing continues. It is a perfect self-regenerating system. After World War II, men were still using and refining skills such as these, first learned over 4,000 years ago.

Today, however, most woodlands are managed differently, with concentration on large timber production. Wildlife actually suffers as a result: flowers are shaded out, butterflies lose their habitat.

LANDSCAPE TODAY Despite the changes of the 20th century, the British landscape presents a remarkable historical tableau. Early settlers slashed and burned down the primeval forests, exhausting the soil and leaving moorlands that still cover much of upland Britain. Agricultural and much common land was subject to enclosure from medieval times to the 19th century; the old "open field" system, where several farmers worked strips within a large single field, was abandoned in favor of smaller enclosures. During that period the hedges (now themselves being removed in many areas) and drystone walls that dominate so much of the lowlands today changed the face of the country.

Gaunt and gray in the British countryside, the shells and ruins of formidable medieval strongholds still defy time and weather. They were sited at strategic points—to control a river crossing, a hill pass, or a harbor, for example. Many of them saw little or no action, which is testimony to their effectiveness. They were not built to provoke attack, but to deter it.

The Norman Conquest of England made 1066 one of the key dates of British history. The triumphant William the Conqueror—known in his own time, though not to his face, as William the Bastard—parceled England out among his Norman, French, Breton, and Flemish followers. The more important built castles to secure their grip on their new estates and by 1100 there were some 500 of these strongholds in England. The early ones consisted of a mound of earth (the motte), built by conscript labor, with a yard (the bailey) around its base, enclosed by an earth rampart and ditch. Wooden buildings housed the castle's lord, his family, and his small private army. The local villagers could take refuge in the bailey in time of danger.

BASTIONS OF STONE Many of these primitive fortresses were soon replaced by daunting strongholds built of stone. A hulking keep was erected on the mound, its walls as

Stark and strong, Corfe Castle in Dorset was built by the Normans

much as 100 feet high and 20 feet thick at the base, pierced by tiny windows through which archers and crossbowmen could fire. The living quarters were in the keep, with the ground floor used for storage and dungeons. Outer walls kept besiegers at a distance and around them might be a water-filled moat crossed by a drawbridge. Castles became ever more elaborate as time went by. The

> ❑ "The rich man in his castle,
>   The poor man at his gate,
> God made them high and lowly,
>   And ordered their estate."
> —19th-century hymn ❑

Tower of London, originally built for William the Conqueror himself, is a particularly impressive specimen.

In Wales, both Norman and native warlords built themselves castles. When Edward I of England conquered the country, a chain of powerful fortresses that could be supplied by sea cemented his hold. **Caernarfon**, **Harlech**, **Conwy**, and **Beaumaris** castles still testify to the skill of his military engineer, James of St. George. Scotland, where central authority was never as strong, bristles with ferocious and romantic strongholds, led by **Edinburgh** and **Stirling**, high on their lofty crags.

THE MANORIAL ESTATE Castles were extremely costly and only the richest nobles could afford them. In medieval England the basic landholding unit was the manor, ruled by its lord, who lived in the large manor house. Often a manor was a village with its surrounding countryside, but some manors

Harlech Castle, impregnable monument to King Edward I

contained more than one village, while others covered only part of one. The villagers cultivated the land, while the lord's function was to protect them and to keep order. Above the lord, in what is now called the **feudal system**, a chain of greater lords led up to the king himself, each link in the chain owing support to the one above it and protection to the one below.

The lord's manor house was at first just a bigger version of the wood-and-mud hovels of his villagers. By the 13th century, though, manor houses were being built of stone and the fortified manor house appeared—cheaper and more comfortable than a castle, but defensible. They centered on one main room, the hall, where the household ate and slept, while the dogs gnawed bones on the straw- or rush-covered floor and smoke from a central hearth drifted out through a hole in the roof.

Over the centuries the medieval lord of the manor became the less powerful, though still dominant, country squire. Just as the power of kings has ebbed away, so the title of lord of the manor has become a picturesque but empty honor.

> ❑ Perhaps England's best example of a fortified manor house is Stokesay Castle, near Shrewsbury in Shropshire (see page 124), which has preserved its medieval atmosphere to a remarkable degree. ❑

At the same time as being beautiful and satisfying to the senses, churches were originally built as earthly houses for God; symbols of the God-given order of the world and the true purpose of human life. Through the centuries, generations of Christians have worshipped in them, joined in the community's spiritual life, been baptized and married and finally, after life's fitful fever, have been laid to rest in eternal peace in the churchyard.

From the humblest parish church to the most sumptuous cathedral, in country and town alike, churches are an essential element of the British scene. Almost all of them have been altered, enlarged, or rebuilt many times over.

STYLES OF ARCHITECTURE A few **Anglo-Saxon** churches are still standing. Small and plain, they are the oldest British ecclesiastical buildings to survive. The **Normans** built on an altogether more massive and powerful scale, notably with thick round columns supporting the roof, and round arches above small doors and windows.

Movingly simple, the Saxon church at Greensted is built of split logs

The **Gothic** style, which arrived in Britain in the 12th century, was lighter, airier, more slender, more uplifting to the spirit. Its earliest phases, Early English and the more ornate Decorated, introduced the pointed arch, the flying buttress, and the tall spire that directed worshippers' eyes and thoughts heavenward. These churches were alive with elaborate decoration, carvings in wood and stone, stained-glass windows, statues and wall paintings—the religious textbooks of an age that could not read. (Much of this decoration, unfortunately, was destroyed or painted over by the Puritans when they took over the government in the 17th century.) In the 14th century came the Perpendicular style, named after the strong vertical lines that carry the eye up to the roof. Tall, soaring shafts support a web of fan-vaulting and enormous windows of the most delicate tracery, while graceful towers rise to a riot of pinnacles. The style reached its apogee in the amazing stone cobweb of **King's College Chapel**, Cambridge. In the 19th century the values of medieval architecture were upheld by such architects as Augustus Pugin in the form of the Gothic Revival style.

THE MONASTIC MOVEMENT Among the most haunting legacies that the Middle Ages left to Britain are the now ruined monasteries—**Fountains**, **Rievaulx**, **Glastonbury**, **Tintern**, and many more. Medieval abbeys and priories ran a virtual welfare system for the poor, treated the sick, kept scholarship and art alive, and gave hospitality to travelers, but their primary function was as centers of prayer and worship. With eight services a day, from matins before dawn to vespers at sunset and compline at bedtime, monks paid humankind's tribute of devotion to God.

The church was always the biggest and finest building in a monastery, usually standing at one side of a quadrangle. Around the other sides were the domestic buildings—the refectory for meals, the kitchen, the dormitory, the infirmary. The monks themselves took vows of poverty, but monasteries accumulated large estates, ran farms, and raised sheep.

Fountains Abbey in Yorkshire, for example, was the North of England's biggest producer of wool.

The **Reformation** of the 16th century created the Church of England as a separate body, no longer owing allegiance to the Pope, and in the 1530s the monasteries were all closed down (the church, however, was often retained by the community as a parish church). Most of the monastic land ended up in the hands of the aristocracy and the country gentry, not only enriching them but making it quite certain that the Dissolution of the Monasteries would never be reversed. Today empty, roofless shells stand quietly where generations of monks once lived and prayed.

The soaring ruins of Tintern Abbey

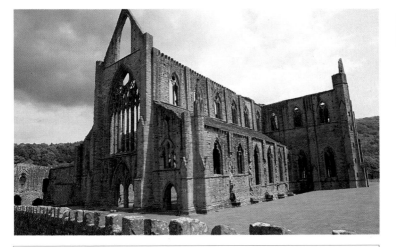

❏ Guidebooks often use the following terms for styles of church architecture in Britain. The dates should be considered as rough indications only.

Style	Dates	Outstanding example
Saxon	650–1066	St. Laurence's, Bradford on Avon
Norman (or Romanesque)	1066–1190	Durham Cathedral
Gothic: Early English	1190–1275	Salisbury Cathedral
Decorated	1275–1375	Exeter Cathedral
Perpendicular	1375–1485	King's College Chapel, Cambridge
Classical	17th–18th centuries	St. Paul's Cathedral, London
Gothic Revival	early 19th century	All Saints, Margaret Street, London W1
Victorian	1837–1901	St. Mary's Cathedral, Edinburgh

A long era of relative peace on British soil since the 1500s has left Britain virtually without equal in the number of grand historic houses open for visitors to enjoy. They're packed from floor to ceiling with treasures of art and triumphs of decoration—paintings, sculptures, furniture, porcelain, books, clocks. Surrounded by exquisite gardens and sumptuously landscaped parks, they testify to five centuries of wealth, taste, and social prominence.

Britain retains a notable number of timber-framed houses dating from medieval times, though most have been adapted and precise dating is difficult; more important buildings were often constructed in stone. Grander medieval examples include **Haddon Hall** in Derbyshire and **Ightham Mote** in Kent.

Tudor Chenies Manor House, near Amersham in Buckinghamshire

THE VERNACULAR The houses of the ordinary people, and also their agricultural and industrial buildings, were constructed following local traditions and in whatever material was readily at hand, be it stone, flint, or cob, thatch, slate, or pantile.

THE ELIZABETHAN AGE The Tudor era was one of peace and prosperity in which the rich Englishman's home no longer needed to be a fortified castle. The wealthy built ostentatious houses, Cardinal Wolsey and Henry

VIII leading the way with the huge brick palace of **Hampton Court**. Capacious bay windows gazed out upon the countryside, while the fantastically elaborate chimneystacks of grand houses of the 16th and 17th centuries joined the gables, turrets, and balustrades that enlivened the roofline to impress the neighbors with the owner's wealth.

Much Tudor building was in brick, but in areas where there was plenty of lumber—as in the Southeast and the western Midlands—houses were half-timbered, with rectangular wooden frames enclosing panels of whitewashed plaster or brick. The most lavish examples, like **Little Moreton Hall** in Cheshire, are a riot of zebra-striped patterns.

THE CLASSICAL IDEAL Outside these houses, a formal symmetrical garden was evidence of the Renaissance enthusiasm for classical Greek and Roman ideals. The first really famous British architects—**Inigo Jones** and **Sir Christopher Wren** in the 17th century—were influenced by classical architecture. Inigo Jones's Queen's House (1616–1635) in Greenwich was one of the first house in Britain to be designed on classical principles. The typical house of Queen Anne's reign was a simple, symmetrical red-brick mansion with large sash windows and a four-sided roof behind a parapet. As the 18th century unfolded, **Sir John Vanbrugh** piled the colossal baroque palaces of **Castle Howard** and **Blenheim** upon the groaning earth, with their splendid domes and porticoes. Most of the English upper class, however, preferred the restrained elegance of the Palladian style of mansion, with its straight lines and pleasing proportions, its classical pillars and pediments. Around the house would stretch a noble park, where smooth lawns escorted the eye to carefully positioned groups of trees, an artificial lake, a bridge, and a temple, such as William Kent's **Holkham Hall**, Norfolk. Horace Walpole's **Strawberry Hill** is a playfully picturesque example of the "Gothick" style.

GEORGIAN ELEGANCE The same style, imposing a calm order upon unruly Nature, created some of Britain's most satisfying townscapes in Bath, London, Edinburgh, and other cities. From the 1760s the interiors of Georgian houses were opulently enriched by the genius of **Robert Adam** and his many imitators, who introduced delicate ornamentation into mansions like **Syon House** in Middlesex, in rooms never intended for living in, but for entertaining. In the early 19th-century Regency period John Nash created the flamboyant **Royal Pavilion** in Brighton and the stucco terraces around **Regent's Park.** His contemporary John Soane adopted a highly original style, exemplified by **Sir John Soane's Museum** in London.

VICTORIAN EXUBERANCE Powerful enthusiasm for medieval Gothic Christian architecture gave many Victorian houses an ecclesiastical

Kiftsgate Court, Gloucestershire: a Georgian house in a lovely garden

❏ All through the 19th century the Gothic and the classical styles vied for supremacy. In Yorkshire, for instance, the city fathers of Leeds built a magnificent classical temple as their town hall, while rival Bradford erected a Gothic town hall of mammoth proportions. ❏

look, with turrets, pointed windows, and stained glass, while Scots magnates built themselves mock baronial palaces. Victorian architects and their patrons took the whole past as their province. They adopted whatever architectural style took their fancy and blended characteristics from different styles to romantic and sometimes wildly excessive effect. In the early 1900s **Richard Norman Shaw** introduced stylized "vernacular," or countryside, styles (as at Cragside, Northumberland) and **Sir Edwin Lutyens** revived the classical style (as at Great Maytham, Kent).

CHANGING IDEALS A fierce reaction against Victorian and Edwardian "pastiche" followed in the 20th century as the modern movement in architecture adopted an austere simplicity of straight lines and concrete, often criticized as concrete monstrosities and provoking a more varied approach from the 1980s on, ranging from neo-classical to mock-vernacular. Yet some high-rise blocks are coming back into fashion: Erno Goldfinger's once-hated and much-vandalized 31-story **Trellick Tower** (1972) in west London is now loved by many residents and acclaimed a masterpiece.

In 1066 William the Conqueror, the Duke of Normandy, invaded from France and became the hugely influential William I of England. Richard III was the last medieval king, having wrested power from Edward V whom he declared illegitimate. Richard was killed at the Battle of Bosworth (1485) and Henry Tudor seized the throne to become Henry VII.

Britain's modern history begins in 1485, when the marriage of **Henry VII** of Lancaster to Elizabeth of York ended the 30-year Wars of the Roses —an inheritance dispute between the dukes of Lancaster and York. His son, **Henry VIII**, with a massive frame and small eyes so famously depicted in the Holbein portrait, is best known for his six wives. Two he divorced—breaking from the Catholic Church in Rome in the process—and two he executed, one died in childbirth, and the sixth outlived him.

ELIZABETH TUDOR It was typical of Henry's daughter **Elizabeth I** that when a deputation arrived at Hatfield House in Hertfordshire in 1558 to tell her she was queen, the 25-year-old princess was found sitting under an oak tree demurely reading a book. She always had a genius for public relations. A consummate politician, with her father's physical and intellectual vigor combined with feminine grace and charm, she successfully

Henry VIII, with Anne of Cleves

Elizabeth I, "Virgin Queen"

❑ "I know I have the body of a weak and feeble woman, but I have the heart and stomach of a king and of a king of England too."—Queen Elizabeth I, speech to the troops on the approach of the Armada, 1588 ❑

steered her country safely through 44 dangerous years.

THE STUARTS Scotland, meanwhile, had seen a long succession of kings of the Stuart dynasty, who since 1371 had struggled to impose their authority on their rebellious aristocracy. The beautiful **Mary, Queen of Scots** was forced to abdicate in 1567. She escaped to England, where she was politely kept prisoner for 20 years until execution in 1587.

Her son, **James VI of Scotland**, succeeded the childless Elizabeth I in 1603 as **James I of England**. The house of Stuart fared little better in

32

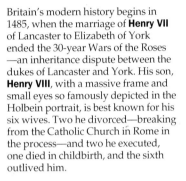

A Van Dyck portrait of Charles I

England than in Scotland. **Charles I**, attempting to uphold royal power against Parliament, was defeated by the Puritans under **Oliver Cromwell** in the **Civil War** and executed in London in 1649. **Charles II** was restored to the throne in 1660, after an interregnum of republican rule that proved deeply unpopular. He is remembered for his charm, his cynicism, and his colorful sex life. His brother was **James II**, who had a brief anti-Protestant reign before fleeing the throne in 1688; Parliament offered the crown, in the bloodless "Glorious Revolution," to the Dutch prince **William of Orange**, who reigned jointly with his wife **Mary**, James's daughter. **Queen Anne**, Mary's sister, was the last Stuart ruler.

THE HANOVERIANS On Anne's death in 1714, the Elector of Hanover became king as **George I**. Although he was a German who could not speak a word of English, as a Protestant he was preferred to the Stuart claimants, who made a dashing but unsuccessful last bid for the lost throne in 1745, led by Prince Charles Edward, sentimentally known as **Bonnie Prince Charlie**.

George III, who was much liked for his hearty geniality, was king when the American colonies broke away to become an independent nation. His son, ultimately **George IV**, acted as regent during George III's mental illness and became influential in fashion, architecture, and the arts, while his grand-daughter, **Queen Victoria**, enjoyed the longest reign of any British sovereign—64 years from 1837 to 1901. Clad invariably in black after the death of her beloved Prince Consort, Albert, in 1861, the widowed queen was ruler of the largest empire in history.

THE HOUSE OF WINDSOR Victoria's grandson, **George V**, sensitive during World War I about the dynasty's German connections, decided to change his family's name (Saxe-Coburg-Gotha) to the House of Windsor. His son **Edward VIII** caused an international scandal by abdicating within months of coming to the throne in 1936, following his marriage to the American divorcée Wallis Simpson, leaving his shy and unprepared brother to rule as **George VI** throughout World War II. Since 1952, **Queen Elizabeth II** has reigned, but the future of the monarchy is constantly under debate.

That Britain is an island has formed and colored its history and character. Britain's greatness was built on seaborne trade, and the British Empire rested on the Royal Navy's command of the sea, celebrated in popular patriotic songs from Rule Britannia *to the Gilbert and Sullivan parody* H.M.S. Pinafore. *The sea and seafaring are in Britain's blood.*

Nelson's flagship, H.M.S. Victory

The sea has played contradictory roles in British history, as both barrier and bridge. Britannia has always needed her "towers along the steep"—coastal fortifications against attack by sea. They can be seen bristling along England's southern and southeastern shoreline, ranging from Roman forts of the Saxon Shore to medieval and Tudor castles, 19th-century Martello towers and Palmerston forts against the French, and World War II defences.

OVERSEAS TRADING At the same time, while the sea has served Britain as a defensive moat, it has also been by sea that people, ideas, and trade have moved between Britain and the rest of the world. As far back as prehistoric times, ships from the Mediterranean came to Cornwall for tin. In Roman days, Britain exported slaves, oysters, and hunting dogs, among other things, to the Continent and imported wine.

The great medieval "wool churches" of England stand as testimony to the wealth generated by the export trade in wool and cloth. It remained a major factor in the economy into the 16th century, when merchants forged thriving trade links with the world beyond Europe—Asia, Africa, and the Americas. The piratical **Sir Francis Drake** sailed away in 1578 in a cockleshell of a ship, which was only the second to circumnavigate the globe. Plundering Spanish possessions on the way, he returned in 1580 with loot estimated at over $37.5 million in today's money.

IN COMMAND OF THE SEAS The British navy can trace its history back to **Alfred the Great** in the 9th century; he was the first English king to lead his own squadron in battle, against the Danes. In medieval times, ships and crews were supplied for the royal fleet by the **Cinque Ports** of southeast England—Dover, Sandwich, Hythe, New Romney, and Hastings. The Tudor and Stuart kings built up a more effective and powerful force. Along with two other formidable Elizabethan seadogs, Hawkins and Frobisher, Drake

---

❑ "Britannia needs no bulwarks,
No towers along the steep;
Her march is o'er the mountain waves,
Her home is on the deep."
—Thomas Campbell,
"Ye Mariners of England"
(1800–1801) ❑

helped defeat the ponderous Spanish Armada in 1588.

Between 1700 and 1780 Britain's foreign trade almost doubled. The port of Bristol took a leading part in the slave trade, which shipped millions of Africans to the American plantations. Meanwhile, Britain became the world's leading colonial power in a struggle against the French in which command of the sea was of paramount importance. The French were driven from India and North America, and the British built up the empire on which the sun never set. The "wooden walls"—the Royal Navy's implacable three-deckers—kept **Napoleon** at arm's length. "I do not say they cannot come," said Admiral Lord St. Vincent of the French invasion barges, "I only say they cannot come by sea."

ILLUSTRIOUS NAMES The navy was the guardian of British liberty, and a succession of naval heroes etched their names on the British consciousness—Anson, Rodney, Hood, Howe, St. Vincent, Collingwood, Cochrane. The most admired and loved of them all was **Horatio Nelson**, killed at the Battle of Trafalgar in 1805 as the H.M.S. *Victory* bore down upon the foe. The great ship is lovingly preserved in Portsmouth.

A Martello tower on the south coast, one of many built to counter the threat of Napoleonic invasion

❑ "A willing foe and sea room." —The Royal Navy's Friday night toast ❑

The British Empire eventually covered a quarter of the land surface of the globe, stretching across the world's heaving waters from Canada to India, Australia, New Zealand, as well as remote islands in the Pacific. It could not be sustained however and World War II demonstrated that command of the sea had eventually passed from Britain to the mightier United States.

Many places in Britain are linked with famous writers and their work. The village of Chawton in Hampshire shelters the modest house where Jane Austen wrote, hiding her papers when any of the household came in. Nearby at Selborne is the home of Gilbert White, the nature writer. Each year, Rochester in Kent honors Charles Dickens, who lived nearby. You can explore George Bernard Shaw's home at Ayot St. Lawrence in Hertfordshire, as well as Lord Byron's and D. H. Lawrence's houses near Nottingham, Rudyard Kipling's at Bateman's in Sussex, and Samuel Johnson's in Lichfield and London.

36

LITERARY SHRINES No writer in English is more admired than **William Shakespeare** and his birthplace town of Stratford-upon-Avon in Warwickshire is the most visited British tourist destination outside London.

In West Yorkshire the once grim little town of Haworth is thronged with pilgrims to the parsonage where **Charlotte**, **Emily**, and **Anne Brontë** and their brother **Branwell** lived. Out on the desolate moorland is the ruined farmhouse that may have been the original *Wuthering Heights*.

The Lake District also draws literary pilgrims, to **William Wordsworth**'s homes at Dove Cottage and Rydal Mount and the Lakeland scenes which inspired his poetry. **John Ruskin**, the Victorian art critic and social reformer, owned a house with a magical view over Coniston Water. **Beatrix Potter** also lived at Near Sawrey.

At Laugharne in South Wales the most famous Welsh poet of the 20th century, **Dylan Thomas**, is fondly remembered at his studio, the Boathouse. Scotland's national poet, **Robert Burns**, is cherished at the humble cottage where he was born in the outskirts of Ayr and also in Dumfries, where he spent his last years. **Sir Walter Scott**'s engaging collection of historical curios—Rob Roy's sword, a lock of the Young Pretender's hair and so on—can be admired at Abbotsford, his home in his beloved Borders, while at Kirriemuir is the birthplace of **Sir James Barrie**, author of *Peter Pan*.

The literary trail of **Jane Austen** includes her house from 1809 to 1817 at Chawton (northeast of Winchester), and the city of Bath, where the Jane Austen Centre recalls her work on such novels as *Persuasion* and *Northanger Abbey*. At Coxwold in North Yorkshire is the house where **Laurence Sterne** wrote *Tristram Shandy* and **John Milton** completed *Paradise Lost* in a cottage at Chalfont St. Giles in Buckinghamshire.

> ❏ Earth has not anything to show
> more fair:
> Dull would he be of soul who could
> pass by
> A sight so touching in its majesty:
> This City now doth like a garment
> wear
> The beauty of the morning; silent,
> bare,
> Ships, towers, domes, theatres
> and temples lie
> Open unto the fields and to the
> sky;
> All bright and glittering in the
> smokeless air.
> —William Wordsworth
> (1770–1850),
> *Upon Westminster Bridge* ❏

RESTING PLACES Interesting literary connections can frequently be found in churchyards. **T. S. Eliot** is buried at East Coker in Somerset, **John Buchan** at Elsfield near Oxford. The country churchyard of **Thomas Gray**'s famous *Elegy* can be found at Stoke Poges in Buckinghamshire. The memory of the evil Count Dracula, **Bram Stoker**'s creation, vampirishly haunts the graveyard at Whitby North Yorkshire. In London, Westminster Abbey's south transept is affectionately known as **Poets' Corner** because Geoffrey Chaucer, Edmund Spenser, Alfred Lord Tennyson, Robert Browning, and many other famous poets are buried or have memorials there. Monuments to Shakespeare, Milton, Wordsworth, Burns, Keats, and Shelley cluster close to memorials to Lord Byron, T. S. Eliot, W. H. Auden and Dylan Thomas.

> ❏ The curfew tolls the knell of
>   parting day,
> The lowing herd winds slowly
>   o'er the lea,
> The ploughman homeward plods
>   his weary way,
> And leaves the world to
>   darkness and to me.
> —Thomas Gray (1716–1771),
> *Elegy in a Country Churchyard* ❏

"...MY COUNTRY STILL" Some writers are associated with a whole area of countryside, seen through their eyes and peopled with their own characters. **Thomas Hardy** Country extends over much of Dorset and the museum in Dorchester has an excellent Hardy collection. The "blue remembered hills" of Shropshire are inseparably linked with the melancholic poetry of **A. E. Housman**.

Alfred, Lord Tennyson is particularly cherished in his native Lincolnshire and there is a noble statue of him outside Lincoln Cathedral. The center of the **George Eliot** industry is Nuneaton in Warwickshire; the southern part of Tyne and Wear now calls itself **Catherine Cookson** Country in homage to the best-selling romantic novelist.

> ❏ The first fire since the
>   summer is lit and is smoking
>   into the room;
> The sun-rays spread it through,
>   like woof-lines in a loom.
> Sparrows spurt from the hedge,
>   whom misgivings appal
> That winter did not leave last
>   year for ever, after all.
> —Thomas Hardy (1840–1928),
> *Shortening Days at the
> Homestead* ❏

Sometimes it is the characters more than the author who cast the spell. It is hardly possible to explore Exmoor without recalling *Lorna Doone*, Cornwall without thinking of the heroes and heroines of **Daphne du Maurier** and **Winston Graham** or Dartmoor without memories of Sherlock Holmes, Doctor Watson, and the hound of the Baskervilles.

37

Thomas Hardy's statue at the end of the high street in Dorchester, the "Casterbridge" of his novels

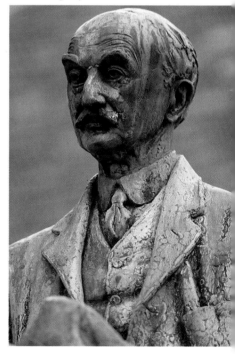

Britain's most characteristic contribution to Western art lies in a long tradition of landscape painting, which inspired such artists as Gainsborough, Constable, and Turner. It is this tradition which created the British idea of what the landscape looks like—or at least of what it ought to look like. Visitors enjoying the countryside today still tend to see it through the eyes of the great painters of the past.

The British tradition of landscape painting was founded by **Richard Wilson**, who was born in Wales in 1714 and was deeply impressed by the work of the French painter Claude Lorraine. Unappreciated and poverty-stricken, he struggled to convince the British eye that wild scenery could be beautiful; his paintings of his native Welsh mountains looming above limpid lakes have a classic grandeur and serenity.

THE GREAT NAMES Far more successful financially was **Thomas Gainsborough**, who originally came from Suffolk. He made his money as a fashionable portrait painter in Bath and London, but his true passion was for landscapes—often general-ized and idyllic, rather than depicting a particular place. The great Victorian art critic John Ruskin said of him: "His touch was as light as the sweep of a cloud and swift as the flash of a sunbeam."

   John Constable, arriving on the scene 50 years later, came from the Suffolk-Essex border and his paint-ings of hayfields, church towers, river scenes, carthorses, and wagons have remained hugely popular ever since. Salisbury Cathedral, Hampstead Heath and the South Coast were also favorite subjects of his. He believed in the most minute study of Nature, to render, as he said, "light—dews—breezes—bloom—and freshness" with loving accuracy and he broke free of the formal Claude-inspired landscape.

   Constable's contemporary, the prodigious **Joseph Mallord William**

Turner, traveled all over Britain, painting romantic landscapes, castles, cathedrals, and great houses. He followed in Richard Wilson's footsteps in Wales, painted extensively at Petworth in Sussex and in the Thames Valley and rejoiced in the scenery of the Lake District and Wharfedale in Yorkshire. As he grew increasingly fascinated by effects of light, his paintings of Norham Castle in Northumberland depict the ruined fortress and the grazing cattle almost disappearing into abstraction in the glowing sunlit mist.

Britain's country houses and London's National Portrait Gallery harbor a rich legacy of portraitists. Foreign artists were patronized in earlier times: **Hans Holbein** painted Henry VIII and his court and **Anthony van Dyck** depicted Charles I. In the 18th century the English artists **Sir Joshua Reynolds** and **George Romney** achieved much success. **Sir William Hogarth** created portraits as well as moralizing commentaries such as *The Rake's Progress.*

PLACES OF INSPIRATION Painters drawn to the Lake District include **Philippe de Loutherburg** and **Joseph Wright. L. S. Lowry** painted Lake District scenes, too, though he is better known for his northern industrial townscapes. Over the centuries, the Thames at London has inspired many foreign artists, including **Canaletto, Rex Whistler,** and **Claude Monet.**

Flatford Mill in Suffolk, still recognizable from Constable's paintings

The young J. M. W. Turner

Some areas have inspired groups of artists, like the **Norwich School** of painters in the early 19th century. **Bristol**'s school of artists was dominated by **Francis Danby** in the 1820s. The **Newlyn School** of artists, based in Cornwall's fishing port, was led by **Stanhope Forbes** from the 1880s, while **St. Ives** in Cornwall was a base for **Barbara Hepworth, Ben Nicholson,** and the potter **Bernard Leach.**

Mystical painter **Samuel Palmer** settled at Shoreham, Kent in the 1820s to explore his "Valley of Vision." **John Singer Sargent** painted Worcestershire landscapes in the 1880s, **Graham Sutherland** painted in Pembrokeshire pre- and post–World War II. **Cookham,** Berkshire owes its fame to the works of **Sir Stanley Spencer.**

The Pre-Raphaelite Brotherhood of 19th-century English artists painted religious and moralistic scenes, steeped in romantic medievalism and brilliantly hued. Leading figures included **Burne-Jones, Rossetti,** and **Millais.** London's Tate Britain and the Birmingham Museum and Art Gallery have superb collections.

Crowded, noisy, dirty, and packed with life, Manchester was the archetype of the new cities created in Britain by the Industrial Revolution. Instead of a skyline of church spires, hundreds of factory chimneys belched out smoke and fumes. Though horrified by the city's abominable slums and its turbid rivers crawling with filth, many visitors saw Manchester as the symbol of a dawning new age of intense creativity and vitality.

The Industrial Revolution was revolutionary in its consequences rather than its speed. The century between 1750 and 1850 ushered in the machine age of factories, mass production and the assembly line, the industrial town and the industrial working class. Why it should all have started in Britain is a disputed question, but the country had certain obvious advantages: ample resources of coal and iron and a growing empire overseas that provided a captive market for British-made products.

THE TEXTILE INDUSTRY The most affected industries in the early stages were textiles, iron and steel, coal mining, and pottery. In textiles, a succession of inventions made it possible to increase output while using less human energy. This transformed the making of cloth from a

small-scale operation, carried on by skilled workmen and their families at home, to large-scale production in factories where unskilled workers, many of them women and children, toiled as acolytes of the insatiable machines. In 1765 **James Hargreaves** patented the "Spinning Jenny"—named after his wife—which could spin several threads simultaneously. Four years later a formidable Lancashireman named **Richard Arkwright**, the first great industrial tycoon, patented a spinning frame powered by water. He built a cotton mill and company town at Cromford in the beautiful Derbyshire valley of the Derwent, where his workers labored in 12-hour shifts as the machines clattered on day and night.

Titus Salt's vast 1853 mill and his model village at Saltaire, Bradford

> ❏ "And if here man has made of the very daylight an infamy, he can boast that he adds to the darkest night the weird beauty of fire and flame-tinted cloud. From roof and hill you may see on every side furnace calling furnace with fiery tongues and wreathing messages of smoke."
> – Arnold Bennett, *The Potteries* (1898) ❏

THE POWER OF STEAM Arkwright's machinery was powered by water, but in 1779 **Samuel Crompton** invented the so-called mule, a spinning machine that could be powered either by water or steam. Steam was the driving force of the Industrial Revolution and the most important figure in its development, the Scottish inventor **James Watt**, patented the first modern steam engine in 1769. Steam was used to drive all kinds of machinery in factories and mines and was later to propel locomotives and ships, as a transport revolution developed in the 19th century.

> ❏ "Since the introduction of inanimate mechanism into British manufactories, man, with few exceptions, has been treated as a secondary and inferior machine."
> —Robert Owen, *A New View of Society* (1813) ❏

COAL AND IRON Steam required coal. Britain's coal production doubled between 1750 and 1800 and then grew by 20 times by the end of the 19th century. **Abraham Darby** initiated the mass production of iron ore at **Ironbridge** and new industrial regions grew up close to the principal coalfields in the **Midlands**, the **North of England**, Scotland's **Clydeside** and **South Wales**. The flow of coal from the valleys turned sleepy little fishing villages like Cardiff, Barry and Swansea into busy, blackened ports. At the entrance to the Great Exhibition of 1851 in London's Hyde Park, there stood, appropriately, a towering 24-ton block of coal.

Towns like Manchester, Birmingham, Glasgow, Leeds, Bradford, and Sheffield covered their surrounding countryside with row upon row of workers' housing. Many a lush valley became an inferno of blast furnaces, slag heaps and "satanic mills." A new Iron Age introduced iron buildings, iron machines, iron bridges, iron boats, even iron tombstones—as well as the iron regimentation of the assembly line.

Victorian Britain had become "the workshop of the world," but other countries soon began to overtake it, notably Germany and the United States. In the 1880s Britain enjoyed 37 percent of the world's trade in manufactured goods, but by 1913 the figure was down to 25 percent. A new phase of the Industrial Revolution had opened, based on steel, chemicals, and electricity and Britain was unable to keep up.

The cotton mill built by Richard Arkwright in Cromford, Derbyshire

London

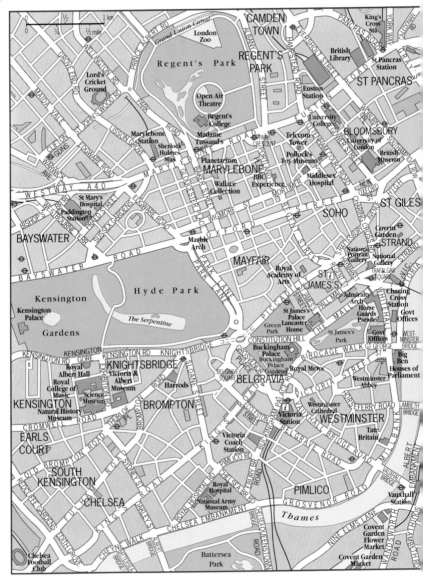

LONDON CONTENTS
Overview 42–46
Museums and art
  galleries 47–49
Houses 50–51
Walks 52–53
Churches 54
Nightlife 55
Shopping 56–57
Hotels 58
Eating out 59

LONDON With a population of seven million, London sprawls across a great basin bisected by the River Thames, which provides classic views, such as Big Ben and the Houses of Parliament from Westminster Bridge and the Tower of London and Tower Bridge from the South Bank. It is not an easy city in which to get your bearings—many Londoners think of the capital in terms of the Underground map rather than the street network—but its sudden changes of mood are the key to its appeal.

THE WEST END The bulk of the capital's attractions are to be found in the **West End**. **Trafalgar Square▶▶▶** is the undisputed center of London, where a statue of Admiral

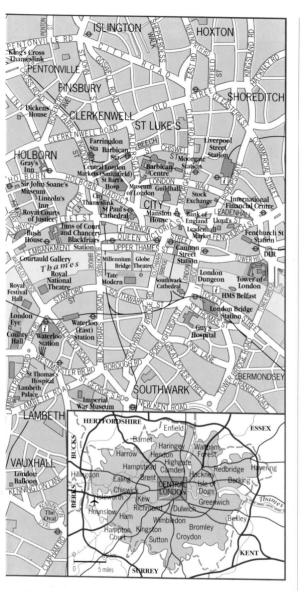

TOURIST INFORMATION
Tel: 09068 663344
(60p per minute)

Nelson stands high on a column guarded by stone lions modeled by the artist Edwin Henry Landseer. **St. Martin-in-the-Fields▶** and the **National Gallery▶▶▶** take up two sides of the square; Admiralty Arch leads through the third into the Mall, the grand approach to **Buckingham Palace▶▶** (begun 1825), the chief residence of the Queen with some rooms open in August and September. Adjacent are the **Queen's Gallery** (*Open* 2002) and the **Royal Mews**. Flanking the Mall are tree-shaded **Green Park** and **St. James's Park▶▶**, an alluring expanse with a lake and bandstand concerts in summer.

The hub of **Westminster** is Parliament Square, dominated by the clocktower housing the huge Big Ben

Taking a break by the fountains of Trafalgar Square against the backdrop of the National Gallery (left) and St. Martin-in-the-Fields Church (right)

▶▶▶ CITY HIGHLIGHTS

British Museum
pages 45 and 47

Covent Garden
pages 44 and 52

Greenwich
pages 46, 47, and 57

Hampton Court *page 51*

Museum of London
pages 46 and 49

St. Paul's Cathedral
pages 46 and 54

**South Kensington
museums** *pages 48–49*

**Tate Britain and Tate
Modern** *page 49*

**Tower of London and
Tower Bridge**
pages 45, 49, and 53

Trafalgar Square
pages 42–43 and 52

bell, which is part of London's most photographed building, the splendid Gothic Revival **Houses of Parliament▶▶▶**. The symbol of the seat of government, they were remodeled by Charles Barry and Augustus Pugin after fire destroyed an earlier building in 1834. When Parliament is in session you can view from the Strangers' Gallery (for times and details of guided tours tel: 020-7219 3000). Across the square is **Westminster Abbey▶▶**.

To the west, some of the best addresses in London are in **Mayfair**, chic **Chelsea**, elegant **Knightsbridge**, and **Kensington**. Here there is a preponderance of 19th-century stucco in addition to the familiar yellow-gray London stock brick. **South Kensington** is the primary museum quarter. **Hyde Park** and adjacent **Kensington Gardens** constitute a green swathe north of the Royal Albert Hall and the mildly preposterous Albert Memorial.

Covent Garden▶▶▶, the former fruit and vegetable market hall, has been imaginatively revamped as a lively piazza, with boutiques, street musicians, and craft stalls—the scheme was inspired by the renaissance of Faneuil Hall in Boston, Massachusetts. Covent Garden Piazza, laid out by Inigo Jones in 1631, was the first true square in London. The name Covent Garden also denotes the Royal Opera House. **Soho▶▶**, further west, is the center of the Chinese community (around Gerrard Street the street names are in Chinese) as well as an amalgam of Italian delicatessens, high-class restaurants, nightclubs, and sex stores.

Bloomsbury▶ represents the hub of intellectual London: blue plaques (placed on buildings throughout London) indicate the former houses of the famous, including the homes of Charles Dickens (a memorial museum is at 48 Doughty Street) and Virginia Woolf and her "Bloomsbury Set." Bloomsbury still has a gracious atmosphere and is a good illustration of how residential London developed into formal squares and terraces in Georgian and Regency times; Bedford Square continues to be as fashionable as when it was first laid out in 1775. Landmarks include the **British Museum**►►► and the unusual **British Telecom Tower**, built in 1964.

Regent's Park►► is a gracious tract that was laid out by Regency architect John Nash in conjunction with the supremely elegant stucco terraces on its east side; within the park are **London Zoo**►►, an open-air theater and a boating lake.

Legal London revolves around **Holborn**, with its Gothic Revival High Courts on the Strand and the Central Criminal Courts in the Old Bailey; both have public galleries within the courtrooms. Barristers are attached to chambers within the **Inns of Court** and **Chancery**►► (Gray's Inn, Middle Temple, Inner Temple and Lincoln's Inn), medieval foundations that originally gave lodging to lawyers and legal students; you can wander into the court-yards on weekdays. In Chancery Lane, the **Public Record Office**► is open on weekdays and exhibits the *Domesday Book*—the detailed survey of England made by William the Conqueror in 1086.

THE CITY The "square mile" of the ancient city of London, the City is where the major financial institutions are con-centrated; it retains its medieval street pattern, and though the city wall has largely disappeared, its gateways live on in place-names (Ludgate, Aldersgate, Moorgate, etc.); these gates, plus plinths bearing the City griffin, still mark the City boundaries. It is best approached from London Bridge, which has a picture-postcard view of **Tower Bridge**►►► and the **Tower of London**►►►. The **Monument**►, designed by Sir Christopher Wren to com-memorate the Great Fire of 1666, is a good viewing platform for those fit enough to manage the narrow steps up. Richard Rodgers' **Lloyd's Building**► in Lime Street is London's most innovative contribution to high-tech archi-tecture. The **Bank of England** (museum inside), the central bank of the U.K., stands opposite the Mansion House, the

A POTTED HISTORY
Becomes the Roman settlement of *Londinium* after the Roman invasion of Britain in AD 43. Hit by the Black Death in 1348–1350 and the Plague in 1665–1666. The Great Fire in 1666 destroys four-fifths of the city, taking the slums, rats, and plague with it. Sir Christopher Wren rebuilds St. Paul's Cathedral and a host of city churches. During World War II, much of central and suburban London is destroyed in the Blitz. Influx of Commonwealth immigrants invited over from the West Indies and Asia in the 1950s and 1960s to help solve a labor shortage. The 1990s recession is accom-panied by a slowdown in major building projects in the City and the Docklands. In 2000 the Millennium Dome fails to capture the public's affec-tion, and Ken Livingstone becomes the first elected Mayor of London.

45

WHITEHALL
Linking Trafalgar Square and Parliament Square, this street contains grandiose 19th-century government offices. London's main royal resi-dence was Whitehall Palace until it was destroyed by fire in 1698; the Banqueting House (designed by Inigo Jones in 1622), with its superb painted ceiling by Rubens, is the sole survivor. In 1649 Charles I walked across the hall and through a window to face his execution. The arch-way at the Horse Guards is the former entrance into the palace: tradition-ally dressed soldiers still keep watch; the Changing of the Guard occurs Apr–Aug, daily at 11 AM; Sep–Mar, every other day.

St. Paul's Cathedral was begun in 1675 and completed 35 years later

Canary Wharf Tower, completed in 1991, rises to 800 feet

GREENWICH

Greenwich Pier, SE10, is home to the "tea-clipper" **Cutty Sark**, launched in 1869 and the last of her kind to survive. She is preserved in dry dock as a museum. In Greenwich Park, the **National Maritime Museum**, Romney Road, celebrates Britain's long maritime history, with a fine array of nautical clocks, sea paintings and ship models. **The Royal Observatory**, was designed by Wren, with astronomical and navigational exhibits. Adjacent is the **Greenwich Meridian** (0° longitude), where you can have one foot in each hemisphere.

official residence of the Lord Mayor; Lombard Street, leading east, is London's Wall Street. Close by **St. Paul's Cathedral►►►**, the somewhat bleak-looking Barbican complex comprises 21 high-rise concrete apartment blocks and a confusing maze of walkways; within is the **Barbican Arts Centre**, home of the London Symphony Orchestra and London base of the Royal Shakespeare Company and the **Museum of London►►►**. To the west and outside the City proper, the quiet streets of **Smithfield►** are a different world, with an endearingly workaday look. The Central London Markets (Smithfield) is an outstanding example of a Victorian market building; adjacent Cloth Fair has a rare wooden house, a survivor of the Great Fire, while the **Church of St. Bartholomew the Great►►** represents London's most impressive Norman church architecture.

THE SUBURBS Docklands► is Europe's biggest urban development area. Once the East End district around the river docks, now a cityscape of gleaming office blocks and Dutch-looking waterside housing, the area covers the Isle of Dogs, North Woolwich, and Rotherhithe on the south bank. The best way to see it is from the elevated Docklands Light Railway (DLR), running from Tower Gateway or Bank to **Canary Wharf Tower**, Britain's tallest building. Canary Wharf and North Greenwich stations are the architectural highlights of the **Jubilee line extension**.

Greenwich►►► The former center of the maritime world (see also panel, page 47), Greenwich Park occupies a hillside above the Thames and within it are the Greenwich meridian line and the **Royal Observatory►►** of 1676, which houses instruments of navigation and astronomy. Just below, the **National Maritime Museum►►** and **Queen's House** (begun in 1616) form a supreme early classical composition by Wren and Inigo Jones. The former Royal Naval College was designed by Wren and the **painted hall►►**, open in the afternoons, has a superb painted ceiling by James Thornhill.

Hampstead and Highgate►► Hampstead Heath remains pleasantly countrified, with hollows, glades, and grassland. Parliament Hill Fields, in the southeast corner of the heath, has a wonderful view over central London. Hampstead village developed as an 18th-century spa and is one of the most fashionable residential districts; psychologist Sigmund Freud and poet John Keats were among its residents—both men's houses can be visited. **Highgate Cemetery►►** (*Guided tours*) has a spectacular derelict area where many rich and famous Victorians are buried.

Richmond and Chiswick►► These charming riverside suburbs, are best seen by taking the summer boat service or by walking along the river, for example westward from Hammersmith Bridge along Chiswick Mall and on to **Chiswick House►** (see page 51) or from Kew to Richmond and westward past **Ham House►** (see page 51). Another excellent boat trip is to **Hampton Court►►►** (see page 51). **Richmond Park►►** is a former royal hunting park, fenced in by Charles I in 1635 and still inhabited by deer; within is the Isabella Plantation, famous for azaleas and heathers. Near the river at Barnes, the **Wetland Centre►►** is a spectacular transformation (created 1995–2000) of reservoirs into a huge watery nature reserve with birdwatchers' blinds. For **Kew Gardens►►►** see page 16.

Museums and art galleries

Many of London's museums are free, or you might consider purchasing The London Pass, which offers entry to over 50 attractions, plus free travel on public transportation, and numerous other discounts (tel: 0870 242 9988, www.londonpass.com).

TRAFALGAR SQUARE The **National Gallery**►►► (*Guided tours* daily at 11:30 and 2:30, plus Wed 6:30 PM from the foyer of the Sainsbury Wing. *Admission free*), in Trafalgar Square, WC2, has a superb collection of paintings, many of which will be instantly familiar, from early Renaissance to the French Impressionists. Around the corner, in St. Martin's Place, WC2, is the **National Portrait Gallery**►► (*Admission free*), as complete a collection of faces of British history as you will find.

COVENT GARDEN AND BLOOMSBURY Somerset House, Strand, WC2 is home to the **Courtauld Gallery**►►, containing one of Britain's finest collections of French Impressionist and post-Impressionist paintings, the **Gilbert Collection**►►, home to a magnificent bequest of

decorative arts, and the **Hermitage Rooms**►► of treasures from the State Hermitage Museum in St. Petersburg. The **London Transport Museum**►►►, in the Piazza, Covent Garden, WC2, is an enthralling place which traces the development of London's buses, trams, trains, and "tubes." Nearby, the **Theatre Museum**►►, 1E Tavistock Street, Covent Garden, WC2, is a home for stage memorabilia.

The **British Museum**►►► (*Admission free; introductory and specialist tours daily*), Great Russell Street, WC1, is one of the greatest collections in the world. The most famous of its artifacts include the Rosetta Stone (which helped historians to decode hieroglyphics), Egyptian mummies, the Elgin Marbles from the Parthenon in Athens, and the Mildenhall and Sutton Hoo treasure hoards. The famous Reading Room, where Marx wrote *Das Kapital*, has been transformed into a reference library, surrounded by the Great Court, spanned by a huge glass roof. The **British Library**►► (*Admission free*) outgrew this space and moved to 96 Euston Road (by St. Pancras railroad station); its John Ritblat Gallery has many great treasures, including Beatles music manuscripts and the oldest wall map of the world.

GETTING AROUND
Forget the car and use public transportation. Day travelcards can be purchased at Underground and railroad stations and from many newssellers and entitle you to unlimited travel by train, Underground, and bus (but not night bus services); Zone 1 tickets cover the center. The Underground (or "tube") is easiest to understand, but the double-decker buses give excellent views (bus route 11 is recommended); free bus maps are available from tourist offices.
For organized tours see page 271.
A street atlas, such as the AA's Street by Street London, is especially useful for exploring the center and suburbs.

The London Transport Museum

EXCURSIONS
The number of possible day trips from the capital is endless. Here we highlight some recommended excursions that can easily be made by train.
Castles: Dover, Windsor.
Historic cities: Cambridge, Canterbury, Oxford, Salisbury, Winchester.
Industrial, railroad, and naval interest: Amberley Museum, Bluebell Railway (near East Grinstead), Royal Naval Base (Chatham), Portsmouth, Watercress Line (Alton to Alresford).
Roman remains: Fishbourne Palace (near Chichester), Lullingstone Villa (near Eynsford), Verulamium (St Albans).
Coastal resorts: Brighton, Broadstairs, Eastbourne, Hastings.
Small towns: Arundel, Lewes, Rye, Sandwich, Tunbridge Wells.

CHANGING EXHIBITIONS OF ART AND DESIGN

The major sites for art exhibitions are the Hayward Gallery on the South Bank, SE1, the Royal Academy in Piccadilly, W1, the ICA in the Mall, SW1, the Saatchi Gallery at 98 Boundary Road NW8, and the Barbican Centre, Silk Street, EC2. The latest aspects of design are on show at the Design Centre in Haymarket (*Admission free*). The Serpentine Gallery in Kensington Gardens has exhibitions focusing on younger contemporary artists (*Admission free*).

The Natural History Museum's pattern of colored terra-cotta and French Romanesque elements was the creation of Alfred Waterhouse

48

REGENT'S PARK AND BAKER STREET London Zoo▶▶ in Regent's Park, NW1, is one of the world's great animal collections and an important research center. It places emphasis on breeding endangered species and on education. In Marylebone Road, NW1, **Madame Tussaud's▶** wax museum tops the charts as a paying tourist attraction; be photographed alongside politicians, pop stars, and sport celebrities. Lines can be long—some may feel the wait and steep admission aren't worth it. Its annex, the **Spirit of London▶** is a "sight, sounds and smells" journey in replica taxi through 400 years of London's history. Next door at the **Planetarium▶** the night sky is projected onto a dome as you are guided around the constellations. The **Sherlock Holmes Museum** at 221b Baker Street, W1, displays memorabilia of the great sleuth at the address used in Arthur Conan Doyle's stories. The **Wallace Collection▶▶** (*Admission free*), has Frans Hals's *The Laughing Cavalier*, plus a superb collection of French paintings and porcelain.

GREAT SPORTING VENUES

London's major sporting venues double as tourist attractions. The Wimbledon Lawn Tennis Museum (Southfields railroad station) recalls the sport's great moments. For Rugby Union fans, the Twickenham Experience (Twickenham railroad station) includes a museum and a stadium tour, while Lord's Cricket Ground (St. John's Wood tube) has a museum open on match days.

SOUTH KENSINGTON Prince Albert headed the Royal Commission that purchased the museum sites in what was dubbed Albertopolis. The **Victoria and Albert Museum▶▶▶** (the "V&A"), Cromwell Road, SW7 (*Admission free*), is a treasurehouse of decorative art and design, displayed by theme (musical instruments, costume, furniture, etc.) and by civilization (Japan, China, India, etc.). There is something for everyone but too much for one visit. Meanwhile, across the road at the **Natural History Museum▶▶▶**, Cromwell Road, SW7 (*Admission free*), dinosaurs, evolution, blue whales...just about everything is here in this splendid Victorian building. The collection is extremely popular with children. The **Science Museum▶▶▶**, around the corner in Exhibition Road, SW7 (*Admission free*), is also a hit with children, but has plenty for everyone.

CHELSEA AND WESTMINSTER The **National Army Museum▶** (*Admission free*), Royal Hospital Road, SW3, tells a 500-year story of soldiers through the ages. The **Cabinet War Rooms▶** in King Charles Street, SW1, were the subterranean emergency offices for Winston Churchill and his cabinet in World War II; the Map Room and the Transatlantic Telephone Room remain intact.

The **Tate Britain▶▶▶** in Millbank, SW1, is the nation's greatest collection of British art; an excellent headphone tour introduces you to the major works. Entry is free but admission is charged for special exhibitions. **The Queen's Gallery▶** at Buckingham Palace, SW1, has items from the royal collection (*Open* 2002), while the **Royal Mews▶** contains the spectacular State Coaches and the Royal Family's sleighs.

SOUTH OF THE RIVER The **Imperial War Museum▶▶▶**, Lambeth Road, SE1, covers the wars that Britain has been involved in since 1914. There is a Blitz reconstruction and a trench dug out, in addition to weapons, memorabilia, uniforms, and a Holocaust exhibition. The latter is particulary harrowing, and is unsuitable for children under 14 years of age. Near Westminster Bridge, County Hall is home to the **London Aquarium▶**. You can hardly miss the slowly rotating 459 feet tall **London Eye▶▶▶**, the world's tallest ferris wheel, erected for the new millennium, whose 30 capusule offer fine views over the city. Further east, by Waterloo Bridge, is the Royal National Theatre complex.

In Southwark, on Bankside, the thatched, circular **Globe Theatre** is a faithful rebuilding of the venue where many of Shakespeare's plays were performed in his own lifetime. There are guided tours, an exhibition, and summer performances in this, the only thatched roof structure to be built in London since the Great Fire. The **Tate Modern▶▶▶** (*Admission free*) is a stunning modern art collection housed in a former power station. The **Design Museum▶** at Butler's Wharf, 28 Shad Thames, SE1, is a stylish riverside building housing thematic exhibitions of modern design. At the **London Dungeon** in Tooley Street, SE1, gloomy vaults reveal the dark stories of punishment, torture, and witchcraft in times past. Next door, **Winston Churchill's Britain at War Experience** evokes London at the height of the Blitz, with the smells and sounds of an air raid. Moored on the Thames close by (reached from Tower Bridge, via the Thames Path) is **H.M.S. Belfast▶▶**, the last of the Royal Navy's big World War II gunships, launched in 1938.

TOWER HILL AND THE CITY The **Tower of London▶▶▶**, Tower Hill, EC3, is the greatest Norman castle in the kingdom, standing silent sentinel in the shadow of adjacent Tower Bridge; the locale has had a long and gory history from Roman times on. Traditionally dressed Beefeaters still patrol the grounds. The White Tower is the main Norman feature, housing St. John's Chapel while the Crown Jewels are in the Jewel House.

At the **Museum of London▶▶▶**, London Wall, EC2, is a time-walk display beginning with Roman London, passing a scale model of St. James's Palace in its heyday, and a full-size street of Victorian stores.

THE EAST END
The **Bethnal Green Museum of Childhood** (*Admission free*), Cambridge Heath Road, Bethnal Green, E2, is an entertaining offshoot of the Victoria and Albert Museum. Toys of all ages and countries are here; among the exhibits are a wonderful collection of dollshouses, a surreal display of dolls' heads and a group of puppet theaters. The **Geffrye Museum** occupies a row of early 18th-century almshouses in Kingsland Road, Hackney, E2. Each of a series of rooms is furnished in a different period style, from the Elizabethan era to 1999. It is a succinct summary of furniture styles through the ages.

SUBURBAN MUSEUMS AND GALLERIES
The **Royal Air Force Museum**, Grahame Park Way, Hendon (Colindale tube) has dozens of aircraft, plus a Red Arrow flight simulator and a Battle of Britain Experience. The **Dulwich Picture Gallery**, Dulwich, SE21, is England's oldest public gallery (1814) and housed in a neo-classical building by Sir John Soane. There are works by Gainsborough, Reynolds, Rembrandt, and others.

The White Tower, the Tower of London

LONDON'S BLUE PLAQUES

A walk around London almost invariably passes at least one building with a blue plaque recalling a famous former occupant. The practice of placing these markers dates back to 1867, when Lord Byron was the first to be thus commemorated. The person must be adjudged to have made "some important positive contribution to human welfare or happiness." Responsibility for erecting plaques now falls to English Heritage (see page 124).

WHERE THE FAMOUS LIE AT REST

The churchyards of Inner London were so crowded by the early 1800s that they had become revolting and unsanitary. To relieve pressure, massive cemeteries were created further out, which are the resting places of some of London's most famous dead. Emmeline Pankhurst, the suffragette leader, is buried in Brompton Cemetery; the music-hall queen Marie Lloyd in Hampstead Cemetery; Isambard Kingdom Brunel and Anthony Trollope at Kensal Green; George Eliot and Karl Marx in Highgate Cemetery.

Left: Hampton Court's Pond Gardens started life as fish ponds supplying the royal kitchens

Houses

London has a wide range of houses open to the public, from grand palaces built for monarchs to the more personal homes of the famous or eccentric.

CENTRAL LONDON Sir John Soane's Museum►► (*Admission free*), 13 Lincoln's Inn Fields, WC2, is wonderfully eccentric; it was designed by the architect Soane (1753–1837), to contain his collection of mostly architectural artifacts. The house is full of inventive lighting effects and quirky details, as well as some great treasures, in particular the paintings of *A Rake's Progress* and *An Election* by Hogarth. At **Dickens' House►**, 48 Doughty Street, WC1, Charles Dickens wrote *Oliver Twist*, the *Pickwick Papers* and *Nicholas Nickleby*. **Dr Johnson's House**, 17 Gough Square, EC4, hidden away down an alley off Fleet Street, is the house where Samuel Johnson lived between 1749 and 1759 and where he completed his celebrated dictionary. Now it is a museum, with mementoes of Johnson's life and work (see panel, page 122).

Apsley House►►, Hyde Park Corner, W1, was the London home of the Duke of Wellington, built in 1778 by Robert Adam with 19th-century alterations by James Wyatt. Its grand interior houses mementoes of the Iron Duke and his campaigns, as well as his impressive collection of paintings. The German composer Georg Friedrich Handel spent many years in London: his house at 25 Brook Street, W1, where he wrote the *Messiah* is now a museum.

Kensington Palace►► Kensington Gardens, W8, was remodeled by Christopher Wren and later William Kent. It was the birthplace of Queen Victoria; it is now the residence of Princess Margaret and was that of Diana,

Princess of Wales. It has the royal collection of pictures and furniture and magnificent court costumes.

Spencer House▶ (1756–1766) was built for the first Earl of Spencer, an ancestor of the Princess of Wales and has sumptuously gilded interiors.

Buckingham Palace▶▶, the official residence of the Queen, is open Aug–Sep, giving a glimpse of the state rooms and garden; try to book ahead on 020-7321 2233.

In Holland Park Road, W14, stands **Leighton House▶ ▶** (*Admission free*), created by the Victorian artist Lord Leighton. Paintings by him and members of the Pre-Raphaelite circle adorn the walls, but the astonishing tiled Arab Hall, styled on a Moorish palace, steals the show.

HAMPSTEAD Kenwood House▶ (*Admission free*), Hampstead Lane, NW8, is handsomely situated on the edge of Hampstead Heath. Robert Adam gave the house its classical proportions; within is a collection of old masters and portraits, including works by Reynolds and Gainsborough. Outdoor summer concerts, often with fireworks, attract big crowds on Saturday evenings. Hampstead's oldest house and one of the grandest, is **Fenton House▶** (N.T.) on Windmill Hill, NW3; it contains antique keyboard instruments, paintings, and furniture. You can visit the houses of the poet **John Keats** and the psychoanalyst **Sigmund Freud**. The great Modernist architect Erno Goldfinger designed **2 Willow Road** in 1939 for himself; it is now owned by the National Trust.

SOUTH AND WEST Hampton Court▶ ▶ ▶, East Molesey, Surrey, is best reached from London by riverboat from Westminster Pier. The palace was begun in the early 16th century by Cardinal Wolsey and later presented to Henry VIII; it is an enjoyable potpourri of styles and history, with a hammer-beamed hall, Wren's Fountain Court, an Orangery with Mantegna cartoons and carvings by Grinling Gibbons. The grounds contain a famous maze.

Ham House▶ ▶ (N.T.), Ham Street, Ham, near the Thames towpath close to Richmond Park, is, for London, an outstanding example of Jacobean architecture, built in 1610.

Kew Palace▶ ▶ was built in 1631 for a London merchant and subsequently leased by George II for Queen Caroline. Since its purchase in 1781 by George III, the house has changed little and retains its old paneling and portraits. A visit here ties in nicely with **Kew Gardens** (see page 16) and a walk along the Thames towpath to Richmond.

Chiswick House▶ (E.H.), Chiswick Park, Chiswick, W4 is a small, formal Palladian villa (1729) once used for soirées and as a library rather than as a house. Modeled on Palladio's Villa Capra in Italy, it stands in delightful parkland, naturalistically landscaped in what came to be regarded as the English manner.

Osterley Park▶ ▶ (N.T.), off Great West Road (A4), Osterley, is a gracious manor house set in parkland, all but engulfed by the suburbia of London's western fringes. Osterley provides an excellent opportunity to see Robert Adam's interiors at their richest. Adam's work dates from 1761 to 1780; the house itself has Tudor origins.

In southeast London, **Eltham Palace▶ ▶** (E.H.) is a unique architectural mixture: the great hall of a medieval palace adjoins an ocean-liner style Art Deco mansion.

Kensington Palace became a royal residence when asthmatic William III elected to move away from the unhealthy riverside air of Whitehall Palace

51

ROBERT ADAM
The state rooms at Syon House and Osterley House are among the finest sets of Robert Adam interiors in the country. The brilliant Scottish designer was born at Kirkcaldy in 1728 and was trained, along with his three brothers, by his architect father, William. He set up practice in London in 1758 and three years later was appointed principal architect to George III. His elegant and graceful classical interiors, lightening the austere accepted Palladian style, were soon all the rage and widely copied. He pioneered several architectural features, notably elliptical rooms. Charlotte Square in Edinburgh (see page 224) is one of his most notable works in his native Scotland. He died in London in 1792.

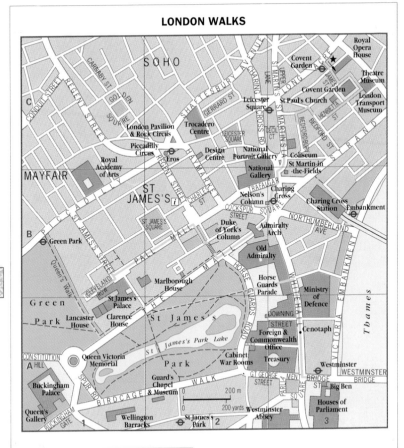

LONDON WALKS

Covent Garden, Royal London and Westminster

Start from Covent Garden tube station. Walk down James Street to **Covent Garden▶▶**, the former fruit and vegetable market, now transformed into a stylish shopping piazza and popular meeting place. The **Theatre Museum▶** and **London Transport Museum▶▶** are close by. From Henrietta Street, an archway on the right leads into the churchyard of St. Paul's, the innovative design of Inigo Jones. At the heart of London's theaterland, St. Paul's is known as the **actors' church▶** and its interior walls are covered with plaques in memory of stars of stage and screen. Leave the churchyard via a gate onto Bedford Street; off the next street to the west, Bedfordbury, an arch leads into Goodwin Court, where bow-windowed houses have changed little since the 18th century. As you reach St. Martin's Lane, opposite is Cecil Court, part of the secondhand bookstore quarter. Enter **Trafalgar Square▶▶▶** at the end of St. Martin's Lane, the great pigeon-populated piazza fronted by the church of **St. Martin-in-the-Fields▶▶** and the **National Gallery▶▶▶**. Cross over to Admiralty Arch and enter the Mall. Steps lead up to the right past the Duke of York's column. Walk along Pall Mall, past the long-established concentration of fashionable gentlemen's clubs, distinguished by unobtrusive signs at the entrances.

Big Ben: not the tower, not the clock, but the massive bell inside

Take a detour to look at the east side of St. James's Street with its trio of old-fashioned stores—Lock's the hat-makers, Berry and Rudd's wine merchants, and Lobb's, makers of custom-fitted shoes. Adjacent Pickering Place was once used for sword duels.

Cleveland Row skirts **St. James's Palace▶**, residence of Prince Charles and others; leave by gates onto Queen's Walk, along the edge of Green Park. Return to the Mall: **Buckingham Palace▶▶**, the main residence of the Queen, is to the right; the Changing of the Guard takes place Apr–Aug, daily at 11:30 AM; Sep–Mar, every other day. Cross the Mall and enter St. James's Park, keeping left. Pass through the arch into **Horse Guards' Parade▶▶** and on to Whitehall; Downing Street, to the right, has at No. 10 the house of the prime minister. In Parliament Square is Big Ben, part of the **Houses of Parliament▶▶▶**. Across the square is **Westminster Abbey**. Return from Westminster tube station.

53

Walk

Along the South Bank to Tower Hill

Start from Westminster Bridge. The above walk can be extended by following the South Bank (which has a walkway for much of the way) from Westminster Bridge, past the **London Eye▶▶▶**—a huge ferris wheel erected for the new millennium—and on to the **Royal Festival Hall▶**. Further on is the **Globe Theatre▶▶** (see page 49). The walkway continues east of Waterloo Bridge past an impressive modern office complex, with outstanding views of the City. Pass **H.M.S. Belfast▶▶** and carry on to **Tower Bridge▶▶** (the Tower Bridge Experience inside the bridge explains its workings and gives access to the high-level walkway, or cross at street level for free); to the right you can see Canary Wharf, Britain's tallest building. On the other side, circle around the moat of the **Tower of London▶▶▶**. Signs to the World Trade Centre lead you to **St. Katharine's Dock▶** yacht haven. Return from Tower Hill tube station.

St. Katharine's Dock

Southwark Cathedral is noted for the many monuments that survived from its days as a monastic church. That of poet John Gower, above, is dated 1408

SIR CHRISTOPHER WREN (1632–1723)
Wren, one of the most celebrated of British architects, was responsible for the rebuilding of St. Paul's Cathedral (in which his monument appears as *lector, si monumentum requiris, circumspice*—"reader, if you seek my monument, look around") and the City churches. He drew up an ambitious plan for the rebuilding of London with Continental-style avenues, but the complexities of land ownership prevented it from being carried out. M.P. for Weymouth in Dorset, he used the local Portland stone liberally in his buildings. The other great architect of the day was Inigo Jones, who designed Covent Garden piazza, the first piazza in London.

The dome of St. Paul's Cathedral

Churches

Although the Great Fire of 1666, the Blitz of 1940 and constant rebuilding have changed London's face repeatedly, there is still an impressive legacy of church architecture, dating from Norman times. There are particularly fine examples of designs of the master architects of the 17th and 18th centuries: Wren, Hawksmoor, and Inigo Jones.

THE EARLIEST CHURCHES The only large-scale church of the Norman period in London is **St. Bartholomew the Great▶▶** in West Smithfield, EC1. It is the survivor of a 12th-century Augustinian priory and although the apsidal east end is a 19th-century rebuilding, the atmosphere is of great antiquity. **Southwark Cathedral▶▶**, Montague Close, the cathedral for the South Bank, was founded as the Augustinian priory church of St. Mary Overie in 1106. Although much restored in the 19th century, it is the most substantial medieval artifact in the district of Southwark. The building attained cathedral status in 1905. Previously it was known as St. Mary Overie (meaning "over" the water from the City).

SIR CHRISTOPHER WREN Wren's domed masterpiece, **St. Paul's Cathedral▶▶▶**, Ludgate Hill, EC4, replaced an earlier Gothic cathedral that perished in the Great Fire of 1666. It no longer dominates the skyline as it did until the mid-20th century, but when seen close up the proportions are overwhelming. Inside the dome, the Whispering Gallery plays acoustic tricks (whispered sounds carry around the great void) and gives splendid interior views. There are tombs of Wren, Nelson, Wellington, Turner, and Reynolds in the crypt, views from the Golden Gallery, woodwork by Gibbons and ironwork by Tijou.
After the Great Fire, Sir Christopher Wren graced the City with 51 churches. Among the most celebrated of **Wren's City churches▶▶** are St. Bride's (Fleet Street), St. Margaret's (Lothbury), St. Martin Ludgate (Ludgate Hill), St. Mary Abchurch (Cannon Street), St. Mary-at-Hill (Eastcheap) and St. Stephen Walbrook (Walbrook).

OTHER GREAT CHURCHES St. Martin-in-the-Fields▶, Trafalgar Square, WC2, is an 18th-century rebuilding by James Gibbs and a particularly satisfying example of the temple-like architecture of the period, with a characteristic galleried interior.
At **Westminster Abbey▶▶▶**, Parliament Square, SW1, British sovereigns are crowned and many great men and women are buried, among them monarchs, statesmen, poets, and scientists. It also has cloisters, a treasury, brass-rubbing center and the oldest garden (*Open* Thu only) in the country. **Westminster Cathedral▶**, in Ashley Place, off Victoria Street, SW1, is Britain's premier Roman Catholic cathedral, a Byzantine brick creation finished in 1903; incense fills the cavernous interior.

Nightlife

THEATER There are dozens of theaters to choose from, offering everything from Shakespeare to Andrew Lloyd Webber musicals; the capital has an impressive legacy of Victorian theater architecture. Discount tickets for the day of performance are available from the tks ticket booth in Leicester Square (see panel).

NIGHTSPOTS Soho and Covent Garden constitute the heart of clubland with clubs like the Hippodrome and Empire discotheque by Leicester Square and The Wag in Wardour Street. Ronnie Scott's (47 Frith Street, W1) is a well-established jazz spot, and Heaven (under Charing Cross Station) is a leading gay club. Cabaret and alternative comedy are performed at The Comedy Store in Leicester Square. Away from the center of town is the highly esteemed Fridge, at Town Hall Parade, Brixton Hill, SW2. Watch listings (see panel) for pop/rock concerts at the Hammersmith Odeon and Brixton Academy.

CLASSICAL MUSIC London has five resident orchestras. The Royal Festival Hall on the South Bank (plus the smaller Purcell Room and Queen Elizabeth Hall) and the Barbican Hall, Silk Street (Moorgate subway), are major concert halls. Wigmore Hall, Wigmore Street hosts performances by up-and-coming artists. Summer visitors should try to take in a Promenade Concert ("the Proms," see page 18), Europe's biggest music festival, at the Royal Albert Hall. Operas at the Royal Opera House in Covent Garden are performed in the original language with subtitles projected above, while the English National Opera in the Coliseum, St. Martin's Lane, gives performances in English. Many churches host lunchtime recitals; most are free, with a collection made at the end.

FILM The big first-run movie house is the Odeon in Leicester Square, which still boasts an organ. The National Film Theatre (N.F.T.) on the South Bank near Waterloo is the leading repertory film theater; programs change daily; one-day memberships are available.

LISTINGS AND BOOKINGS
The weekly magazine *Time Out* gives listings for all London's entertainments, events, and exhibitions and has excellent previews. The *London Theatre Guide*, updated every two weeks, lists theatrical events and is available free of charge from West End theatres, libraries, and tourist information centers.
Buy tickets directly from the box office to avoid paying commissions. Ticket agencies include Ticketmaster (tel: 020-7344 4444); check for credit card surcharges. Never buy tickets from touts on the street or unofficial agencies. Discounted tickets are available, on the day of performance only, from tkts in Leicester Square (*Open* Mon–Sat 10–7, Sun noon–3).

The lights of Leicester Square

James Smith's redoubtable stick and umbrella store

LONDON VIEWS

Take the elevator up the bell tower of Westminster Cathedral, ride the London Eye; reservations advised (tel: 0870 400 3040), or climb the steps to the top of St. Paul's Cathedral or the Monument (both in the City). There are superb views for free from Waterloo and Hungerford bridges, Primrose Hill, (north of Regent's Park), and Parliament Hill Fields (Hampstead Heath).

Shopping

PRINCIPAL SHOPPING AREAS The major West End department stores are clustered along **Oxford Street**, with Selfridges the biggest of them. John Lewis (whose "never knowingly undersold" policy guarantees a refund if you find the same goods on sale cheaper elsewhere) has a fine stock of furnishings, fashions, and decorative items, while the ubiquitous Marks and Spencer is known for good-value clothing and good food halls. Virgin Megastore and HMV have big selections of CDs and cassettes.

Around the corner, **Regent Street** comes into its own in the weeks before Christmas when the illuminations are switched on; during this period, Hamleys, the undisputed king of the toystores, fills to bursting and has spectacular displays. Nearby is Liberty, renowned for Liberty print fabrics and clothes; the mock-Tudor building itself is worth a look.

Stereos and electrical goods are available at discount prices in the stores along **Tottenham Court Road**. The **British Museum** store has stylish reproductions of some of its treasures; nearby at 53 New Oxford Street, **James Smith's** umbrella store has an eye-catching Victorian storefront boasting "Life Preservers, Jagger Canes and Swordsticks."

Charing Cross Road constitutes the heart of London's bookstore territory. Foyles, the largest bookstore, has an impressive stock though the layout can be confusing. There is a particularly fascinating array of specialist secondhand bookstores just off Charing Cross Road on Cecil Court. Around the corner in Trafalgar Square, the **National Gallery store** has a good selection of art posters, cards, and books. **Soho** is densely packed with ethnic food stores, including Chinese supermarkets in Chinatown, and numerous Italian delis.

Covent Garden has a wide variety of stores and boutiques, including the Tea Shop in Neal Street, a cheese store and bakery in Neal's Yard and a dollhouse store in the piazza itself.

St. James's Street, off Piccadilly, has old-fashioned stores: Berry and Rudd wine merchants, Lock's the hatmakers, and Lobb's the shoemakers.

Kings Road in Chelsea is the place for chic fashions, stylish interior design stores, and people-watching; a nice antiques market (Mon–Sat) extends along one part.

GREAT FOR WINDOW SHOPPING Harrods, Brompton Road, is the grandest department store of them all; many visitors go just to get a shopping bag. Harrods prides itself on its range and quality of stock; the food halls conjure up Edwardian splendor. **Burlington Arcade**, off Piccadilly, is a perfectly preserved Regency shopping arcade, retaining its early 19th-century air with considerable dignity. An immaculately attired beadle patrols the alley and notices forbid "hurrying or whistling." **Fortnum and Mason**, on Piccadilly, is the food store *par excellence*. The famous exterior clock features Mr. Fortnum and Mr. Mason, who bow to each other on the hour. **New Bond Street** is the home of Sotheby's, the prestigious fine art auctioneers.

Street markets always provide good entertainment. Easily the most atmospheric is **Brick Lane** (Sunday mornings only), off Bethnal Green Road in the heart of Cockney London, now the Bengali community. It is unashamedly shabby and hugely crowded, with wares ranging from cheap stereos to secondhand junk. Note this is not the same as the nearby (and overrated) Petticoat Lane Market. Weekend-long antiques markets are at **Camden Lock** and **Greenwich. Portobello Road**, W11, operates Monday to Saturday (junk stalls on Friday, antiques on Saturday); both get absolutely packed. **Grays Antique Market** (Mon–Fri) at 1–7 Davies Mews, W1, has some 180 dealers within two Victorian warehouses.

Below: some chic window displays verge on the inscrutable

57

SPEAKERS' CORNER
At the corner of Hyde Park, close to Marble Arch at the western end of Oxford Street, Speakers' Corner is a bastion of free speech. It provides memorable free entertainment, at lunchtime Monday to Friday and is at full throttle on Sunday morning. Anyone can set up a soapbox and speak on anything he or she likes as long as there is no blasphemy, defamation, treason, or breach of the peace laws.

Only the best: a selection of Fortnum and Mason's gift baskets while a frock-coated assistant looks on

RESERVING HOTELS

London Tourist Board has lists of hotels and operates a reservation service. For recorded information, tel: 0906 850 5487 (premium rate). For reservations tel: 020-7223 7226, 020-7223 7229 or 020-7223 8666. You can also rent a flat; the tourist board has details of agencies.

In a city of pricey hotels, London's top hotels can be a very expensive experience

Service at its most discreet…

Hotels

HOTELS London is one of the most expensive European capitals for hotel rooms. Those who can afford high prices will appreciate the style and service at such long-established and prestigious establishments as the Ritz, Claridge's, the Savoy, the Dorchester, and the Connaught; be prepared for lots of British formality, however, and do not expect air-conditioning as a matter of course. The top modern hotels are generally all in the same price bracket. Among the best areas to stay in the capital are the West

End (W1, NW1, SW1, WC2), Bloomsbury (WC1), Kensington (SW7, W2, W8, W11), Knightsbridge (SW1) and Chelsea (SW3).

BED AND BREAKFAST Even a modest B.&B. accommodation costs roughly twice what you would pay outside London. There is a reasonable selection around Victoria (SW1) and Bloomsbury (WC1); the King's Cross area (also WC1) is cheap and drab (Argyle Street WC1, is a reasonable bet if you're really stuck) and there are plenty of places (including some private hostels) in the Earl's Court area (SW5). Out to the west, Hammersmith (W6) is an unprepossessing area but has some large hotels and good Underground connections to central London. Small hotels and B&Bs exist in many suburbs and can cut your hotel costs; aim for a location convenient to the Underground and check the journey time and the timing of the last train back.

HOSTELS AND CAMPSITES The central locations for youth hostelers are on Noel Street, W1, Bolton Gardens, SW5, Holland Park, W8, Euston Road, N1 and Carter Lane, EC4; three further-flung hostels are on Highgate West Hill, N6, Wellgarth Road, NW11 and Salter Road, Rotherhithe, SE16. Reservations are advised (national YHA tel: 0870 870 8808). Additionally, numerous colleges offer accommodations in the summer. Campsites are obviously further out; Crystal Palace Caravan (trailer) Site, SE19, is pleasantly situated, with good public transportation links.

Eating out

BREAKFAST For a leisurely start to the day, splurge on **breakfast** at one of the big hotels such as the Savoy (the Strand, WC2; tel: 020-7836 4343). Devotees of Chinese *dim sum* brunch should look no further than New World (1 Gerrard Place, W1; tel: 020-7434 2508).

LUNCH For quick lunches, sandwich bars and no-frills restaurants are a good bet; there are several of these in the West End. Many pubs and wine bars offer food, though some get crowded and smokey; Gordon's Wine Bar (47 Villiers Street, WC2; tel: 020-7930 1408) is set in a subterranean vault by the Thames. Look around Soho and Covent Garden for Asian restaurants, which offer good-value lunches. You can lunch at some top restaurants for roughly half the price of an evening meal. Big museums and galleries, including the National Gallery, Tate Gallery, and Festival Hall, have good self-service cafeterias. A number of inexpensive southern Indian vegetarian restaurants, along Drummond Street, NW1, are handy for Regent's Park. Panton Street, WC2, off Leicester Square, has several budget eateries.

AFTERNOON TEA Tea is served with considerable flair at such prestigious hotels as the Ritz (reservation advisable; Piccadilly, W1; tel: 020-7493 8181) and Brown's (Dover Street, W1; tel: 020-7493 6020), although prices are high and there is a formal dress code. Less expensive options are Fortnum and Mason's (tel: 020-7734 8040) and the Charing Cross Hotel (Strand, WC2; tel: 020-7839 7282).

THE EVENING For a treat, try one of the great Continental-style restaurants such as Bibendum (Michelin House, 81 Fulham Road, SW3; tel: 020-7581 5817) in the eye-catching Michelin Building, or Nico Central (35 Great Portland Street, W1; tel: 020-7436 8846). Those who wish to live it up without breaking the bank may like Kettner's (29 Romilly Street, W1; no reservations), in the heart of Soho, part of the Pizza Express chain. London's residential districts Hampstead, Camden Town, Islington, Bayswater, Chelsea, and Kensington have a good choice of places to eat. See also accommodations and restaurants, pages 276–284.

PUBS IN LONDON
Pubs of special character include the **Cittie of York** (with Britain's longest bar, 22 High Holborn, WC2); the **Lamb and Flag** (in Covent Garden, 33 Rose Street, WC2); the **Museum Tavern** (near the British Museum, Museum Street, WC1); the **Princess Louise** (spectacular Victorian tiled interior, 208 High Holborn, WC1); the **Lamb** (Bloomsbury, with old fittings, Lamb's Conduit Street, WC1); **Ye Olde Cheshire Cheese** (ancient tavern, former haunt of writers Dickens and Johnson, Wine Office Court, 145 Fleet Street, EC4); the **George Inn** (London's last galleried inn, Borough High Street, SE1); the **Black Friar** (London's finest Art Nouveau pub interior, 174 Queen Victoria Street, EC4, opposite Blackfriars station); and the **Dove** (riverside pub with terrace, 19 Upper Mall, Chiswick, W6). Fuller's and Young's are two excellent "real ale" London brews.

The Ritz was London's very first steel-framed building when erected in 1906

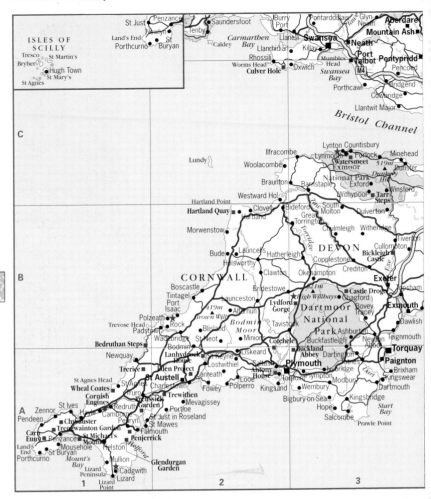

★ Walk start point

0	10	20	30	40	50 km
0		10		20	30 miles

THE WEST COUNTRY The tapering southwestern peninsula of England culminates in the rugged clifflands of western Cornwall, where Land's End forms the big toe of Great Britain. Called the West Country, the area offers perhaps a fuller range of activities, landscapes, and experiences than any other in Britain and, as a result, you'll find many other visitors here, especially during the summer, when the crowds are sometimes overwhelming. People from all over Britain spend their vacations here, in indolent ease or in a whirl of activity. For many of them, the region's diversity is the key to its appeal.

The climate is mild and the sprawling resorts of Torquay and Bournemouth head the sunshine league; this is also a major retirement area. To many, the West Country is synonymous with dairy country; the locals are big cheese-eaters, and you can indulge in a cream tea or even mail home some delicious "clotted" cream, a cholesterol-watcher's nightmare. Another regional speciality is lardy cake, a gooey raisin-topped bakery product largely confined to the southern and western counties.

Opposite: Land's End, Cornwall

The West Country

RECOMMENDED COASTAL TOWNS AND VILLAGES

Cornwall: Boscastle, Port Isaac, Padstow, St. Ives, Mousehole, Cadgwith, St. Anthony in Roseland, Portloe, Mevagissey, Charlestown, Fowey, Polperro, Kingsand.
Devon: Lynmouth, Clovelly, Sidmouth, Dartmouth, Salcombe, Newton Ferrers, Plymouth.
Dorset: Lyme Regis, Abbotsbury, Weymouth.

SMALL TOWNS INLAND
Cornwall: Launceston
Somerset: Dulverton, Wells, Dunster, Glastonbury.
Dorset: Beaminster, Sherborne, Shaftesbury.
Wiltshire: Marlborough, Bradford on Avon, Devizes.

HISTORIC CITIES
Bath, Bristol, Exeter, Salisbury.

COASTAL FEATURES
Cornwall: Tintagel Castle, Bedruthan Steps, Gurnards Head (near Zennor), Porthcurno open-air theatre, Logan Rock (near Treen), St. Michael's Mount, Mullion Cove, Fal Estuary, Dodman Point, Rame Head.
Devon: Valley of Rocks, Baggy Point (near Croyde), Hartland Quay, Hobby Drive (near Clovelly), Hooken Cliffs (near Beer), Bolt Head, Bolt Tail (both near Salcombe).
Somerset Porlock Toll Road, Selworthy Beacon, Brean Down

(continued on page 63)

▶▶▶ REGION HIGHLIGHTS

Avebury page 65
Bath pages 65 and 66
Cheddar Gorge page 85
Cornish Coast pages 68–71
Dartmoor National Park pages 73–74
Dorset coast page 77
Exmoor National Park pages 78–79
Salisbury pages 82–83
Stonehenge page 84
Wells page 84

CORNWALL Until the opening of the Tamar railway bridge on the Devon border in the 19th century, Cornwall was the remotest county in England. That may be hard to believe at the peak of summer, as tourists descend upon the coastal villages and the narrow lanes jam with traffic, but the area still has a distinct sense of locale—partly real, partly manufactured by the tourist industry. The Cornish language has gone, the last tin mine has now closed, and Tintagel has but a tenuous link with King Arthur's Camelot. But plenty is real enough: Cornish place-names live on and the superlative coastline encompasses awe-inspiring headlands and secret coves that bring to life tales of smugglers and shipwrecks. Cornwall is a summer playground, ideal for watersports and family fun, less promising for scenic drives (the roads seldom follow the coast close enough) and more interesting for its archaeology, holy wells (structures built over springs that have supposed miraculous curative properties) and ancient stone crosses than for its architecture. Cornish villages are plain, sturdy-looking affairs of granite walls beneath Delabole slate roofs. There is nothing very ancient-feeling about much of central Cornwall, which largely grew up around the mining and china clay industries. However, no part of the county is more than a half-hour away from the coast (in normal driving conditions!), where you can usually walk along a coastal path in comparative solitude, surrounded by unrivaled beauty.

DEVON South Devon has the best beaches (such as Blackpool Sands near Stoke Fleming and Bigbury-on-Sea) and some popular coastal resorts—Torquay, Paignton, Teignmouth, Dawlish, Brixham and Exmouth, each pleasant enough at the shore but not worth going out of your way to see. Sidmouth has a conspicuously well-preserved Regency seafront. Much of the action focuses around the estuaries, notably the grand finale of the River Dart at Dartmouth and the Kingsbridge Estuary. Of central Devon, Dartmoor is by far the best-known part, a world of windswept wastes and wilderness, tors and relics of early settlers. Granite is the predominant building material, although on the edges you will see cob walls and thatched roofs, a Devon vernacular hallmark. Exeter, unfortunately, was bombed in World War II, and you have to search around for its best corners; but the city repays such exploration (particularly the cathedral) and makes a good base. The rest of central Devon is less well known, a terrain of hilly farmlands, sandstone walls and swift-flowing rivers. In the far north, moorland meets the sea in Exmoor, which has primeval grandeur, England's highest cliffs and Devon's longest stretch of unspoiled coast—but a damp climate.

SOMERSET While the Somerset coast has little to speak of outside Exmoor (which straddles the Devon border), there is much to explore inland. The little-visited Quantock Hills have a fine heritage of country churches; the Mendip Hills are unspectacular until you encounter Wells, the Cheddar Gorge, and Burrington Combe. Southward lie the Levels, a flat, drained marshland once beneath the sea; Glastonbury Tor and the low-rise Polden Hills protrude above the far side. Taunton, the main town in the heart of (hard) cider-making country, has a bland streetscape redeemed by an impressive church and an absorbing museum.

Bath is the obvious first choice among cities to visit in Somerset (although until recently it was in the county of Avon, named after the river that flows through it). It is a delightful city for wandering around, but hellish to drive in. Bristol (now in its own county of Bristol) is a large old port with a great maritime heritage and the elegant suburb of Clifton.

DORSET The home of Dorset Blue Vinny cheese, the county often has the tag "Hardy's Wessex" applied to it, though the ancient kingdom of Wessex in fact extended into Wiltshire, Somerset, and Hampshire. There is scarcely a corner of Dorset that does not appear under a pseudonym in Thomas Hardy's literary output. Although over three-quarters of the county's heathlands have disappeared since 1945, the inland areas still have an ancient, primitive look, with sweeping downs, clumps of beech trees, thatched villages, and prehistoric burial sites (tumuli) and hill forts. Villages such as Abbotsbury and Corfe Castle make delightful bases for the best of the remarkably varied and largely undeveloped coast.

RECOMMENDED
(continued from page 62)
Dorset: Lyme Regis undercliff, Chesil Beach, Portland Bill, Lulworth Cove, St Aldhlem's Head, Old Harry Rocks, Poole Harbour.
WALKING
The 500 mile South West Coast Path follows the coast from Minehead (Somerset) to Poole (Dorset); Exmoor, north Cornwall and east Dorset are the most dramatic parts; Dartmoor is best for inland walking; otherwise inland Exmoor, the Dorset Downs, the Mendips, the Quantocks.
OFFSHORE ESCAPISM
Isles of Scilly, Lundy Island.
PREHISTORIC SITES
Wiltshire Downs, west Cornwall.

63

WILTSHIRE An inland county, Wiltshire has a gentle landscape of prairie-like chalk downlands, with its northern reaches of honey-stone villages just in the Cotswolds. Most of its interest is manmade—as in the curious hill "carvings" of horses and regimental badges on the hillsides. More famous is the legacy of early inhabitants, notably at Stonehenge and perhaps even more memorably at Avebury. Salisbury Cathedral is the pinnacle of the Early English style; a bus service from Salisbury station to Stonehenge helps make it a feasible day-trip from London. Wiltshire's largest town, Swindon, grew up in the railway era (its railway museum is a magnet for train buffs) and witnessed an economic boom in the 1980s; smaller places, including Devizes, Marlborough, and Bradford on Avon, are much more attractive.

Thatched roofs and whitewashed walls in Lustleigh: the unspoiled face of Devon

"There is in the Cornish character, smouldering beneath the surface, ever ready to ignite, a fiery independence, a stubborn pride."
—Daphne du Maurier, *Vanishing Cornwall* (1967)

Walks

Cheddar Gorge, Somerset   61C4

Parking lot adjacent to Butchers Arms near gorge entrance. Walk along the road at the bottom of the gorge; at the far end (1 mile) across from the gate into a nature reserve, take the West Mendip Way on the right, up through woods. Fork right to follow the top edge of the gorge; the views are impressive. Descend by the steps at Prospect Tower. (2 hours)

Lizard, Cornwall   60A1

Start at Lizard village. For the best of this celebrated coast, take the road east to Church Cove and turn right along the coastal path, past Lizard Point, the southernmost point on the mainland and to idyllic Kynance Cove. Follow the toll road inland, branching right by a National Trust sign onto a path back to Lizard village. (2 hours)

Lulworth Cove, Dorset   61B5

Car park at Lulworth Cove. Take the broad path from the car park, joining the coast to reach Durdle Door, a wave-eroded natural arch; on return-ing, keep along the coast past Stair Hole, for a view of Lulworth Cove. The rugged coast east of the Cove towards Kimmeridge is army training land (open most weekends, Easter and all of August); a path heads down to the cliff where there is a fossil forest. (1 to 2 hours)

Lydford Gorge, Dartmoor National Park, Devon   60B3

Parking lots by gorge; entrance fee. Walk through this densely wooded gorge with the White Lady Waterfall at one end and the Devil's Cauldron, where the River Lyd swirls in a gloomy chasm, at the other. The full trail takes 1.5 hours, or you can take short walks from the parking lots.

Valley of Rocks, Exmoor National Park, Devon   60C3

Start at Lynton. Take the small road between the Valley of Rocks Hotel and the church; it becomes the coastal path. The Valley of Rocks and its wild goats soon come into view. Climb Castle Rock, the most prominent fea-ture, for the view and return along the road, branching left after .25 miles by a stone shelter to ascend Hollerday Hill and drop into Lynton. (1.5 hours)

Avebury's stones stand silent as daily life goes on around them

▶▶▶ **Avebury**   *61C5*
(tel: 01672 539425)

Avebury village is surrounded by an astonishingly large 4000-year-old stone circle and grassy banked henge. In the 1930s the marmalade magnate Alexander Keiller bought the entire village, and set about re-erecting the stones—toppled in medieval times by locals who thought the site was the work of the Devil. Near **Avebury Manor** (NT), the **Alexander Keiller Museum** (NT/EH) fleshes out the background of this and the vicinity's other mysterious prehistoric monuments (see panel).

▶▶▶ **Bath**   *61C5*
(Tourist information center tel: 01225 477101)

A popular spa center since Roman times, Bath regained favor in the 18th century as a place for "taking the waters," and it remains the finest Georgian townscape in Britain. Parks, terraces, squares, and a Royal Crescent—much of it the design of John Wood the Elder and Younger (father and son)—were laid out in the heyday of fashionable society. The city has elegant uniformity thanks to the use of the golden-hued Bath stone.

Museums include the **Museum of Costume**▶▶▶ in the Assembly Rooms, the **Jane Austen Centre**▶, evoking the author's times in Bath, the **Bath Industrial Heritage Centre**▶▶ with a re-created Victorian factory, the **Building of Bath Museum**▶, the **Victoria Art Gallery**, the **William Herschel Museum**▶ (former home of the astronomer Herschel, who discovered Uranus from his garden), and the **Holburne Museum of Art**▶. At Claverton Manor the **American Museum in Britain**▶ has 17th–19th-century New World interiors. When it is not hosting functions, you can look inside the **Guildhall Banqueting Room**▶, for its Adam-style décor. The **Pump Room**▶▶, **Roman Baths**▶▶▶ and **Bath Abbey**▶▶ form the historical core (see page 66). Set in a valley overlooking the city, **Prior Park Landscape Garden**▶▶ (N.T.) is an 18th-century creation by Lancelot "Capability" Brown; take bus 2 or 4 (there is no parking lot).

PREHISTORIC LANDMARKS AT AVEBURY
Avebury's stone circle, which can be walked around in its entirety, connects to the so-called **Stone Avenue**, parallel rows of stones that lead south to the site of another circle, the **Sanctuary**. Across from the parking lot, a path leading south passes close by **Silbury Hill**, the largest prehistoric earthwork in Europe; it is thought to have played an astronomical or religious role. The path continues south of the A4 to **West Kennet Long Barrow**, an ancient burial chamber, which can be entered.

BATH REVIVES ITS SPA
Bath's major Millennium project funded by the National Lottery is the reinstatement of its spa and from October 2002 visitors can take the waters. The centerpiece of the complex is a new spa building with thermal pools, steam rooms, and massage facilities; adjacent is the Hot Bath, offering a range of orthodox and complementary spa treatments, and nearby is the historic Cross Bath, a small bathing house also restored to use.

BATH

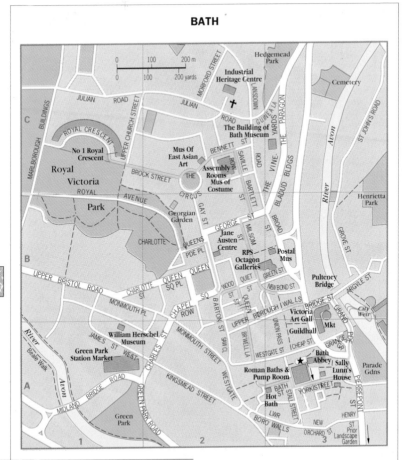

Bath city center

At the **abbey▶▶**, look at the west front depicting Bishop Oliver's dream of angels that inspired him to rebuild the abbey in 1499. Then walk past the **Roman Baths▶▶▶**, Britain's finest Roman remains: baths, cold plunges, a hypocaust room, and part of a Temple to Sulis Minerva, goddess of the springs, can be seen. Adjacent is the **Pump Room▶▶**, the epitome of Bath's timeless spirit; take afternoon tea to the strains of chamber music by the statue of Beau Nash.

Continue along Old Lilliput Alley. **Sally Lunn's House**, a bakery producing the original Sally Lunn cakes from a secret recipe, is the oldest house in Bath (1482); a kitchen museum tells the story. Follow Grand Parade as far as **Pulteney Bridge▶▶** (1774, designed by Robert Adam), with stores along both sides.

Walk up Saville Row past the **Assembly Rooms** and **Museum of Costume▶▶▶**. Walk around **The Circus▶▶▶** (John Wood the Elder, begun 1754) and continue onto **Royal Crescent▶▶▶** (John Wood the Younger, 1767–1774), No. 1 is open to the public. Go through Royal Victoria Park, past the **Georgian Garden▶** (re-created from its 1770s plan), past the **Jane Austen Centre▶** and **Queen Square** (1729–1736). Return via Bath Street to the abbey.

▶ Bodmin Moor   60B2

(Launceston tourist information center tel: 01566 772321)

The top of Cornwall resembles a smaller version of Dartmoor; bleak open moors dotted with granite tors, ponies, and sheep. Brown Willy (1,377 feet) is the county's highest point. Trails onto the moor from the windswept hamlet of **Minions** give excellent views and lead past **The Hurlers** stone circle▶ (Bronze Age).

At nearby Darite, **Trethevy Quoit▶** is a Bronze Age burial chamber with its capstone still in place. Villages ringing the moor are well off the beaten path. **Altarnun▶** is a tranquil haven off the busy A30; its church has magnificent 16th-century bench ends with carvings of a jester, piper and dancers, while the church at **St. Neot** has the finest medieval stained glass in Cornwall.

Launceston▶ occupies a hilltop crowned by a Norman castle keep; one town gateway survives. Near Bodmin are **Lanhydrock House▶ ▶** (N.T.), epitomizing aristocratic living at the end of the 19th century, and **Restormel Castle▶** (E.H.), an impressive Norman fortress.

▶▶ Bradford on Avon   61C5

(Tourist information center tel: 01225 865797)

A charming base for the southern Cotswolds, this stone-built town rises steeply, terrace by terrace, with

Bradford on Avon's nine-arched Town Bridge dates from the 14th century; two of its original arches remain

flagged steps connecting its narrow lanes. Former cloth merchants' mansions and humble medieval and 18th-century weavers' cottages set the tone. The oddly named Top Rank Tory is the street with the best views. In Barton Farm Park stands a splendid 14th-century tithe barn.

Lacock Abbey▶ (N.T.), some 9 miles northeast, retains 13th-century cloisters, chapter house, and sacristy. A barn houses the Fox Talbot Museum, in memory of the pioneering photographer who lived here from 1827 to 1877. The village itself has an 18th-century time-warp feeling, and is National Trust property.

THE EDEN PROJECT

West of Bodmin Moor towards St. Austell, on the high plateau scarred by the snow-white spoil heaps of the china clay industry, the Eden Project, opened in 2001, is one of the largest schemes funded by the Millennium Commission. Gigantic glass structures known as "biomes" house re-creations of Mediterranean and tropical plant life; the third, called the "Roofless Biome," represents the temperate zone. The Eden Project aims to promote an awareness of how much we depend on plants and how we should manage them to achieve a sustainable future.

A LOST CHURCH

Bradford on Avon's Church of St. Laurence, thought to be 7th–8th century, is one of Britain's most complete Saxon churches, yet it lay completely forgotten for many years. Looking over the town from a house above the church, a 19th-century vicar noticed the cruciform shape of the building, parts of which had been incorporated into a school, a house, and a factory wall. In 1858, restoration was carried out and its interior can once more be seen.

The harsh Atlantic winds buffet a wild, rocky coast, a graveyard for hundreds of wrecked ships. Eerie ruins of tin mines perch on treeless hillsides. The long coast is popular for its beautiful scenery, sights, and excellent swimming and surfing beaches. Accordingly, you have to be prepared for crowds at the peak of the season and also for some unsightly resort development, especially between Padstow and Newquay. But it is still easy to get away from it all if you are prepared to walk a mile or two along the coastal path.

PENWITH'S RICH ARCHAEOLOGY
Inland Penwith is peppered with reminders of early peoples. Major sites include two Iron Age villages, Carn Euny and Chysauster. Chûn Castle is an Iron Age fort, while Lanyon Quoit is a good Bronze Age burial chamber and Men-an-Tol is a stone hoop of unknown purpose, used in recent times as a folk remedy for rickets; all three sites lie near the Madron–Morvah road. Close by St. Buryan, near the road, Merry Maidens stone circle is Bronze Age, the maidens supposedly turned to stone for dancing on the Sabbath.

ARTHUR'S FABLES
The deeds of King Arthur—his castle Camelot, the sword Excalibur, his Knights of the Round Table and his quest for the Holy Grail—mix fact and fiction. He was a real 6th-century chieftain (reputedly born in Tintagel and buried at Glastonbury). But later writers embroidered his exploits—the anonymous *Sir Gawayne and the Greene Knight* (1346), Sir Thomas Malory's *Le Morte d'Arthur* (1485), Tennyson's *Idylls of the King* (1857–1885) and works by T. H. White and Mark Twain.

The Devon border to Padstow The village of **Morwenstow▶** bears the indelible stamp of Rev. Robert Hawker, Celtic poet and priest here from 1834 to 1875. He adorned the vicarage with chimneypots in the form of miniature church towers and, on the cliffs nearby, erected a driftwood shack for meditation and opium-smoking (it still stands). His memorial is in the church, which has Norman arches and 16th-century bench ends.

Bude is an unremarkable resort town and a major surfing base, with a large beach; a small museum on the quay tells the story of the Bude Canal, which ends here. Inland, **Launcells Church▶**, standing all by itself, escaped the fervor of Victorian restorers and has changed little since the 15th century.

Boscastle▶ occupies a craggy, precipitous creek; the best views are from the clifftop just west of the harbor. **Tintagel▶** achieved fame for its legendary connections with King Arthur; the ruined medieval castle postdates Arthur, but the site is nevertheless magnificent, atop an impregnable headland, reached by a steep staircase. The adjacent village is a tourist trap, redeemed somewhat by the Old Post Office (N.T.), a small-scale manor house preserved as an outstanding example of Cornish domestic architecture. **Port Isaac▶▶** may stake a claim as the most authentic-feeling Cornish fishing village, a hodge-podge of cottages and narrow alleyways, with a wholesome whiff of seaweed.

Padstow▶ is a busy resort town of considerable charm. It lacks a beach (try Harlyn Bay, west of town) but has a harbor packed with brightly painted boats; fresh fish are on sale at quay warehouses and served at a number of good seafood restaurants. Prideaux Place, at the top of the town, looks Elizabethan, but house tours in the summer months reveal whimsical Strawberry Hill Gothick alterations (see Shobdon, page 122) as well as the original Elizabethan plaster ceilings. The adjacent Camel Estuary offers sailing and gentle walks.

Bedruthan Steps to Land's End West from Padstow the summer crowds thicken rapidly. Many of Cornwall's safest and cleanest beaches are found between Padstow and Newquay. The immediate hinterland is spoiled by modern development, but **Bedruthan Steps▶▶** is an impressive coastal feature, comprising massive rock buttresses detached from the cliff itself. **Newquay** has a brash bustle: nightspots, loud-music pubs, theme parks, and surfers' stores. It also offers good beaches, a well-stocked zoo and a pretty harbor. Out of town, **Trerice►** (N.T.) is a handsome Elizabethan manor house with a minstrels' gallery and intricate plasterwork ceilings.

St. Ives►►, a delightful port turned resort, has attracted artists and beach-loving vacationers for a century. Although it has been considerably cleaned up since its heyday as a fishing port, its back streets have unmistakably Cornish character. Sculptress Barbara Hepworth was one of many 20th-century artists who settled here; her studio is now a museum with her sculptures gracing its garden. A branch of the Tate Gallery features the St. Ives school of artists in one of the most striking settings of any gallery.

The westernmost part of Cornwall is known as **Penwith►►►** and has some of the most dramatic coastal scenery in England, with lonely heather moors inland. At **Zennor** the folk museum has an appealing selection of Cornish bygones while the church is home to a legendary mermaid, carved on an ancient bench end. **Land's End**, Britain's southwesternmost mainland point, is the place to come if you collect geographical extremities. A signpost gives distances to places throughout the world (add amusement home town and pose for the photo); the crowds and theme park dwindle to nothing within ten minutes' walk along the cliff southward, where the scenery gets better. The impressive outdoor **Minack Theatre►** clings to a breathtaking cliff site at Porthcurno, while eastward the headland of **Treryn Dinas**, near Treen, is one of the most dramatic features of Cornwall's coastline. **Mousehole** (pronounced "Mouzal"), as quaint as its name suggests, was the home of the last solely Cornish speaker, Dolly Pentreath, who died in 1777 aged 102.

A shopkeeper holds some Cornish pasties (hefty meat and vegetable turnovers)

69

MINING IN CORNWALL
Until the 19th century Cornwall was a world leader in copper and tin production (lead was also produced), when Redruth, Camborne and St. Just were busy centers. The industry has gone, but there is a striking legacy of abandoned mines and engine houses, such as Wheal Coates near St Agnes Head. At Pool, near Redruth, the National Trust preserves two huge beam engines that pumped water from the mines. In medieval times tin was weighed and stamped at stannary towns, which included Penzance and Truro. Mine accidents were numerous. Cornish innovations which made the job easier included Sir Humphry Davy's miner's safety lamp, Richard Trevithick's steam-powered beam engine and the rock drill.

St. Ives' distinctive Mediterranean light qualities attracted artists such as Naum Gabo, Ben Nicholson, and Bernard Leach

Eastwards from Penzance, the coast gets more sheltered; the cliffs are less mighty, the seaboard is lusher and more populated than the north coast. Deep-water harbors are packed with craft: industrial ships, private yachts, and ferries—every village and town seems to have a sign advertising fishing and sharking trips by boat. Visitors in spring and early summer will be on time for Cornwall's famous gardens.

70

LIZARD TRANSMITTERS

The Lizard peninsula is an important past and present telecommunications center. A memorial near Poldhu Cove commemorates the birth of transatlantic transmissions—it was from here that in 1901 Marconi sent three dots (a morse "S") to Newfoundland; his first message which followed was "What hath God wrought." Inland, "the Lizard" is dominated by the space-age form of the Goonhilly Earth Station, the receiving center for satellite-relayed telephone calls. A tour of the site takes you into an old control tower and you can see the nerve center of the whole operation.

Penzance to Falmouth The town of **Penzance** was knocked around by the 20th century, but it retains corners of Georgian streetscape, at its best on Chapel Street with its capricious Egyptian House, an early 19th-century precursor to art deco. The National Lighthouse Centre records the essential function of lighthouses on a perilous coast. Surveying the main street is the statue of Sir Humphry Davy, inventor of the miner's safety lamp and the town's foremost son in its tin-mining heyday.

St. Michael's Mount ▶ ▶ ▶ (N.T.) shimmers in the sea, an isle capped by a castle. Those who have seen Mont St. Michel in Brittany can be excused a sense of *déjà vu* and in fact it was the Benedictines from Brittany who founded a church on the site, which became a fortress after the Dissolution in 1539. The owners today are the same family that snatched possession after the Civil War. At low tide you can walk to it along a causeway across the sands; at other times take the little ferry.

The **Lizard peninsula** forms Britain's southernmost acres. **Kynance Cove ▶** epitomizes the best of the tumbledown cliffscape of the western Lizard, with a wonderfully sited beach amid the so-called Serpentine Rocks. There are several rock workshops at **Lizard** village, which is itself of little appeal. Eastern Lizard, beyond **Cadgwith ▶**, with its thatched cottages stepping down to the sea, has hidden, verdant creeks in the vicinity of the **Helford River**.

These days fishing boats in Mevagissey are still busy, but tourism is the main source of income

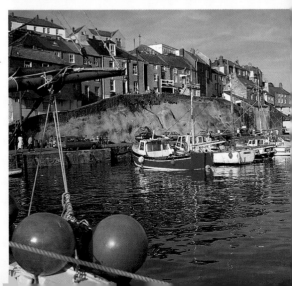

Falmouth, Cornwall's largest town, is no great beauty but it's the base for boat trips up Carrick Roads, alternatively known as the **Fal Estuary**▶ including excursions upriver to **Truro**, the Cornish capital (not itself of major interest, although it has a 19th-century cathedral). Perfectly preserved Tudor castles, St. Mawes and Pendennis, guard the great estuary. Subtropical plants abound at the delightful churchyard of **St. Just in Roseland**▶, which dips down to the water's edge.

Portloe to the Tamar Charming **Portloe**▶ is an unspoiled fishing hamlet, hard to get to—and long may it continue to be; it has real character and nothing to attract large-scale commercialization. **Veryan**, inland, is known for its five early 19th-century round houses. **Charlestown**▶, a carefully preserved port, is still used by the china clay industry, whose white refuse heaps dominate the area.

Fowey▶▶ rises above the deep-anchorage of Fowey Harbor, terrace by terrace, with Polruan across the water. Blockhouses that used to guard the harbour stand silent sentinel. An appealing resort town, Fowey comes to life during the late summer regatta.

Mevagissey has become too popular for some people's tastes, with busloads of visitors cramming into its little harbour, but the place resumes its quiet charm when they have gone; just outside the village the **Lost Gardens of Heligan**▶▶ are being painstakingly restored to their Victorian glory. Another unmissable plant attraction, in the unlikely moonscape setting of a china clay pit near St. Austell, is the **Eden Project**▶▶▶ (see panel, page 67).

Polperro▶▶▶ is even prettier and more groomed than Mevagissey, though no less popular, with a maze of alleys around its photogenic harbour; park at Talland Bay to the east and walk in along the level coastal path rather than struggle with traffic jams.

The **Tamar Estuary** forms the Devon/Cornwall border; the river can be explored by boat trip from Plymouth. **Antony**▶ (N.T.) is the earliest and finest classical-style house in Cornwall, with fine woodland gardens. **Cotehele**▶▶ (N.T.) is an extraordinary medieval relic, a completely unmodernized house; its estate buildings (saddler, smithy, wheelwright, etc.) are well preserved. By the Tamar is moored *Shamrock*, the last Tamar barge in existence. The **Mount Edgcumbe estate**▶, tucked in the far corner of southeastern Cornwall, is a country park looking across to Plymouth; paths through its grounds lead towards quietly characterful Kingsand and Cawsand.

Rising like a dream from Mounts Bay, St. Michael's Mount acquired its monastery after the Archangel Michael appeared in a vision to local fishermen

71

SUBTROPICAL GARDENS
Penjerrick, Glendurgan (N.T.) and Trebah gardens, close together west of Falmouth, were all the creation of the Foxes, a Quaker family, who aimed to create Paradise on Earth. For other gardens to visit in south Cornwall, see Gardens, page 16—do not miss the Lost Gardens of Heligan.

Looe, a lively resort in a pleasant setting

CLIFTON

Venture out to the Georgian suburb of Clifton when visiting Bristol. It resembles a mini-Bath with its handsome stone-built squares, crescents, and terraces (notably Royal York Crescent). Brunel's majestic Clifton Suspension Bridge (built 1836–1864) spans the Avon gorge. Nearby, an 18th-century camera obscura offers views over the city.

Brunel's Clifton Suspension Bridge: when it was completed in 1864, its 702-foot span was the world's greatest

▶▶ Bristol   61C4

(Tourist information center tel: 0117 926 0767)

The city center was badly bombed in 1940 and postwar planning was unimaginative. However, a huge facelift was made for the new millennium, with construction of tree-lined avenues and the restoration of Queen Square as a traffic-free haven. The city preserves many gems, among them **Christmas Steps**, a 17th-century relic; the **Church of St. Mary Redcliffe▶** with its majestic proportions; the **cathedral▶** (begun 1142), notable for its Norman chapter house and organ case carved by Grinling Gibbons; and the **New Room**, Britain's first Wesleyan (Methodist) chapel. A curious architectural folly, the **Cabot Tower▶** provides an excellent city view.

Docking activity is now concentrated in Avonmouth, but the revamped dockland area still has a July regatta and boat tours around the harbor. Here too is the **Industrial Museum**, which acknowledges the life of Isambard Kingdom Brunel, the 19th-century engineer who designed the world's first ocean-going propeller ship, the **S.S. Great Britain▶ ▶**. Launched in 1843, she is now on show in the dry dock where she was built. Entrance also covers the **Maritime Centre**, which charts the city's shipbuilding, the replica of **Matthew** (in which Cabot voyaged to Newfoundland) and the **Bristol Blue Glass Workshop**. The harbor is also home to **Explore@Bristol** (a hands-on science center) and **Wildscreen@Bristol** (looking at wildlife photography, with **IMAX cinema** and interactive exhibits). Here also is the **Arnolfini** arts center.

▶ Clovelly   60B2

(Bideford tourist information center tel: 01237 477626)

A captivating fishing village, overrun in summer, Clovelly is so steep that cars must park at the top. The Hobby Drive was built by a 19th-century owner of Clovelly Court as a scenic road; it's well worth the modest toll. Donkeys and sleds make the descent through its cobbled, time-warp main street.

Hartland Quay▶ ▶, to the east, gives access to some of the most formidable cliffs in the West Country, the strata fantastically contorted into bizarre cross-sections.

AN L OF AN ACCENT

The hallmark of Bristol speech is the adding of the letter *L* to the ends of words. Thus *area* becomes *areal*, *Australia* becomes *Australial* and *Bristowe*, the old city name, becomes *Bristol*.

►►► Dartmoor National Park 60B3

(Dartmoor National Park tel: 01822 890414)

Southern England's largest area of wild country, Dartmoor is a great expanse of blustery moors punctuated by weathered granite outcroppings known as tors. Sheep and Dartmoor ponies graze the open grasslands, wandering between Bronze Age hut circles and burial mounds. The moor can be a bleak place—"nine months winter and three months bad weather"—but there are cozy cob-and-thatch villages to come down to in the lusher valleys (some offering Devon cream teas) and several fine country-house style hotels. Indoor attractions are few: this is a place to be outdoors—picnicking, touring, walking, or horseback riding.

On Dartmoor's east side, lush farmland meets the barren moors. **Hay Tor**►► is the most visited viewpoint, easily accessible. **Hound Tor**►►, close by, is well marked by signs and lies next to a well-preserved abandoned medieval village, where you can still make out the fireplaces. West of **Buckland**, whose church clock has the letters MY DEAR MOTHER instead of numerals, **Bel Tor** presides over the Webburn Valley. The **Dart Valley**► is full of choice corners, including Combestone Tor and the medieval "clapper" bridge, made of great granite slabs, at Dartsmeet, the confluence of the West and East Dart rivers.

Widecombe in the Moor► draws visitors for its valley setting, its fame from the folk song "Widecombe Fair" and for its church, the "cathedral of the moor." **North Bovey**► is much quieter and quite uncommercialised, with a pretty green, thatched cottages, a stone cross, and a village pump. **Chagford** is a large but sleepy village, with enough character and a good location to make it a recommendable base; **Moretonhampstead**, a crossroads town, is a shade busier and has a fine row of 17th-century almshouses.

In northeast Dartmoor the River Teign has carved a course through a deep valley with an enchanting deciduous forest. From **Fingle Bridge**►, an old packhorse bridge, paths lead along the river and up onto moorland viewpoints; the Hunter's Path passes the back entrance to **Castle Drogo**►► (N.T.), architect Edwin Lutyens' early 20th-century masterpiece, an improbable marriage of granite medievalism and Edwardian Arts and Crafts style. The main entrance is near **Drewsteignton**, which has a charming village square.

Two main roads cross the central moor; the B3212 passes through **Postbridge**, with its notable medieval "clapper bridge," and grim **Princetown**, dominated by a high-security prison originally built for Napoleonic prisoners of war. For an overview of Dartmoor, go to the **High Moorland Visitor Centre** in Princetown. (Access to the high northern moor is restricted due to military training.)

Two outstanding features justify a visit to the western fringes: **Brent Tor**►, a plain church atop a huge rock and looking far into Cornwall and **Lydford Gorge**►► (see Walks, page 64; N.T.), a deep and tortuous ravine with a waterfall and whirlpool.

The towns encircling Dartmoor National Park are not of great interest, although **Ashburton** has some attractive streets and **Buckfastleigh** boasts a modern Benedictine abbey, a butterfly park and otter sanctuary and the

Hound Tor: weathering has attacked the joints in the great granite outcrops that dominate the wastes of Dartmoor

DARTMOOR'S LETTERBOXES
Many visitors to Dartmoor in the 19th century liked to try to locate Cranmere Pool, scarcely more than a puddle and remotely situated in the moors above Chagford. Someone had the idea of placing a mailbox here, so that a self-addressed postcard would be left here by one walker and picked up and sent on by the next. The fad caught on and now there are some 6,000 official, unofficial, and mobile boxes in various places. Today you can record your visit with the rubber stamp provided.

PREHISTORIC PROCESSIONAL ROUTES
Rows of stones erected in the Bronze Age are believed to have marked processional routes. Above the Erme Valley in south Dartmoor, one of these stretches 2 miles from Stall Moor to Green Hill.

EARLY SETTLERS ON DARTMOOR

The moorland gravels yielded copious quantities of tin, exploited by Bronze Age settlers. Among the most striking of their relics are **Scorhill Stone Circle**, on Shovel Down above Gidleigh (near Chagford), a Bronze Age stone circle of 23 uprights and **Spinsters' Rock**, off the A382 south of its intersection with the A30, a neolithic tomb with its capstone held in place by three uprights.

Grimspound, between Widecombe in the Moor and the B3212, reached by a path up from the road onto Hamel Down, consists of a large walled enclosure with 24 discernible hut circles.

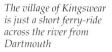

74

terminal of the steam-powered South Devon Railway which wends its way 7 miles to Totnes. The **Museum of Dartmoor Life** at **Okehampton** tells of country life and ways; a fragment of a medieval **castle** (E.H.) caps a hillock on the edge of town.

Buckland Abbey▶, a former Cistercian monastery, was once home to Sir Francis Drake, born at nearby Tavistock. The house has some relics from his famous ship, *Golden Hind* (including a drum and banners), but it was more Sir Richard Grenville, an earlier occupant, who stamped his character on the house; he added the intricate plasterwork in the Great Hall.

▶▶ Dartmouth
60A3

(Tourist information center tel: 01803 834224)

An old naval town, set on steep slopes which drop to the River Dart, Dartmouth has real atmosphere, with small craft on the river and harbor and a maze of back streets. The August regatta sees the town at its most exuberant.

Beside Duke Street is the arcaded **Butterwalk**, a former dairy market and now a local museum. In the quayside gardens stands the world's first steam pumping-engine, built in 1725 by Thomas Newcomen, a Dartmouth resident. Two Tudor castles guard either side of the harbor entrance; **Dartmouth Castle▶** has a magnificent view from its roof terrace.

Dartmouth is a good base for excursions, including **Totnes▶** with its Norman castle and steep medieval streets and **Salcombe▶**, a yachting center with a handsome location on an estuary. Ferries cross the Dart to Kingswear, where steam locomotives haul trainloads of day visitors along the **Paignton and Dartmouth Steam Railway**.

The village of Kingswear is just a short ferry-ride across the river from Dartmouth

WALKS NEAR DARTMOUTH

Where you can actually walk along the coast, it is nearly always highly rewarding. But the official coast path in places veers well inland, where the landscape is often unremarkable. The path south from Dartmouth Castle wriggles round some magnificent coves and rugged cliffs before steering inland at Warren Cove. Other fine uninterrupted coastal stretches are south of Brixham and between Bolt Tail and Start Point either side of Salcombe Harbor; East Prawle is a useful starting point for circular walks.

▶ Dorchester

61B4

(Tourist information center tel: 01305 267992)

Although not outstandingly attractive, Dorchester is the center of the countryside of Thomas Hardy's novels, in which the town features as Casterbridge; it is often visited for that reason. The **Dorset County Museum**▶ celebrates aspects of the county and displaying Hardy's study and a collection of material relating to him. Hardy was also a trained architect and designed **Max Gate** (N.T.), open to the public; he lived there from 1885 until his death in 1928.

Dorchester, a typical country town, is still recognizable as Thomas Hardy's "Casterbridge"

75

Maiden Castle▶▶, on the southwestern edge of Dorchester is Britain's largest Iron Age hillfort; its massive concentric ramparts date from the 1st century BC.

Hardy's Birthplace▶, the humble thatched cottage where Thomas Hardy was born in 1840, is furnished as it may have looked in his lifetime. Start from the parking lot at Higher Bockhampton; either walk along the main track or take the longer Thorncombe Trail, a nature walk through woodland and a fragment of the "untamed and untameable wild" of Egdon Heath in Hardy's work. Although Hardy is buried at Westminster Abbey, his heart is buried in the family plot at **Stinsford Church**▶, Mellstock Church of his novel *Under the Greenwood Tree.*

A prominent tower some 5 miles southwest of Dorchester, confusingly called the **Hardy Monument**▶, commemorates Admiral Thomas Hardy, Nelson's flag-captain at the Battle of Trafalgar. From here there's a view over Chesil Beach and Portland Bill.

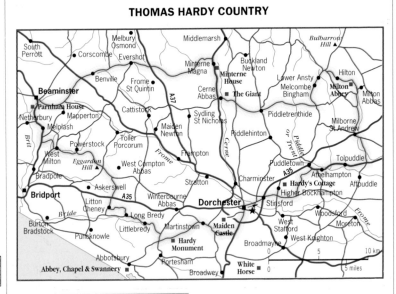

THOMAS HARDY COUNTRY

Drive

Thomas Hardy country

This tour (about 70 miles in total) explores the heartland of the country-side immortalized in the writings of Thomas Hardy. Local life has changed beyond recognition, but many elements are still there—thatched villages, rolling downlands, manor houses, ancient monuments.

From **Dorchester** take the A35 east, branching off for **Stinsford▶** and detouring to Hardy's Birthplace at **Higher Bockhampton▶** (see page 75). At **Tolpuddle** the cottage museum pays homage to the Tolpuddle Martyrs who formed a trade union and were transported for their pains.

Take minor roads heading northwards to **Milton Abbas▶▶**, an 18th-century estate village of rustic thatch and whitewash: the owner of Milton Abbey house nearby (which is now a school) had the village rebuilt here to improve the view from his house. The abbey church and finely roofed Abbot's Hall are open.

Take lanes west to **Cerne Abbas▶▶** to look at the famous Giant, best seen from a vista point on the A352 road north. Follow the A352 to **Minterne Magna**, where a late 19th-century house harbors a fine collection of trees and shrubs (open in season).

❏ Looming over the demure village of Cerne Abbas is an extraordinary prehistoric hill-carving of a naked club-bearing man (known as the Cerne Giant) revealing all for the world to see. Its origins and purpose are unclear, but it is thought to be a fertility or cult symbol. ❏

Continue west to **Beaminster▶**, a delightful scene of small-town rural England with an attractive square, and past **Parnham House▶**. Drunken lanes meander southeast through **Powerstock**, attractively placed on a hillside and past **Eggardon Hill▶**, an impressively bleak Iron Age hill fort site. Continue on through Littlebredy and up to the **Hardy Monument▶** (see page 75). Drive east via the B3159 and minor roads to pass **Maiden Castle▶** (parking lot on Dorchester side). The A354 leads northwards into Dorchester.

Lulworth Cove, a great semicircular scoop in the coast, displays layers of chalk, sandstone, and Portland limestone

THE FOWLES CONNECTION
At Lyme Regis a sinuous sea wall known as The Cobb gained fame through the film of John Fowles's novel *The French Lieutenant's Woman*, where crazed Sarah Woodruff (played by Meryl Streep) stared out to sea in despair while Charles Smithson (Jeremy Irons) explored natural history in the undercliff just west of town. The Cobb is of medieval origin, and the undercliff, still a wild place and riddled with landslips, is designated a National Nature Reserve.

▶▶ **Dorset Coast**   61B4–B5
(Tourist information center tel: 01305 267992 for west; 01929 552740 for east)

Beyond Dorset's mighty cliffs lie unspoiled hinterlands that seem to have emerged only recently from the primeval past. The coast is famous for fossils, no place more than **Lyme Regis▶▶**, a charming resort beloved of novelist Jane Austen. The narrow lanes and Regency seafront cottages have changed little since her visits at the turn of the 19th century. Huge ammonite fossils can be seen in garden walls, in **Dinosaurland** (a museum which also gives guided fossil walks along the beach) and in fossil stores. The thatched honey-stone village of **Abbotsbury▶▶** crouches beneath a hillock crowned by a lone chapel; dedicated to St. Catherine, it was once the property of the Benedictine abbey which gave the village its name. A tithe barn and the swannery (very much alive) are other abbey leftovers.

   Close by, **Chesil Beach** (or Bank) is one of the most extraordinary features of the British coastline (see panel). **Weymouth▶**, an elegant resort with an early 19th-century flavour, made popular by George III, lies behind a curving bay. Further east lies **Lulworth Cove▶▶▶**, abutted by amazing cliffs that offer ideal cross-sections for the aspiring geologists who flock here along with fishermen, skindivers, and walkers heading for **Durdle Door** (see Walks, page 64), a fine natural arch. East of Lulworth, army ranges permit only occasional access to rugged cliffs as far as Kimmeridge. **St. Aldhelm's Head** juts into the sea and has a primitive chapel on its summit. Beyond the coastal resort of **Swanage** lie **Old Harry Rocks▶**, chalk stacks detached from the cliff, and the multicolored sands of **Studland**, with its fine Norman church; the village lies near the largest remaining heathlands in Dorset. Seaward, views extend to the Isle of Wight. The **Purbeck Ridge** offers a panorama of Poole Harbor and the largest of Dorset's heathlands. The ridge is interrupted dramatically at **Corfe Castle▶▶**, where the pinnacle of a Norman castle rises above the village.

THE CHESIL BEACH NATURAL PHENOMENON
The 18 mile shingle bank was created by the deposit of millions of pebbles through the process of long-shore drift, the lateral shift of material as a result of the waves meeting the shore at an oblique angle. The beach links Portland Bill to the mainland and encloses a lagoon known as the Fleet, a peaceful haven for birds. Because of the steeply shelving seaward side of the beach, it attracts anglers (but swimmers must stay clear: this is one of Britain's most dangerous beaches). The pebbles increase in size from west to east.

Tarr Steps was allegedly built in a single night by the Devil

A LA RONDE

At Exmouth, south of Exeter, A la Ronde (N.T.) is a delightfully eccentric 16-sided house of 1796, built by Jane and Mary Parminter on returning from a Grand Tour of Europe. It is based on the Byzantine church of San Vitale in Ravenna, Italy and displays many items the sisters collected on their travels.

LUNDY ISLAND

A popular day-trip by ferry from Bideford (in summer also from Barnstaple) is to Lundy (N.T.), a little island some 39 miles north of Hartland Point. Its cliffs are a major site for birdlife; over 400 species are recorded, including puffins (*lunde* being Norse for puffin).
From 1925 to 1954 Lundy's owner Martin Harman tried to make it a separate kingdom; he did not succeed, but the island still issues its own stamps. Lundy's isolation in the Bristol Channel has given it a long history of smuggling. The Marisco Tavern serves beer brewed on the island.

► **Exeter**   *60B3*

(Tourist information center tel: 01392 265700)
Prior to destruction in a World War II air raid (one of a series targeted on historic sites), Exeter was among southern England's most attractive cities. Amazingly, the **cathedral** ► ► escaped almost unscathed, and makes it worth the effort to visit the otherwise largely rebuilt center. The twin towers are Norman, and its nave displays the longest span of Gothic vaulting in the world. Look too for the astronomical clock in the north transept, the bishop's throne and the intricately carved misericords.

The porticoed **Guildhall** in the High Street is England's oldest municipal building. Within Boots Arcade is the entrance to a 13th-century subterranean water system known as the **Underground Passages** ► (*Guided tours*).

► ► **Exmoor National Park**   *60C3*

(Exmoor National Park tel: 01398 323841)
A small but varied national park, Exmoor encompasses unspoiled coast, moors, and quiet farmland straddling the Devon and Somerset borders. The coast is the main focus of interest, but inland there are lonely moors and fine river valleys. Unusually for England, the moors often reach the clifftops, and the Exmoor coast is a fine place for walks, where you can set off on the coastal path and return over windswept hillsides.

THE COAST ROAD (A39) In the northwest of the national park, **Parracombe's Church of St. Petrock** ► is a completely unaltered medieval building, threatened with demolition in the last century but preserved thanks to a campaign led by John Ruskin, influential writer, critic, and social reformer. **Trentishoe Church** has a tiny musicians' gallery (notice the notch cut out to allow for a double bass's bow); just east, **Heddon's Mouth** is a charming, walkers-only valley which leads from the isolated Hunter's Inn to an abandoned lime kiln on a pebbly beach. At **Lynton**, a sleepy but amiable resort, strangely shaped crags adorn the **Valley of Rocks** ► ►, where wild goats sniff the sea breezes (see Walks, page 64); **Heddon Valley** is another popular area for walks. A cliff railroad connects Lynton with **Lynmouth** below, prettily situated by a small harbor and, in season, it's more animated than its neighbor. Eastward, the River Lyn lines a magnificent wooded valley; you can walk along the river to an idyllically sited café at **Watersmeet** ► ►, at the joining of the East Lyn River and Farley Water, or head for the hills for the best views; close by, the cliffs near **Countisbury** exceed 1,000 feet and are some of England's highest. **Oare** and **Malmsmead** are at the heart of Doone Country, the setting of R. D. Blackmore's *Lorna Doone*, based on a real family of outlaws (see panel). **Culbone**, north of the main road, boasts England's smallest church in regular use, alone in the woods. **Allerford▶** has a pretty packhorse bridge and a fascinating local museum within its old school, while tiny **Selworthy▶▶** has a group of immaculate thatched cottages and a large church with a fine wagon roof.

INLAND EXMOOR Sheep and ponies roam the breezy hills, red deer the eastern forests. Over the years the moors have dwindled in extent, encroached upon by farmland and pastures, but recent National Park measures have safeguarded what remains. A road tour from Dunkery Hill to Exford, then to Dulverton and west along the Park boundary to Twitchen, gives a good idea of the moor. **Winsford▶**, **Exford** and **Withypool** are three attractive villages in this area; **Dulverton▶** has lots of small-town charm. South of Withypool, **Tarr Steps▶** is a 1,000-year-old clapper bridge spanning the River Barle. **Dunkery Beacon▶▶** is an easily climbed hill, a 10-minute walk from the road, which on a clear day offers a far-ranging view across Devon and Somerset and over the Bristol Channel into South Wales. **Dunster▶▶▶** rates as one of the most perfect small towns in England, with its ancient yarn market at the hub of its tapering street of medieval buildings, and **Dunster Castle▶▶** (N.T.) towering above. The fashionable 19th-century architect Anthony Salvin upgraded the castle interior, but it retains earlier features, including a 17th-century staircase and leather wall-hangings that tell the story of Antony and Cleopatra. On the edge of town is a working 18th-century watermill (N.T.) and there are glorious walks through Dunster Park and along the ridge of Grabbist Hill.

WALKING ON EXMOOR
In addition to the routes into the Valley of Rocks (see page 64) and Hunter's Inn (see page 78), there is outstanding terrain along all of the Exmoor coast. From Lynton head east along the wooded Lyn valley to Watersmeet, and return high above the south side of the valley for coastal views. From Allerford, head to the coast and climb Selworthy Beacon for a huge panorama. Attractive inland walks include Horner Wood beneath Dunkery Beacon, the Grabbist Hill ridge near Dunster, and the moorland valley of Badgeworthy Water in "Doone Country" south of Malmsmead.

79

Dunster Castle: there has been a castle on this site since Norman times

LORNA DOONE
Blackmore's Victorian adventure novel takes place in the wilds of Exmoor. The hero, John Ridd, seeks revenge on the Doones for shooting his father and is in love with Lorna Doone, whom the Doones have kidnapped for her large inheritance. Tragedy later strikes at Lorna's wedding at Oare Church. Despite failing to sell for more than a year after publication, *Lorna Doone* has become a minor classic that for many is synonymous with Exmoor.

SIR FRANCIS DRAKE

One of the most immortal examples of cool-headedness was when Sir Francis Drake (c1541–1596) insisted on finishing a lawn bowling match on Plymouth Hoe before turning his attention to the Spanish Armada. Devon-born, he was the first Englishman to sail around the world and, as a darling of Elizabeth I, he was knighted for his efforts. In 1588 he achieved the great victory over the Armada; the weather played a major role—a third of the Spanish vessels were shipwrecked. This was Drake's last great naval exploit, although he pioneered a leat (channel) bringing fresh water from Dartmoor to Plymouth.

Gilded ceilings and other adornments at Longleat House were added in the 19th century by the 4th Marquess of Bath

►► Glastonbury   61C4
(tel: 01458 832954)

The town huddles around the base of Glastonbury Tor, a hillock capped by St. Michael's Chapel. Visible from afar, the Tor was an island in early times, when the sea extended across the Somerset Levels. The **abbey►** has long been a place of pilgrimage: the Legend of Glastonbury records Joseph of Arimathaea burying the chalice used at the Last Supper. There are links too with Arthurian legend: Arthur's corpse was brought here by Sir Lancelot.

►► Longleat   61C5
(tel: 01985 844400)

In 1949 Longleat was Britain's first country house to open its doors full-time; side attractions include a Mirror Maze and a safari park. The house, completed in 1580, was ahead of its time: it looks out to its park rather than gazing into a courtyard. Inside are some 16th-century tapestries, portraits, and rare manuscripts; 19th-century embellishments—marquetry, fireplaces and gilded ceilings—were added by Italian craftsmen after the 4th Marquess of Bath returned from a Grand Tour. The kitchen dates from this period. Capability Brown landscaped the grounds in 1757 with the world's largest maze.

► Plymouth   60A2
(tel: 01752 304849)

A major naval base for centuries, Plymouth sprawls in a natural harbor. After World War II bombing, much of the center was rebuilt in a monolithic style. Head for the Barbican, west of Sutton Harbour, with the **National Marine Aquarium►**, the timber-framed **Elizabethan House**, the **Plymouth Gin Distillery** (in operation since 1793) and the **Pilgrim Fathers Memorial**. Continue past the **Royal Citadel** to **The Hoe►►** waterfront area: **Plymouth Dome►** is a hi-tech evocation of the city's past; entrance covers **Smeaton's Tower**, a re-erected 18th-century lighthouse. On Finewell Street is 15th-century **Prysten House** (with a model of 17th-century Plymouth). The **Tamar Bridges** cross into Cornwall: the 1961 road suspension bridge and Brunel's 1859 railway bridge.

In Dorset you can walk from Ryme Intrinseca to Beer Hackett; in Kent you can try getting your tongue around Trottiscliffe (pronounced Trozlee); in County Durham you can go to Pity Me; while in Worcestershire, there is a village called Upton Snodsbury. England's place-names have long amused and bemused visitors and locals alike, inspiring both affectionate parody and rhapsodic poetry.

Historical pointers By the time of the Norman invasion in 1066, the settlement pattern in England was already largely established. Place-names give a host of clues as to how and when England developed. Generally the suffix gives the key element, with the prefix acting as a descriptive defining element—Doncaster, for example, tells us of a Roman camp (*castra*) on the River Don.

Settlers from the East As Saxons began to settle in England, they introduced their own place-names rather than using the existing Celtic ones—most of the native place-names that survived adopted natural features such as hills, rivers, and valleys. Early Saxon names included heathen names such as those of gods, for instance Woden (Wednesbury) and Thunor (Thunderfield). The suffix -*ing* survives from that period, particularly in Surrey and East Anglia, while later Saxon names included the commonest suffixes, -*ham* (home) and -*ton* (enclosure, farm, or manor).

Scandinavian settlers ensconced themselves in eastern England, where today there are still many names ending with -*by* (Grimsby, Whitby, Wragby, etc.): the vast majority are in the eastern and northwestern counties. Remote areas had names unto themselves: Lympne and Lyminge in east Kent and numerous Cornish names (Trelissick, Marazion, Nanjizal) are unique to those parts. The prefix Chipping (Chipping Campden, Chipping Sodbury, Chippenham, etc.) indicates a marketplace; the word is related to the German *kaufen* (to buy) and appears to be the root of Copenhagen.

Later changes In the 19th century, mining and other industrial settlements created new names—ranging from matter-of-fact New Mills to the intriguing likes of Indian Queens and Booze. The Somerset coastal resort of Weston upgraded itself into Latin and was renamed Weston-super-Mare. The odd euphemism evolved—the Devil's Arse cave was tamed to Peak Cavern and Pigg Hill became Peak Hill. Craven Arms in Shropshire was originally just a pub; a railroad town grew around it and the name stuck.

81

PLACE-NAME QUIRKS
● Some places were merely mapmaker's accidents: Unnear appears on several early 19th-century maps of Mid Wales, but was no more than the corruption of a mapmaker's query—Quaere.
● Few 20th-century place-names exist; the new towns of Peterlee (named after a trade union leader) and Telford (after Thomas Telford, a Scottish civil engineer) are exceptions.
● Westward Ho! is Britain's only place-name bearing an exclamation mark.
● Coldharbour (meaning a shelter from bad weather) is the most common minor place-name.

CASTLE ACRE

THE LYRIC POETS IN SOMERSET
The Quantocks and hills near Culbone inspired *The Lyrical Ballads* (1798) of William Wordsworth and Samuel Taylor Coleridge. Dorothy Wordsworth recorded: "There is everything here; sea, woods wild as fancy ever painted, brooks clear and pebbly as in Cumberland, villages so romantic." Coleridge wrote *The Rime of the Ancient Mariner* and Part One of *Christabel* at Nether Stowey. His great poem *Kubla Khan* was written at a cottage near Culbone in Exmoor and was inspired by an opium dream, rudely broken off by the alleged arrival of a "person from Porlock" about some minor matter. The work was never completed.

Salisbury Cathedral

▶ Quantock Hills 61C4

(Taunton tourist information center tel: 01823 336344)

A forgotten corner of rural England. The hedges grow high around the sunken, crooked lanes, the churchyards hide behind banks of cow parsley and manor houses lurk behind estate walls. Villages are sleepy, typically of sandstone and color-washed cottages. Dense woodlands cloak the lower slopes. On the top is a plateau of heather moors crossed by ancient trackways.

Medieval wool-trade prosperity left a legacy of fine churches in the Quantocks: 16th-century carved bench ends are a speciality; the best include those at **Broomfield**, **Spaxton**, **Crowcombe**, and **Bicknoller**.

William Wordsworth and his sister Dorothy stayed in 1797 at Alfoxton Park at **Holford**, keeping fellow poet Samuel Taylor Coleridge company (see panel). The latter lived for some years at **Nether Stowey▶**, where his cottage has been restored by the National Trust and filled with mementoes of his life and works.

The **West Somerset Railway▶**, the longest private line in Britain, operates steam and diesel trains along the track from Bishop's Lydeard (near Taunton) to Minehead on the coast. Washford station has a small museum devoted to railway memorabilia.

▶▶ Salisbury 61C5

(Tourist information center tel: 01722 334956)

Built between 1220 and 1258, entirely in the Early English Gothic style, Salisbury's **cathedral▶▶▶** was the subject of a number of paintings by Constable. Its noble spire, added in 1334–1380, soars 404 feet, higher than any other in the country. On clear days, it is worth the effort to climb the tower to the base of the spire. Reached through the cloisters, the octagonal chapter house boasts a medieval carved frieze depicting scenes from the books of Genesis and Exodus and the best-preserved of four manuscripts of the Magna Carta, the first bill of rights foisted by barons on King John in 1215. England's largest **cathedral close** surrounds the precincts; houses open to the public are the 13th-century **King's House**, now home to the **Salisbury and South Wiltshire Museum** (exhibits relate to Stonehenge, Old Sarum, ceramics and a pre-National Health Service doctor's office),

Silver sands at Gimble Porth, Tresco, part of the Isles of Scilly whose entire population numbers just 2,000

Malmesbury House, and **Mompesson House**▶ (N.T.), a Queen Anne house with a walled garden, period furnishings and a rare collection of English drinking glasses. The rest of the town, laid out on a spacious grid plan by Bishop Poore in the 13th century, has many attractive corners.

Wilton House▶▶ The 17th-century home of the Earls of Pembroke in nearby Wilton is not on the grandest scale but shows exemplary taste; Inigo Jones designed most of it, including the Double Cube Room, hung with Van Dyck portraits. Here too is the room where some of the D-Day invasion planning took place.

From Salisbury there are buses (tel: 01722 336855) to **Old Sarum**▶▶ (see panel) and **Stonehenge**▶▶▶ (see page 84).

▶▶ Scilly, Isles of 60C1

(Tourist information center tel: 01720 422536)

An idyllic retreat beyond the southwestern tip of the British mainland, the Scillies comprise five inhabited, strikingly contrasting islands. There is much to interest the naturalist, particularly birdlife. Daffodils, narcissi, irises, and tulips are commercially grown.

Hugh Town is the principal township on **St. Mary's**, the largest island (with a maximum width of only 3 miles); Star Castle, built in 1593–1594 as a fortress against a possible Spanish invasion, is now a hotel. Paths follow the coastline; there is a remarkable concentration of prehistoric burial chambers to explore, while at Peninnis Head are curiously weathered rocks. The island of **Bryher** is windswept, with simple facilities and gorse-clad hillsides. **St. Agnes**, the smallest inhabited island, has an old lighthouse of 1680 (now a private house but still providing flashes). Troy Town Maze, a piece of folk art with stones laid out on the turf, may have been created by an 18th-century lighthouse-keeper with time on his hands. **St. Martin's** is treeless, with a prominent day-mark cone (1683) on its highest point and has splendid beaches; Higher and Lower Towns between them muster a population of around 100. **Tresco**▶▶ is renowned for the subtropical gardens of Tresco Abbey, the major attraction of the Scillies, created by Dorrien Smith. The island is fun to explore (no cars, just tractors), with forts and several white-sand beaches.

OLD SARUM
Old Sarum (EH), the original site of Salisbury, was finally abandoned in Norman times because of its exposed hilltop position. Old Sarum Church was founded in 1078, but five days afterwards was struck by lightning and largely destroyed. The town moved to New Sarum (present-day Salisbury) soon after, yet up to 1832 the old town was the classic "rotten borough" represented by two Members of Parliament (including, towards the end, William Pitt) to serve a nonexistent electorate. Old Sarum is on the edge of Salisbury.

SCILLY PRACTICALITIES
The archipelago, 28 miles west of Land's End, is reached from Penzance heliport (just out of town on the A330) by a 20-minute helicopter trip, by plane (from Land's End, Newquay, or Exeter), or by a 2.5-hour boat ride to St. Mary's. There is a good boat service between the other islands. Bicycles can be hired on St. Mary's.

Stonehenge, immense and silent, is thought to have been constructed in three phases

STONEHENGE—THE FACTS

Stonehenge began as a simple ditch and bank (2800 BC); sarsen stones from Wiltshire and stones from the Preseli Hills in Wales were added around 2000 BC. In the Bronze Age, around 1600–1500 BC, the whole site was remodeled with uprights and cross-lintels. The central axis aligns with the sun on Midsummer's Day and other alignments may have enabled the circle to function as a kind of calender.

STONEHENGE—THE ENIGMA

Archaeologists may never know the precise mystical, religious, or ceremonial significance of Stonehenge. More extreme theories have included notions of inspirations from beings from outer space, a creation by King Arthur and his circle of models of male and female sexuality, a bird trap, a model of the solar system, and a cosmic scheme related to the Egyptian pyramids and built by the people of Atlantis.

▶▶▶ Stonehenge   61C5
(tel: 01980 624715)

Britain's most famous prehistoric stone circle (E.H.), a World Heritage Site, stands alone on Salisbury Plain, a sparsely populated area of chalk downland studded with mementoes of early inhabitants. Its origins remain a mystery (see panel). Entry includes an audio tour. Visitors flock here in the thousands; a new visitor center and an upgrade in facilities are being planned.

▶▶ Stourhead   61C5
(tel: 01747 841152)

In 1741, inspired by a Grand Tour of Europe, Henry Hoare II, the son of a wealthy banker, returned home to Stourhead and decided to re-landscape his grounds with classical temples, a triangular lake, and rare plants. He created one of the highest achievements of English landscape gardening. The Palladian mansion suffered a fire in 1902 but still has good Chippendale furniture, paintings, and a library. This and the adjacent village of Stourton are owned by the National Trust.

▶▶▶ Wells   61C4
(Tourist information center tel: 01749 672552)

England's smallest cathedral city is set near the eastern end of the Mendip Hills. The streets of limestone houses are dwarfed by the **cathedral▶▶**, significant above all for the richness of its early 13th-century west front (recently restored), adorned with 356 statues. Building started on the choir in about 1180 and finished with the cloisters in 1508, following the designs of Bishop Reginald de Bohun. A problem of subsidence at the crossing was resolved by the innovation of inverted "scissor" arches, which despite the obvious Gothic provenance look timeless in style. Here too is the world's second oldest clock, with its 14th-century face showing phases of the moon and the position of the sun. The stained glass, chapter house, and carving deserve time to be savored.

Close by is the moated **Bishop's Palace▶▶** with its drawbridge, turrets, and medieval hall; a rope dangles for swans to pull when they want to be fed (a trick passed down from one generation to another). Just off the cathedral close, an archway leads into **Vicars Close▶▶**, a medieval street dating from 1381.

Cheddar Gorge▶▶▶ is the most outstanding feature of the Mendip Hills, themselves a gently rolling whaleback plateau perforated with limestone caverns, some of which have collapsed to form gorges. A road follows the bottom of Cheddar Gorge beneath the massive grey cliffs; fanciful names have been given to many of the crags. A staircase at the entrance to the gorge, on its south side, leads up to a tin prospect tower; views are even better from above. (See Walks, page 64.) Also by the gorge entrance are the **Cheddar Caves**▶, of which Gough Cave is recommended for its weird limestone formations. Cheddar itself has a fine medieval market cross.

Axbridge▶ is a pleasing, small town that sees far fewer visitors than Cheddar Gorge or Wells. Its fetching, rather irregular central square is overlooked by the half-timbered King John Hunting Lodge, a 15th-century merchant's house that is home to a local history museum.

Burrington Combe▶ is a lesser version of Cheddar Gorge. During a storm here in 1792, Reverend Augustus Toplady sheltered beneath a rock and composed the hymn "Rock of Ages." **Dolebury Warren**▶, a grassy ridge between Burrington Combe and the A38, has good views from its Iron Age hill fort, extending over the Severn Estuary to South Wales and northwards towards Bristol. Jutting out into the Severn Estuary south of Weston-super-Mare, **Brean Down**▶▶ gives phenomenal views of hills and estuary; this too has the site of an ancient hill fort on its summit. **Wookey Hole**▶ is a colorfully lit cavern, said to have housed the Witch of Wookey (her alabaster ball and comb and the bones of her goat are in the town museum in Wells). It's a fun place to bring children, with an exhibition re-creating the world of a 9,000-year old skeleton on display, as well as such contrivances as a mirror maze and an assembly of vintage penny-in-the-slot machines. Near Wookey Hole, Ebbor Gorge is a secretive limestone ravine with a nature trail through charming woods.

CHEDDAR CHEESE
Cheddar itself is of course best known for Cheddar cheese. The hard cows'-milk cheese was first made here in the early 12th century, perhaps even earlier. The traditional method is to "cheddar" or cut the firm curd into small pieces and to drain the whey before packing the residual matter into cylinders some 12–15 inches in diameter; the cheese is then wrapped in cheesecloth and coated with wax. It is left to mature (originally this was done in local caves) for anything from three months to two years according to the strength desired. The Cheddar Gorge Cheese Co. Rural Village, Cheddar, makes the authentic product.

85

A genre of folk art: antique merry-go-round horses in the old Papermill at Wookey Hole

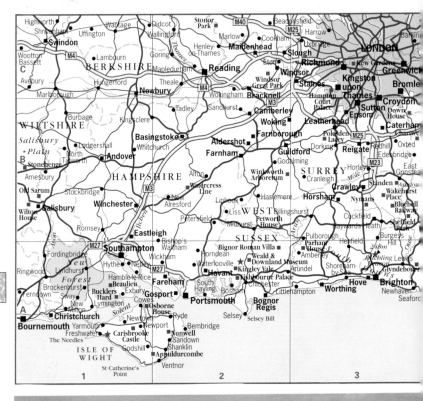

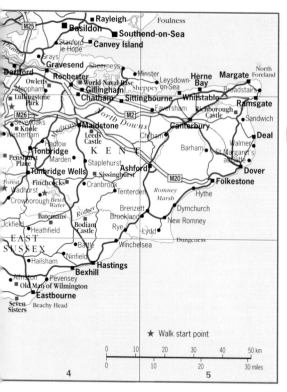

★ Walk start point

```
0      10      20      30      40      50 km
0          10          20          30 miles
```

4   5

SOUTHERN ENGLAND

The southeastern counties make up a comparatively affluent corner of Britain. Proximity to the capital and a green-belt policy restricting growth around London have pushed up property prices in this cherished ring of countryside, so that the villages have become affluent commuter caches; beyond the green belt spreads a sizeable stretch of suburbia. Yet for all the urban pressures, the region has surprisingly deep pockets of rural countryside; west Kent, southern Surrey, and much of Sussex represent some of the most varied lowlands in Britain.

THE WEALD AND THE DOWNS Many of the region's lushest gardens (see pages 16–17), finest country houses (see pages 102–103) and most appealing villages are found in the Weald, a term given to a somewhat ill-defined area stretching south of London towards the coast. Geologically it is identifiable as being between the North and South Downs, two ranges of chalk hills—or "downs"—that run west to east and end spectacularly in sheer, crumbly cliffs at Dover (the famous White Cliffs) and at Beachy Head near Eastbourne. The Downs rise to no great height, but are much-loved weekend walking grounds, with the long-distance North Downs Way and South Downs Way benefiting from wide views over the Weald itself.

Weald comes from a word meaning "wood", and though many of the trees have been cleared, it has the character of a wooded area, with stands of trees and hedge-lined fields. Here the villages tend to be traditional

Opposite: Wye Down, part of the North Downs, in Kent

looking, many with timber framed structures, some hung with pantiles and others exposing their beams, plus cottages built with flints, brick, or local stone. In Kent you will see oast houses—circular brick kilns built for drying hops for brewing, and now converted to other uses; regimented poles of hops growing in "hop gardens," as well as apple and cherry orchards, are also particularly Kentish. Jutting between the North and South Downs are the hills (of a Wealden sandstone known as greensand) of the High Weald, which include the Ashdown Forest, the wonderfully timeless heathland landscape of the Winnie-the-Pooh stories of A. A. Milne.

KENT, EAST AND WEST SUSSEX, AND SURREY Kent is a mixed bag; the north coast is part marshy, part industrial, although the historic dockyard in Chatham and the center of Rochester are attractive. Inland Kent has numerous pretty villages such as Penshurst, Chiddingstone, Chilham, and Shoreham; of its inland towns, Canterbury, Sandwich, Cranbrook, Tunbridge Wells, and Tenterden stand out the most.

On the coast, Dover deserves more than a fleeting glance for its castle, and Broadstairs and Folkestone are pleasant resorts. The Channel Tunnel runs from Folkestone to Sangatte (see panel, page 98).

The **Sussex** shoreline is almost entirely built up, though the cliffs west of Eastbourne and east of Hastings are notable exceptions. The only decent sandy beach is at Camber, near Rye. Coastal curios include the assembly of houseboats on the tidal mud flats at Shoreham, in West Sussex, and the De La Warre Pavilion, a Bauhaus-inspired design, in the unlikely setting of Bexhill.

The most appealing coastal towns by far are Hastings and Eastbourne, in contrasting styles but both abutting fine cliffs; and Brighton, a semi-shabby seaside resort, still has tremendous atmosphere, with its Royal Pavilion rating as one of the country's most extravagant follies. Chichester Harbour is the big yacht haven for Sussex. Chichester, West Sussex's cathedral city, lies within easy reach of the county's finest Roman monuments—Fishbourne Palace and Bignor Villa.

RECOMMENDED HISTORIC CITIES
Canterbury, Rochester, Winchester.

CASTLES AND ROYALTY
Berkshire: Windsor.
Hampshire: Portchester, Solent defences at Portsmouth, Southsea, etc.
Isle of Wight: Carisbrooke, Osborne House.
Kent: Deal, Dover, Rochester, Walmer.
Sussex: Bodiam, Pevensey.

ROMAN REMAINS
Kent: Lighthouse and painted house at Dover, Lullingstone Villa (near Eynsford), Richborough Castle (near Sandwich).
Sussex: Bignor Villa (near Amberley), Fishbourne Palace (near Chichester).

SMALL TOWNS Arundel, Chichester, Cranbrook, Faversham, Lewes, Petworth, Rye, Sandwich, Tunbridge Wells.

SEASIDE TOWNS
Brighton, Broadstairs, Eastbourne, Hastings.

NAVAL HERITAGE
Chatham, Portsmouth.

COASTAL SCENERY
Sussex: Seven Sisters and Beachy Head (near Eastbourne), Fairlight Cove (Hastings).
Kent: Cliffs between Folkestone and Walmer.

Oast houses are unique to Kent and the Hereford and Worcester areas

A number of small-scale vineyards are now well-established in the south

"In quitting the great Wen [London] we go through Surrey…There are erected within these four years, two entire miles of stock-jobbers' houses on this one road and the work goes on with accelerated force!…What an at once horrible and ridiculous thing this country would become, if this thing could go on only for a few years!"
—William Cobbett (1822), *Rural Rides*

▶▶▶ REGION HIGHLIGHTS

Beachy Head and the Seven Sisters *pages 98–99*

Brighton *pages 90–91*

Canterbury *page 93*

Dover Castle *page 98*

Portsmouth *page 104*

Rye *pages 104–105*

The Weald *pages 102–103 and 106–107*

Winchester *pages 107–108*

Windsor *page 109*

Inland Sussex has some prosperous-looking villages and a fair scattering of antiques stores, and pleasant country pubs. Highlights include Arundel, with its massive castle towering over its steep main street; Battle, the historic battlefield of 1066 and the abbey founded by William the Conqueror; Rye and Winchelsea, two remarkably unspoilt former ports; Lewes, with its architectural variety and Norman castle; and Alfriston, memorably set beneath the South Downs.

Surrey has been largely developed into an affluent commuter suburb, but it has some delicious countryside, ideal for walking—notably in the greensand country around Haslemere and the vicinities of Shere and Leith Hill, at 965 feet the highest point in the Southeast.

HAMPSHIRE, THE ISLE OF WIGHT, AND BERKSHIRE The county of **Hampshire** rolls gently inland, the best of its country in the far east around Selborne and in the far west by the heaths and woodlands of the New Forest. Winchester has a compact but fascinating medieval center. The coast doesn't offer much aesthetically, but Portsmouth has an important naval heritage. Southampton, a large industrial and commercial center that was heavily bombed in World War II, has a few corners of historic interest (medieval town walls, Tudor House, and the oldest bowling green in the world) as well as aviation and maritime museums and a fine art gallery. Both these cities and Lymington, have ferries to the **Isle of Wight**, a pleasant base, with plenty of attractions and scenery to tempt families and walkers, despite the suburbanization along its eastern coast. The island has an excellent public transportation system (some may wish to leave the car on the mainland to avoid the expense of taking it on the ferry) and its south coast is one of Britain's sunniest spots.

Berkshire has a split identity, divided north–south by the M4 motorway, with downlands merging into Wiltshire and Hampshire to the west, while at its flatter eastern edge is Windsor Great Park. At Windsor Castle you can see inside the state apartments of the Queen's favorite residence. Crowds throng the town all year round; you can escape from the bustle by taking a boat trip along the Thames or a walk into Eton or the park. The Thames defines Berkshire's northern border from Windsor to Streatley; the river, which runs down from Buckinghamshire and Oxfordshire, has a placid beauty and a boating scene that can only be found in England.

I will go out against the sun
Where the rolled scarp retires,
And the Long Man of Wilmington
Looks naked toward the shires;
And east till doubling Rother crawls
To find the fickle tide,
By dry and sea-forgotten walls,
Our ports of stranded pride.
—Rudyard Kipling (1865–1936), on the Sussex landscape

Horsted Keynes Station on the Bluebell Line—so-called because of the bluebell woods through which the railroad passes

BRIGHTON'S PAST
In 1754 Dr. Richard Russell came to the fishing village of Brighthelmstone and prescribed seawater as a cure for a variety of complaints; many people took his advice and the village acquired spa status. Georgian and Regency terraces followed as the élite arrived in the footsteps of the Prince Regent. Brighton later got a reputation as a rendezvous for lovers' illicit weekends; the railroad added a sleazy element. Graham Greene's novel *Brighton Rock* is set in the world of 1930s gang warfare.

▶▶ **Bluebell Railway**   86B3
(tel: 01825 722370)
In 1960 the Bluebell was the first standard-gauge steam railway to be reopened as a tourist attraction; in many ways it is the pick of the bunch, with some of its carriages dating from the 1890s and stations furnished with Victorian advertising signs, fire buckets, and gas lamps. Its 18 mile round trip takes an hour (special restaurant trains and other events at weekends) and runs between Sheffield Park and Kingscote via Horsted Keynes (there are bus links to East Grinstead rail station, where the line may eventually extend). Sheffield Park Garden (see page 17) makes a pleasant destination.

▶▶▶ **Brighton**   86A3
(Tourist information office tel: 0906 711255 (50p/minute))
This is one of the oldest and most interesting British coastal resorts. The Prince Regent, later King George IV, came here after his secret marriage to Mrs. Fitzherbert and initiated the fashion for seaside holidays and bathing. He converted a farmhouse bought in 1784 into his capricious **Royal Pavilion**▶▶▶, an oriental extravaganza covered with minarets and onion domes (see panel, page 91).

Despite the obvious decay (itself a Brighton hallmark) of the **seafront**▶▶, you can still see traces of its elegant heyday. **West Pier**, Britain's finest such structure, has long been derelict, but a National Lottery award has been allocated to help restore it. Meanwhile, the newer **Palace Pier** is very much alive, with fish-and-chips take-outs, tacky souvenir booths, and fortune-tellers. Summer weekends still draw the crowds to the amusements, aquarium, and privately run seafront train, and throughout May the city hosts a huge arts festival. The nude beach, Britain's first, lies out of sight from the pier; the main beach is shingle. Cream and sky-blue period streetlamps and rows of white stucco houses and hotels proliferate. The best streets lie to the east at **Kemp Town▶**, an example of early 19th-century town planning, with Lewes Crescent at its far end. Toward Hove to the west there are elegant bow-fronted Regency terraces, in Brunswick Square and north of Western Road.

The Lanes▶▶ survive from the once humble fishing village of Brighthelmstone; ironically this is now the most chic area of Brighton, with expensive antiques stores, sidewalk cafés, and galleries in its warren of narrow alleys. Brighton's main **museum▶▶** (*Admission free*), housed in the former stable block of the Royal Pavilion and similarly fantastic in style, has some eye-catching furniture, including Art Nouveau pieces, as well as a display about the town's early resort days. The **North Laine** (between the station and North Street) is the vibrant heart of funky Brighton, with buskers and alternative stores.

A conspicuously attractive town by the South Downs, to the northeast of Brighton, **Lewes▶▶** is graced with some very pleasing streets and paths known as "twittens," which include steep, cobbled Keere Street. The hilltop castle is Norman and was adapted into a romantic garden feature in the 18th century; it gives a fascinating rooftop view. Many of the half-timbered houses were given a fake brick veneer, fashionable in the 18th century, with the widespread use of "mathematical tiles," thin fascia tiles resembling bricks. The town is famed for the best and heartiest November 5 fireworks night in the country. On a more genteel note, Lewes also has a notable concentration of antiques stores and auction rooms.

▶▶ Broadstairs 87C5

(Tourist information center tel: 01843 862242)

The prettiest of the coastal resorts in Thanet in East Kent is Broadstairs; all its charm is concentrated on the seafront, with seven sandy coves beneath low cliffs. It is a combination of sedate resort and fishing port; you can still watch fish being unloaded and eat shellfish on the harbor wall. The town has a pleasantly old-fashioned air. Charles Dickens knew Broadstairs well; he spent several summers at what has since been named "Bleak House," with the desk at which he wrote *David Copperfield*.

Nearby **Ramsgate▶** is more run down, but it is worth a stroll for the Regency streets. The coastal walk from Broadstairs to Ramsgate takes about 30 minutes.

THE ROYAL PAVILION
The Prince Regent employed the great architect John Nash to transform an unspectacular house into a fantasy palace that formed the nucleus of his flamboyant social life—centered on parties, horse-racing, concerts, and vast dinners. The building takes its inspiration from India externally and China internally. Queen Victoria was unenthusiastic about the Pavilion and Brighton: "There were far too many of the wrong sort of people and they were all staring at me." She sold the building in 1850.

91

BLOOMSBURY CONNECTIONS
Three places associated with the Bloomsbury Group are found beneath the South Downs around Lewes. **Monk's House** at Rodmell (south of Lewes) was the home of Leonard and Virginia Woolf. **Charleston Farmhouse**, near Alciston, was the home of Duncan Grant and Clive and Vanessa Bell (the latter being Virginia's sister), and its walls and furniture are still decorated with their paintings; the garden is reminiscent of the Bloomsbury days. The Group added further decorations in the form of murals in **Berwick Church**.

At this desk at "Bleak House", Dickens completed David Copperfield

Tennyson Down, Isle of Wight   86A1

Start from Freshwater Bay. The coastal path leads west along a grassy ridge, with sea views on three sides. Pass the Tennyson monument and continue to the island's western tip; an old fort, Needles Old Battery, gives views of The Needles, a set of rock pinnacles battered by the waves. Return the same way. (2.5 hours)

Ditchling Beacon, West Sussex   86A3

Start from parking lot adjacent to Ditchling Beacon. Here the South Downs rise to their third highest point and are capped by the site of an Iron Age hill fort. Follow the South Downs Way west along the escarpment edge. After 2 miles you reach the famous Jack and Jill windmills. Return the same way. (2.5 hours)

Bewl Water, Kent/East Sussex border   87B4

Start from visitor center parking lot. An attractive reservoir, Bewl Water is the largest lake in Southeast England and is circled by a well-marked and scenically varied path. It is too long for an entire day's walk, but very pleasant for strolls.

Lullingstone Park, Kent   87B4

Start from car park at visitor center off the A225. Trails from the center take in landscapes of river, woodland and grassland plus Lullingstone Roman Villa and Lullingstone Castle (about 1.5 hours). Longer walks can incorporate the pretty villages of Shoreham, Otford, and Eynsford.

Ashdown Forest, East Sussex   87B4

Start at the Poohsticks Bridge parking lot in Ashdown Forest (take the B2026 south of Hartfield 1.25 miles, turn west at intersection with minor road; the parking lot is 200 yards on north side of road). This is the heartland of A. A. Milne's *Winnie-the-Pooh* stories. A path leads to the bridge where the game of Poohsticks was once played; return to the parking lot and follow the gravel path eastward; ignore left forks. Cross the road and take a path rising onto heathland (where Piglet supposedly lived). Walk up to the monument to Milne on Gill's Lap: this is the Enchanted Place of the stories, an ideal picnic spot with a view encapsulating the splendor of the "forest." Return the same way. (1.5 hours)

Poohsticks Bridge, Ashdown Forest

▶▶▶ Canterbury 87B5

(Tourist information center tel: 01227 766567)

Canterbury has witnessed two very dark hours. One was the murder of Thomas à Becket in the cathedral in 1170, the other a World War II "Baedeker raid" in 1942 (so called because targets were historic rather than military). The medieval city center was destroyed, but the cathedral, seat of the Archbishop of Canterbury and the premier church of England, was miraculously unscathed.

Yet today the city's sense of history is as compelling as ever. You can walk through the **West Gate** (museum inside), as pilgrims have done for eight centuries and pass a number of charitable hospitals founded in medieval times as places to accommodate pilgrims (St. Thomas's Hospital and the **Poor Priests' Hospital** are open to the public, the latter housing the hi-tech **Canterbury Heritage Museum▶**).

The old city center is largely contained within the **city wall**, but just outside lie **St. Augustine's Abbey** (EH), founded in 597, its church and cloister foundations still apparent and **St. Martin's Church**, England's oldest

Canterbury's rich architectural heritage is in evidence around the early 16th-century Christ Church Gate

church in continuous use and once the headquarters of St. Augustine—red Roman bricks can be seen in the walls.

The **cathedral▶▶▶** precincts are entered by Christ Church Gate. The cathedral, built in Caen limestone, boasts several outstanding features, among them Bell Harry, the 23 foot-high central tower, a collection of 12th- and 13th-century stained glass, a Norman crypt, and the Black Prince's tomb. Adjacent is the 15th-century Great Cloister, with a stone marking the spot where Thomas à Becket died.

Behind the cathedral, Green Court is fronted by the Norman Staircase, ruins of the monks' dormitory and the buildings of **King's School**. The **Roman Museum▶** on Longmarket sets the scene of Roman Canterbury, with reconstructions of some dealers' stalls and domestic interiors, before reaching a real Roman house with hypocaust system and mosaics. **The Canterbury Tales** brings Chaucer's characters to life in re-creations of Canterbury in medieval times.

To the southwest, the village of **Chilham▶▶** has a half-timbered square, with church at one end and castle entrance at the other.

CANTERBURY'S STREETSCAPE
The city's surviving older streets show a rich mixture of medieval, Georgian, and Victorian styles. Some of the first buildings in the center are: Queen Elizabeth's Guest Chamber, a former inn with a wonderfully over-the-top stucco façade; The Weavers, which is ancient, although its "half-timbering" is fake and relatively modern; and the Beaney Institute, an elaborate library, a statement of high Victorian exuberance. The major Roman remains are within the Roman Museum in Longmarket.

THE CANTERBURY TALES
In Chaucer's *Canterbury Tales*, the high point of English medieval literature, a party of pilgrims meet at the Tabard Inn, Southwark (now part of London). They agree to travel together and to tell stories to pass the time:
   "And specially, from every shires ende
   Of Engelonde to Caunterbury they wende."
Chaucer's works are brought to life in theme-park fashion, with tableaux and re-created sounds and smells, in *The Canterbury Tales* in St. Margaret's Street.

The seaside vacation is one of those great British institutions, which, like other good things, has spread down the class ladder. In the 18th century the only people who could afford a holiday of more than one day were the rich. Later, resorts like Bournemouth and Eastbourne were planned to attract middle-class business. The coming of the railroads and the invention of the nationwide "bank holidays" in Victorian times spurred the development of resorts for the working class—Blackpool, Margate, Skegness, and their like.

BEACH BELLES

When the fashion for "sea-bathing" began in the 18th century, men and women customarily swam naked, but as it spread, so did modesty. The "bathing machine" carried people, shielded from view, right out into the waves, but even so, women took to wearing all-enveloping flannel gowns tied with a drawstring at the neck. Elaborate Victorian and Edwardian costumes made of flannel, worsted, or serge looked much like day dresses, with frilly caps, stockings, even shoes. The one-piece swimsuit for ladies came in before World War I; it had sleeves and reached to the knees.

Before the 18th century Britons occasionally swam in rivers and lakes, but eyed the sea askance. It was dangerous and it tasted nasty. Even in the Royal Navy, a seaman who could swim was a rarity. When sea bathing began, it was for health rather than pleasure. A drawing of 1735 shows men and women in the sea at Scarborough, a health spa with a mineral spring on the Yorkshire coast. The spring enriched the local doctors and it seems to have occurred to them then that perhaps the rolling brine so plentifully at hand, the salt-laden water, and brisk North Sea breezes might be profitably exploited as well.

"Beside the seaside" Certainly this was what happened on the Sussex coast, where the obscure fishing hamlet of Brighthelmstone was transformed into glamorous **Brighton**, queen of the briny. A doctor named Richard Russell, who moved there in 1753, proclaimed the virtues of crabs' eyes, cuttlefish bones, and wood lice washed down with a hearty pint of seawater. His successor, an Irishman named Anthony Relham, opportunely discovered the salubrious qualities of fresh sea air, heightened, he said, by Brighton's fortunate lack of noxiously perspiring trees.

The effect of all this nonsense was to draw well-to-do invalids and hypochondriacs to the Sussex shore. When the Prince Regent took to visiting and built for himself the glamorous Royal Pavilion, the new resort's success was assured.

Some fishing villages and minor ports grew gradually into resorts, while others were planned for profit by shrewd local landowners

and developers. **Llandudno** on the North Wales coast was laid out by the local Mostyn family and remains a charming Victorian resort, lording it over brash **Rhyl** and **Prestatyn**, which were developed later for Lancashire mill-hands. At **Skegness** on the Lincolnshire coast, the Earl of Scarborough built a resort in the 1870s with the intention of attracting the middle classes, but the Great Northern Railway brought hordes of tourists from the Midlands industrial towns and Skegness became a leading working-class resort. The first in a chain of Butlin's "holiday camps" opened there in 1937.

Places with a sandy beach naturally cashed in, as did towns with a mild climate and plenty of summer sunshine. The Thames Estuary resorts of **Margate** and **Southend** enjoy Britain's highest July/August temperatures, followed by those along the south coast from **Torquay** to **Folkestone**. The highest figures for hours of sunshine per day are held by **Sandown** and **Shanklin** on the Isle of Wight.

"*So* bracing" Health remained a factor—"Skegness Is So Bracing," the posters proclaimed—but sheer fun took precedence as resorts sprouted piers and promenades, amusement parks, cliff railroads, zoos, excessively flowery gardens, bandstands, dance halls, freak shows, tattoo parlors, tacky postcards, fortune-tellers' booths, ice cream, and rock kiosks (see panel) to spice up the simpler pleasures of swimming, sunbathing, sand castles, and donkey rides. The seaside landlady became a comic cliché, with her iron-bound notions of gentility, strictly regulated mealtimes, and green plants in a fussy parlor. On August Bank Holiday Monday in 1937 more than half a million people swarmed into **Blackpool** in 50,000 motor vehicles and 700 trains, the earliest of which arrived at 3:55 AM.

Since World War II, with growing affluence, more cars and much longer vacations, patterns have changed. Some people still go faithfully to the same resort every year. Blackpool and Brighton are both going strong, but most British seaside resorts have found themselves unable to compete with the allure of the climate and competitive pricing of package tours abroad. Bad publicity about polluted beaches has not helped either. The traditional seaside vacation seems increasingly to be a pleasure of the past.

PIERS OF THE REALM
The pier, that familiar feature of the seaside, is descended from the much earlier quay, built to land cargo and passengers on an open shore. In 1823 Brighton constructed its famous Chain Pier, like a suspension bridge tiptoeing gracefully into the English Channel (which destroyed it in a storm in 1896). Though built for boat-passengers to and from Dieppe, it was a pleasure pier as well. It had souvenir booths and a camera obscura and was appreciated as a way of enjoying the sea without being seasick. Sadly, piers are an endangered species now, desperately expensive to repair and maintain.

95

Above left: ice cream and beach huts, Walton on the Naze. Above: just sitting, Brighton Palace Pier

ALL THE WAY THROUGH
A traditional seaside delight is "rock", a stick of hard mint candy that is usually white in color with the resort's name in pink letters, mysteriously running through the stick's length. Blackpool and Morecambe both claim to have invented the treat, but there is also a tradition that it originated in the inland industrial town of Dewsbury in the 1860s. As late as the 1970s Blackpool was manufacturing two tons of rock a day in the summer.

THE MEDWAY TOWNS
The three Medway towns of Rochester, Chatham, and Gillingham together form a large industrial sprawl in the north of Kent. The most historic of these is Rochester. Pre-industrial Rochester is compact but impressive, with a medieval cathedral, an absorbing museum within the Guildhall, and the ruins of a Norman castle (E.H.) giving mighty panoramas over the River Medway below. The writer Charles Dickens lived in Rochester for a period; the Charles Dickens Centre is in Eastgate House, which features in the *Pickwick Papers* and *Edwin Drood*.

FISHBOURNE'S UNEARTHING
What visitors see at Fishbourne—the mosaics, hypocaust and partition walls—is only one side of a vast palace of AD 75, the largest Roman building yet discovered in northern Europe. Part of the rest is under houses and nearby excavations completed in 1999 revealed a military building of similar date to the Roman Conquest in AD 43 that some historians believe confirms that the Conquest began at Fishbourne (where local tribes were friendly with the Romans) and not in east Kent as commonly thought.

Vernacular building styles on show at the Weald and Downland Open Air Museum at Singleton

▶▶ Chatham: World Naval Base   87C4
(tel: 01634 823800)
The historic dockyard here was once a naval center of ship-building and -fitting; today it incorporates Britain's largest concentration of landmarked buildings. The site includes lifeboats, a shipbuilding exhibition, warehouses, a rope works, shipbuilding sheds, a visitor center and three vessels—a destroyer, a submarine and a Victorian sloop. Combined with Rochester (see panel), this makes an excellent day out (speedy train services from London).

▶▶ Chichester   86A2
(Tourist information center tel: 01243 775888)
The cathedral city for Sussex, Chichester, is based on a simple criss cross layout centered on a fine 16th-century market cross and, with ancient city walls and handsome Georgian streets, it is an enjoyable place to explore. Its medieval **cathedral▶** (early Norman with Early English additions) is unusual—it is not tucked away within its own close and it has a freestanding belfry. The interior has some distinguished modern features: a tapestry by John Piper, a painting by Graham Sutherland and glass by Marc Chagall, and unusual older tombs (most famously the medieval Arundel Knight, who breaks with tradition and holds hands with his lady). The **Mechanical Music and Doll Collection** is the most offbeat of the city's museums, while **Pallant House** specializes in modern British art, displayed within an elegant early 18th-century house.

Fishbourne Roman Palace▶▶, on the edge of Chichester, is thought to have been built for one Cogidubnus, a Briton who supported the Romans and was made senator. Now much has been re-created, with a dining room, mosaics in full view; remarkably, excavations revealed the exact shape of the bedding trenches in the garden—this has been faithfully replanted and there is a Roman herbarium, with the kinds of plants that would have been familiar to the Romans. (See also panel.)

To the southwest of the town, **Chichester Harbour▶** is a big yachting center. Extending over a huge area, its east side is natural mud flats and complex, marshy inlets. **Bosham** is one of the best places to appreciate the setting: the much-painted village has a picturesque church steeple, waterfront cottages, and boating scenes. East Head juts into the southeast corner of the harbor: here sand dunes and salt marshes make a good setting for an exhilarating stroll.

Boat-building: one of several crafts found at Amberley Museum

Daily boat tours (in season; also winter birdwatching trips at some weekends) from Itchenor take 1.5 hours (for a recorded schedule tel: 01243 786418). Due north of Chichester is the **Weald and Downland Open Air Museum▶▶**, Singleton, a rural museum with reconstructed buildings rescued from Kent and Sussex—including a farmhouse, smithy, school, and water mill.

A sleepy, unblemished village, much of it thatched, **Amberley▶▶** is beautifully set beneath the South Downs some 13 miles northeast of Chichester. Glimpse through the churchyard gate to the 16th-century manor (private) within a massive medieval castle wall, the former residence of bishops of Chichester. It perches on the edge of Amberley Wild Brooks, an area of water meadows known for its rich birdlife and marshland plants. Near the station at the south end of the village, the **Amberley Museum▶** has displays of small-scale Sussex industries and crafts, situated in a former chalk pit; here are a blacksmith, potter, boat-builder, printer, narrow-gauge railroad, vintage buses, wheelwright, and even a collection of antique radios. Nearby is the Elizabethan manor house **Parham House▶**, begun in 1577 by Sir Thomas Parham, who later sailed with Sir Francis Drake to Cadiz; its deer park has lakes and a walled garden.

Arundel▶▶ is a handsome, compact town. The main street climbs from the canalized River Arun up to the sprawling, much-restored medieval-Victorian castle—home of the Dukes of Norfolk and their ancestors for over 700 years—and the nearby superb Roman Catholic cathedral. The castle, rich in furnishings and art treasures, is open to the public, as is the adjoining park. At the **Wildfowl and Wetland Trust▶** (just north of town), you can observe hundreds of geese, swans, and ducks at close quarters from specially constructed hides.

To the north, **Bignor Roman Villa▶**, one of Britain's largest Roman houses, has mosaic floors (depicting gladiators, Ganymede and the eagle, etc.). The villa was occupied during the 2nd to 4th centuries. Stane Street, a Roman road now turned into a path, cuts across the downland close by. Its finest section starts from the car park on Bignor Hill (reached by a dead-end lane).

KINGLEY VALE
Europe's largest yew forest spreads over a shoulder of the South Downs, a wonderful ancient-feeling place, dark and eerie, where trees have collapsed and then continued to grow from their horizontal positions, making a bizarre collection of shapes and forms. A nature trail circles the site. The forest's origins are a mystery; could it have been a plantation? Yews were once valued for making bows and arrows. The view from the Bronze Age bell barrows (burial mounds) on the summit extends over Chichester Harbour.

Chichester: flint walls on St. Richard's Walk

THE CHANNEL TUNNEL

The project to build a link from England to France germinated during Napoleonic times. The final tunnel was completed in 1994 at a cost of £10 billion; **Eurotunnel shuttles** take cars between Folkestone and Calais and the **Eurostar** passenger train runs from London Waterloo to Paris, Lille, Calais, and Brussels. The Eurotunnel Exhibition Centre in Folkestone gives you an overview of the "Chunnel" (as it was originally called). The spoil created Samphire Hoe, Britain's newest land—a coastal grassland beautifully sited beneath the cliff, reached by road tunnel west of Dover.

Eastbourne's Victorian pier

▶▶ Dover   87B5

(Tourist information center tel: 01304 205108)

The major cross-Channel port since Roman times (when it was known as Dubris), Dover has long assumed a military role. It was badly bombed in World War II and re-development has been lackluster—a wasted opportunity, given its cliff and valley setting. But the famous white cliffs (a symbol of homecoming for Britons) still beckon across the Channel. The **castle▶▶▶**, high above the town, stands as one of Britain's finest examples of an intact Norman keep, within which are sight and sound experiences re-creating the castle under siege in 1216 and during a visit by Henry VIII in 1539. The castle has the longest history of any in the country and has much scope for wandering around gun emplacements, watch towers and parapets. Within the site a Saxon church stands beside the Pharos, a Roman lighthouse (Britain's tallest Roman building). Take the audio tour of the Battlements Walk and the medieval tunnels. Arrive early to reserve a tour of the Secret Wartime Tunnels, from where the evacuation of Dunkirk in 1940 was coordinated; Cap Griz Nez on the French coast looks surprisingly near on a clear day. In the town center, a few Georgian and Regency terraces remain unscathed; the major sight is the **Roman Painted House▶**, with its central-heating system and painted walls. The **White Cliffs Experience** gives an interactive view of Dover's history: you can row a Roman galley and walk through a Blitz-damaged street.

THE FIRST CROSS-CHANNEL FLIGHT

The cliff walk northeast from Dover passes Blériot's monument, commemorating the first powered flight across the Channel. Louis Blériot (1872–1936), whose early flying experiments included towing gliders along the River Seine, made the historic flight from Calais to Dover on July 25, 1909.

Deal and Walmer▶ are both on the coast to the north of Dover and both have castles built by Henry VIII in the plan of a Tudor rose. Walmer is all neat houses looking over a stony beach; Deal has a pretty ex-fishermen's quarter of narrow streets.

▶ Eastbourne   87A4

(Tourist information center tel: 01323 411400)

A town of chintz-decorated hotels, genteel stucco, and brass bands on the promenade, Eastbourne is a well-preserved example of a 19th-century English seaside resort.

The South Downs end in style just west of Eastbourne at **Beachy Head** and the **Seven Sisters▶▶▶**. There is a sheer drop of 525 feet at Beachy Head, the chalk cliffs towering above a lighthouse. Further west, the Seven Sisters are a series of dry valleys chopped off by the sea to form a roller-coaster cliff. There is access to the coastal path at **Birling Gap** and at the **Seven Sisters Country Park** by Cuckmere Haven. Beware of the unfenced edge.

Alfriston►► has a strong medieval atmosphere, with tile-hung and timber houses, cafés, and antiques stores. The 14th-century Clergy House, a pre-Reformation vicarage, was the first building acquired by the National Trust and is a restored half-timbered house with its original clay floor. Adjacent, the church, dubbed the Cathedral of the Downs, has 14th-century features. The street also has two fine inns, the Star and the George and the stump of a market cross is a memento of busier days. Nearby and best seen from south of Wilmington village is the **Long Man of Wilmington**►►, an enigmatic chalk carving on the downs of a man bearing a staff in either hand. It is probably Anglo-Saxon or earlier, although no written record before the 18th century has been found. Eastward along the coast is **Pevensey Castle**► (E.H.). Its 4th-century Roman walls enclose a medieval castle and keep. William the Conqueror landed nearby in 1066 to launch his invasion of England (see panel).

► Hastings

87A4

(Tourist information center tel: 01424 781111)

Dramatically hilly, Hastings is a mixture of a faded seaside resort and an old fishing port thick with character. The picturesque and warren-like **old town** lies in a valley east of the center; the former fishermen's quarter lies close to a group of tall wooden sheds, called deezes, built for storing fishing nets, and there are caves and a castle to visit. Pleasant walks onto the sandstone cliffs extend eastward to **Fairlight Cove** along a wild coastline and a cliff-hugging train hauls you up the slope of the old town.

Battle►► (see panels) is a handsome small town, famed for **Battle Abbey and Battlefield**►► (E.H.); the medieval Almonry houses the **Town Model**, and the **Battle Museum** and **Buckley's Yesterdays World** (shop and room displays) justify a full day's visit.

Bodiam Castle►► (N.T.), 12 miles inland from Hastings, dates from the 14th century—surrounded by a wide moat filled with water lilies and with walls at their original height. A visit can be combined with a steam-hauled ride on the **Kent and East Sussex Railway** to Tenterden.

THE BATTLE OF HASTINGS
The best-known date in British history is 1066, when the Battle of Hastings between William of Normandy and King Harold took place at Battle (as it is now called). Oddly, the great turning point in English history was a surprisingly haphazard affair: the English should have trounced the Normans, who were vastly outnumbered and fighting uphill. However, the English made a strategic blunder in storming downhill when they thought some of the Normans were retreating; this left a hole in the English defences on the top of the slope, which the Normans promptly filled.

BATTLE ABBEY
William I, "the Conqueror," vowed that if he was victorious he would found an abbey here, on the battlefield where he defeated Harold's English forces; the high altar marks the spot where Harold is said to have fallen, pierced in the eye with a Frenchman's arrow. Today a battlefield trail and an audiovisual display detail the story of the battle. Of the abbey, the gatehouse of 1338, and the east range are still intact.

Low tide at Birling Gap gives access to the beach below the brilliant-white Seven Sisters cliffs, which are slowly being eroded back

The Royal Yacht Squadron has its headquarters at Cowes

ISLAND HOUSES

Osborne House (E.H.) was built as a retreat for Queen Victoria, in 1845 and she died here in 1901. The State Apartments provide a rewarding insight into Victoria's lifestyle.

Dating from the 18th century, **Appuldurcombe House** (E.H.) stands as a spooky skeleton, with a triumphal gateway to nowhere in its Capability Brown-landscaped grounds.

THE TENNYSON CONNECTION

Alfred, Lord Tennyson lived at Farringford Park House (now a hotel) near Freshwater Bay; his Victorian fan club (autograph hunters and all) tracked him down here and he is still remembered by the monument on Tennyson Down.

Cowes High Street

▶▶ **Isle of Wight**   86A1-A2

(Tourist information center tel: 01983 813818)

Just 2 miles over the Solent from the mainland at its nearest point, the diamond-shaped island is reached by ferry or catamaran from Portsmouth (landing in Ryde and Fishbourne), Southampton (landing in Cowes), or Lymington (landing in Yarmouth). Although developed, the isle has plenty of scenic variety, with chalk downs and splendid coastal cliffs. Public transport is excellent; many visitors leave their cars on the mainland.

On the south coast, grassy whaleback hills provide outstanding views for walkers; at the western end of **Tennyson Down▶▶** (see Walks, page 92) is a set of chalk pinnacles known as **The Needles**. Close by, the multicolored sands of Alum Bay are sold in souvenir glass bottles of every shape and size. The island's southernmost point, **St. Catherine's Point▶**, has a lighthouse open to visitors; St. Catherine's Hill is capped by an oratory in the tower of a 14th-century chapel. Farther north, **Yarmouth▶** is the most appealing town on the island, a pretty port with whitewashed cottages and one of the numerous forts built by Henry VIII to defend the Solent. The coast and rivers have some attractive marshy landscapes, as found along the **River Yar** and **Newtown Estuary**.

The east coast is mostly developed: **Ryde**, **Shanklin**, **Sandown**, and **Bembridge** are good spots for low-key holidays. **Dinosaur Isle** in Sandown claims to be one of the biggest exhibition on the subject. Shanklin has preserved its old village near Shanklin Chine, a gorge leading to the sea. **Cowes** has a sailboat atmosphere; in late June the Round the Island Yacht Race features over a thousand competitors, and in August Cowes hosts a regatta. **Ventnor** snuggles beneath an undercliff and has a subtropical **Botanic Garden▶▶**.

Near Newport, the island's capital, **Carisbrooke Castle▶▶** (E.H.) is one of the best-preserved Norman shells in the kingdom, with inner rooms dating from 1470; Charles I spent time here pending his execution. The castle has Britain's only surviving donkey wheel, used to haul water from a deep well. **Godshill** is a pretty village of stone and thatch; its church has a rare 15th-century wall painting of the "Lily Cross."

▶ New Forest 86A1

(Lyndhurst tourist information center tel: 01703 282269)

Set to become a national park, the New Forest has survived into the 21st century surprisingly intact. Established in 1079 as a hunting forest for Norman royalty, it still feels incredibly remote. Essentially it is a tract of lowland heath and mixed forest; it is splendid territory for walking, camping, and picnicking. There are no major hills, but there is enough variety to spark interest; it tends to be more open on the west side. Wild ponies and red deer are commonly seen; the former graze on heathlands and are owned by commoners with historic grazing rights. The **New Forest Museum** at Lyndhurst sets the scene.

Lined with conifers planted in the 19th century, the **Bolderwood** and **Rhinefield ornamental drives**▶ are forest drives; species include giant fir, redwood, and swamp cypress. Lord Montagu's **National Motor Museum**▶▶ at Beaulieu, the finest collection of its kind, celebrates the golden age of automobiles; adjacent are **Beaulieu Abbey**▶ (founded 1204) and **Palace House**▶ (the former abbey gatehouse), Montagu's stately home (complete with monorail and vintage bus rides). Downriver, **Bucklers Hard**▶ is a hamlet with a nautical flavor; the story of this former boat-building center is told in its Maritime Museum. **Exbury Gardens** includes a collection of azaleas, rhododendrons, magnolias, and camelias.

Rhinefield, in the New Forest

▶▶ Petworth 86B2

(tel: 01798 342207)

This grand, late 17th-century mansion (N.T.), built by the Duke of Somerset, has been Percy family property since Norman times. Today the National Trust maintains its interior, which includes virtuoso woodcarving and a collection of paintings unrivaled by any other National Trust property; there are works by Turner, Blake, Rembrandt, Reynolds, and others. The grounds, landscaped by Capability Brown, offer delightful walks. Petworth town lies immediately adjacent to the house; the old streets are most attractive, but suffer appallingly from traffic.

SQUATTERS' RIGHTS
A few scattered thatched hamlets are found in New Forest clearings. Typically such settlements owe their origins to squatters' rights, whereby common land could be occupied by anyone building a house within one day, provided smoke was seen to be rising from the chimney by dusk.

The counties of Kent, West Sussex, East Sussex, and Surrey boast a remarkably varied range of houses that are open to the public. Many of those described below make pleasant day-trips from London. Several are included in the Drive on pages 106–107. Some houses may be closed during the winter months, so it is always worth checking on opening times with local tourist information centers.

THE NATIONAL TRUST (N.T.)

The National Trust is a major landowner; it was formed in 1895 to safeguard Britain's places of historic interest and natural beauty. Property it acquires is held in trust for the nation. Many of the N.T.'s hundreds of country houses, gardens, and other places of interest are open to the public. Cards giving free admission to any property are available, on payment of a membership fee, from these and from N.T. information centres, or by mail from P.O. Box 39, Bromley, Kent BR1 3XL; or tel: 020-8315 1111. Most properties close in winter. Membership also gives you free entry to properties owned by the National Trust for Scotland (N.T.S.), based at 28 Charlotte Square, Edinburgh EH2 4ET, tel: 0131-226 5922. In this book, N.T. and N.T.S. denote staffed properties that charge entrance fees. Website: www.nationaltrust.org.uk

The Italian Garden at Hever Castle: part of Astor's 20th-century design

102

Standen▶ (N.T.), near East Grinstead, West Sussex, is a delightful Arts and Crafts house, designed in the 1890s by Philip Webb, a friend of leading artist-craftsman William Morris. It still has its original electric light fittings and has a collection of ceramics by William de Morgan. Toward Tonbridge, **Penshurst Place▶▶**, Penshurst, Kent, lies amid charming lowland countryside, an outstanding example of 14th-century domestic architecture owned by the Sidney family, Earls of Leicester, whose forebears include Sir Philip Sidney, the Elizabethan poet. It has a splendid hall with a chestnut ceiling and a fine, long gallery. Nearby **Hever Castle▶▶**, Hever, Kent, was the birthplace of Anne Boleyn, second wife of Henry VIII. The moated Tudor house owes much of its present appearance to the 20th-century renovation by William Waldorf Astor, a wealthy American. He added mock-medieval features and laid out delightful grounds with great avenues of chestnuts and lindens, a yew maze, yew topiary in the form of chessmen and an Italian garden filled with sculpture. Some 5 miles north, **Chartwell▶▶** (N.T.), near Westerham, Kent, was Sir Winston Churchill's home from 1922 until his death in 1965. The house appears as it was when Churchill and his family lived here, a homely place filled with mementoes of one of the great men of the 20th century. General Wolfe, general of the British army at the capture of Quebec from the French, was born in 1726 at **Quebec House▶** (N.T.), Westerham, Kent, close by; an exhibition illustrates the campaign that led to British supremacy in Canada.

Charles Darwin lived the last 40 years of his life at **Down House▶▶** (E.H.) near Downe, Kent. Here he wrote

his seminal work *On the Origin of Species* (1859), the book that changed mainstream thinking on evolution. The rooms are set up as in Darwin's day, and you can imagine the great man ensconced in his study or thinking his theories through on his regular walks in the garden.

Immediately southeast of Sevenoaks, Kent, **Knole**▶ ▶ ▶ (N.T.) is England's largest house, with 365 rooms, 7 courtyards and 52 corridors; little has been altered since the early 17th century. A former archbishop's palace which later fell into the hands of Henry VIII, Knole has been in the hands of the Sackvilles from the time of Elizabeth I. The huge deer park is always open to the public. **Ightham Mote**▶ ▶ ▶ (N.T.), near Shipbourne, Kent, is a 14th-century moated building of great character, with a Tudor chapel with painted ceiling, a splendid Great Hall, and a 14th-century chapel and crypt.

Close by the North Downs in northern Kent, **Owletts**▶ (N.T.), near Cobham, is a restrained red-brick 17th-century house, which boasts a plasterwork ceiling and a staircase of the same period. Do not miss the collection of memorial brasses in nearby Cobham Church. Near the village of Shoreham in Kent's Darent Valley, **Lullingstone Castle**▶ is a Tudor and Queen Anne family mansion with state rooms and one of the earliest brick gateways (ca1497) in the country; a visit can be combined with Lullingstone Roman Villa (see walk on page 92).

Leeds Castle▶ ▶, to the east of Maidstone, Kent, was once a residence of Henry VIII but is not as genuine a stately home as some: the furniture and contents were later brought in with the aim of re-creating a country house; but the grounds and building themselves are real enough and the place has warmth and an idyllic lake setting. About 13 miles south near Goudhurst, Kent (not far from **Sissinghurst**, see Gardens, page 17), is **Finchcocks**▶ ▶, an early Georgian house noted for its collection of keyboard instruments. Be sure to catch the demonstration, where the owner gives a witty talk and plays some of the instruments. Some 12 miles south again at Burwash, East Sussex, is **Bateman's**▶ (N.T.), the 17th-century house where author Rudyard Kipling lived from 1902 to 1936 and completed *Puck of Pook's Hill* and *Rewards and Fairies*. The mill next door houses one of the oldest water-driven turbines, still grinding flour for sale. Kipling's 1928 Rolls-Royce is on display.

The Arcadian beauty of Penshurst Place, famed for its medieval Baron's Hall

103

THE WEALDEN FORESTS
The Weald has not always been the countryside of fine mansions, charming villages, rich farms, and hop-fields that we see today. In centuries gone by, it was deeply forested, its oaks supplying the timber that built the British navy. The trees were also felled by charcoal burners to smelt the Sussex iron. Patches of this ancient forest remain, in the forests of St. Leonards and Ashdown.

Nelson's flagship,
H.M.S. Victory

PORTSMOUTH'S HISTORIC SHIPS

H.M.S. *Victory* was Lord Nelson's flagship at Trafalgar and is still in commission (thus manned by serving officers). Henry VIII's favorite battleship, the *Mary Rose*, keeled over in the harbor in 1545, in sight of the king. In 1982 the wreck was brought to the surface and is now kept under special conditions, an intriguing time capsule of Tudor life. H.M.S. *Warrior* (1860) was the world's first iron-hulled warship, now restored to its former glory; visitors are free to walk around the decks.

NAVAL DEFENCES AT PORTSMOUTH

Among those which can be visited are Southsea Castle, built in 1544, which still has tunnels (exhibits include fish-bone ship models made by Napoleonic prisoners of war); Spitbank Fort, out to sea and reached by a short boat trip, with a labyrinth of passages; and Fort Nelson at Fareham. In 1944 Portsmouth was the nerve center of the Normandy invasion and in 1982 the South Atlantic Task Force was prepared here for battle in the Falklands War.

Church Square, Rye

▶▶▶ Portsmouth 86A2

(Tourist information center tel: 023-9282 6722)

A sprawling port and industrial city, heavily bombarded in World War II, Portsmouth is unique among British towns in being built on its own island. This has been a naval base since the 12th century, and in 1495 was host to the world's first dry dock. For the visitor, Portsmouth rates alongside Greenwich (see page 46) as the center for finding out about Britain's maritime history.

The **Historic Dockyard▶▶▶**, close to Portsmouth Harbour station, is the chief attraction, where a trio of famous warships are berthed (see panel). The **Royal Naval Museum** (*Admission charge* separate, or combined with ticket for H.M.S. *Victory*) charts naval history from 1485 to the Falklands War and features the Trafalgar campaign and the Siege of Malta. **Port cruises** operate between April and October, weather permitting. For the Millennium, Portsmouth smartened up its waterside, with an ambitious new development at **Gunwharf Quays**, public promenades along each side of the harbor and the much-delayed 500 foot **Millennium Tower**.

Eastwards lies **Southsea**, an Edwardian coastal resort, where the **D-Day Museum▶** commemorates the Allied invasion of Normandy on June 6, 1944, with the sights and sounds of Britain at war and the 272-foot Overlord Embroidery (a latter-day Bayeux Tapestry). The **Royal Marines Museum** within a grandiose Victorian building that formerly served as the officers' mess, traces the 300-year history of the Marines. Also in Southsea, the **Portsmouth Sea Life Centre** is an aquarium with a ceiling-high "window onto the ocean."

Elsewhere in town are **Charles Dickens' birthplace** (Commercial Road), where the writer was born in 1812, now a three-room museum; **Portchester Castle▶▶** (E.H.), from which the Romans coordinated the defence of southeast England and including remains of a Norman church and a palace built by Richard II; and the **City Museum** (Museum Road) with old storefronts and more.

▶▶▶ Rye 87B4

(Tourist information center tel: 01797 226696)

This small town of cobblestones and half-timbered houses perches on a rise above Romney Marsh. Mermaid Street is one of the prettiest thoroughfares in southeast England. Once a Cinque Port (see panel, page 105), Rye now lies inland by some 2miles. In medieval times the town was frequently attacked by the French, who set fire to it in 1377; the Ypres Tower is a rare pre-fire survivor and now houses the local museum. Medieval Landgate guards what was once the only landward entrance. The Gun Garden below looks down the River Rother toward Rye Harbour. The novelists Henry James and E. F. Benson lived at Lamb House (N.T.) at different times; many of Benson's Mapp and Lucia stories are set in Rye. Antique hunters should head for the stores near the old quay.

To the northeast lies **Romney Marsh▶**. The sea has receded, leaving the marsh, now drained, and fertile farmland grazed by chunky Romney sheep. A long way inland, the old Saxon shore is visible as an abrupt escarpment edge; at its foot runs the Royal Military Canal, built in Napoleonic times as a defence. Romney Marsh is sparsely populated but has some good medieval churches, including the drunkenly askew church at **Brookland**, with its freestanding belfry. **Camber Sands** offers one of the cleanest beaches in the southeast.

Winchelsea▶ ▶ is a quiet hilltop village just southeast of Rye, still ranged around its medieval grid plan, with many handsome old houses and a superb church. The original town was much plundered by the French in the 14th and 15th centuries. Three town gates survive.

Beyond Romney Marsh, the **Romney, Hythe, and Dymchurch Railway**, a mere 15 inch gauge, runs between the picturesque hillside town of **Hythe** (there's a bizarre collection of human skulls in the church crypt) and Dungeness, a most surreal place, where fishermen's shacks and converted train carriages crouch on a vast rocky bank beneath the shadow of Dungeness B nuclear power station (*Guided tours free*).

▶▶ Sandwich 87B5
(Tourist information center tel: 01304 613565)

Though it is of modest size, Sandwich has a remarkably intact medieval center, all the better for being off the tourist beat. Take a walk beside the river on the earth ramparts, visiting the Barbican, a toll bridge-cum-gateway. **Richborough Castle▶** (E.H.) was erected after the Roman invasion of AD 43 and a busy town once existed here, dominated by a huge arch that greeted Roman legions at this threshold to Britain. The entrance fee includes an informative audio tour that explains the site.

THE CINQUE PORTS
During the reign of Edward the Confessor (1042–1066) a confederation of Channel ports was formed for the defence of the coast and for 300 years these Cinque Ports (French for "five ports") had the monopoly on supplying ships and men for the royal fleet, enjoying privileges in return. The original five ports—Sandwich, Hastings, Hythe, New Romney and Dover—were later joined by Winchelsea and Rye and several other towns were also attached. After the 14th century, as harbors silted up and the coastline shifted, the Cinque Ports declined in importance. Today, only Dover is an active port.

105

MARTELLO TOWERS
A feature of the Kent and Sussex coasts is the string of 74 Martello towers (of a type formerly widespread in Europe and named after Cape Mortella in Corsica, where the British Navy captured such a tower in 1794), built 1805–1812 to resist a possible French invasion; some are derelict, others are converted to private houses; English Heritage maintains one at Dymchurch, in Romney Marsh (Kent) and opens it to the public in summer.

Fishing boats on the beach at Dungeness

THE WEALD

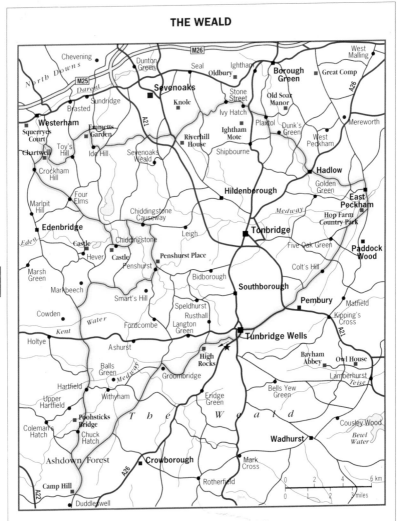

The Pantiles, an attractive shopping area in Tunbridge Wells

The Weald

Starting at Tunbridge Wells, this is a circular tour of approximately 70 miles. You'll see the weatherboarded and pantile-hung cottages, the undulating woodlands and farmland of the Weald, and you can visit a host of country houses and attractive gardens. Allow at least a day if you plan to stop at all the places mentioned.

Start at **Tunbridge Wells▶**, a very pleasant old spa town with echoes of its 18th-century heyday (evoked in the exhibition "A Day at the Wells"), including the delightful Pantiles, a Regency arcade. Leave by the A26, but soon fork right and then left to pass **High Rocks▶**, a popular place for climbers.

At **Groombridge** take the B2188 which rises onto the sandy heathlands of the **Ashdown Forest▶**, the landscape of A. A. Milne's much-loved *Winnie-the-Pooh* stories (see walk on page 92). Detour south along the B2026—just before the next road junction, Camp Hill on the right offers a fine viewpoint.

Return north along the B2026 through **Hartfield** and turn off past Cowden railroad station to follow back lanes to **Penshurst▶ ▶**, known for its great house (see page 102) and picturesque cottages.

Continue on the B2176 and then a minor road to **Chiddingstone▶**, where a splendid half-timbered group of buildings owned by the National Trust includes the Castle Inn, named for being close to an eye-catching Gothic castle.

Weave around minor lanes past **Chartwell▶ ▶**, Churchill's former house (see page 102), through pretty **Ide Hill** village, with its spacious green, around the south side of **Knole Park▶ ▶** and close to **Ightham Mote▶ ▶ ▶** (see page 103).

Return to Tunbridge Wells via **Plaxtol**, **Hadlow** with its ruined 19th-century folly tower and **East Peckham**, where oast houses mark the site of Whitbread Brewery's **Hop Farm Country Park**.

107

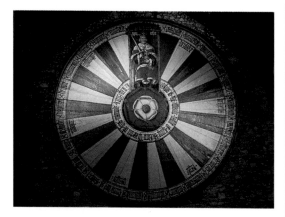

▶ ▶ ▶ Winchester
86B1
(tel: 01962 840500)

The capital of Saxon England, Winchester became a major religious and commercial center in medieval times. Its importance has ebbed, but its medieval core is well preserved. Its college is one of Britain's great public schools.

Visitors often spend most of their time in the vicinity of the **cathedral▶ ▶ ▶**, the longest medieval cathedral in Europe. It has an outstanding Norman crypt, much

King Arthur's "Round Table"

WINCHESTER COLLEGE

Students of Winchester College, one of the country's leading "public" schools (see panel on Eton College, page 109), are known as Wykehamists, harkening to its 14th-century foundation by the Bishop of Winchester, William of Wykeham. Seventy scholars were taught classics and other disciplines here before studying at New College, Oxford (another Wykeham foundation). The school probably was used as a model for Eton College, founded by Henry VI. Both have quadrangles, a chapel, and a hall.

THE WATERCRESS LINE

Also known as the Mid-Hants Railway, the privately owned 10 mile railroad runs through the Hampshire countryside from New Alresford to Alton (where it connects with the main railroad line), giving a good idea of train travel in the age of steam. The carriages are old British Rail ones, the staff dress in period costume, and the stations look and feel right. The watercress beds which gave the line its nickname can still be seen around New Alresford and watercress soup is served on the line's evening diner train. For details, tel: 01962 734866.

Winchester Cathedral contains the remains of Canute, successor to King Alfred

Perpendicular work, and monuments to Jane Austen and to Isaak Walton, of *Compleat Angler* fame; the chantry of William Wykeham, who funded restoration work, is perhaps the finest monument of all. Walton resided in No. 7 in the **cathedral close**, a charming precinct abutted by the flying buttresses of the cathedral, and by the rambling half-timbered Cheyney Court (dating from 1148). Close by is the **Winchester City Museum▶**, with a strong Roman section.

The **High Street** and **Broadway** have been the main axis of the city since Roman times. At the top end, **West Gate**, one of two surviving city gates, occupies a Roman site; a small museum upstairs has a drawing of Wren's scheme for a royal palace (which never got off the ground). Nearby is the Great Hall, where hangs "King Arthur's Round Table," which lists the names of all his knights but is actually a resplendent medieval fake made about 700 years after his death. Down along Broadway is a 1901 statue of King Alfred, King of Wessex, who is buried nearby and the Abbey Gardens, a quiet haven close to the Gothic revival guildhall (1871) housing the tourist information center.

The half-timbered **Winchester City Mill** straddles the River Itchen nearby. On **College Street**, a plaque records the house in which Jane Austen died in 1817, aged 42. **Winchester College▶** (*Guided tours* Apr–Sep) has a "quad" like those found at the colleges of Oxford and Cambridge universities. **Wolvesey Castle▶** (E.H.), a gaunt shell of a bishop's palace built in 1130 and dismantled by Parliamentarians in the Civil War, stands next to elegant **Wolvesey Palace** (1684), which superseded it.

A 15–20 minute walk along the riverside meadows to the south brings you to **St. Cross Hospital▶▶**, founded in 1136 as a charitable almshouse institution, an extraordinary time-warp place with cloistered seclusion, a fine Norman chapel, and an antiquated kitchen. By an ancient rule of the charitable trust, Wayfarer's Dole— bread and ale—is still given to anyone who asks for it specifically.

On the banks of the River Test, 10 miles southwest of Winchester, is the pleasant, small town of **Romsey**, well worth a visit for its wonderful Norman **abbey church▶▶**, built mainly in the 12th century by Henry de Blois, Bishop of Winchester, and with Saxon sculptures among its treasures.

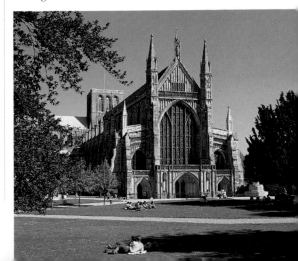

Eton College rowers with Windsor Castle beyond

TOO INNOVATIVE
FOR SOME
Windsor's 17th-century
guildhall, started by Sir
Robert Fitch and
completed by Sir
Christopher Wren, needed
no structural columns
beneath its raised floor.
The alarmed town
burghers insisted that
Wren supply some; this he
did, but he deliberately
built them too short, to
prove they were actually
unnecessary.

►►► Windsor and Eton   86C2

(Tourist information center tel: 01753 743900)

The two towns are a short walk apart, separated only by the Thames. Although within easy reach of London by train, Windsor and Eton demand a very full day if you want to get around all of the sights. Visitors often tie in a trip to the gardens at **Wisley►►** (see page 16).

The town of **Windsor** is dominated by the presence of **Windsor Castle►►►**, Europe's largest, a royal family residence which opens its doors to visitors. The castle dates from the 12th century, but was extended over the next 700 years and was restored following a massive fire in 1992. St. George's Chapel (begun in the 15th century by Edward IV and a superb example of the Perpendicular style, with a fan-vaulted aisle and three-tier stalls), the State Apartments and the extraordinarily detailed Queen Mary's Dolls' House are high points. During the restoration, parts of the building were re-discovered, including an undercroft and medieval well (restoration tours by appointment, tel: 01753 868286 extension 2347).

Another royal site is **Frogmore House** (*Open* occasionally), the 17th-century home of Queen Charlotte and Queen Victoria's mother and the burial place of Victoria herself, alongside Prince Albert. **Windsor Park►►** is worth exploring on foot (there is public access to most of it), with follies, lakes, and a totem pole to discover. **Legoland Windsor** theme park includes a Lego driving school and a miniature re-creation of Amsterdam, London, Brussels, and Paris; reserve ahead to avoid long lines (tel: 0870 5040404).

Over the river lies **Eton**, its appealing main street fronted by **Eton College►►** (see panel; tours given). Eton was founded in 1440 by Henry VI. The chapel is a fine example of the Perpendicular style, reminiscent of King's College Chapel, Cambridge. The quad also looks like an Oxford University college. Entrance to the college includes admission to the Museum of Eton Life.

From **Windsor**, boat trips run to **Boveney Lock** in the heart of the **Thames Valley►►**. At **Maidenhead**, villas and gardens back onto the river. **Cookham►** has been immortalized by the artist Stanley Spencer; a gallery here has a number of his works. **Henley-on-Thames►** is famed for its Royal Regatta, first rowed in 1839.

ETON COLLEGE
This is the most famous
of Britain's public schools
(that is those prestigious
private, fee-paying
establishments whose
headmasters attend the
Headmasters' Conference:
they are actually quite
independent of the state
system). The high street
has numerous barbers and
tailors; one of them,
T. Brown, has changed little over the years. Here,
the boys are fitted out at
the start of term in long-
tailed jackets and
wing-collars. "Old
Etonians" include William
Gladstone (19th-century
prime minster), George
Orwell (real name Eric
Blair; author of *1984*), Ian
Fleming (author of the
James Bond books), and
Thomas Arne (composer of
Rule Britannia).

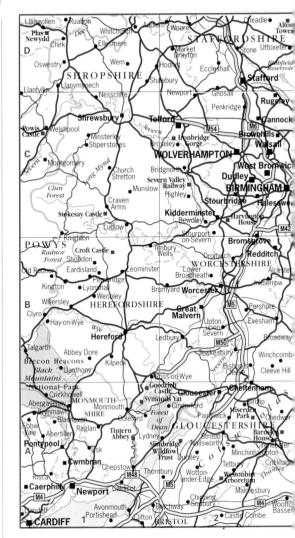

THE HEART OF ENGLAND This is a region that reflects, as deeply as any other, that elusively diverse nature of the English landscape: for it includes both the Cotswolds, the epitome of rural England, and the industrial "Black Country," the economic hub of the Midlands.

THE WEST MIDLANDS AND THE BLACK COUNTRY The Midlands is a nebulous term, often applied to the central industrial manufacturing belt encompassing the cities of Birmingham, Wolverhampton, Coventry, Leicester, Derby, Stoke-on-Trent and Nottingham (some of which fall outside the scope of this chapter). Most first-time visitors to Britain would skip the bulk of the area, but there is plenty of interest in the cityscapes, industrial sights, museums, and even areas of unspoilt countryside.

The county of **West Midlands** encompasses the so-called Black Country, dominated by the conurbation of

RECOMMENDED HISTORIC CITIES AND COUNTRY TOWNS

Gloucestershire: Cheltenham, Chipping Campden, Cirencester, Gloucester, Painswick, Tewkesbury, Winchcombe.

Herefordshire: Bewdley, Hereford, Ledbury, Leominster.

Worcestershire: Stourport, Worcester.

Oxfordshire: Abingdon, Burford, Dorchester, Henley, Oxford.

Shropshire: Bishop's Castle, Clun, Bridgnorth, Ludlow, Much Wenlock, Shrewsbury.

Staffordshire: Lichfield.

Warwickshire: Stratford-upon-Avon, Warwick.

INDUSTRIAL HERITAGE

Birmingham, Black Country Living Museum, Didcot Railway Centre, Ironbridge, Severn Valley Railway.

WALKS

Abberley Hills, Cannock Chase, Chiltern Hills, Cotswold Hills (Cotswold Way and western escarpment), Clent Hills, Forest of Dean, Ironbridge Gorge, Lickey Hills, Malvern Hills, South Shropshire, Lower Wye Valley (page 171), the Wrekin, Wyre Forest.

VILLAGE-TO-VILLAGE DRIVES

Chiltern Hills, Cotswolds, Herefordshire, Shropshire.

Eastnor, below the Malvern Hills

Wolverhampton, West Bromwich and others, much of which developed in the 19th century through the exploitation of coal and iron deposits. Some towns developed specialized industries—leather in Walsall, glass in Stourbridge, and locks in Willenhall. The industrial heritage is celebrated at the Black Country Living Museum in Dudley (see page 20), and at the Leather Museum in Walsall.

To the east the conurbation merges into **Birmingham** (nicknamed "Brum"), England's second city, and at first sight an unappealing jungle of motorway overpasses, and suburban and industrial sprawl. However, in the last decade or so a remarkable renaissance has come about in its central area, with a new lease of life for its canalside buildings and its Jewellery Quarter as well as its civic and industrial heritage. The City of Birmingham Symphony Orchestra, based at Symphony Hall, has emerged as one of the world's greatest orchestras, while the National Exhibition Centre and International Convention Centre bring in many business travelers. The heaths and woodlands of Cannock Chase and the modest heights of the Clent Hills have pleasant walks just outside the built-up area. East of Birmingham, **Coventry** had its heart knocked out by bombing in 1940, and the ruins of its medieval cathedral stand beside Basil Spence's innovative postwar replacement—endowed with some striking modern art, including glass by John Piper and a huge tapestry by Graham Sutherland.

THE ENGLISH MARCHES Shropshire, **Herefordshire**, and **Worcestershire** encompass much in the way of unspoiled countryside, black-and-white and red-brick villages, and the assertive south Shropshire Hills; it is ideal for those who like to make their own discoveries. To the west it adjoins the even lesser-known, and much less populated, Welsh Marches or borderlands. Only the pleasant market town of Ludlow and Ironbridge Gorge, birthplace of the Industrial Revolution, are firmly on the tourist trail; Shrewsbury, Hereford, and numerous smaller towns and villages such as Much Wenlock and Ledbury are well-kept secrets. Walkers may like to head for the hills around Church Stretton and for the Malvern Hills. The russet-earthed territory of rural Herefordshire, its pastures

grazed by docile Hereford cattle, is amiably sleepy and has a wealth of half-timbered "black and white" buildings as well as several outstanding churches, some tucked well away. **Worcestershire** has the cathedral city of Worcester for its centerpiece.

THE COTSWOLDS AND THEIR FRINGES East of the fruit and vegetable heartlands of the Vale of Evesham, the buildings change color dramatically as one climbs up into the **Cotswold Hills** (mostly belonging to **Gloucestershire** and **Oxfordshire**). Its honey-yellow stone villages and towns have enchanted generations of visitors; the area is rich in both places to visit and hotels.

Non-Cotswold Gloucestershire includes Gloucester, Cheltenham, and the lowlands abutting the Severn Estuary, the final stages of Britain's longest river. On a waterside site, the naturalist Peter Scott set up the celebrated wildfowl reserve at Slimbridge. In the Forest of Dean, once a coal and charcoal producing area, the villages are not particularly attractive, but there are verdant walks, including the Sculpture Trail (west of Cinderford). The Lower Wye Valley (see under Wales) is close at hand.

The fringes of the Cotswolds harbor some of the greatest visitor attractions of central England, including Oxford, Blenheim Palace, and Shakespeare's Stratford-upon-Avon. These are close enough to London for day-trips. Notable arrays of stately homes and manor houses open to the public are found in **Warwickshire** (Baddesley Clinton, Charlecote Park, Coughton Court, Farnborough Hall, Kenilworth Castle, Packwood House, Upton House, Warwick Castle) and **Buckinghamshire** (Chenies Manor, Chicheley Hall, Claydon House, Nancy Astor's Cliveden, Dorney Court, Disraeli's Hughenden Manor, Wycombe Park, and above all the Rothschilds' properties—Ascott House, Mentmore Towers, and Waddesdon). Closer to the capital lie the **Chiltern Hills**, whose gently rolling chalk hills and majestic beech woods have been carefully preserved by Green Belt legislation and whose villages look distinctly prosperous.

There are old musical instruments at Snowshill Manor as well as a collection of Japanese Samurai armor, toys, and bicycles

113

▶▶▶ REGION HIGHLIGHTS

Blenheim Palace
page 115

The Cotswolds
pages 118–121

Ironbridge Gorge Museum *page 123*

Ludlow *page 124*

Malvern Hills *page 125*

Oxford *pages 126–127*

Shropshire Hills
page 130

Stratford-upon-Avon
pages 131–132

Waddesdon Manor
page 132

Warwick *page 133*

OXFORD ALUMNI
Oxford University's many notable graduates include Sir William Walton (composer) and Lewis Carroll (author), both at Christ Church College; T. S. Eliot (poet), Merton College; Oscar Wilde (playwright) and Sir John Betjeman (poet), both at Magdalen College; and T. E. Lawrence ("Lawrence of Arabia"), Jesus College.

*Birmingham Museum
and Art Gallery*

▶▶ **Birmingham**   *110C2*

(Tourist information center tel: 0121 693 6300)
England's second city, one of the largest manufacturing centers in the country and a major convention venue, is undergoing a dramatic facelift (trying to rid its image of 1960s brutalist architecture and run-down streetscapes).

SOHO HOUSE
Situated in Soho Avenue off Soho Road, north of central Birmingham (buses 74, 78, and 79 from Bull Street), Soho House was, from 1766 to 1809, the home of Matthew Boulton, one of the industrial pioneers of his day. He set up a huge manufactory (where buckles, buttons, Sheffield plate, silver, and ormulu objects were made) and mint, and with James Watt, developed the steam engine. Eminent scientific luminaries from the Lunar Society met here and the house became a hotbed of scientific thought. His house has been preserved; it boasted such comforts as central heating and a water closet.

At its heart, Victoria Square speaks of civic pride, with its domed Victorian Council House (city hall), at the back of which is the **Birmingham Museum and Art Gallery**▶▶ *(Admission free)*, with one of the world's greatest collections of Pre-Raphaelite paintings, plus superb fossils, silverware and wooden marquetry. A walk west from here leads into Centenary Square, flanked by Symphony Hall, which is the home of the City of Birmingham Symphony Orchestra.

The canals are part of the city's renaissance, with a blend of restored Victorian brick buildings and gleaming new blocks; along the canals are the fish-shaped **National Sea Life Centre**▶, with aquatic life from the River Severn displayed in a manner well-geared to children and the **Gas Street Basin**, with narrowboats moored near waterside pubs. North of the city center, the jewelry quarter has some 4,000 workshops and dozens of jewelry shops; the **Museum of the Jewellery Quarter**▶▶ includes a tour of Smith and Pepper's workshops, closed in 1981 and little changed since starting business in 1899—production processes are shown by the guides (see panel, page 115).

At Birmingham University, the **Barber Institute for Fine Arts**▶▶ *(Admission free;* train from New Street station to

University) is a choice collection with many of the great European artists represented. **Aston Hall▶▶** (*Admission free*), after which Aston Villa Football Club is named, is a splendid Jacobean mansion of 1618–1635, with plaster ceilings and a fine Long Gallery.

At Bourneville, the Cadbury family set up their chocolate factory in 1879 and near the original garden village built for workers is **Cadbury World▶** (reservations recommended, tel: 0121 451 4180)—not a factory tour, but you see handmade chocolates being made and are allowed to sample the result; a history of the foodstuff is told in the attached museum.

▶▶▶ Blenheim Palace   111A3
(tel: 01993 811325)

This is more of a gilded palace than an English country house, impersonal in scale but undeniably impressive, with sumptuous state rooms, furnishings, tapestries, and door-cases carved by Grinling Gibbons. It is considered the finest true baroque house in Britain.

Blenheim was designed by John Vanbrugh for the 1st Duke of Marlborough, one John Churchill. It was a reward from Queen Anne in recognition of his crushing victory over the French at Blenheim in Bavaria in 1704. More recently, in 1874, it was the birthplace of Winston Churchill and the contents include some fascinating Churchilliana. He is buried nearby in Bladon Church.

The palace stands in a great park laid out by Henry Wise, gardener to Queen Anne, and later modified by Capability Brown. Explore the numerous walks, beech woods, and formal features that include the Triumphal Way, Italian Garden, maze, ornamental bridge, and Column of Victory. Adjacent is the town of **Woodstock**, home to the **Oxfordshire Museum**.

▶ Bridgnorth   110C2
(Tourist information center tel: 01746 763257)

Bridgnorth perches high on a sandstone cliff above the Severn, with a cliff railway connecting the low town. Stroll along Castle Walk past the ruin of a Norman castle, blown up in 1646 during the Civil War. From here the **Severn Valley Railway▶▶** runs 16 miles to Kidderminster, recapturing travel of yesteryear, with steam locomotives passing a series of old stations. The journey takes just over an hour and passes through **Bewdley▶**, where the Old Shambles houses the local museum. To the east, on the A456, is the **West Midlands Safari and Leisure Park**, which has themed rides in its Leisure Park.

BIRMINGHAM'S JEWELRY QUARTER
This character-laden district just north of the city center narrowly escaped postwar redevelopment. The many jewelry workshops mostly employ only one or two people, and are highly specialized, depending on each other as part of the process—one may be a polisher, another a gem-setter or wedding ring maker, while another manufactures bangles or butterfly wings. The Smith and Pepper bangle workshop, now the Museum of the Jewellery Quarter, is the most astonishing time-warp of all. In recent years, numerous jewelry retailers have set up locally, too.

THE BOTANICAL GARDENS
Central Birmingham is strikingly devoid of trees and parks, so the Botanical Gardens (just west of the center in Westbourne Road) makes a welcoming oasis of lush greenery. Ferns, banana trees, cacti, and other exotica fill the glass houses, and there are historic and cottage gardens as well as tree collections. Admission is very expensive, so it is worth making a day of it. From April to September Sunday bandstand concerts enhance the atmosphere further.

A home fit for a world leader: Blenheim Palace was the birthplace of Winston Churchill

WEST WYCOMBE AND THE DASHWOODS

The most notorious member of the Dashwood family was undoubtedly Sir Francis Dashwood (1708–1791), who set up the Hell Fire Club, a black-magic brotherhood more interested in drinking and whoring than satanic rites. Its meeting places included the West Wycombe Caves (open to the public, just north of the village street) and the hollow gold ball on top of the Church of St. Lawrence. The Dashwood memorials are within the curious roofless, hexagonal mausoleum (1764) next to the church.

Mapledurham Mill, the last working water mill on the Thames

WHIPSNADE WILD ANIMAL PARK

Planned by the Zoological Society of London, Whipsnade is one of Europe's foremost animal collections, situated in a spacious park; close by, Whipsnade Tree Cathedral was created by Edmund Kell Blyth in 1931 as a war memorial, with trees laid out in aisles, transepts, and cloisters.

As one who long in
  populous city pent,
Where houses thick and
  sewers annoy the air,
Forth issuing on a
  summer's morn to
  breathe
Among the pleasant
  villages and farms
Adjoin'd, from each thing
  met conceives delight.
—John Milton
(1608–1674), *Paradise Lost*

▶ Chiltern Hills   111A4

(High Wycombe tourist information center tel: 01494 421892)

Stretching some 50 miles from the Thames Valley west of Reading to the vicinity of Luton at their northern edge, the Chilterns are a rising of chalk downs to the northwest of London. Although the area is part of the city commuter belt, once you are clear of the suburban developments you find yourself in countryside, with pretty brick-and-flint cottages, fine manor houses, and country pubs. The beech woods that made the area an important furniture-making center are still a feature of the landscape.

At **Mapledurham▶**, by the Thames, you can visit a working water mill and Elizabethan Mapledurham

House, while the 18th-century brick facade of **Stonor House▶**, the home of the Stonors for 600 years, incorporates a private chapel and a medieval solar. Almost all of **West Wycombe▶** was purchased by the National Trust in 1929 to save it from a road-widening project; its main street has predominantly 17th- and 18th-century houses. Adjacent stands **West Wycombe Park▶** (N.T.), a mansion built in 1765 for Sir John Dashwood (see panel). Humphry Repton landscaped the park in 1803, adorning it with follies and classical temples. Benjamin Disraeli, the 19th-century prime minister, lived at **Hughenden Manor▶** (N.T.) north of High Wycombe; his library and study have been preserved. **Beaconsfield**, **Princes Risborough**, **Berkhamsted**, and **Wendover** are commuter towns today, but each has an old and attractive center.

In 1665 John Milton came to **Chalfont St. Giles** as an old and blind man, escaping plague-ridden London to a cottage (now a **museum▶**) where he completed *Paradise Lost* and began *Paradise Regain'd*. Close by, traditional Chiltern buildings can be seen at the **Chiltern Open Air Museum▶**; including an Iron Age dwelling, a 19th-century farm, and a 1940s prefab. **Chenies** is a 19th-century village which was built for estate workers of the medieval step-gabled brick **manor▶** (*Open* to the public) of the Russell family.

116

► **Gloucester** *110A2*

(Tourist information center tel: 01452 421188)

Gloucester's down-to-earth red-brick textures contrast sharply with the dreamy golden hues of the nearby Cotswolds, but offers rewards in its small yet absorbing medieval center and its revived 19th-century docks. From June to August the Gloucester Civic Trust give free guided tours of the historic center.

Just off the historic axis of Westgate Street, with its **Folk Museum**, lie the precincts of the **cathedral►►**. It became a place of pilgrimage after the installation of the tomb of Edward II, who was murdered at nearby Berkeley Castle in 1327. From the outside it is a pleasing medieval mishmash; within, its glory is the glass of its east window, one of England's largest and the 14th-century fan-vaulting in the cloisters, England's earliest.

Meanwhile, in the **docks**, the warehouses, towers of red bricks, have been partly converted to offices, stores, and cafés; you can take 40-minute trips around the site on an old Thames craft. Here the **National Waterways Museum►** charts the development of Britain's canals, the entertaining **Robert Opie Collection of Advertising and Packaging►** wallows in nostalgia for vintage ephemera, and the **Soldiers of Gloucestershire Museum** details 300 years of regimental history.

Gloucester's neighbor, **Cheltenham►**, is an elegant Regency spa, with its pump room designed in the best 19th-century Greek Revival tradition. A mineral spring was discovered here in 1715, allegedly by observing the comings and goings of a healthy-looking pigeon population; pigeons feature on the town's crest today. Cheltenham later received the royal approval of George III and acquired its handsome terraces, wrought-iron balconies, and leafy thoroughfares. Other attractions are the art gallery and museum, the **Holst Birthplace Museum** (where the composer of *The Planets* was born in 1874), the annual festivals of music (July) and of literature (October) and the racecourse.

To the northwest, **Tewkesbury►**, where the Avon and Severn meet, is a handsome town of high-medieval and later facades. The **abbey church►** is one of England's finest examples of Norman ecclesiastical architecture.

"Baker's bells," a distinctive carillon in Gloucester's Southgate Street

THREE CHOIRS FESTIVAL
This major music festival takes place in the last week of August and rotates in a three-year cycle between Gloucester, Worcester, and Hereford cathedrals. Its origins go back to the early 18th century; from the 1890s three organist-conductors (one from each cathedral) were appointed and a distinguished list of works by some of the country's greatest composers were given their first performance, including *Fantasia on a Theme of Thomas Tallis* (1910) by Vaughan Williams, the *Colour Symphony* (1922) by Bliss, and the *Choral Fantasia* (1931) of Holst. Elgar directed his own music here until his death in 1934.

Touring country par excellence, the Cotswold Hills are an area of beautiful honey-colored limestone villages, tucked-away manor houses, cottage gardens, russet-earth fields enclosed by drystone walls, and lonely, winding country roads leading to nowhere in particular.

Cirencester tourist information center tel: 01285 654180. Stow-on-the-Wold tourist information center tel: 01451 831082

SOUTH COTSWOLDS HOUSES
Buscot Park (N.T.), near Faringdon, is an 18th-century house renowned for its paintings and porcelain. Also near Faringdon is **Great Coxwell Tithe Barn** (N.T.), built by the monks of Beaulieu and considered one of England's finest: in medieval times a tenth of agricultural produce of each parish was handed over as a tax or "tithe" to the church and was stored in tithe barns. **Owlpen Manor**, a Tudor manor in an old hillside garden of roses and box parterres was restored in the 1920s by Norman Jewson, a follower of the Arts and Crafts movement and is a fascinating mixture of centuries.

118

Cotswold architecture: honey-hued walls and stone-mullioned windows

SOUTH COTSWOLDS GARDENS
Among many outstanding gardens are the **Rococo Garden** outside Painswick, **Westonbirt Arboretum** (a Forestry Commission collection of over 17,000 trees), **Barnsley House Garden** (Georgian summerhouses, laburnum walk, herbaceous borders), **Batsford Arboretum** (rare trees) and **Miserden Park Gardens** (topiary, shrubs, borders and more, in a woodland setting).

The Cotswolds present timeless tableaux of rural England. The scenery is pleasant rather than dramatic, with the best views from the western edges. There are plenty of hotels, some very high class, and the area is strong on sights (with plenty of interest for children). Wool was the key to the area's medieval prosperity and the wealth it created is commemorated in a striking legacy of grand churches. Almost every town and village seems to have a Sheep Street.

The area is described in two parts, one lying south of the A40, the other north.

The south The undoubted capital of the south Cotswolds is **Cirencester►►**, a handsome town with more bustle than most of its neighbors and plenty of speciality stores for browsing. In Roman times, only London (*Londinium*) was bigger than Cirencester (*Corinium*) and these and later days are celebrated in the excellent Corinium Museum, which displays original mosaic paving and reconstructions of Roman domestic interiors. Dominating the market square is the cathedral-like parish church, with its fan-vaulted porch and grand interior. One of the finest streets is Cecily Hill, its far end leading into Cirencester Park (pedestrians only), the grounds of Lord Bathurst's stately home.

At **Bibury**▶▶ a triple-arched footbridge over the River Coln leads to Arlington Row, a group of former weavers' cottages. The village is full of pretty cottage gardens and unspoiled corners. The Victorian artist-craftsman William Morris and his Pre-Raphaelite friends "discovered" the Cotswolds, and in 1871 he came to live at nearby Kelmscott. Morris declared Bibury to be the most beautiful village in England. The former Arlington Mill houses the Cotswold Museum. More low-key, cozy charm is found in abundance in the **Colns** (Coln St. Aldwyn, Coln Rogers and Coln St. Dennis) and the **Duntisbournes** (Duntisbourne Abbots, Duntisbourne Leer and Duntisbourne Rouse, the latter having a little Saxon church). **Fairford**▶ prides itself on its splendid "wool church," famed for its late 15th-century stained glass.

Painswick▶▶ has an appealing, sloping knot of central lanes and grey-stone walls; grand houses jostle cheek by jowl with minute cottages. Best of all is the churchyard, dominated by 99 yews; an explanatory leaflet describes the fine 16th- to 19th-century tombstones. The surrounding area is lush and deep-set, the numerous viewpoints including **Painswick Beacon** and **Haresfield Beacon**. **Slad** was the village of writer Laurie Lee, who captured the pre-automobile age so evocatively in *Cider with Rosie*. Stroud is not particularly attractive, but the atmospherically derelict **Thames and Severn Canal**, near Sapperton, is worth exploring. Further south are some finely sited towns and villages, including **Wotton-under-Edge** and **Dursley**, snug beneath the escarpment and **Minchinhampton**, on a breezy hilltop site.

Chedworth Roman Villa▶ (N.T.), which was excavated between 1864–1866, stands alone in the woods near Chedworth and gives an excellent insight into the period. Mosaics and bath and heating systems have been found; it is thought that the villa functioned like a hotel for people visiting its water shrine. **Hetty Pegler's Tump**, named after the wife of its 17th-century owner, is a neolithic burial mound with its stone slabs still in place.

The drystone wall is the main type of field boundary in the Cotswolds

FAMILY ATTRACTIONS (SOUTH)
South of Burford, the **Cotswold Wildlife Park** features white rhinos, tigers, and more. At **Prinknash Abbey**, a living community of Benedictine monks, there is a bird sanctuary and pottery. At Northleach are two absorbing attractions, **Keith Harding's World of Mechanical Music** (antique mechanical instruments) and the **Cotswold Heritage Centre** (exhibits from yesteryear housed in a former prison). Further afield, the **Wildfowl and Wetlands Trust** at Slimbridge on the Severn Estuary has a huge collection of wildfowl and **Berkeley Castle** is famous for the dungeon in which Edward II was murdered in 1327.

FAMILY ATTRACTIONS (NORTH)

The **North Gloucestershire Railway** operates steam trains between Toddington and Winchcombe, while the **Cotswold Farm Park** (west of Stow-on-the-Wold) is home to rare animal breeds. Just outside Witney, the **Cogges Manor Farm Museum** offers a look at rural Edwardian life in Oxfordshire, with craft and farming demonstrations.

120

Angular gables, stone roofs, and trim lawns: typical of many Cotswold manor houses

NORTH COTSWOLDS HOUSES

Stanway House is a good example of Jacobean architecture, while **Broughton Castle** near Banbury is a moated medieval manor and **Snowshill Manor** (N.T.) contains a collection of bicycles, and Japanese Samurai armor. By contrast, **Sezincote** was remodeled in the 1800s as an Indian fantasy; the Prince Regent found in it inspiration for his Royal Pavilion in Brighton (see page 90). **Chastleton House** (N.T.) is a Jacobean manor (must book timed tickets, tel: 01494 755572). **Sudeley Castle**, an imposing part-ruined stately home at Winchcombe, was the burial place of Henry VIII's sixth wife, Catherine Parr.

NORTH COTSWOLDS GARDENS

The magically hidden-away gardens of **Hidcote Manor** (N.T.), north of Chipping Campden, are pure joy: a 20th-century creation of a series of "rooms" bounded by hedges and walls. Close by, **Kiftsgate Court Gardens** have rare shrubs and a fine rose collection.

The north In the far north, **Chipping Campden▶▶▶** should not be missed for its showpiece main street, primitive open-sided market hall, and a fine church with Gloucestershire's largest memorial brass. The great manor house of Campden has gone, but its Jacobean lodges and gateway remain. Chipping Campden is just large enough to be a town, but its pace is unhurried and its charms preserved without being commercialized. By contrast, **Broadway▶** is a tourist magnet, its elegant (but traffic-ridden) main street well lined with gift boutiques and tearooms. The village lies beneath the Cotswold escarpment on the brink of the Vale of Evesham, a major fruit-growing area with roadside stalls selling produce in season; the abrupt transition from Cotswold stone to Midland red brick is quite striking.

Other quieter villages nearby have plenty of charm, including **Buckland** and **Stanton**. Within the town center of **Winchcombe▶** you can find a gargoyle-covered church (look for the splendid weathercock) and an old-fashioned

ambience; attractions include a folk and police museum, and a museum of railroad memorabilia. Just out of town by the B4632, **Cleeve Hill▶** is a blustery highland (only 1,040 feet, but it feels higher), a place for strolls, kite-flying, and enjoying the view westwards to the Malvern Hills (see page 125). Beautifully set beneath the Cotswold escarpment, the Cistercian ruin of **Hailes Abbey▶** (E.H./N.T.) was in its day a major pilgrimage site.

Stow-on-the-Wold and **Chipping Norton** are conveniently placed market towns in the area, the latter with a superb 19th-century tweed mill. With its series of tiny bridges spanning the Windrush, **Bourton-on-the-Water** is almost too pretty to be believed; it is also the most commercialized village in the Cotswolds, drawing crowds to its miniature model village, perfumery exhibition, model railroad, Birdland aviary, motor museum, and Miniature World exhibition. By contrast, neighboring **Lower Slaughter▶** is an amazingly unspoiled delight, with cottages and an old mill overlooking a rippling brook. **Burford** has an impressive church and a distinguished main street lined with shops and inns, sloping down to an ancient stone bridge. Close to Witney is **Minster Lovell▶** with its spooky, ruined 15th-century hall.

THE COTSWOLDS

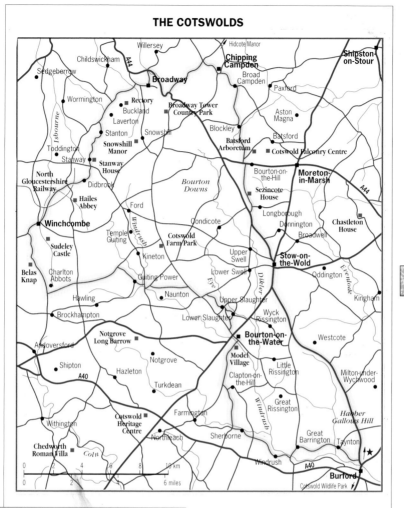

The Cotswolds

This tour promises golden stone-built villages, dignified manor houses and fine views (approx 55 miles).

Start from **Burford▶**, descending the main street and continue past **Stow-on-the-Wold** to branch off, past **Sezincote House▶▶** and **Blockley**, which still has a few of its old silk-throwing mills. Continue to **Chipping Campden▶▶**; head south-west to the A44 where you turn right (Broadway Tower, a famous scenic viewpoint, is soon off left) to **Broadway▶**. Take the B4632 to skirt peaceful **Buckland▶**; branch off left through **Stanton▶** and **Stanway▶** and rejoin the B4632 close to the turning to **Hailes Abbey▶**. Continue into **Winchcombe▶**, stopping off for **Sudeley Castle▶**. Pass **Belas Knap** prehistoric burial mound and **Guiting Power**. The villages of **Upper Slaughter** and **Lower Slaughter▶** lead up to busy **Bourton-on-the-Water**.

Finish your drive by exploring the quiet countryside around **Great Barrington**.

122

CIDER IN HEREFORDSHIRE
The alcoholic apple drink has a venerable tradition in the county; in former days, many farms produced hard cider specially for farm laborers. True farmhouse "scrumpy" cider is now a rarity, but the drink has enjoyed a revival in recent years. Bulmer's Cider, one of the largest operations, produces in Hereford (there is a factory store; tours by appointment, tel: 01432 352000; best when the cider mill is in operation, late September to mid November). Hereford's Cider Museum displays cider-making methods ancient and modern. Near Pembridge, a village on the Black and White Villages Trail, Dunkerton's Cider is an engagingly rustic outfit, operating from a barn, and Weston's, a much larger company, produces at Much Marcle.

The finely worked 900-year-old carving on the south doorway of Kilpeck Church

DR. JOHNSON (1709–1784)
In Lichfield's market square stand statues of this formidably learned and witty man, and his biographer James Boswell. His early years in Lichfield were not dazzling: he dropped out of his studies at Oxford, and had an unsuccessful career as a teacher. But in London he made a living as an essayist and journalist, compiling his famous Dictionary over eight years up to 1755 (see Dr. Johnson's House, page 50), and became one of the capital's greatest literary figures. In 1763 he met Boswell and penned *A Journey to the Western Isles of Scotland* after their travels together.

▶ **Hereford**   *110B1*
(Tourist information center tel: 01432 268430)
The capital of Herefordshire, renowned for its eponymous cattle breed and for cider making, stands on the banks of the River Wye. A ring road cuts too close to the center, but there are some good medieval streets. The highlight is the sandstone **cathedral**▶ (begun in 1107) with its library of over 1,400 chained books and its priceless Mappa Mundi, a 13th-century map of the world.

Southwest of the town is **Abbey Dore**▶. Only a portion of what was a huge Cistercian abbey remains, but you can imagine it in its heyday. Nearby **Kilpeck Church**▶▶ is a perfect Norman building, embellished inside and out with carvings of birds, beasts and angels. Prudish Victorians failed to remove all of the more salacious ones.

The **Black and White Villages Trail**▶▶ is a well-marked car tour west of Hereford through some beautiful, unspoiled half-timbered villages, including **Weobley, Pembridge, Eardisland**, and **Lyonshall**.

At **Shobdon**▶ the stonework of the old church, which may well have been by the same person who sculpted Kilpeck, was turned into a garden ornament in the mid-18th century for a nearby house; the "new" church built in its place has an interior of wedding-cake "Strawberry Hill Gothick", a style of architecture named after that used in writer Horace Walpole's 1747 house at Strawberry Hill in Twickenham, near London. Farther north, **Croft Castle**▶ (N.T.) is a fascinating mixture of medievalism and Georgian Gothic. Walks in the adjacent National Trust estate include the ascent of Croft Ambrey, a well-sited Iron Age hill fort with visible ramparts.

▶ **Lichfield**   *111C3*
(Tourist information center tel: 01543 308209)
The trio of sandstone spires of the mostly 12th- to 15th-century **cathedral**▶ dominates a gracious close of 17th- to 19th-century buildings. There is much Early English and Decorated work. The west front has 113 statues, including 24 English kings. The city's most famous son was man of letters Dr. Johnson (see panel), subject of Boswell's biography; his birthplace is now a museum.

The wooded gorge of the River Severn gave birth to the Industrial Revolution in the early 18th century. What happened at Ironbridge signaled the emergence of Britain as the first industrial nation in the world, and was the catalyst for a dramatic change in the face of the country, as the Midlands and northern England became a great industrial heartland.

Here in 1709 Abraham Darby first smelted iron ore with coke instead of charcoal, making mass production of iron possible. The gorge soon filled with industrial activity. Today it is a picturesque area, and you have to imagine the din and smoke of the great ironworks and other industries—but the first-rate **Ironbridge Gorge Museum** (tel: 01952 433522) spread over eight sites, skillfully brings it alive. Ironbridge is near Telford (map: *110C2*).

What to see The **Iron Bridge** itself was the world's earliest iron structure of its kind (built in 1779). Staff in period costume enhance the atmosphere of **Blists Hill Victorian Town▶▶▶**, the largest site, including a toll-house, period shops, a colliery, and an inclined railway that linked two canals. **Jackfield Tile Museum▶▶** is housed in a huge Victorian tile factory that had lain abandoned; today it has been reopened and tiles are put on display. The **Coalport China Museum▶▶** marks the original site of the Coalport china factory, based here from the 1790s until the 1920s; today there is a display of china as well as early brick beehive kilns. You have to wear a hard hat to enter the gloomy **Tar Tunnel▶**, where bitumen was once extracted. You can also visit the **Darby Houses**, where the ironmasters lived, the **Museum of the Gorge** and the **Broseley Pipe Works**, which manufactured clay smoking pipes ("Broseleys"). At the **Museum of Iron▶▶▶** you are in historic territory, the very spot where Darby sparked the industrialization of Britain.

History today: the daily round at Blists Hill

DON'T MISS
There is too much to see in a day in the gorge; if you have only a short time, concentrate on Blists Hill, the Iron Bridge, and Coalbrookdale. You can buy separate tickets for each site, or a "passport" that allows return visits on different occasions. Buses run between the sites. For information: Ironbridge Gorge Museum tel: 01952 433522 (website: www.ironbridge.org).

The Iron Bridge gives its name to the town of Ironbridge, which rises steeply from it

Ludlow Castle: the keep

124

E.H., CADW AND H.S.
Stokesay Castle is just one of hundreds of historic properties that are in the guardianship of the government organization English Heritage (E.H.). Its sister organizations are Cadw: Welsh Historic Monuments (for Wales, see page 167), Historic Scotland (H.S.; for Scotland), and Manx National Heritage (for the Isle of Man). Properties include prehistoric and Roman remains, medieval castles and abbeys, and working industrial monuments as well as some stately homes. Membership in any one of these groups provides half-price (free after first year's membership) admission to the historic sites protected by the other organizations. Overseas Visitors Passes are valid for seven or 14 days. For information tel: 020-7973 3434 (website: www.english-heritage.org.uk; e-mail: members@english-heritage.org.uk). Most properties open year-round. In this book, E.H., Cadw and H.S. denote staffed properties that charge entrance fees.

The Feathers, one of the finest examples of 17th-century half-timbering in Britain

▶▶▶ **Ludlow**   110C1
(Tourist information center tel: 01584 875053)
This is often acclaimed as England's most perfect country town—and it is easy to see why. On its hilltop site its streets spread elegantly out from the ancient butter cross and marketplace, on which is found the absorbing **museum** of local history. Just behind the market cross stands the cathedral-like **Church of St. Laurence**▶▶. Within its soaring interior, the patron saint's life and miracles are celebrated in the great east window and there is a renowned set of 15th-century carved misericords. Poet A. E. Housman of *Shropshire Lad* fame (see page 130) is buried in the churchyard.

Broad Street is Ludlow's most celebrated thoroughfare, with its half-timbered Tudor buildings and 17th- to 19th-century brick facades combining happily along the gentle slope to a gateway at the bottom end. The **Feathers Hotel**, a riot of half-timbering, is an outstanding house of its period. **Ludlow Castle**▶▶, founded by Roger Montgomery, Earl of Shrewsbury, in 1085, was built to withstand both Welsh and Norman incursions; its long list of distinguished visitors includes Sir Philip Sidney, Edward IV, and Catherine of Aragon. A Norman chapel within the castle has an unusual circular nave. During the Ludlow Festival in June and July, outdoor performances of Shakespeare plays are held in the inner bailey.

Ludlow is splendidly situated for exploring the Welsh Marches, and the South Shropshire Hills (see page 130) are within close reach. **Stokesay Castle**▶▶ (E.H.), near Craven Arms, is an outstandingly well-preserved example of a 13th-century fortified manor house; it was designed with windows unusually large for those lawless times. The adjacent church dates mostly from the 17th century but has a Norman doorway.

▶▶ Malvern Hills   110B2

(Great Malvern tourist information center tel: 01684 892289)
The jagged Malvern ridge rises between the low plains of Herefordshire and the Vale of Evesham. From a distance it looks like a mountain range; close up it reveals itself as a friendly upland stripe offering superb views from the easily accessible paths along its spine.

Its advantages as a defensive site were exploited by Iron Age people: Worcestershire Beacon (the highest point, 1,381 feet) and Herefordshire Beacon are both well-preserved hill forts. To the west there are views of **Eastnor Castle**, a 19th-century mock-medieval extravaganza designed by Robert Smirke and A. W. N. Pugin in the Gothic Revival style. In the distance are the hills of the Welsh Marches; to the east is the Cotswold escarpment.

Malvern Wells and **Great Malvern▶** lie right under the Malvern Hills. Malvern water put the area on the map as a spa after a Dr. Wall wrote in 1756 of the waters' medicinal value. Within a modest stone pavilion is St. Ann's Well, the original source. The priory church, the glory of Great Malvern, has fine 15th-century stained glass.

Southwest is **Ledbury▶**. The town's broad main street focuses on John Abel's 16th-century half-timbered market house. Pretty Church Lane leads to the church, with its "gold vane surveying half the shire," in the words of locally born John Masefield, former Poet Laureate.

Worcester▶ is famous as the home of Royal Worcester porcelain (factory tours Mon–Fri; tel: 01905 23221) and Worcestershire Sauce. It was an important center in the Civil War, as you can learn from the exhibition in the **Commandery** in Sidbury Road, Charles II's headquarters during the Battle of Worcester. The city is a mix of the sublime and the mundane: a fine **cathedral▶▶** (look in for the monuments, crypt, cloister garden, and marble pulpit), but insensitive post-war development that mars the center. The **county cricket ground**, stationed by the Severn with a magnificent view of the cathedral, is a classic place for trying to fathom the English summer game.

Just west of Worcester, **Lower Broadheath▶** was the birthplace on June 2, 1857 of composer Edward Elgar (see panel). The modest cottage commemorates his life with scores, photographs, and concert programs.

A Royal Worcester vase

SIR EDWARD ELGAR (1857–1934)
Elgar's musical education was derived mainly from his experience as a violin player, as a singer at the church where his father was organist, and from browsing the scores in his father's music store in Worcester. For a long time he felt the musical world was set against him, yet the fact that he was mainly self-taught probably gave him a freshness of vision and made him perhaps the greatest English composer since Henry Purcell.
Elgar's early works were recognized only locally, but his international reputation was assured when Richard Strauss acclaimed the ever-popular *Enigma Variations* (1899). *The Dream of Gerontius* (1900) enjoyed success in the Three Choirs Festival (see panel, page 117) in 1902. The *First Symphony* (1908) and the *Pomp and Circumstance Marches* (1901–1930) won widespread popularity.

Worcester's spectacular Guildhall, dated 1722

CHRIST CHURCH COLLEGE

Tom Quad, the main quadrangle, is so called because of Tom Tower, designed by Sir Christopher Wren and named after the bell, Great Tom, which strikes the hour. Ever since 1682, at 9:05 PM it has rung 101 times, commemorating the original number of students; this signaled the time for students to be back in college. The 16th-century college hall has portraits of some of the college's distinguished former members, including William Gladstone, Lewis Carroll, John Ruskin, and W. H. Auden.

126

OXFORD VERSUS CAMBRIDGE

The two universities maintain an ancient rivalry, most obviously displayed in the University Boat Race, rowed on the Thames in west London every spring and in the Varsity rugby match, played at Twickenham in the autumn.

"OXBRIDGE" SUBTLETIES

Oxford and Cambridge universities are referred to jointly as "Oxbridge."
● When steering a "punt," a shallow boat, on the river in Oxford, you stand inside the boat; in Cambridge you stand on its platform.
● Only at Oxford does formal academic dress feature a mortar board as well as a gown.
● In Cambridge, colleges have courtyards; in Oxford they are known as quadrangles (or quads).
● At Cambridge, students' academic work is charted by directors of studies; at Oxford the terminology is tutors.
● There are more colleges at Oxford and they mostly have fewer students than their Cambridge counterparts.

▶▶▶ Oxford

111A3

(Tourist information center tel: 01865 726871)

Home of one of the world's greatest universities (founded about 1200), Oxford has a stunning heritage of historic buildings. Close to the bustling city center lie placid swathes of riverside greenery along Christ Church Meadow. As with Cambridge, there is no single campus in Oxford: the colleges are set in cloistered seclusion behind high walls; most are open to visitors in the afternoon.

Most notable among the university buildings are the **Sheldonian Theatre**, built in 1664 as a ceremonial assembly hall and the **Radcliffe Camera**, a domed building, now a reading room for the **Bodleian Library**, which contains well over 5.5 million volumes. The Bodleian is one of five "copyright" libraries in the United Kingdom, entitled to receive a copy of every book published in the country. The view from the tower of **St. Mary the Virgin**, the university church on the High Street, extends over the city.

Christ Church▶▶, founded as Cardinal College by Cardinal Wolsey in 1525, is the largest college, has the biggest quadrangle, and its chapel (which predates the college) is England's smallest cathedral; the college picture gallery contains works by Dürer and Michelangelo. **Magdalen College**▶▶ (pronounced "mawdlin") has its own deer park. **All Souls College** has a highly scholarly reputation and admits only post-graduate students, while **St. John's College** is the wealthiest of all and has luscious gardens. **New College**▶ (founded 1379) has a splendid chapel with a statue of Lazarus by Jacob Epstein. Also seek out **Oriel**▶, **Merton**▶▶, **Queen's**▶ and **Keble**▶ colleges, the latter a relative newcomer whose ornamental red-brick buildings are Victorian masterpieces.

Of Oxford's museums, the outstanding attraction is the **Ashmolean**▶▶▶, a treasure-house of art and antiquities whose exhibits include a 9th-century brooch made for King Alfred, while in its wonderful Victorian setting the **Pitt Rivers Museum**▶▶ *(Admission free)* is ranked as one of the world's top six ethnographic collections. The city's history, both town and gown, is illustrated in the **Museum of Oxford**, St. Aldates, while a livelier, less traditional approach is provided by the **Oxford Story**, Broad Street, where you sit at moving desks on a voyage through the city's past.

OXFORD

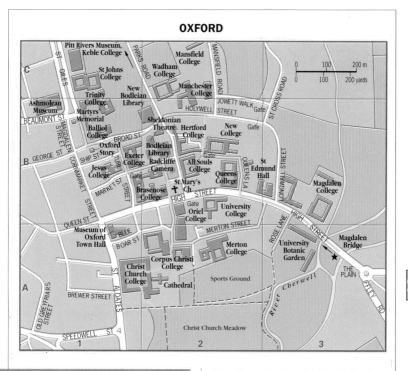

Walk

Start from Magdalen Bridge, pass **Magdalen College**▶▶ and turn right into Queen's Lane, which weaves past

Despite its name, New College was founded in 1379

Magdalen Bridge to the Botanic Garden

St. Edmund's Hall▶ (founded 1220) and **New College**▶ (1379). Just before the Bridge of Sighs (which spans the street), take an alley on the right, passing the Turf Tavern, an old pub with an appealing courtyard. Turn left along Holywell Street and continue past the **Sheldonian Theatre**, with its array of sculpted heads of Roman emperors and along **Broad Street** to the **Martyrs' Memorial**, where three bishops were burned for their Protestant beliefs in the 1550s. Diagonally opposite is the **Ashmolean Museum**▶▶▶. Double back along Broad Street and turn right down Turl Street to the **Radcliffe Camera** and **Bodleian Library**. Cross the High Street, taking Oriel Street on its south side to enter **Christ Church**▶▶ by the gate near the college's picture gallery (if closed, continue along Merton Street to the start of the walk), crossing Tom Quad and leaving by the turnstile at the south side of the college to follow Broad Walk along **Christ Church Meadow**. The **Botanic Garden**▶ is the oldest of its kind in the country.

There are few more pleasant ways to explore Britain's scenery, wildlife, and history than an easygoing voyage along the inland waterways. The slow, unhurried pace of a narrowboat gives a chance for once to take a long look at things. Canals run through towns as well as the countryside and supply unexpected perspectives. Spectacular flights of locks, aqueducts, tunnels and bridges, warehouses and workshops, pleasant pubs, and inns are the legacy of a time when the canal system seemed to hold the future of Britain's transport system.

128

WATERWAYS VACATIONS
Britain's canals are now used primarily for leisure—boating trips, fishing and towpath walks.
For information and details about waterways vacations, contact: Customer Services, British Waterways, Willow Grange, Church Road, Watford, Hertfordshire WD17 4QA (tel: 01923 201120).

CANAL ART
During the 19th century a rich tradition of canal art developed. Boat owners covered the boats and their interiors and utensils with a riot of roses and castles, daisies, and marigolds in simple patterns and vivid primary colors—a popular art form similar to the one which developed in the same period in traveling fairs.

Some 2,000 miles of navigable inland waterways have been described as the British tourist industry's best-kept secret. From prehistoric times down to the 18th century, travel by river was generally faster, safer, and more comfortable than travel by road. Rivers like the Severn, the Thames, and the Trent bustled with boats carrying goods and people, and the towns along their banks prospered as inland ports.

The Canal Age dawns The trouble with rivers is that they do not always go where you want them to, they silt up, water levels vary, and shallows block navigation, as do periodic floods. Attempts to control and improve rivers were made from early times and artificial cuts were made to shorten routes, straighten bends, and evade shallows. The Canal Age in the 18th and 19th centuries brought much more radical action. A network of artificial rivers was constructed to mesh with the natural waterways and create an efficient system covering much of the country. The canals were the principal arteries of the first stage of the Industrial Revolution.

The first canal of this period was begun in Lancashire in the 1750s to link St. Helens with the Mersey, but much more excitement arose in the 1760s when the Duke of Bridgewater ordered the construction of a canal to be built to carry coal mined on his estates at Worsley, a distance of 7.5 miles into Manchester. The duke's engineer was an illiterate genius from Derbyshire named James Brindley. The Bridgewater Canal was soon extended to the Mersey, linking Manchester with Liverpool. (The Manchester end is now part of the Castlefield urban heritage area.)

Not only did the duke's canal halve the price of coal in Manchester, but the spectacle of canal boats crossing the River Irwell at Barton on an aqueduct, above the barges on the river, fired the public imagination. A bold plan was swiftly hatched to build a canal joining the Trent and the Mersey—Josiah Wedgwood, the great chinamaker, was one of its most eager promoters—from which other canals would run to the Thames and the Severn. This would link Britain's four most important rivers and provide an inland waterway connection between London, Birmingham, Hull, Liverpool, and Bristol.

Brindley was the engineer for the Trent and Mersey, which was completed in 1777, five years after his death and the other components of the plan soon followed.

The heyday The success of the early ventures set off "canal mania," a frenzy that had people flocking to meetings all over the country to invest in new waterways. It reached its peak in 1793, when Parliament passed 24 canal construction acts in that single year. One politician of the time said he hoped his grandchildren would be born with webbed feet, since no dry land would be left in England for them to walk on.

A total of 170 miles of canal in 1770 grew to 16,000 miles by the end of the century and 4,250 miles in the 1850s as armies of "navvies" (navigators)—tough, brawling, hard-drinking laborers—drove the new waterways across country on giant embankments and through cuttings and tunnels. The earliest tunnels had no towpaths and the boats had to be "legged" through by the crew, lying on their backs or sides, walking along the brickwork.

The canals' brief heyday was ended by the railroads from the 1830s on and the development of road transport almost finished them off. Even so, some 4 million tons of goods are still carried on the waterways every year, though they are used far more today for recreation. Some have been revived: projects include restoring the Rochdale Canal from Manchester to Halifax, and the Huddersfield Narrow Canal through the country's longest canal tunnel.

NARROWBOATS IN THE SKY

Among the most spectacular engineering feats of the canal engineers were flights of locks and aqueducts. The most famous staircase of locks is probably the Bingley Five Rise on the Leeds and Liverpool Canal, which climbs 60 feet. The most sensational of aqueducts is the Pontcysyllte near Llangollen in North Wales, designed by the great engineer Thomas Telford in the 1790s. The canal is carried across the aqueduct for 335 yards, in an iron trough almost 12 feet wide, with an iron towpath set above it. Boats still go across and visitors can also walk across on the towpath.

129

The Rochdale Canal at Hebden Bridge: boats were once pulled by horses plodding along the towpath

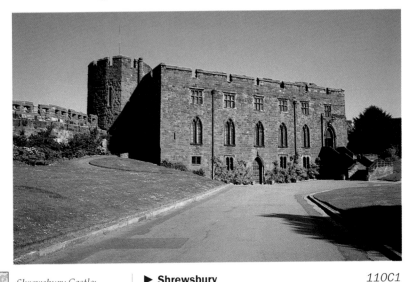

Shrewsbury Castle: rebuilt in the 18th century by Thomas Telford, has Norman origins

▶ Shrewsbury

110C1

(Tourist information center tel: 01743 281200)

The town has a natural defensive site, within a tight loop of the meandering River Severn, with a **castle** to guard the land-linked neck of land. Shrewsbury's collection of Tudor half-timbering and red-brick Georgian buildings, reminders of prosperity brought by the wool trade, is remarkable. Look, for example, at **Owen's Mansion** and **Ireland's Mansion** (both near the arcaded old market hall), and **Council House Court**: the half-timbering includes decorative cable-molding and quatrefoils.

Finds from the Roman city of Wroxeter (*Uriconium*), a short way out of town, are displayed in **Rowley's House Museum. Bear Steps**, a tiny alley, looks medieval, with a hall founded in 1389 as a guild for wool merchants. The Benedictine **abbey** has Norman features and a statue of Edward III on its tower. Street names can bemuse. Butcher Row is self-explanatory (although the butchers are not in evidence) and Grope Lane suggests a variety of possibilities, but Wyle Cop, where Henry VII had a house, may baffle you—it means "hill top." The meaning of Dog Pole is uncertain: perhaps a low gate or "ducken poll" where one had to stoop to get through.

East of Shrewsbury, **Wroxeter Roman City▶** (E.H.) was, in its day, the fourth largest town in England. The most striking remains are the 2nd-century municipal baths; a museum highlights finds from the site.

The **Shropshire Hills▶▶** are south of Shrewsbury, the heartland of the territory immortalized in A. E. Housman's 1896 collection of poems, *A Shropshire Lad*. **Church Stretton** is the starting point of the **Long Mynd** area, a massif of bracken- and bilberry-clad hills deeply cut by valleys such as Ashes Hollow and Carding Mill Valley (parking available in the latter); these and nearby Caer Caradoc, itself best reached by walking from Hope Bowdler, offer magnificent walking. The **Stiperstones** are a series of quartzite rocks atop a breezy ridge close to **Snailbeach**, a village with many relics of a lead-mining industry that flourished in the 18th and 19th centuries.

Decorative quatrefoils in the Square, Shrewsbury

▶▶ Stratford-upon-Avon   *111B3*

(Tourist information center tel: 01789 293127)

Long since celebrated as the birthplace and deathplace of William Shakespeare, Stratford-upon-Avon is swamped with visitors. The Shakespeare connection looms large at every turn; the souvenir shops are stocked with miniature ceramic models of Anne Hathaway's cottage, there is a shopping mall christened Bard's Walk. For devotees of the Bard the town is a must; but be warned, some find it a disappointment. The attractions can be divided into three categories: the historic Shakespeare sites, the town itself and the ancillary attractions tacked on for visitors who wonder why they have come here. The town is agreeable enough, with half-timbered buildings, and a pleasant boating scene on the Avon; look in Holy Trinity Church for a famous memorial to Shakespeare, quill pen in hand.

An **open-topped bus** tours the sites every 15–30 minutes (board at any point on its route). The places in town can be easily reached on foot, but the bus is handy if you want to take in Anne Hathaway's Cottage and Mary Arden's House; a ticket (valid for one day only) allows its holder cut-price entry to Shakespeare properties. You can get around them all in one full day if you start early.

I know a bank whereon
   the wild thyme blows.
Where oxlips and the nod-
   ding violet grows
Quite over-canopied with
   luscious woodbine,
With sweet musk-roses,
   and with eglantine:
There sleeps Titania some
   time of the night,
Lull'd in these flowers
   with dances and delight;
And there the snake
   throws her enamell'd
   skin,
Weed wide enough to
   wrap a fairy in.
—William Shakespeare,
A Midsummer Night's Dream

Britain's most hallowed literary shrine: Shakespeare's Birthplace

Foremost among the sites maintained by the Shakespeare Birthplace Trust is obviously **Shakespeare's Birthplace▶▶** itself. Entrance is through a visitor center and the cottage's garden. Inside, an auction notice describes the property ("a truly heart-stirring relic") when it came up for sale in 1847 and was purchased, for the sum of £3,000, as a national memorial. A miscellanea of Shakespearean bits and pieces make up the exhibits. Shakespeare's daughter Susanna and her husband Dr. Hall lived at **Hall's Croft▶**, a somewhat grander house, now furnished with Tudor trappings and home to an exhibition about medicine in Shakespeare's day and the career of Dr. Hall.

Shakespeare died in New Place, a house adjacent to **Nash's House▶**; New Place is no longer, but an Elizabethan-style knot garden marks the site, and Nash's House itself displays Tudor furniture and exhibits relating to Stratford's past. Shakespeare was baptized and buried at **Holy Trinity Church**.

131

A NATIONAL TREASURE
Before the auction in 1847, Shakespeare's Birthplace had been in the keeping of two widowed ladies, who had made a good thing out of showing such relics as "the identical lantern with which Friar Laurence discovered Romeo and Juliet at the tomb." The house was a ruinous mess but, spurred by the approaching tricentennial in 1864 of Shakespeare's birth and a rumour that a wealthy American planned to ship the house across the Atlantic, the people of Stratford determined to buy the property. The place was cleaned up, judicious restoration was done, and a shilling (5 pence) was charged for admission. The town can never have regretted its investment.

Shall I compare thee to a
summer's day?
Thou art more lovely and
more temperate:
Rough winds do shake the
darling buds of May,
And summer's lease hath
all too short a date...

But thy eternal summer
shall not fade,
Nor lose possession of
that fair thou ow'st
Nor shall death brag thou
wander'st in his shade,
When in eternal lines to
time thou grow'st...
—William Shakespeare,
Sonnet XVIII

Out of town at the village of Shottery, **Anne Hathaway's Cottage▶** was the home of Shakespeare's wife Anne before her marriage; it is a picturesque thatched timber building that reaches the bursting point at peak times (you may have to line up to get in). Nevertheless the old-world atmosphere has been kept intact, thanks to the Trust's foresight in purchasing the cottage back in 1892. Less hectic, but an equally good example of domestic Tudor architecture (minus the thatch), is **Mary Arden's House▶**, the farmhouse childhood home of Shakespeare's mother, at the village of Wilmcote. This has been set up as a farm and countryside museum, with falconry flying demonstrations, rare farm breeds, and exhibits evoking rural life in the last century.

Shakespeare productions are performed at the **Royal Shakespeare Theatre** by the Royal Shakespeare Company (tel: 01789 403403); **Behind the Scenes with the RSC▶▶** exhibits over 1,000 props and costumes used for past performances. The company has a London base at the Barbican (see page 46). There is a fascinating **backstage tour▶▶** of the Royal Shakespeare and Swan theaters.

Cox's Yard, which has its own micro-brewery, includes **Stratford Tales**, telling the story of Stratford from medieval times to the present, using audiovisuals and tableaux, while the **Butterfly Farm** re-creates a jungle environment as a setting for some 1,000 exotic butterfly species. Stratford is also home to the **Teddy Bear Museum**.

132

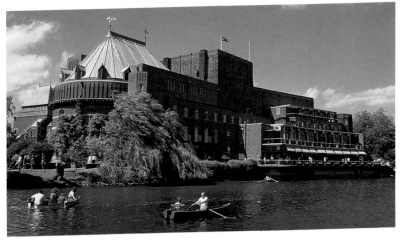

The Royal Shakespeare Theatre, one of the venues used by the Royal Shakespeare Company

▶▶ Waddesdon Manor   *111A4*
(tel: 01296 653211)
Ferdinand de Rothschild spared no expense when he had this French Renaissance-style château built in the Buckinghamshire countryside in the 1870s and 1880s. It is breathtaking in its opulence—the contents as much as the house itself. Harkening back to the golden days of collecting, the treasures include clocks, Sèvres porcelain, lace, and paintings by Rubens, Gainsborough, and others. Within the grounds are two fountains and an aviary. Waddesdon, in the care of the National Trust, is the grandest of a trio of local Rothschild mansions (*Open* to the public): the others are **Mentmore Towers▶** and **Ascott▶** (N.T.).

▶▶ Warwick   111B3
(Tourist information center tel: 01926 492212)

Warwick Castle rises sheer from the River Avon

Warwick is a pleasant country town with a magnificent castle, one of Britain's most visited stately homes. Indeed, on weekends and at vacation periods your visit may be spoiled by the crowds. The center of the town was rebuilt after a fire in 1694; a walk around **High Street** and **Northgate Street** takes you past some of the finest buildings, including Court House and Landor House. The **Warwickshire Museum** (*Admission free*) in the market square is a good place for children, with displays including natural history, a model of old Warwick, and the historic Sheldon tapestry map of Warwickshire; its **Doll Museum**, on a separate site, displays antique toys and games. Two of Warwick's medieval **gateways** survive, complete with chapels. Westgate Chapel forms part of **Leycester's Hospital▶**, a tottering half-timbered range enclosing a pretty courtyard; since 1571, the building has been used as a hospice for retired soldiers, and part of the interior houses the Queen's Own Hussars regimental museum. Pre-fire features of the collegiate **Church of St. Mary▶** include the fan-vaulted Beauchamp Chapel, with a collection of Warwick tombs, and a Norman crypt.

Warwick Castle▶▶ looks its very best from Castle Bridge, where the 14th-century walls are reflected in the waters of the Avon. There is a walk along the ramparts and, inside, a tour of the palatial mansion takes you from the grim austerity of the original dungeons to the gloomy but sumptuous opulence of rooms later adapted for comfortable living. There are wax figures of a royal weekend party and the Kingmaker Exhibition (with the sounds, sights, and smells of the castle getting ready for battle). In the grounds are a re-created Victorian rose garden, the formal Peacock Gardens, and an expanse of open parkland, landscaped by Capability Brown.

KENILWORTH CASTLE
On the western edge of Kenilworth, this huge sandstone castle is the site for events featuring medieval pageantry, drama, and music. The castle was built as a fortress in Norman times but was much adapted by the Earl of Leicester, Queen Elizabeth's favorite, whose neglected wife Amy Robsart died nearby in mysterious circumstances (it was never discovered whether her fall down stairs was murder, accident, or suicide). The Virgin Queen was compelled by the resulting controversy to distance herself from Leicester, whom she eventually had executed for treason.

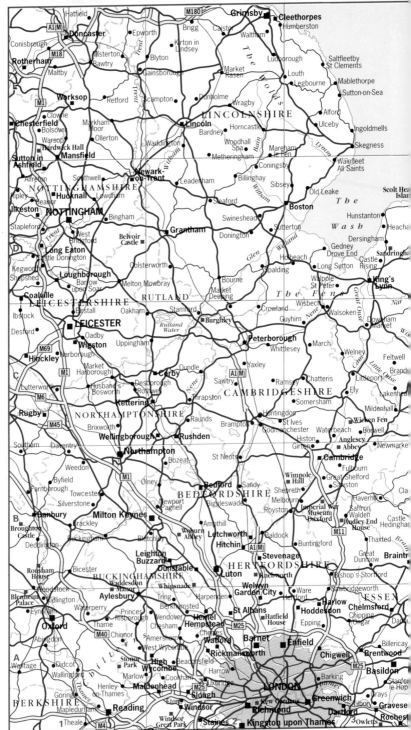

▶▶▶ REGION HIGHLIGHTS

Audley End House *page 143*
Blickling Hall *page 142*
Cambridge *pages 138–139*
Ely *page 140*
Hatfield House *page 146*
Lincoln *page 141*
North Norfolk coast
page 142
Norwich *page 143*
Southwold and area
page 146
Stamford *page 147*
Woburn Abbey *page 147*

The River Ant near How Hill: typical of the waterscapes of the Norfolk Broads

"On a still day, the light can have the delicate outlines of a Japanese picture. On a stormy day, even in summer, the grey sea batters itself against the shelf [of pebbles], dragging the shingle down with a scrunching, grating, slithering sound. To anyone born on the Suffolk coast, this sound has always meant home."
– Imogen Holst, *Britten*, in the "Great Composers" series (1966)

EASTERN ENGLAND This region extends from the northern edge of London to the brink of Humberside. There are no uplands: the rural landscape is flat or gently undulating agricultural country, with only the Lincolnshire Wolds, Bedfordshire's Dunstable Downs, and Leicestershire's Charnwood Forest rising to any appreciable height. Fields are often prairie-like in scale. Although much of the landscape is uninspiring, the region does have rewarding corners.

EAST ANGLIA The most consistently picturesque area of eastern England is East Anglia, the collective term for **Norfolk**, **Suffolk**, northern **Essex**, and eastern **Cambridgeshire**: here, above all, the prosperity brought about by the medieval wool trade left a noble legacy of church architecture and villages and towns of handsome half-timbered and plaster-fronted cottages. A speciality of the countryside immortalized by the paintings of John Constable on the Essex/Suffolk border is pastel-colored plasterwork ornately decorated with relief patterns known as "pargeting." In **Norfolk**, flint walls and Dutch gable ends, reflecting former trading links with the Low Countries, are a common sight. Windmills are ubiquitous, the skies are vast, and the light effects subtle.

Scenically, the coast is the most appealing part: south Essex is drably developed around the Thames Estuary, but east of Ipswich **Suffolk** has lots of interest for the walker and naturalist, although the presence of Sizewell nuclear power station is unfortunate. The **Norfolk Broads** is an excellent place to rent a sail-it-yourself boat. More solitary beauty is abundant along the unspoiled north Norfolk coast. North of Cambridge lie the **Fens**, a vast expanse of fertile, flat, black-soil farmland, formerly beneath water but drained by cuts and sluices; much of that landscape transformation was begun by the Dutch engineer Cornelius Vermuyden in the 17th century. Wicken Fen near Ely gives an idea of what the Fens were like before this great agricultural upgrading.

THE INLAND SHIRES There are various pockets of interest inland. **Hertfordshire** has some fine country houses and oases of rural charm such as Ayot St. Lawrence and Benington, but Hertford, Hemel Hempstead, and others are commuter satellites. **Bedfordshire** has grand houses such as Luton Hoo and Woburn Abbey, but the former hat-making center of Luton and Bedford itself are uninteresting. Northampton is famed for shoemaking and the best of the gentle **Northamptonshire** countryside includes Rockingham Forest and the ironstone villages of Badby and Everdon, while there is an appealing canal scene and canal museum at Stoke Bruerne. Milton Keynes is the newest of Britain's new towns. **Althorp** is the seat of the Spencer family; Diana, Princess of Wales, is buried on a lake island and visitors can pay their respects at a shrine; the house and grounds open in July and August (reservations essential; tel: 0870 1679000). **Leicestershire** is endowed with some large country estates and rolling countryside on its eastern side, but further west many of its towns belong to the industrial East Midlands; Leicester, the county town, is an industrial center, though it does have an excavated Roman site within the Jewry Wall Museum and all the museums are free, making it a good place for day visits. Belvoir Castle, home of the Duke of Rutland, is one of the grandest 19th-century statements of wealth and social prominence. **Nottinghamshire** is the county of Robin Hood, although what is left of Sherwood Forest is inevitably smaller and tamer than in the famous outlaw's day; the great country estates known as the Dukeries include Newstead Abbey and others, while Clumber Park is a popular strolling ground. The writer D. H. Lawrence lived at Eastwood, in the Nottinghamshire coalfield and his house is open as a museum. Nottingham itself is no great beauty but the Lace Market district is attractive and there is an excellent crop of museums.

CAMBRIDGE AND THE CATHEDRAL CITIES Visitors come above all to the university city of **Cambridge**, whose colleges and river combine in perfect composition. Alumni include Oliver Cromwell, John Milton, Isaac Newton, Lord Byron, and Charles Darwin. **Ely**, **Norwich**, **Peterborough**, **St Albans**, **Southwell**, and **Lincoln** each have splendid cathedrals, abbeys, or minsters. Of these places, Norwich and Lincoln are less well known, because of their relative isolation, than many of England's other great cathedral cities and deserve a longer look.

BEST PLACES TO GO:
HISTORIC CITIES
Cambridge, Lincoln, Norwich.
SMALL TOWNS
Bury St. Edmunds, Ely, Lavenham, Little Walsingham, Louth, Newark-on-Trent, Saffron Walden, St Albans, Southwell, Stamford, Thaxted, Woodbridge, Wymondham.
COASTAL TOWNS AND VILLAGES
Aldeburgh, Burnham Overy Staithe, Cley, Dunwich, Southwold, Wells-next-the-Sea.
WALKS
Bedfordshire: Dunstable Downs, Ampthill Park.
Cambridgeshire: Wicken Fen, Cambridge to Grantchester via the river, Grafham Water, Hemingford Grey and St. Ives.
Essex: Sea wall at Tollesbury, Epping Forest, Hatfield Forest.
Hertfordshire: King's Walden and St. Paul's Walden, Ivinghoe Beacon, Tring Reservoirs, Essendon.
Leicestershire: Bradgate Park, Beacon Hill, Burrough Hill, Rutland Water, Grand Union Canal.
Lincolnshire: Lincolnshire Wolds.
Norfolk: Holkham Gap, Cley, Horsey Mere, Yare Estuary, Sandringham country park.
Northamptonshire: Canal towpath at Stoke Bruerne, Knightley Way from Preston Capes to Fawsley Hall.
Nottinghamshire: Clumber Park, Cresswell Crags.
Suffolk: Southwold, Minsmere, Flatford Mill.

St. Albans Abbey and the parkland containing remains of the Roman city of Verulamium

THE COLLEGIATE SYSTEM

Colleges are the life and soul of the University of Cambridge, just as they are at Oxford (see page 126). The colleges are where most students live, eat, and have their supervisions (in which small groups of students discuss their work with teachers). Lectures, examinations, and societies are organized on a university basis, but there are comparatively few "university" buildings as such.

138

EXCURSIONS FROM CAMBRIDGE

Wimpole Hall (N.T.) is Cambridgeshire's grandest house, a formal Georgian composition. It has restored Victorian stables and a large park with lots of walks. Rare breeds of domestic animals and two centuries of farm machinery can be seen at adjacent Home Farm. **Anglesey Abbey** (N.T.), built around 1600, has impressive grounds laid out this century. The **Imperial War Museum Duxford** claims to hold Europe's largest collection of historic military aircraft; it also includes the American Air Museum. The museum (tel: 01223 835000) runs free hourly buses from Cambridge train station.

The classical grandeur of the Fitzwilliam Museum

▶▶▶ **Cambridge** *134B3*

(Tourist information center tel: 01223 322640)

Home of one of the world's oldest and greatest universities (founded in 1284), Cambridge is a city ideal for wandering. It is a place of tranquillity, students on bicycles, and riverside beauty, as well as a bustling market town. You can go into many colleges, but respect "Private" notices; some close to visitors from April to June. The tourist information center, Wheeler Street, offers guided tours.

The university comprises about 30 colleges scattered around the city, of which 16 have medieval origins. **King's College** has the most famous building; its **chapel**▶▶▶, a symphony of fan-vaulting and magnificent stained glass, is regarded as the finest example of the Perpendicular (15th-century Gothic) style. Nearby **Clare College**▶ is a formal composition, like a Renaissance palace. The grand Palladian **Senate House** is used for formal functions, including graduation ceremonies. **Trinity College**▶▶ has the largest courtyard in Oxford or Cambridge and Christopher Wren's famous library (*Open* to the public) in Nevile Court. **St. John's College**▶▶ has two Tudor courts; beyond them the Bridge of Sighs leads into 19th-century Gothic New Court. More modest in scale is **Queens' College**▶, with its half-timbered courtyard and painted hall.

The Mathematical Bridge is a wooden structure originally built without any bolts—until engineers dismantled it and were unable to reassemble it as it was!

Behind Trinity and King's, the River Cam slices through a delectable swath of greenery, fringed by neat gardens and lawns; this area is known as The Backs. Punts (boats originally designed for gathering reeds for thatching) can be rented near Silver Street Bridge. Walk south through riverside meadows for 2 miles to Grantchester, or head north from Magdalene Street Bridge to watch college rowing crews training.

The **Fitzwilliam Museum**▶▶▶ (*Admission free*) is a major collection of art, medieval manuscripts, armor, and more. The **Cambridge and County Folk Museum**▶ is packed with local memorabilia and **Kettle's Yard**▶ is an idiosyncratic private house and modern art gallery.

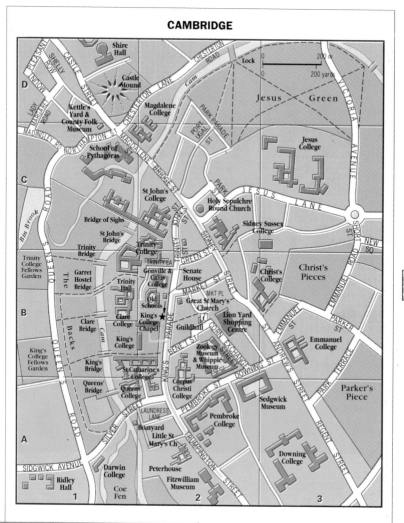

CAMBRIDGE

139

Walk

The colleges, river and streets

With the **Church of Great St. Mary's** (fine view from **tower▶**) on your left, follow King's Parade (which becomes Trumpington Street. On the right is **King's College** with its **chapel▶▶▶**. Pass **Corpus Christi** (its Old Court is hidden at the back) and **Pembroke** (chapel by Wren); further on are

Peterhouse (founded 1284, the oldest college) and the **Fitzwilliam Museum▶▶▶**. Enter Little St. Mary's Lane, turn right by the river (you can rent a punt). Pass Mill Inn, cross Silver Street Bridge to pass **Queens' College▶**. Take a path on right across grass for views from **The Backs**. Garret Hostel Lane leads over the river to Trinity Lane. Turn left past **Trinity Hall▶**. Enter **Trinity▶▶** and **St. John's▶▶** colleges from Trinity Street; at river, take walkway on right to a foot-bridge by the **Lock** and turn right across Jesus Green to Portugal Street. Return past the **Round Church▶** and **Sidney Sussex College** in Sidney Street.

GRIME'S GRAVES
A major center of England's neolithic flint industry occupies a site in Thetford Warren, the conifer forest on the low-lying sandy tracts of the Breckland (east of Ely). Over 400 shafts have been discovered; neolithic men climbed down these shafts to work in cramped tunnels, chipping away the flint for use in tools and weapons. One shaft is open to the public.

For centuries, Ely was dependent on the Ouse as a waterway

WICKEN FEN
Britain's oldest nature reserve, situated south of Ely and now owned by the National Trust, gives an idea of what the fens were like before they were drained. Villagers left the fen undrained to preserve its supply of reeds for thatching; it is in parts wooded, wetland, and meadow, with waterways enclosing the site. A nature trail takes you past a re-erected pumping mill, some bog oaks (logs submerged for thousands of years under the fen and recently unearthed), and the birdwatchers' blind.

▶▶ **Ely** *134C3*
(Tourist information center tel: 01353 662062)
The little town is dwarfed by its great cathedral, occupying a slightly elevated site that lets it dominate the pancake-flat Fenland plain for far around. The region is still called the Isle of Ely—a reminder of the days when the town was more or less an island in the undrained marsh. There is little to see in town, but the **cathedral**▶▶▶ ranks among the greats.

Part of the building shows Norman work, including the west front and tower, but restoration was soon needed: in 1250 the east end was rebuilt in Purbeck marble. In 1321 Alan of Walsingham supervised the building of the Lady Chapel; when the central tower collapsed the next year he created the wonderful octagonal lantern, lodged on eight oak pillars, that graces the building today (divine intervention must have prevented a further collapse: the structure has little to support it). Attached to the cathedral are a stained-glass museum and a brass-rubbing center. Around the precincts are the houses of the King's School, an eminent "public" school founded by Henry VIII.

▶ **King's Lynn** *134D3*
(Tourist information center tel: 01553 763044)
Once a member of the Hanseatic League (a powerful commercial association of towns in northern Germany formed in the 14th century), King's Lynn still has a continental look in its darkened red-brick buildings. It traded with northern Europe for many centuries and its docks and industrial area are still very much functional. St. George's Guildhall (1420) is the oldest guildhall in England and has a splendid beamed roof; this and twin-towered St. Margaret's Church (Norman, with fine memorial brasses) make a visit to the town worthwhile. Lifestyles of yesteryear are evoked within **True's Yard Heritage Centre**, where a pair of fisherman's cottages house a museum.

The villages of **Castle Rising** and **Castle Acre**▶, respectively 4 miles north and 13 miles east of King's Lynn, both have Norman castles. West of Castle Acre, the priory church of a Cluniac foundation survives almost intact. Castle Rising has jousting contests in summer.

Fenland churches▶▶ Among the finest of these are **Walpole St. Peter**, with superb benches, font and pulpit and **Walsoken**, a Norman church with a magnificent roof and a 16th-century painting of the *Judgement of Solomon*.

140

Lincoln Cathedral: one of the great masterpieces of Gothic architecture

▶ ▶ ▶ **Lincoln**   134E2

(Tourist information center tel: 01522 529828)

The massive towers of Lincoln's superb cathedral soar high from a hilltop site. The cathedral, castle, museums and historic streets provide plenty of attractions for a full-day visit. However, outside the small historic core much of the city is quite undistinguished.

The **cathedral▶ ▶ ▶**, one of England's finest, was largely rebuilt in the 13th and 14th centuries after an earthquake in 1185 destroyed an earlier structure. Highlights are the elaborate west façade, the carved choir stalls, and the stained-glass rose windows known as the Dean's Eye and the Bishop's Eye. High up, the Lincolnshire Imp carving steals the show; the story goes that he got too close to the angels and was turned to stone for his sins. Steps lead up the central tower to a viewing spot.

Minster Yard, the cathedral close, has Georgian and medieval houses. Near the cathedral's east end, the **Bishop's Old Palace** dates from the 12th to 15th centuries. **Steep Hill** lives up to its name, climbing from the River Witham, past the Jew's House, inhabited from Norman times and so named because of a Jewish community that once existed there, and continuing beyond the cathedral as **Bailgate**. The street is spanned by Newport Arch, a Roman gateway into the city. Opposite the cathedral's west façade, **Exchequergate** leads to **Lincoln Castle▶** which dates from Norman times and has thick walls, gateways, towers, and a 19th-century prisoners' chapel.

▶ **Norfolk Broads**   135C5

(The Broads National Park tel: 01603 610734)

Ever popular with boat enthusiasts and birdwatchers, the Broads is an area of fertile fens, waterways, and reedy lakes (called "broads") formed from peat excavations. Windmills, erected to pump water to drain the farmland and now mostly defunct, proliferate. The broads are difficult to see except from a boat; one of the best waterside walks is in the vicinity of Horsey, where the pumping mill is open to the public. The National Trust owns the broad of Horsey Mere; marsh harriers, bitterns, and otters make up part of the population. Other strolls include the banks of the rivers Bure, Thurne, and Yare.

MUSEUMS IN LINCOLN

Lincoln's indoor attractions include the **Museum of Lincolnshire Life**, with a sizeable collection of horse-drawn vehicles, and domestic and agricultural bygones and the **Usher Gallery**, which exhibits applied arts, including a collection of watches, memorabilia relating to poet Lord Tennyson (born at Somersby in the Lincolnshire Wolds) and paintings by Lincolnshire artist Peter de Wint.

141

SPALDING

A former bulb-growing center in the Fens, Spalding hosts the Flower Parade (usually first Sat in May; check with the tourist office, tel: 01775 725468). It's one of the great free shows of eastern England, where often as many as three million tulips are used to decorate the floats in a procession accompanied by bands and general bonhomie. During the same weekend, many churches in the surrounding South Holland area have spectacular flower festivals.

The virtue and the joy of this little-explored corner of English coast is its isolation. The area also has a tremendous sense of place and history, and lots to interest the naturalist. Dutch gables, flint walls, huge medieval "wool" churches, and weather-beaten coastal villages supply the human elements—salt marshes (Europe's largest expanse), vast sandy beaches, prolific birdlife, and dramatic skyscapes are among the natural attractions.

NORFOLK HOUSES

Blickling Hall (N.T.) is a lovely red-brick 17th-century house, famed for the Jacobean plasterwork in its Long Gallery. **Holkham Hall** is a neat Palladian mansion built for Thomas Coke, 18th-century agricultural pioneer. **Felbrigg** (N.T.), a tall-chimneyed, 17th-century house in a wooded park, has Georgian furnishings and a fine 18th-century library. **Houghton Hall** exudes Palladian elegance and was the seat of Sir Robert Walpole, the first English prime minister. **Sandringham** (*Open* only when the Royals are not in residence; park and drives always open) was built in the 19th century as a country home for the Prince of Wales, the future Edward VII.

A shrimping boat at Wells-next-the-Sea

142

THE VILLAGES Cromer, famed for its crabs, and **Sheringham** are demure Edwardian resorts atop crumbly cliffs; from the latter a private steam railroad heads towards Holt. Inland lies Norfolk's highest land (heathy rises rather than full-fledged hills). **Cley**▶ has an often-photographed windmill (*Open* periodically). While **Blakeney** is a yachting center, where mast-stays flap in the wind and a gravelly bank leads to Blakeney Point (still building up westward). Inland, **Binham**▶ has a superb 13th-century priory church beside the ruins of an 11th-century Benedictine priory.

Wells-next-the-Sea produces 80 percent of English whelks; the attractive port looks out over wide salt marshes. A walk westward brings you to **Holkham Gap**, where Corsican pines stabilize the dunes, flanking an immense beach. Another steam railroad connects Wells with **Little Walsingham**▶, a pilgrimage center for 900 years with both Roman Catholic and (incense-filled) Anglican shrines to Our Lady of Walsingham. It's fascinating even to non-pilgrims.

The "Seven Burnhams" are a scattering of hamlets and villages all named with the prefix Burnham. **Burnham Overy Staithe**▶ broods over salt marshes with a fetching harbor scene—close by are a tower windmill and pretty watermill. **Burnham Thorpe** is famed as Admiral Lord Nelson's birthplace—every other pub hereabouts seems to be called the Nelson or the Hero. The nation's greatest sailor died on board H.M.S. *Victory* (see page 104) after defeating the French and Spanish at Trafalgar in 1805; he was buried in St. Paul's Cathedral in London, but there are memorials in Burnham Thorpe Church. **Burnham Market** is an attractive village set around a spacious green. **Hunstanton** is a quiet resort beside chalk cliffs, with its **Sea Life Centre** tunnel-style aquarium.

THE WILDLIFE Among the best places for observing Norfolk's wildlife are the reserves at **Holme-next-the-Sea**, at **Cley**, a site with reedbeds and shallow lagoons, and **Blakeney Point**, reached by boat from Morston or by a long coastal walk over sand and rocky beach from Blakeney. The coast supports a huge population of waders, with wood and curlew sandpipers in summer; great tern colonies exist at Scolt Head island, common and grey seals breed here, and there are sizeable numbers of autumnal migrants and wintering birds.

►►► Norwich   135C4
(Tourist information center tel: 01603 666071)

Tucked away in the northeast corner of East Anglia, Norwich is less touristy than most other great cathedral cities in England. It is the major commercial center for the region and a university city, too, which gives it a workaday bustle. For the visitor there is enough to fill a weekend and you can escape to the Norfolk Broads for peace and space (see page 141). The marketplace (one of England's grandest), antiques showrooms, and speciality stores (including the Colman's Mustard store) make for fascinating browsing and there is a fair range of theaters. The medieval center has a mix of good streets—the finest being **Elm Hill**, **Bridewell Alley**, and Colegate—a number of ancient buildings (head for the **Guildhall** and **Pull's Ferry**) and a multitude of medieval churches, notably **St. Peter Mancroft** (Perpendicular) and **St. Peter Hungate**, which has a fine hammerbeam roof, a museum of church art and a brass-rubbing center.

Top of the sights is the **cathedral►►►** (founded 1096), surrounded by a close of houses and boasting remarkable detailing in the roof-bosses, misericords, glass and stone vaulting; the Norman cloister is the largest in the country. More prominent is the **castle►**; guided tours take you around the Norman keep, battlements, and dungeons.

MUSEUMS IN NORWICH
Bridewell Museum, Bridewell Alley, shows the trades and industries of Norwich over two centuries, in a former prison. **Castle Museum**, Castle Meadow, displays a celebrated collection of paintings by the Norwich school; ceramics (including hundreds of teapots), archaeology and natural history (Norfolk's last pair of great bustards are here, in stuffed form). **Sainsbury Centre for Visual Arts**, University of East Anglia campus (western edge of the city), has an outstanding art collection, innovatively displayed in a striking building by Sir Norman Foster. On King Street, **Dragon Hall** is a medieval merchant's hall with a fine roof and vaulted undercroft. In Oak Street, **Inspire** is a hands-on science center in a former church.

143

Pull's Ferry, a 15th-century watergate on the River Wensum at Norwich

► Saffron Walden   134B3
(Tourist information center tel: 01799 510444)

From medieval times until the 18th century this was a center for the saffron crocus industry. The legacy of its wealth is a knot of historic streets around the largest parish church in Essex, which is in the Perpendicular Gothic style and has notable carvings, roofs, and brasses. The former Sun Inn on Church Street is outstanding among many examples of the East Anglian craft of pargeting (decorative external plasterwork). On the Common is an enigmatic turf maze.

Just west of the town is **Audley End House►►**. Although only a fraction of its original size, it represents Jacobean architecture on its grandest scale. Vanbrugh and Robert Adam were responsible for the early 18th-century alterations; Capability Brown landscaped the park.

AROUND SAFFRON WALDEN
The area's pretty villages make for excellent touring by car or bike, with quiet backroads through gently rolling farmland. To the west are **Clavering**, with its ford and Saxon castle site and **Brent Pelham**, where thatched cottages overlook the old stocks and whipping post. To the south, **Newport's** main street displays many examples of pargeting (ornamental plasterwork).

That national asset, the British countryside, is adored for its infinite variety. Yet the landscapes of Thomas Hardy and John Constable have already been transformed in the name of progress. In recent years public attitudes have become more preservationist, but is it too late?

THE NATIONAL PARKS
Apart from the **Peak** (see opposite), the other National Parks are: the **Lake District**, the **Yorkshire Dales**, **Northumberland**, and the **North York Moors** (in northern England); **Snowdonia**, the **Pembrokeshire Coast**, and the **Brecon Beacons** (in Wales); **Exmoor** and **Dartmoor** (in the West Country); proposed additions are the **South Downs** (Sussex) and **New Forest**. The Broads has a similar status to a National Park. There are also Areas of Outstanding Natural Beauty such as the Lincolnshire Wolds and the Forest of Bowland, which have strict planning controls. Scotland's first National Park—Loch Lomond and the Trossachs—was established in 2002.

Britain's footpaths need a constant watch to ensure that they are in usable condition

SAVING THE LAKES
Early in the 19th century, poet William Wordsworth was anxious about the development of the Lake District and expressed his wish that it should be deemed "a sort of national property, in which every man has a right and interest who has an eye to perceive and a heart to enjoy." The children's author Beatrix Potter was another who loved the area and used revenue from her books to acquire local farms and estates, which she donated to the National Trust.

THE SHAPING OF THE LANDSCAPE The countryside is made by a combination of human and natural activity. Patches of the primeval tree cover that once cloaked much of the country exist here and there, but "slash-and-burn" policies led to a legacy of barren moorland, while farming produced a patchwork of hedge-lined fields and wealthy landowners created great estates and hunting grounds. Yet so embedded in Britain's national culture is the landscape that this unique blend of elements has become "nature" in the public imagination. No value can be placed on landscape beauty, but the populace tends to expect it to be available for them to enjoy.

THE THREATS AND THE SAVIORS Delicate eco-systems that have thrived for centuries in Britain's varied landscape have suffered greatly in the past half century, with agricultural mass-production, road-building, urban development, and other changes in land use. Since 1945, the British countryside has lost 40 percent of its heathlands, 80 percent of its chalk downland pastures and 95 percent of its herb-rich hay meadows. Fortunately the countryside is so prominent in the national conscience that there has been abundant support for saving what remains, from local campaigns to government environmental policies and conservationist bodies like the National Trust.

NATIONAL PARKS AND PUBLIC ACCESS The major catalyst in the formation of National Parks in England and Wales was in 1932, when hikers (or "ramblers" as they called themselves) mounted a mass trespass against the denial of public access to the hills of the Peak District. Fights broke out with landowners' gamekeepers, who jealously guarded the privately owned moorlands; six ramblers were arrested and five received prison sentences. This event brought the issues of access to the fore and after World War II the Peak became Britain's first such designated area—seen as both valuable and vulnerable for its proximity to industrial cities.

The National Parks that were created in the 1950s (see sidebar) had several aims, including provision of access and facilities for the public, preserving the landscape, protecting wildlife and buildings, and maintaining established farming use. However, walkers do not have total freedom of access (although the law may soon allow the "right to roam" in open country) and the national parks differ from their counterparts in the U.S.A. and most other countries in that most of the land is privately owned.

At the same time a unique system of registering public rights of way over private land was set up—giving anyone the right to walk on some 140,000 miles of paths and bridleways in England and Wales—all now shown on Ordnance Survey maps.

HELPING HANDS The National Trust, a charitable body (see panel, page 102) has since 1895 acquired large areas of coast, downland, upland and forest, which it has the statutory power to declare inalienable (making it impossible ever to be sold) for public enjoyment in perpetuity. In this way large areas of coastal Devon and Cornwall's magnificent coastal cliffs have been saved for the nation, and access guaranteed. There is free access on foot to all the Trust's countryside sites.

Some of Britain's most valuable wildlife sites are protected as **National Nature Reserves**. On the South Downs in Sussex, for example, many of the hillsides that attracted a wealth of wildlife have been ploughed up and agriculturally "improved" since the 1940s; however, a few pockets have been preserved as nature reserves, such as Mount Caburn (near Lewes), with its rare orchids and butterflies, and Lullington Heath (near Alfriston), with its unusual mixture of acid and chalky soils, giving rise to a diverse flora. **The Royal Society for the Protection of Birds** (R.S.P.B.) is the principal body concerned with wild birds and their environments in the U.K. and has 120 reserves, many—among them Minsmere in Suffolk—with blinds for birdwatchers. For information contact the R.S.P.B. at The Lodge, Sandy, Bedfordshire SG19 2DL, tel: 01767 680551 (website: www.rspb.org.uk).

Additionally, numerous specialist bodies play a role in safeguarding wildlife. Based at **Slimbridge** on the Severn Estuary in Gloucestershire, the **Wildfowl and Wetlands Trust** is dedicated to the protection of wetland sites—with a huge population of geese, swans and ducks on site—and has wildfowl collections at seven other centers in the U.K. Meanwhile the **Tamar Otter Park** at North Petherwin in Cornwall breeds otters with the aim of reintroducing this once-familiar animal to England's rivers.

LONG-DISTANCE PATHS
A web of long-distance paths spans the length and breadth of Britain. It includes the **Pennine Way** along the "spine" of upland England from Derbyshire to the Scottish Borders: the **West Highland Way** from the edge of Glasgow to the heart of the Scottish Highlands; the **Peddar's Way and the North Norfolk Coast Path** in the milder scenery of East Anglia. The **South Downs Way** is open to horse riders and mountain bikers as well as walkers. For information on walking in Britain, contact the Ramblers' Association, Camelford House, 87–90 Albert Embankment, London SE1 7TW, tel: 020-7339 8500 (website: www.ramblers.org.uk).

145

VOLUNTARY WORK
The British Trust for Conservation Volunteers (36 St Mary's Street, Wallingford, Oxfordshire OX10 0EU, tel: 01491 839766; website: www.btcv.org) runs over 500 conservation working vacations and many one-day projects (footpath maintenance, drystone walling and so on); participants pay a small amount towards food and accommodation.

NATURE ON THE SUFFOLK COAST

Walberswick, a scattered hamlet, abuts reedbeds, mud flats, and heath, a habitat for bearded tits, reed warblers, bitterns, water rails, and marshland plants. Much of the former port of Dunwich has disappeared beneath the sea; Dunwich and Westleton heaths are nearby and Minsmere is a freshwater lake owned by the Royal Society for the Protection of Birds (over 280 bird species have been recorded locally, including bearded tits, nightjars, woodpeckers, and nightingales). Access to Minsmere Reserve is tightly controlled, but birdwatchers' blinds are open to the public.

146

Southwold: choose from today's catch at the harbor

▶ St Albans 134A2
(Tourist information center tel: 01727 864511)

Less than 20 miles from London, St. Albans has preserved its provincial character surprisingly well. Its **abbey church▶** is a medieval foundation built on the site where Alban, the first British martyr, was executed in the 4th century. Its brick-and-flint architecture dates from the 11th century and has been added to in every century since. The Roman city of **Verulamium▶** lies in a nearby park; excavations include a semicircular amphitheater, part of the city walls, foundations of houses, and a temple. Site finds are well displayed in the Verulamium Museum.

The **Gardens of the Rose▶**, the Royal National Rose Society's home at Chiswell Green, southwest of St. Albans, has some 30,000 bushes, at their best in July. Five miles east of St. Albans, **Hatfield House▶▶** has been in the same family since it was built for Robert Cecil in 1611. It has state rooms and knot and scented gardens.

▶ Southwell 134D1
(Newark-on-Trent tourist information center tel: 01636 655765)

The medieval minster in this small Nottinghamshire town is not England's best-known, but the chapter house (begun in 1292) boasts some of the country's most breathtakingly intricate carving: a celebration of Sherwood Forest's foliage in stone, featuring oak, maple, vine and ivy leaves. Two of the three Norman towers were rebuilt after a fire in 1711, but the nave, crossing, and transept display characteristic Norman simplicity.

▶▶ Southwold 135C5
(Tourist information center tel: 01502 724729)

An old-fashioned coastal town, Southwold is a center for exploring the best of Suffolk's coast. The former home town of novelist George Orwell, it was rebuilt after a fire in 1659 around a charming series of greens edged by flint, brick, and color-washed cottages. The great Perpendicular church has a superb interior, a lighthouse gleams behind the Sole Bay Inn and the town museum and Sailors' Reading Room have displays on maritime life. Just south of town, the River Blyth has an attractive boating scene. Around Southwold lie numerous marshlands, some unspoiled low-lying coast, and heathy grassland—the traditional sandlings, or sheepwalks, on which Suffolk's economy depended in the wool-prosperous Middle Ages—making an area of interest for naturalists.

Southwards 16 miles, **Aldeburgh▶** is a small coastal town, the birthplace of George Crabbe, an 18th-century poet. His poem *The Borough* was adapted by Benjamin Britten for his opera *Peter Grimes*, a brilliant evocation of life on this coast, which premièred in 1945. Britten (1913–1976) is buried in the churchyard of St. Peter and St. Paul; a memorial window was designed by John Piper. Britten co-founded Aldeburgh's esteemed June music festival, which is centered on The Maltings at Snape.

Just north of Aldeburgh is **Thorpeness▶**, a resort village planned in the early 20th century as a weatherboarded and half-timbered "olde-English" haven. Beside the Meare, the village's artificial lake, is a former grain windmill, moved here to pump water to the adjacent tall former water tower, known as the House in the Clouds.

▶▶ Stamford 134C2

(Tourist information center tel: 01780 755611)

An oasis of mellow, Cotswold-like limestone buildings, Stamford was the first conservation area designated in England. Its clutch of medieval churches includes **St. Martin's**, a complete Perpendicular church with a notable 16th-century alabaster monument to Lord Burghley. Of Stamford's inns **The George** is the most conspicuous, with its "gallows" inn-sign spanning the street. Look for two good examples of almshouses, 15th-century **Browne's Hospital** and Elizabethan **Lord Burghley's Hospital**.

Capability Brown's landscaped park at **Burghley House▶▶** laps the brink of Stamford. The palatial mansion was built by one William Cecil, chief minister to Elizabeth I, and later Lord Burghley. The Elizabethan exterior belies an interior refurbished 100 years later, full of baroque flourishes, including a dazzling array of Italian plasterwork and painted ceilings by Verrio and Laguerre in the "Heaven" and "Hell" rooms, magnificent porcelain, paintings by Veronese and Gainsborough, and notable portraits. **Rutland Water▶**, to the west, is a huge reservoir and major recreation area. Further afield, 14 miles southeast, **Peterborough** is sprawling and industrial but worth a visit for its Norman **cathedral▶▶** that boasts a superb painted wooden ceiling—Europe's largest. Some 3 miles from Stamford is **Flag Fen▶** (see panel).

▶▶ Woburn Abbey 134B2

(tel: 01525 290666)

Britain's largest animal safari park forms part of the grounds of this stately home, the seat of the Russells, the Dukes of Bedford, since 1550. Despite its abbey origins—a Cistercian foundation prior to the Reformation—the house is an 18th-century Palladian composition set in a deer park. Within is the finest set of Canaletto paintings to be found anywhere. You can feel the family connection with the house (which claims to be the birthplace of afternoon tea), with portraits and possessions spanning many centuries.

FLAG FEN

Discovered in the fens in 1982, the remarkable Flag Fen Bronze Age Monument is the only English site of its era where archeological excavations are open to the public. The site was once a settlement by a lake, and a wooden causeway consisting of a platform and a line of posts extending about 0.5 miles once crossed the water. From this remarkable structure deliberately slighted metal objects seem to have been thrown as part of some mysterious ritual. The museum displays some of the best of the many such artifacts unearthed, including the oldest wooden wheel ever found in Britain. Try to take in the guided site tour, and visit the reconstructed Bronze Age and Iron Age houses.

A windmill stands among the tranquil marshes flanking the Blyth Estuary near Southwold

147

CONSTABLE COUNTRY

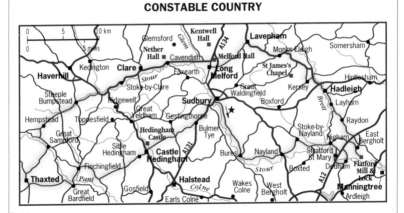

Drive

Constable country

The candy colors of local plasterwork, the village greens, and the great medieval churches, paid for by the prosperous wool trade, have changed little since Constable's day. The countryside is mild and agreeable if unspectacular: it is the towns and villages, well endowed with tearooms, and craft and antiques stores, that have most appeal in this tour (approx 90 miles).

Start at **Sudbury** (Tourist information center tel: 01787 881320), where Thomas Gainsborough's birthplace is now a museum. The route follows the

Gainsborough's House, Sudbury

River Stour, along the B1508 to **Bures**, then eastwards through **Stoke-by-Nayland►**, where the church tower (a familiar feature in Constable's paintings) presides over the Maltings and Guildhall.

Dedham► ► has an attractively broad main street and the building of Constable's school survives; the artist Alfred Munnings lived here and his works are displayed in his former house. Near **East Bergholt**, Constable's birthplace, is **Flatford Mill► ►** (also reached by a pretty 1.25 mile river path or by boats rented in Dedham); Willy Lott's Cottage by the millpond is still recognizable as the setting for Constable's painting *The Haywain*.

Turn northwest along the B1070 through **Hadleigh►**, a handsome town by the River Brett with a fine church and half-timbered Guildhall. Detour through **Kersey►**, a charming village of one street and join the A1141 to **Lavenham► ►**, with its resplendent half-timbering, a huddle of inns and an outstanding church. Westwards, **Long Melford►** has antiques stores, a magnificent church, and two fine stately homes adjacent.

The A1092 heads past **Cavendish**, a confection of pink rendering and thatch around the green and **Clare**, with its marketplace and flint-built church noted for its woodcarving. Seek out the church, windmill, and Recorders' House at **Thaxted► ►**.

Eastwards lies **Finchingfield►** with a delightful green and a windmill. **Castle Hedingham► ►** has a mighty Norman keep.

The landscape of East Anglia has always held a special fascination for painters. Gainsborough and Constable both came from Suffolk and Gainsborough's birthplace in Sudbury is now a museum. Constable was born at East Bergholt and pictures like The Haywain *and* Flatford Mill *made the winding valley of the Stour "Constable country" even during the painter's own lifetime.*

While Constable and Gainsborough are the two biggest names (see page 38), many other distinguished artists recorded the East Anglian scene. Philip Wilson Steer painted the Suffolk coast in the 1880s. **Sir Alfred Munnings** painted equestrian scenes and his house at Dedham is now a museum. **John Nash**, a major

landscape artist, lived and worked in Essex for years before his death in 1977.

THE NORWICH SCHOOL Norwich's Castle Museum has a splendid collection of paintings by the Norwich School of painters, which began in 1803. Its chief figures were **John Crome** and **John Sell Cotman**. Crome was much more successful, to the anguished jealousy of Cotman, who is now regarded as the greater painter, admired for his ability to impose simple and satisfying patterns on the natural scene. The work of the Norwich School echoes the Dutch school of landscape painting. They responded to a similar setting—a flat landscape studded by windmills and grazed by cattle beneath a sky of towering cloudscapes.

The wealth and the comparatively isolated position of Norwich in the early 19th century meant that most of its painters were known only locally. The local gentry wanted representations of the scenes they knew—the tranquil Norfolk landscape, picturesquely dilapidated cottages, ruined towers and crumbling abbeys, cattle and sheep, river and coastal views. The Norwich School painted the rural scene as it was in the last days before the Industrial Revolution changed the face of Britain.

Above: from
Wood scene *by John Crome, 1810*

Fishing boats off Yarmouth *by John Sell Cotman*

EAST ANGLIAN ART ON SHOW
In addition to Gainsborough's house in Sudbury, there are notable collections of works by East Anglian artists at the Castle Museum and the Sainsbury Centre, both in Norwich, the Fitzwilliam Museum in Cambridge and at Tate Britain and the National Gallery in London—the latter has Constable's *The Haywain.*

"How much real delight have I had with the study of Landscape this summer. Either I am myself much improved in "the Art of seeing Nature" (which Sir Joshua Reynolds calls painting) or Nature has unveiled her beauties to me with a less fastidious hand—perhaps there may be something of both so we will divide these fine compliments between us..."
—John Constable, to his future wife (1812)

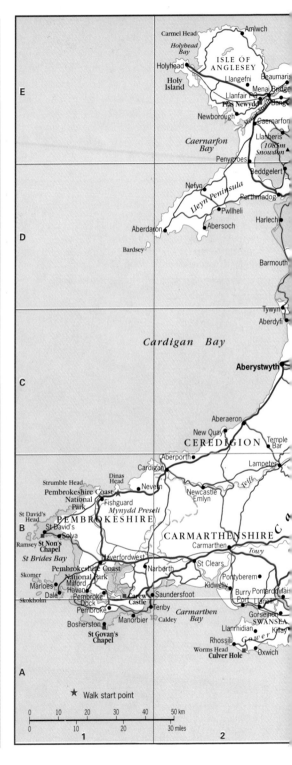

Carmel Head
Amlwch
Holyhead Bay
ISLE OF ANGLESEY
Holyhead
Llangefni
Beaumaris
Holy Island
E
Llanfair P.G.
Menai Bridge
Bangor
Plas Newydd
Newborough
Caernarfon
Caernarfon Bay
Llanberis
(1085m Snowdon)
Penygroes
Beddgelert

Nefyn
Lleyn Peninsula
Porthmadog
D
Pwllheli
Harlech
Aberdaron
Abersoch
Bardsey
Barmouth

Tywyn
Aberdyfi

Cardigan Bay
C
Aberystwyth

Aberaeron
New Quay
Temple Bar
CEREDIGION
Aberporth
Lampeter
Cardigan
Teifi
Strumble Head
Dinas Head
Nevern
Pembrokeshire Coast National Park
Fishguard
Newcastle Emlyn
St David's Head
Mynydd Preseli
B
St David's
PEMBROKESHIRE
CARMARTHENSHIRE
Solva
Carmarthen
Ramsey
St Non's Chapel
Towy
St Brides Bay
Haverfordwest
Narberth
St Clears
Skomer
Pembrokeshire Coast National Park
Pontyberem
Marloes
Milford Haven
Kidwelly
Burry Port
Pontarddulais
Dale
Llanelli
Skokholm
Pembroke Dock
Carew Castle
Saundersfoot
Gorseinon
Pembroke
Tenby
SWANSEA
Manorbier
Caldey
Carmarthen Bay
Llanrhidian
Bosherston
Killay
St Govan's Chapel
Rhossili
Gower
Worms Head
Oxwich
A
Culver Hole

★ Walk start point

0   10   20   30   40   50 km
0   10   20   30 miles

1   2

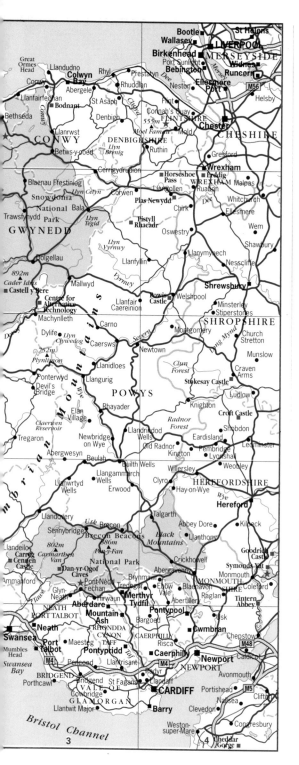

Wales

▶▶▶ **REGION HIGHLIGHTS**

Beaumaris *page 154*

Brecon Beacons National Park *page 155*

Elan Valley *page 159*

Pembrokeshire Coast National Park *pages 165–166*

Plas Newydd *page 164*

Powis Castle *page 166*

Snowdonia National Park *page 167–170*

Welsh Folk Museum *page 157*

Wye Valley *page 171*

Traditional Armenian dancing at the Llangollen Eisteddfod

WALES Constitutionally Wales is closer to England than is Scotland; there is no separate legal system, and the two countries have been unified since 1535. Yet the Welsh are proudly independent in culture and outlook; the Welsh language is very much alive (much more so than Gaelic in Scotland) and is taught in schools. Welsh is the first language of many, particularly in North and West Wales; signs ("dim parcio/no parking", "croeso i Gymru/ welcome to Wales") are predominantly bilingual; roughly one in five of its inhabitants is a Welsh speaker. Wales also prides itself on its educational system; it has the highest teacher/pupil ratios in the UK.

Plaid Cymru, a Welsh nationalist party, has sent members to Parliament since 1966, and devolution—restoration of some powers to the local Welsh government—is a current talking point. In September 1997, the Welsh people voted by a narrow margin to establish a Welsh Assembly in Cardiff, which came into existence in 1999. There are strong traditions of choral singing and of Nonconformism (that is, the Protestant denominations such as Methodism that have broken away from the Established Church), virtually every village having at least one chapel. The Welsh love of music, literature, and art manifests itself in the numerous *eisteddfodau* (festivals), in which music, poetry, drama, and fine arts feature. Welsh domestic architecture on the other hand is humble—typically sturdy stone-built farmsteads and houses beneath slate roofs; the railway age added red and yellow brick façades. Grand houses are few, but there are plenty of medieval castles to visit.

SOUTH WALES For all its proximity to northwest and central England, Wales is strikingly remote. Cross into South or Mid Wales from the English border and the hills rise immediately. The southern borderland (the border country often being termed as the Marches) is defined precisely by the gorge of the **Lower Wye**, whose scenic reaches are punctuated by features such as Tintern Abbey,

THE WELSH LANGUAGE
Visitors to Wales will not need to speak Welsh, but the language—one of Europe's oldest—is in evidence everywhere; on signposts, official notices, on TV and radio, and in place names. It is, however, useful to pick up the pronunciation to make it clear what town or village you are talking about. Many places begin with *Llan* (meaning church), the *ll* pronounced as a soft ch followed by an *l* sound—put the side of your tongue against your teeth and blow. Other useful rules are: *u* as in wheel; *y* as in tin or turn; *f* as in van; ff as in fun; th as in thought; *dd* as in then; ch as in loch; *au* as in mid; and *w* as in look. So Fforest Fawr is pronounced *forest vowr*, Llanwrtyd as *chlanuhrtid*; and Caersws as *kairsooce*.

Chepstow Castle, and Symonds Yat rock. Criss-crossing the English border from the South Wales coast to its northern one, the exhilarating and extremely hilly 177-mile **Offa's Dyke Path** roughly follows the line of a 9th-century boundary dike built by Offa, King of Mercia. Further into South Wales lie the former coalfields and the dying industrial heartlands of the **valleys**, which though hardly picturesque have their own fascination. **Cardiff**, the Welsh capital, is the administrative and cultural capital. The coast becomes increasingly seductive as you proceed westwards; Nash Point near Llantwit Major on the Vale of Glamorgan coast displays extraordinary candy-striped rocks, while **Gower**, on the back doorstep of the industrial city of Swansea, is a peninsula endowed with castles, magnificent bays, and cliffs. **Pembrokeshire**, too distant for mere day-trips, is a favorite destination for seaside holidays without the host of commercialized trappings found in so many of the English resorts.

MID WALES This nebulous term is applied to a relatively unknown region, sparsely populated except by sheep, which are encountered everywhere (one-quarter of the E.U.'s sheep population is here). The **Brecon Beacons National Park** offers the grandest scenery, with its best-known tracts on its eastern side—the Black Mountains, the Brecon Beacons themselves and the secondhand bookstore town of Hay-on-Wye. Further west, the **Cambrian Mountains** are scarcely inhabited and largely impenetrable by car, except by a handful of spectacularly lonely mountain roads laid along routes used by drovers taking sheep to market in the pre-automobile era. Aberystwyth is the principal coastal town of Ceredigian (or Cardigan), whose shoreline, though not as scenic as Pembrokeshire, does have a few pleasant places, such as Llangranog, New Quay, and Aberaeron.

NORTH WALES Along the north coast stretches a line of resorts, largely undistinguished with the notable exception of Llandudno. But more significantly, North Wales contains the **Snowdonia National Park**; here are the highest mountains in England and Wales and a good range of attractions, including castles, mines, and steam trains. Nevertheless, this can be a frustrating area for motorists: roads are often sunk down in the valleys and the scenery slips by quickly; but there are outstanding walks at varying levels of difficulty, from easy forest strolls to tough scrambles up challenging scree-covered mountain slopes.

RECOMMENDED
SMALL TOWNS
Carmarthenshire: Llandeilo.
Conwy: Conwy.
Monmouthshire: Chepstow, Monmouth.
Pembrokeshire: St. David's.
Powys: Hay-on-Wye, Llandrindod Wells, Llanidloes, Montgomery, Presteigne.
CASTLES
Caernarfon, Caerphilly, Conwy, Harlech.
COASTAL TOWNS
Llandudno, Tenby.
WALKING AREAS
Brecon Beacons National Park, Gower, Offa's Dyke Path, Pembrokeshire Coast National Park, Snowdonia National Park, Lower Wye Valley. (See Walks, page 158.)
INDUSTRIAL INTEREST
Snowdonia National Park, the South Wales mining valleys especially Blaenavon World Heritage Site.
SCENIC DRIVES
Mid Wales: Elan Valley, Beulah to Tregaron, Llanidloes via Dylife to Machynlleth, Rhayader to Aberystwyth.
Brecon Beacons National Park: Gospel Pass (Hay-on-Wye to Llanthony).
Snowdonia National Park: see Drive, page 170.

Rounding up sheep the Welsh way—but sheep dogs normally do the precision work

Anglesey Sea Zoo: all-weather fun

THE DRUIDS OF ANGLESEY
The religious leaders of the Celts were the Druids, and Anglesey was famed far and wide as a druidic center. Tacitus, the Roman historian writing in the 1st century AD, speaks of Anglesey as the place where youths aspiring to the priesthood were sent to be schooled in philosophy, religion, and poetry. In more sinister mode, he also speaks of human blood being smeared on the Druids' altars and human entrails being used for prophecies.

154

▶ **Anglesey, Isle of**   *150E2*
(Holyhead tourist information center tel: 01407 762622)
Wales' largest island is flat and fertile and it is its shores that provide most of its attractions to visitors. Good beaches include **Newborough Warren**, which offers distant views of Snowdonia and **Amlwch Bay**.

Pioneering neolithic man built an amazing number of chamber tombs on Anglesey, the most notable being **Bryn-celli Ddu** and **Barcloddiad y Gawres**. The island's geographical position en route to Ireland and its gold and copper inevitably attracted the Celts too; a great hoard of Iron Age chariot fittings and weapons was found at Llyn Cerrig Bach. In medieval times, when the island's farmland provided valuable supplies for granaries in England, Anglesey was held by the English. In the 1290s, Edward I built a stronghold at **Beaumaris▶▶**; the castle (Cadw) was never attacked and the moated shell survives to this day. The town's former prison houses a museum where you can find ghoulish delights such as the treadmill, the condemned cell, and the route to the scaffold.

Between Anglesey and the mainland is the Menai Strait, spanned by Thomas Telford's suspension bridge, the longest such structure in the world when it was built (1826) and one of the engineer's greatest achievements. Overlooking the strait is **Plas Newydd▶** (N.T.), the Pagets' 18th- and 19th-century family home; it has a *trompe l'oeil* mural in the dining room, painted by Rex Whistler in the 1930s. **Holy Island**, attached to Anglesey by a 0.5 mile causeway, is good for birdwatching and, although the industrial port of Holyhead is disappointing, there are good walks on Holyhead Mountain, the island's highest point, which has the remains of a Roman watchtower and traces of 3rd- and 4th-century hut circles. Ferries leave from Holyhead for Dublin in Ireland.

Rugged cliffs embrace Porth Dafarch, on Anglesey's Holy Island peninsula, a popular beach for divers and canoeists

►► Brecon Beacons National Park   151B3

(tel: 01874 624437)

The park is an east–west upland of four distinct areas, the Black Mountains, Fforest Fawr, the Brecon Beacons themselves and the Black Mountain. It is less rugged than Snowdonia but has some fine views and excellent walks.

The eastern flanks comprise the **Black Mountains**, a series of ridges enclosing deep sheep-grazed valleys. Drive up from **Hay-on-Wye►**, a small town crowded around its castle and a mecca of secondhand bookstores. Above Hay the **Gospel Pass►►** is perhaps the most scenic drive in the park, with easy access to the summit of Hay Bluff. The road dips into a valley, past the ruins of 13th-century **Llanthony Abbey►**. Up an obscure side valley **Patrishow Church►** boasts a rare musicians' gallery and an eerie mural of a skeleton bearing a shovel, scythe, and hourglass. Further west, the A479 skirts the massif between the attractive towns of **Crickhowell** and **Talgarth** before passing through **Tretower►**, with its fortified medieval manor (Cadw) by the ruin of an earlier castle.

The **Brecon Beacons** are really a sandstone ridge that culminates in Pen y Fan (2,906 feet), the highest point in Wales outside Snowdonia. The graceful M shape of the twin summits is seen from far around. To the south is the little **Brecon Mountain Railway**. **Brecon** itself is an amiable market town with a small cathedral and the **Brecknock Museum►**. Out of town, the **Brecon Beacons Mountain Centre** is the main national park information outlet.

Predominantly grassy upland, **Fforest Fawr** includes, near Pont Nedd Fechan, the superlative "**waterfall country**"►► of the wooded Nedd, Hepste, and Mellte gorges (see Walks, page 158). **Dan-yr-ogof Caves►** nearby are part of Britain's largest known cave system; one has a re-creation of a Bronze Age dwelling, another presents a history of caving in a sound-and-light show.

To the west, the **Black Mountain** is an expanse of moors and forests dominated by the craggy ridge of **Carmarthen Fan**. Much of it is for the serious walker only, but **Carreg Cennen Castle►►** (Cadw), a majestically placed ruin in a valley close to Llandeilo, merits a detour.

The national park includes the highest land in South Wales

LOVE SPOONS
Throughout rural Wales during the 17th, 18th, and 19th centuries, young men would spend many long, dark evenings carving ornamental wooden "love spoons." These would be presented as tokens to the girls or women they courted; if accepted, it was a sign that courtship would lead to marriage. They are still produced as souvenirs; the Brecknock Museum in Brecon and the Welsh Folk Museum at St. Fagans (see page 157) have fine collections of this genre of folk art.

The industrial valleys of South Wales present a startling transition from the lonely wilds of the Brecon Beacons to the north. Here, stretching from Pontypool in the east (close to the English border) towards Llanelli in the west, is one of the most strongly characterised industrial regions in the whole of Britain.

How green was my valley Between narrow fingers of rising ridges extend the valleys—running deep and roughly north to south, each grooved with long rows of houses built in the heyday of the areas' industrial prosperity.

Towards the end of the 18th century, the Industrial Revolution heralded a new dawn; peasants from rural areas migrated *en masse* into the Valleys as ironmasters established works at Aberdare, Dowlais, Hirwaun, and Merthyr Tydfil. In 1804 Richard Trevithick gave birth to the age of rail with his steam railway from Merthyr to Abercynon. The Merthyr ironworks supplied cannon for the British forces in the Napoleonic wars and track for railways across the globe.

Coal, choirs, and rugby Later, iron production ceased and the Valleys specialized in coal extraction; the coalfield witnessed a great influx of new population. Work was hard and often dangerous, but community life brought its rewards—passions for rugby and choral singing; the Valleys choirs still carry away the honors at the International Eisteddfod (see panels, pages 160 and 163). Numerous leading socialists were born and bred here, including Aneurin Bevan, a miner's son who was to be the instigator of the National Health Service (see panel) and Neil Kinnock, former leader of the Labour Party.

Facing the future At the height of the Valleys' industrialization, people joked disbelievingly that it would have once been possible for a monkey to have swung from tree to tree along the Rhondda Valley. Now the smoke has gone with closure of the collieries as seams are largely exhausted and greenery is returning: evergreen plantations cloak the upper slopes. Tower Colliery at Hirwaun, the last of the nationally owned pits, is now owned by its workforce; open-cast mining continues, but only one deep mine and a handful of open-cast mines operate in Wales, providing employment for merely a few hundred people. Unemployment overall is running high, and many houses stand empty. Service industries are alive however and the area has awakened to its tourist potential. Former miners take visitors around the inside of abandoned coal mines at the Big Pit Mining Museum in Blaenavon, and in the Rhondda Heritage Park near Pontypridd, where there are also displays recalling mining through three generations. The 18th-century Blaenavon Ironworks have been preserved under the guardianship of Cadw, and in 2000 the town of Blaenavon gained World Heritage Site status: things may indeed be looking up.

156

"NYE" AND THE NHS
Aneurin Bevan, or Nye as he was fondly called, was born the son of a miner in 1897. As a boy he was himself a miner and had early trade union experience in the South Wales Miners Federation. In 1929 he was elected M.P. for Ebbw Vale and held the seat until he died in 1960. One of parliament's greatest orators, he has gone down in history as the minister who in 1948 introduced the National Health Service, providing the people of Britain with a comprehensive medical, dental, and welfare service funded largely by general taxation.

An old pit head

▶▶ Cardiff 151A4
(tel: 029 2022 7281)

Although it is situated in the industrial heartland of Wales, Cardiff is a surprisingly clean and livable place. Despite its status as Welsh capital and as home of Welsh rugby union and of the (much-acclaimed) Welsh National Opera, Cardiff is not a particularly Welsh city. Bute Park cuts a swath by the banks of the Taff, close to the civic center, a gleaming complex in Portland stone begun in the 1890s. **Cardiff Castle▶▶** dates from Norman times but had money poured into it in the 1860s and onwards by the fabulously wealthy 2nd Marquess of Bute (who built the city's docks and made Cardiff the world's prime coal port); the result was a mock-medieval fantasy of Ludwig II proportions, designed by William Burges.

Cardiff has a excellent array of **museums▶▶**. At the wide-ranging **National Museum of Wales**, collections include paintings by French Impressionists as well as silver, ceramics, fossils, dinosaur skeletons, and shells, while the Millennium Stadium has a **Rugby Experience** museum. Cardiff Bay, where the harbor and docklands are being newly developed, now has numerous attractions: a three-dimensional model of the bay can be seen in the futuristic **Cardiff Bay Visitor Centre**; and **Techniquest** is one of the largest hands-on science centers in the country, a "wonderland of science and technology" for all age and experience levels. The Welsh Assembly is also based at Cardiff Bay.

The medieval **Llandaff Cathedral▶** is dominated by the figure of *Christ in Majesty* by Jacob Epstein, an impressive creation in concrete. The **Welsh Folk Museum▶▶▶** at nearby **St. Fagans** has a collection of rural dwellings from all over Wales, including a farmhouse, a terrace from the mining valleys, a Unitarian chapel, and a Working Men's Institute.

North of Cardiff, double-moated **Caerphilly Castle▶▶** (Cadw), dating from the 13th and 14th centuries, is the largest castle in England and Wales after Windsor. South of Abergavenny, **Big Pit Mining Museum, Blaenavon▶▶**, is the best attraction in the industrial Valleys, capturing the atmosphere of a working mine (see opposite page).

The past is brought to life at the Welsh Folk Museum (left); it is a steep climb to Cardiff Castle's 12-sided Norman keep

157

CASTELL COCH
Another fairy-tale concoction of William Burges was Castell Coch (Cadw), on the edge of Cardiff, designed for the 3rd Marquess of Bute. It was never completed, but there are hints at what might have been in the breathtaking splendor of the giltwork, painting, tiles, statues and carvings. Murals of Aesop's fables and the family's coats of arms (below) decorate the drawing room, while the ceiling of Lady Bute's bedroom is painted with the story of Sleeping Beauty.

Walks

from the road to the partly collapsed Jubilee Tower gives views westwards to Snowdonia and eastwards to the Peak District. Start from the picnic site and walk through the forest (following the blue or red markers); return along the open ridge to drop down to the road, then turn left to the starting point. (1.5 hours)

Dinas Island,   150B1
Pembrokeshire Coast
National Park, Pembrokeshire

Off the A487 east of Fishguard; parking lot near Sailors' Safety Inn. The "island" is in fact a peninsula, ideal for an exhilarating circular walk of 1 to 1.5 hours along the clifftop path, passing Dinas Head, the highest point, and Needle Rock, with its large birdlife population. A well-walked public footpath cuts across the narrow neck of land to complete the circuit.

158

Llyn Idwal, Snowdonia   151E3
National Park, Gwynedd

Parking lot by Idwal Cottage Youth Hostel on the A5. The nature trail around Llyn (lake) Idwal gives straightforward access to supremely dramatic scenery, passing the crags of the Devil's Kitchen beneath Glyder Fawr (1.5 hours). The slopes support rare flora, including alpine species and the area is an officially designated National Nature Reserve. Trail guide available on site.

Moel Famau,   151E4
Denbighshire

Parking lot and picnic site on the B5429 between Llanbedr-Dyffryn-Clwyd and Llandyrnog. The walk up

The Nedd, Hepste, and   151B3
Mellte Waterfalls, Brecon
Beacons National Park, Powys

Parking lot at Pontneddfechan, east of Glyn Neath. These mighty waterfalls crash their way along wooded gorges in the southern fringes of the national park. The Hepste and Mellte falls can be reached by a woodland path from Craig y Ddinas car park at the east end of Pontneddfechan or from Porth yr Ogof to the north; the highlight here is Sgwd yr Ira, where you can walk behind the curtain of the fall. (1–2 hours)

Symonds Yat, Lower   151B4
Wye Valley, Herefordshire border

Parking lot at end of the B4432, north of Coleford. This renowned scenic viewpoint over the Wye gives access to one of the prettiest parts of the gorge. Descend to the west, past a refreshment stand and on a marked path to the riverside Saracen's Head Inn, where a chain ferry takes you across. On the far bank turn left to the wire suspension bridge (it will bounce as you cross); return along the old railroad track on the east bank. (1.5 hours)

▶▶ Elan Valley, Aberystwyth and the Cambrian Mountains
151C3

(Aberystwyth tourist information center tel: 01970 612125)

One of the best places for spotting the red kite (a huge bird of prey identifiable by its forked tail—see panel), the **Elan Valley** is a chain of reservoirs which graces the great unpopulated wilds of the Cambrian Mountains. The lakes supply water to Birmingham, and both the dams and Elan village, built for the reservoir workers, are in characteristically solid Edwardian style. The Elan Valley visitor center in Elan village has details of walks; the trackbed of an old railroad used in the construction of the reservoirs is a good route for lakeside strolls.

An exciting **mountain road▶▶** climbs the Cambrian range, leaving Rhayader for the Elan Valley and continuing past abandoned lead and zinc mines to **Devil's Bridge▶**, where three bridges, stacked one upon the other, span a gorge. Tiny steam trains run along the scenic narrow-gauge **Vale of Rheidol Railway▶** from here to **Aberystwyth**, the main seaside resort for Cardigan Bay. A crescent of bay-windowed Victorian guest houses on the seafront overlook a rocky beach, which is hemmed in by the bulky bluff of Constitution Hill from where you can see Snowdonia and the Preseli Hills. A cliff railroad makes an effortless ascent to the top, and a camera obscura enhances the panorama on sunny days.

▶▶ Erddig
151D4

(tel: 01978 355314)

Although not an architecturally distinguished house, Erddig (N.T.), 2 miles south of Wrexham, is an excellent introduction to life "below stairs" in a country mansion. The National Trust rescued the house when mining subsidence threatened the structure; all the service buildings and most of the contents had survived intact and it is now preserved as a fascinating picture of the workings of a country estate in the 18th and 19th centuries.

The Yorke family, which lived here from 1733 to 1973, treated its servants kindly and as a visitor you see the house somewhat through a servant's eyes, entering not by the main door but through the servants' quarters.

Pennygarreg Reservoir Dam, Elan Valley

THE RED KITE
Less than 20 years ago this majestic bird of prey had become extremely scarce, but has been successfully reintroduced in some areas of Britain and numbers are on the increase. Close to the Elan Valley reservoirs, a good place to see them is just outside Rhayader at Gigrin Farm. The farm has established a Red Kite Centre where the birds make an appearance at feeding time (daily at 2 PM GMT, 3 PM British Summer Time), and where bird blinds have been erected.

DOLAUCOTHI GOLD MINES
Remotely sited near Pumsaint, just off the A482 southeast of Lampeter, the mines (N.T.) were periodically worked from Roman times up to the 20th century. Some of the 1930s machinery is still in place and, equipped with helmets and miners' lamps, visitors tour the mine tunnels and pan for gold. During July and August get there as early as possible or reserve ahead (tel: 01558 650359).

Far left: the family bicycle collection at Erddig

Look at any vacation brochure or tourist poster for Wales and you are likely to come across the same well-worn images: male voice choirs; young girls playing the harp in Welsh hats; mist-shrouded mountains and lakes; and rugged mining valleys. Like all clichés, they convey only a superficial picture. The reality is far more vital: a combination of reverence for the past and passionate concern for the future. One element links all the strands of politics and culture: a fervent sense of Welsh identity.

THE NATIONAL EISTEDDFOD

Welsh-language culture is seen at its most robust at an *eisteddfod*. All over the country, local *eisteddfodau* (literally "sittings") are set up in schools and chapels, where singers, dancers, musicians, actors, artists, and writers of all ages compete to reach the next level in the categories of Awdl (a complex, ancient form of Welsh poetry) and Pryddest (free verse). The nationwide contest culminates, in the first week of August, in the National Eisteddfod, presided over by the Gorsedd of Bards in their druidic robes.

DYLAN THOMAS AND LAUGHARNE

One of Wales's cultural giants, Dylan Thomas (1914–1953) penned *A Child's Christmas in Wales* as well as the autobiographical short stories of *Portrait of the Artist as a Young Dog* (1940). Born in Swansea, he worked as a newspaper reporter and from 1938 he stayed and eventually settled in the village of Laugharne (northwest of Swansea). The boathouse which he made his haven and the adjacent shed in which he wrote (and drank heavily) now form a museum, with photographs and furniture on display. He is buried in the churchyard.

Dylan Thomas summed up perfectly the eccentricity and claustrophobia of small-town Welsh life in his play *Under Milk Wood*. The action is set in Llareggub, a mythical fishing community whose name read backwards is the rude phrase "bugger all." One of its residents, the Reverend Eli Jenkins, captures the emotional exuberance of Welsh culture with his cry "Praise the Lord! We are a musical nation!" Music and poetry have an influence which is recognised and nurtured in Wales. The famous male-voice choirs, some of which now perform and record all over the world, are still rooted in the close-knit mining communities of South Wales and the farming and slate-mining areas of the north; and the *Eisteddfod* (presided over by Bards chosen for their contributions to Welsh life), a well-known celebration of Welsh culture, is an important focus for the 500,000 or so Welsh-speakers in Wales (see panel).

The Welsh language The survival of this ancient Celtic language—one of Europe's oldest—does much to explain the defensive pride of the Welsh. Banned from use in official channels by Henry VIII, one of the Welsh Tudor dynasty, the language lived on in the home and in the arts. Fluency in English became essential for anyone wishing to get ahead in life and many parents with ambitions for their children favored and encouraged its use. But Welsh continued to be the language of worship and as Nonconformist chapels (especially Baptist and Methodist denominations) sprang up in the wake of religious revival, it survived as the linchpin of many communities.

Political issues With new generations came new attitudes, and the 20th century saw a battle to reestablish Welsh education. Plaid Cymru, a Welsh nationalist party (which now has four M.P.s in Westminster), began in the 1920s calling for a return to the agrarian, Welsh-speaking way of life—a call not welcomed by the struggling industrial communities of South Wales, where socialism still has a firm hold.

In the 1960s and 1970s, nationalism took a more radical turn, as young members of Cymdeithas yr Iaith Gymraeg (the Welsh Language Society) kept the "language issue" in the headlines with acts such as painting out anglicized place-names on road signs. In

recent years the language has enjoyed a revival—it's now included in the statutory school curriculum, a Welsh TV channel has been established, and a lively pop culture has developed, willing to absorb the dreaded Anglo-American influence. Today you will hear Welsh spoken by both children and their elders in much of North and West Wales particularly and Welsh is taught at schools.

The current hot political issue in Wales is the influx of English people and the decline of traditional Welsh communities. For example, English "incomers" living on the northern Lleyn peninsula have been issued with threats and deadlines for leaving the country, but the intermittent arson attacks on such buildings seem to have ceased. Most Welsh people are quick to condemn these acts, which veil the very real fears of communities whose younger generations are leaving in search of work, while cottages are sold at unaffordable prices to absent landlords and stand empty for half the year, turning once vibrant areas into sad and ghostly places.

Conflict in the field For a glimpse of the whole Welsh nation at its sentimental and raucous best, try to get hold of a ticket for one of the international rugby matches at the Millennium Stadium in winter—preferably Wales vs England, when rivalry is strong and emotions are high. Hearing a stadium full of fans singing the Welsh anthem before watching their national game can bring a lump to the throat—whatever the final score might be.

Part of the Eisteddfod *ceremony: a handmaiden makes her offering to the crown bard*

THE "WELSH NOT"
In 1847 education commissioners visited schools in Wales. There they heard children using their native Welsh language, which they attacked as immoral and backwards. A campaign to stamp out the use of Welsh was rigorously pursued—often by the Welsh themselves. Pupils overheard slipping into the language were forced to wear wooden boards around their necks bearing the words "Welsh Not." The commission's report, bound between blue covers, was never really forgiven and has passed into Welsh history as the Treason of the Blue Books.

162

CASTLES OF GOWER

Like southern Pembrokeshire, Gower has been a "little England beyond Wales," with a long history of English-speaking. In the 12th century the Normans held Gower and built a chain of castles, of which remains exist at Oxwich, Oystermouth, Pennard, Penrice, and Weobley. Cadw maintain Oxwich, a 16th-century courtyard house, and Weobley, a medieval fortified manor house perched by the marshy north coast.

TAKING THE WATERS

Llandrindod Wells, Builth Wells, Llangammarch Wells, and Llanwrtyd Wells are the spa towns of Mid Wales. Back in 1732, Rev. Theophilus Evans tried the highly sulphurous waters and thus found a cure for his skin ailment. Chalybeate and saline springs were discovered close by and the area became known as a place for taking the waters. A Mrs. Jenkins found a sulphur source in 1736 at Llandrindod and by the 1830s Llangammarch was offering barium chloride as a remedy for heart conditions.

Llandrindod Wells: its hotels recall its heyday as a spa

►► Gower 150A2

(Swansea tourist information centre tel: 01792 468321)

The Gower Peninsula stretches out west of Swansea. The residential and industrial outskirts of that city abruptly give way to green countryside, and a coast that, on its southern seaboard, is the rival of Pembrokeshire (see pages 165–166). It has great limestone cliffs and superb sandy beaches, followed for their length by a coastal path, while the north seaboard is low-lying and marshy.

The western tip is the best part of all: here **Rhossili Down►►**, a moorland ridge with views of the entire peninsula, dips to a seemingly endless beach; westwards stretches **Worms Head**, a high-tide island accessible on foot by those courageous enough. Nearby, **Mewslade Bay►►** shows rock strata tilted and folded. Further east are more good beaches at **Oxwich Bay** and at tiny **Brandy Cove**. Gower oddities include **Llanrhidian village**, with a mysteriously carved leper stone in the church and a village green dominated by a pair of gigantic stones.

► Llandrindod Wells 151C3

(Tourist information centre tel: 01597 822600)

A rare instance of a spa town whose traditions are still alive. A few years ago Llandrindod's Victorian pump-room was semiderelict; today it stands proudly in restored state, and you can sample the rusty-tasting waters spurting from a nearby fountain. Grand red-brick terraces and spa hotels, ornate wrought-iron arcades and balconies, and spacious tree-lined streets suggest something larger than a town of under 5,000 in the heart of Mid Wales sheep country.

Cefnllys► is an Iron Age hill fort situated above the River Ithon beside a lone church and the (now robust) Shaky Bridge. There is a nature trail along the river. The **Beulah to Abergwesyn road►►**, an old drovers' road to the southwest of the town, takes a spectacular course over the wilderness of the Cambrian Mountains.

Towards New Radnor, the quaintly named waterfall **Water-Break-Its-Neck►** is to be found north of the A44 in Radnor Forest, a lonely massif of rounded hills and steep-sided valleys. **Old Radnor Church►** is possibly the finest parish church in Wales, with a medieval screen, Britain's oldest organ case, and a font hewn from a prehistoric monolith. Little has changed for 200 years in the border town of **Presteigne►**, which has another impressive

church. In Broad Street the **Judge's Lodging▶ ▶** adjoins the former (criminal) assize court, which are the subject of a lively museum, with an audio tour taking you around the house where circuit judges used to stay.

▶ ▶ Llangollen, Vale of   150D4

(Llangollen tourist information centre tel: 01978 860828)
This deep valley, hemmed in by natural terraces of limestone crags, is a landmark on the A5. From it the A542 rises up the hairpin bends of the **Horseshoe Pass**, engineered by Thomas Telford. **Llangollen** itself, site of the international musical *eisteddfod* (see panel), is of little intrinsic interest but is a busy tourist centre, a convenient base for a number of attractions. On the valley floor stand the picturesque ruins of **Valle Crucis Abbey▶** (Cadw), a Cistercian foundation of 1201; notable features are the Early English west facade and the vaulted 14th-century chapter house. A wooden roof installed in St. Gollen's in Llangollen is said to have been taken from here. On the edge of Llangollen, horse-drawn barge trips operate along the **Llangollen Canal**; the canal's proudest moment occurs farther east as it crosses 126 feet above the valley on the Pontcysyllte Aqueduct, built by Telford in 1805. Steam and diesel trains on the **Llangollen Railway** run 9 miles along the valley. Above town is the so-called **Panorama Walk**, really a small road. You can get even better views, extending to the Berwyn Hills, by climbing up to the spectacularly sited 13th-century ruins of **Castell Dinas Bran▶ ▶**.

The view from Castell Dinas Bran, looking towards the limestone buttresses that tower above the Vale of Llangollen

THE LLANGOLLEN INTERNATIONAL EISTEDDFOD
Established in 1947, this *eisteddfod* (see panel, page 160) has become a major international musical competition, now attracting competitors from some 30 countries. The hugely popular event takes place in the first week of July. During this time, informal performances by groups of musicians and dancers take place on the Dee Bridge.

Wind turbine at the Centre for Alternative Technology

Right: Pistyll Rhayader, Wales' most spectacular waterfall

THE CENTRE FOR ALTERNATIVE TECHNOLOGY
The center was established in 1974 as a place for promoting environmentally friendly technologies. A water-powered cliffside train whisks you up to the site entrance and a trail takes you around an informative exhibition that includes an energy-efficient house, ecologically oriented gardens, and displays of solar heating and other alternative energy sources. Although obviously an idealized setup, the center is a great place for talking to people (several workers live on site) and learning how to cut your energy bills, improve your garden, and give a greener tinge to your lifestyle. Plenty of appeal for children, too.

Just south of town, **Plas Newydd**▶ ▶ (N.T.) is a remarkable mock-Tudor inspiration, home for half a century starting in 1780 to eccentric recluses Lady Eleanor Butler and Miss Sarah Ponsonby, the "Ladies of Llangollen." They transformed a cottage into this remarkable half-timbered house, where they entertained a distinguished number of guests, including Sir Walter Scott and the Duke of Wellington. The house is whimsical in the extreme and full of personal touches.

Pistyll Rhayader▶, Wales's tallest waterfall, is at the head of a remote valley south of Llangollen. The fall has been engineered to give the water a twist as it tumbles, but the effect is pleasing. There is easy access by road.

▶**Machynlleth**   *151C3*
(Tourist information centre tel: 01654 702401)
A market town centered on a clock tower (of a design that seems to be mandatory for Welsh towns), Machynlleth is comfortably set in the peaceful hills south of the Snowdonia National Park. It is an uneventful place in a pleasant kind of way. The town's hinterland is partly inhabited by a significant hippie population. Topping the bill of local attractions is the excellent **Centre for Alternative Technology**▶ ▶ (see panel).

The scenic **Machynlleth–Dylife road**▶ runs over the shoulder of Plynlimon, a boggy upland from which rise the Wye and the Severn, the two great rivers of Wales. At **Dylife** a stream plummets into a gorge via Ffrwd Fawr, a splendid waterfall. A scenic viewpoint at a curve in the road takes in Cader Idris, the major summit in southern Snowdonia. It is worth continuing past **Llyn Clywedog reservoir** to the unspoiled town of **Llanidloes**▶.

▶▶▶ **Pembrokeshire Coast National Park**   *150B1*
(tel: 01437 764636)

As its name implies, the national park is largely confined to a coastal strip. Here are magnificent cliffs, sandy coves (many excellent for swimming if you can stand the chilly water), complex natural harbors, and a diversity of wildlife which ranks on a par with the best of Cornwall. The south and north parts of the park are strikingly different: a wave-cut platform, now raised high above sea level, leaves the southern cliffs mostly level-topped, while further north the scene is more exciting, with assertive bluffs, soaring headlands, and dramatic variations in height. Southern Pembrokeshire was for a long time a "little England beyond Wales," owned by the English, who left a legacy of English place-names and Norman castles for keeping watch over the unruly Welsh. Regrettably, the army's foothold on the south coast in the vicinity of Castlemartin means restricted access. Walking is the main draw of the north, which is less populated and consequently less busy in season. Scenic drives are few—the roads generally keep too far inland; a better bet is to take in some of the coastal path, which snakes around the intricate seaboard for some 180 miles. A car will get you into the wilds of the Preseli Hills (see page 166).

TOWNS AND VILLAGES Most famous is undoubtedly **St. David's▶▶▶**. Scarcely more than a large village of craft stores, galleries, and cafés, it keeps its great Norman cathedral half-hidden in a valley, alongside the considerable ruins of a 14th-century bishop's palace (Cadw). Allegedly, relics of St. David, patron saint of Wales, lie beneath the altar. Of the coastal towns, **Tenby▶▶** is perhaps the most appealing, with its maze of narrow streets, a harbor surrounded by tiers of color-washed Georgian and Tudor merchants' houses, a castle up the hill and a five-arched gate in the town wall. It is very pretty—and it suffers badly for that in summer, with bumper-to-bumper traffic. **Pembroke▶** is less important than its name suggests, a one-street market town completely dominated by an exceptional Norman castle, which has a 75-foot tower and tunnels to explore.

A boat trip leaves Martin's Haven for Skomer Island

ISLAND HOPS
Skokholm and Skomer are major bird sanctuaries, supporting the largest concentration of Manx shearwaters in Britain. Puffins abound on Skomer while Skokholm has a population of storm petrels. Boat trips start from Martin's Haven. Ramsey Island has lots of grey seals, (which can also be seen off the mainland) and cliff-nesting birds including choughs; boat trips begin from St. Justinian. Caldey Island, reached by boat from Tenby, is home to a community of Cistercian monks.

165

CASTELL HENLLYS
A finely placed Iron Age hill-fort east of Newport, Castell Henllys now is a museum re-creating the lifestyles of its original inhabitants. Iron Age round huts have been reconstructed, and actors demonstrate such crafts as weaving and iron forging.

St. David's Cathedral: 39 steps (or "Articles") lead down to its door

166

THE PRESELI HILLS
The national park also encompasses the Preseli Hills (or Mynydd Preseli), a tract of remote upland near Fishguard that is scattered with the burial mounds and hill forts of early settlers. It was from here that the bluestone rocks were transported to Wiltshire for the construction of Stonehenge (see page 84), a feat that has baffled archaeologists. The rocks may have been moved by raft (this is technically feasible), but more plausible perhaps is the theory that they were naturally moved closer to Stonehenge by glaciers during the last ice age, possibly as far as the Somerset Mendips.

Fishguard is split in two by the lie of the land, with the lower town crowded around the harbor and the upper town grouped around sloping streets. Ferries depart from Goodwick to Rosslare in Ireland (99 mins by catamaran). The village of **Solva**▶ is a boating center and one-time port prettily set at the end of a narrow, steep-sided bay.

THE BEST OF THE COAST In the south, the indented headlands and bays around **Dale** and **Milford Haven** (itself an industrial port adjacent to oil refineries, but worth seeing for its natural harbor site) have constantly changing views, while **Wooltack Point**▶▶ near Marloes has views across to Skomer and Skokholm islands. At **Bosherston** a series of **lily ponds**▶ makes a popular walk which can be tacked onto a visit to a fine beach. On the margins of some luscious estuary landscape east of Milford Haven is **Carew Castle**, adjacent to a tide mill and a superb 11th-century Celtic cross. Perched among Pembrokeshire's cliffs are three primitive hermitage chapels, **St. Govan's**, just west of St. Govan's Head, **St. Justinian's** and **St. Non's** (both near St. David's). **St. David's Head**▶▶ and **Strumble Head**▶ have rugged grandeur; it is sometimes possible to see the Wicklow Mountains in Ireland from these. Among the most popular swimming beaches are **St Bride's Bay**, **Tenby, Saundersfoot,** and **Whitesands Bay**, but there are numerous smaller ones offering greater privacy.

▶▶ Powis Castle   151D4
(tel: 01938 557018)

A great border stronghold, owned by the Herbert family from 1587 to 1952, Powis (N.T.) stands just outside Welshpool. It is memorable for its superb gardens (terraced in the 18th century), its architectural diversity through centuries of changes and its lavish state apartments.

Montgomery▶ is more English than Welsh in character: the tiny town center focuses on a gracious square with an 18th-century town hall and an assemblage of red-brick Elizabethan facades. The castle mound above town was the stronghold of Roger de Montgomery, who in the 13th century launched assaults on the Welsh.

THE WELSHPOOL AND LLANFAIR LIGHT RAILWAY
The privately operated steam train operates along 8 miles of track between Welshpool and Llanfair Caereinion. Its chief distinguishing features are the narrow 30-inch gauge, and the antique wooden cars from the Zillertal in Austria and 1961 carriages from Sierra Leone.

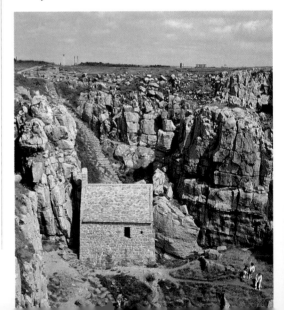

Tiny St. Govan's Chapel, tucked into the cliffs, can be reached on foot by taking the coastal path from Bosherston Lily Ponds

MOUNTAIN SAFETY
Beware! The Snowdonia mountains may not compete in height with the Alps or the Rockies, but they are full of dangers and have claimed many lives. Be sure to be appropriately dressed and equipped; check the weather forecast, take a good map, compass, and provisions, and tackle only those walks well within your abilities. Leave a note with your hotel of where you are going and when you intend to return.

Classic postglacial scenery: the towering form of Y Garn, seen across Llyn (Lake) Ogwen

touring southern Snowdonia and it has some excellent easier walks on its doorstep, including Cregennan Lakes at the foot of Cader Idris, the old railroad track along the magnificent Mawddach Estuary and the Precipice Walk (hair-raising for those with young children) above the Mawddach Gorge. Further west, near the coastal resort of Barmouth, the railroad bridge across the Mawddach includes a footpath that makes a highly memorable walk in its own right.

THE MAJOR PEAKS The king of them all, **Snowdon** (Yr Wddfa in Welsh) rises high and majestic to 3,560 feet, five ridges (known collectively as Eryri, "abode of eagles") radiating from its central pyramid. Not surprisingly, this is the most popular mountain ascent, not just because it is the highest but also because of the views both on the way up and from the top. Paths approach from all directions, or you can cheat and use the Snowdon Mountain Railway (see page 167); the route from Llanberis, parallel to the railroad, is the easiest but least interesting path, while the Horseshoe Route (along knife-edge ridges) is the most enthralling and demanding, definitely not for the inexperienced. The first half of the Miners' Track from Pen y Pass (see page 170) takes you into the wilds, rising past lakes and abandoned copper mines to a splendid corrie beneath the summit and main ascent—this initial stage provides an unchallenging way of sampling a great mountain route.

▶▶▶ Snowdonia National Park 151D3
(tel: 01776 770274)

Snowdonia is unsurpassed among the national parks of England and Wales for the wild drama of its scenery. Ideal for walking, rock-climbing, and horseback riding, it has a fair offering of scenic drives, although these tend to be confined to valley routes and are limited in scope.

The main mountain group is quite compact, centered on Snowdon, the highest point in England and Wales. Perhaps the hallmark of Snowdonia is the individuality of each of the main summits: each has its distinctive shape, and visitors soon find their personal favorites. Snowdonia's coast is disappointing, ribboned as it is by main roads and with no cliffs to speak of. Sightseeing interest, on the other hand, is particularly rich, with a host of nostalgic railroads, old mines, and castles built by Edward I in the 13th century to control the Welsh.

THE MAIN CENTERS In northern Snowdonia **Betws-y-coed** (pronounced Bettus-ee coe-ed) is a touristy village of Victorian hotels and craft stores. It has grand scenery on its doorstep and walks along the River Llugwy and the Swallow Falls and a series of attractive reservoirs close by to the west; the big mountains keep hidden, however. Also central and with a touch more charm, the Victorian mountain resort village of **Beddgelert▶** lies close to the Aberglaslyn Gorge, Moel Hebog, and Snowdon. A much-publicized but probably bogus attraction here is Gelert's Grave, Gelert being the noble 13th-century Prince Llywelyn's dog. A tour can be taken around **Sygun Copper Mine▶▶**, which has formations of stalactites and stalagmites. Bala gets busy in high season; Wales' largest lake adjoins it, but the scenery is not quite so stupendous.

Of the resorts on the north coast **Llandudno▶** is by far the most attractive. It's one of Britain's best-preserved Victorian coastal towns, with its elegant curving bay, its pier, Punch and Judy shows on the sands, and a mountain tram up to Great Ormes Head. **Conwy▶▶▶**, also on the coast but a historic walled town, is the most rewarding town for casual wandering, with a splendid castle (Cadw), an elegant suspension bridge designed by Thomas Telford (N.T.), and a house that claims to be Britain's smallest. **Caernarfon▶▶**, too, boasts a great castle and is a place everyone should try to visit (although for some it may be too far out to serve as a base). **Harlech▶▶** straddles a slope above marshland, one of the few portions of this coast not to be followed by a main road; good beaches lie to the south. The castle is the spectacular attraction.

Mountains of slate scraps surround **Blaenau Ffestiniog**, at the heart of the Snowdonia slate industry. Although not pretty it has curiosity value and is in the center; it is establishing itself as a tourist town now that the **Llechwedd Slate Caverns▶▶** have been opened to the public . At **Llanberis** is the **Welsh Slate Museum▶** and a branch of the National Museum of Wales, **Dinorwic Discovery▶** which offers trips to the "Electric Mountain," underground hydroelectric storage station. There are also tours at the active Ffestiniog Power Station near Blaenau Ffestiniog.

Dolgellau▶, the only town inside the national park, is a place of gray-stone houses and narrow streets; life revolves around its marketplace. It makes a good base for

167

GREAT LITTLE TRAINS OF SNOWDONIA
The **Snowdon Mountain Railway** climbs 3,280 feet from Llanberis to the summit. Many people walk back down. **Ffestiniog Railway**, built for the slate industry and now one of the most scenic of all Britain's private railroads, runs from Porthmadog to Blaenau Ffestiniog, while the **Talyllyn Railway** runs inland from Tywyn to Nant Gwernol. **Bala Lake** and **Llanberis Lake** railroads run alongside the lakes from which they take their names. The shorter **Welsh Highland Railway** starts from Porthmadog.

CADW MEMBERSHIP
Most of the great castles of Wales—including Conwy, Caernarfon, Harlech, Beaumaris, and Dolbadarn—and other ancient monuments are in the care of Cadw, the Welsh Historic Monuments Commission. Cadw (tel: 029 2082 6174) offers 3-day, weekly, and annual passes for its properties.

Almost as high as Snowdon and just as spectacular are **Glyder Fawr** (3,277 feet) and **Glyder Fach** (3,261 feet), two peaks on a great ridge with rock pinnacles and precipitous drops; the **Carneddau group** and (lower but with good views) **Moel Siabod** (2,861 feet). The southern giant is **Cader Idris** (2,930 feet), a sprawling mass with some reassuringly gentle slopes but huge panoramas.

Caernarfon Castle, where the monarch invests with the eldest royal son with the title of Prince of Wales

HOUSES, CASTLES AND GARDENS Penrhyn Castle▶▶ (N.T.) is an imposing mock-Norman structure built by slate magnate Lord Penrhyn in the mid-19th century; architect Thomas Hopper gave it battlements and turrets and a grandiose interior which epitomizes high living of the period. Genuine castles abound in Snowdonia. Most famous of all is **Caernarfon Castle**▶▶▶ (Cadw), begun in 1283 after Edward I's conquest of Wales. It was the setting in 1969 for the investiture of the Prince of Wales; his investiture robes are on show here, together with a display of the dynasty of the Welsh princes. **Harlech Castle**▶▶ (Cadw), also founded in 1283, has a fine site above the coast; although seemingly impregnable it was taken by Owain Glyndwr in 1404. **Conwy Castle**▶▶▶ (Cadw), another of Edward I's foundations, is sited in the town wall; it has 21 semicircular towers and overlooks a castellated suspension bridge, one of some 1,200 bridges designed by Thomas Telford between 1792 and his death in 1834. Less substantial, but set among the hills, are the castles of **Dolwyddelan**▶ (Cadw, near Blaenau Ffestiniog) and **Castell y Bere**▶ (Cadw, near Abergynolwyn).

Bodnant Garden▶▶ (N.T.), near Llanrwst, rates among Britain's finest horticultural creations. Try to visit **Portmeirion**▶▶, an Italianate fantasy village created in the 20th century by Clough Williams-Ellis to show that a scenic site could be developed and retain its beauty. It has often been used as a film set; the cult TV series *The Prisoner* was made here.

The Canal Terrace, Bodnant Garden

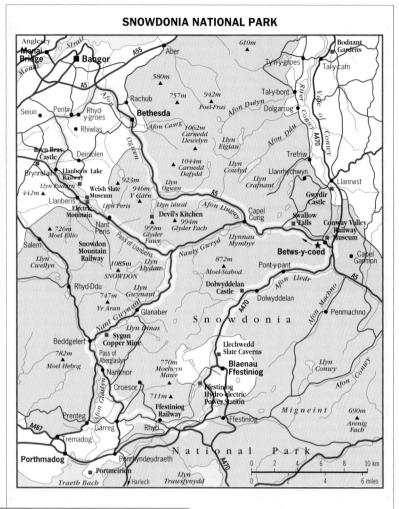

SNOWDONIA NATIONAL PARK

Drive

Snowdonia National Park

A circuit of the grandest uplands in Wales (approx 65 miles).

Start at **Betws-y-coed** and take the A5 past the entrance to the spectacular **Swallow Falls**▶ to Capel Curig. Continue past Llyn (lake) Ogwen; from the parking lot at its far end, a short path leads to **Llyn Idwal**▶▶, beneath the vast crags of the Devil's Kitchen (see Walks, page 158). Beyond the mining town of **Bethesda** take the B4409, then the A4086 past **Llanberis**, base station for the **Snowdon Mountain Railway**▶. At the top of the **Llanberis Pass**, the Miners' Track and Pyg Track leave for an exciting ascent of **Snowdon**. Continue on the A498 past **Beddgelert**▶ and along the **Pass of Aberglaslyn**. Take the B4410 and A496 to **Blaenau Ffestiniog**, passing **Ffestiniog Power Station**▶ and **Llechwedd Slate Caverns**▶▶. **Dolwyddelan Castle**▶, further up the valley (A470), is supposedly the birthplace of Prince Llewellyn the Great.

The River Wye, as seen from Symonds Yat, near the end of its journey

SONS OF MONMOUTH
Henry V was born in Monmouth Castle, of which nothing now remains, in 1387. Before the Battle of Agincourt he gained the nickname Harry of Monmouth. The central plaza is named Agincourt Square in his honor.
Charles Rolls was a pioneer of early aviation, engineering and motoring who was a partner in Rolls-Royce. In 1910 he became the first Briton to die in a flying accident. His statue outside the town hall holds aloft a model airplane, and the town museum has a section devoted to his life.

▶▶ Wye Valley   151B4

(Monmouth tourist information center tel: 01600 713899)

The River Wye defines the English/Welsh border for its glorious finale as it enters a sandstone gorge whose slopes are cloaked with woodlands that display breathtaking colors in the autumn. Once the gorge was a hive of industrial activity, the trees supplying charcoal for iron-smelting; brass was invented here in 1568. The valley established a name for itself during the late 18th-century Romantic movement, whose poets sought a deeper appreciation of the beauties of nature. **Ross-on-Wye**, though not in the gorge proper, has a mock-Gothic town wall built in the 1830s at the time of this "picturesque discovery." Its arcaded market house is two centuries older. **Symonds Yat▶**, a rock reached by a stairway, overlooks a bend of the Wye; paths lead down to the river, which is crossed by chain ferry (see Walks on page 158). **Goodrich Castle▶** (E.H.) is an impressive 12th-century sandstone bulk, intact until a Parliamentary siege in the Civil War.

The Monnow flows into the Wye at **Monmouth▶**, the Monnow spanned by a medieval bridge with a fortified gateway. The **Nelson Museum** is a collection devoted to Nelson, including his letters and sword. Above the town, a rustic folly commemorating admirals of the Napoleonic wars caps **Kymin Hill▶**, a good place for views. Turner painted and Wordsworth revered the ruins of **Tintern Abbey▶▶▶** (Cadw), an ancient Cistercian foundation set on the valley floor. It is roofless, but standing to its original height and with exquisite tracery in its east window.

Chepstow has a formidable Norman **castle▶▶** (Cadw) with keep and mighty outer wall. The main street rises up to a gateway in the Port Walls, the town wall. Above the east bank, **Wintour's Leap** is a quarried cliff face by the road with a dizzying drop to the river, while the **Wynd Cliff▶**, on the west bank, offers a wider view.

One of the world's first iron bridges—the Regency Bridge over the Wye, at Chepstow

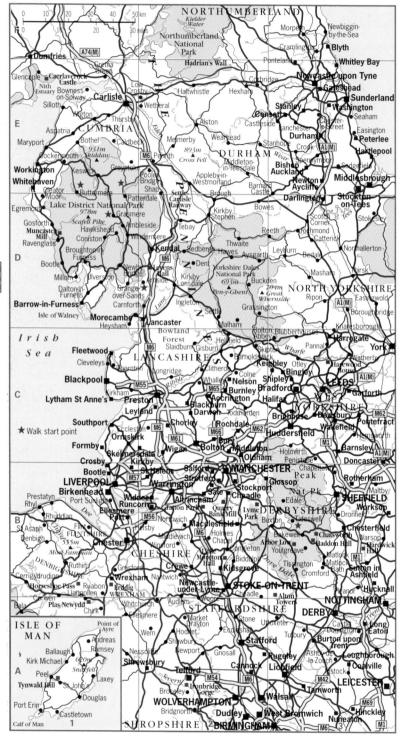

NORTHWEST ENGLAND This strip covers the region from the industrial northern Midlands to the Scottish border. The most hallowed feature is doubtless the **Lake District**, within the northerly county of Cumbria.

LAKE DISTRICT DELIGHTS Here the lakes, high fells (mountains), pastures, and woodlands offer constantly changing vistas of peerless scenic beauty. It is all at a perfect scale for exploration on foot, as equally suited for those wanting a gentle saunter with the mountains as a backdrop as for aspiring rock-climbers. Another option available is to take a boat trip on one of the lakes. Roads and parking lots get annoyingly busy in peak periods, but out of season driving is a delight. Public transport is also feasible (Ambleside and Keswick would make good bases), though it restricts what can be visited. The Lake District scores highly for quantity and quality of hotels, for the range of sights suitable for those all-too-frequent rainy days, and for the scope of other outdoor activities, which include sailing, mountain biking, horseback riding, and angling (swimming in the lakes is discouraged because of undercurrents). As a general rule, the western Lake District has more in the way of spectacle and wildness, while the east is milder, more crowded and has more indoor sights.

THE REST OF CUMBRIA Outside the Lake District, the rest of Cumbria offers a long and not especially beautiful coastline, but an interesting one: along it are the early industrial town of Whitehaven, well worth a visit; St. Bees Head (ideal for birdwatching); and the free visitor center at Sellafield nuclear reprocessing plant, set up to woo support for the nuclear industry. Northern Cumbria is fairly flat, but it has nice views across the Solway Firth to southern Scotland and the historic city of Carlisle. Southern Cumbria is fringed by the great expanse of Morecambe Bay, an important site for wading birds and the setting for Britain's fastest incoming tides; tourist offices have details of guided walks over the bay (follow routes precisely to avoid the quicksand).

LANCASHIRE, MERSEYSIDE, AND GREATER MANCHESTER The more built-up parts of Morecambe Bay lie within **Lancashire**—Blackpool, Morecambe, and Southport were developed as resorts to serve the cotton-mill towns that

Below (left): Dove Dale, the best-known limestone valley in the Peak District, deserves time to be savored in full

Below: maintaining the dry-stone walls of the region's farmland

Northwest England

RECOMMENDED HISTORIC TOWNS AND CITIES
Cheshire: Chester.
Derbyshire: Buxton.
Cumbria: Carlisle, Cockermouth, Kendal, Kirkby Lonsdale, Whitehaven.
SCENERY
Lake District, Peak District, Isle of Man, Forest of Bowland, Morecambe Bay (north side).
TRAIN RIDES
Settle to Carlisle; Arnside to Ulverston; Barrow-in-Furness to Whitehaven; Ravenglass to Boot (narrow gauge).

View across Morecambe Bay

▶▶▶ **REGION HIGHLIGHTS**

Chester *page 177*
The Lake District National Park *pages 178–181*
Little Moreton Hall *page 189*
Liverpool *page 182*
Peak National Park *pages 186–187*
Quarry Bank Mill *page 189*
Stoke-on-Trent Potteries *page 189*

sprang up in the 19th century. Those mill towns changed the face of the county and heralded a major phase in the industrialization of Britain. The mills have closed or changed to other uses, but these urban landscapes, immortalised by the paintings of L. S. Lowry (see panel, page 183), still exist, the straight lines of millworkers' terraces being their dominant feature: Burnley and Accrington are examples. Manchester and Liverpool were the great cities created by this expansion; today Manchester is more prosperous, but Liverpool wins on museums and atmosphere. The Forest of Bowland in northern Lancashire is, despite its name, a tract of high, open country, with fine, rugged walks and exhilarating views.

CHESHIRE, DERBYSHIRE, AND STAFFORDSHIRE Cheshire extends from the Welsh border to the brink of the Peak National Park; between lies a fertile plain, pockmarked by tiny lakes and ponds called meres. Black and white half-timbering and red brick are predominant building materials, seen to best advantage in Chester, remarkable for its intact city walls. Cheshire, Staffordshire, Derbyshire and South Yorkshire share the **Peak District**, a very accessible and popular national park; although it cannot match the Lake District for scenery, it has limestone dales, austere gritstone moors, caverns, the contrasting houses of Chatsworth and Haddon Hall, and some charming villages, many of which indulge in the ancient annual custom of "well dressing" (see panel on page 186). Other houses in **Derbyshire** include Calke Abbey and Hardwick Hall. Although undistinguished visually, Derby has a number of good museums; Derby porcelain is on display at the Derby Museum and at Royal Crown Derby, and an 18th-century silk mill houses the Industrial Museum. Stoke-on-Trent (**Staffordshire**) is the china-making capital.

Walks

Arnside Knott, Cumbria · 172D2

Parking lot by seafront at Arnside.
The wooded limestone hill is laced with paths to its summit, where a view opens out over the southern Lake District and Morecambe Bay, one of Europe's most important sites for waterbirds of the wader family. The quickest way up is southwards through the village, on residential roads that give way to paths. (1 hour)

Buttermere, Lake · 172E1
District National Park, Cumbria

Parking lot at Buttermere village.
A well-traveled path leads to Buttermere. The path which runs around the lake is straightforward and level, but is graced with a fine mountain backdrop; the path weaves out of forest, through a section of tunnel and along the water's edge (1.5 hours). Optional add-ons include the ascent of Haystacks, the jagged, dark-topped fell to the south.

Grasmere and · 172D1
Rydal Water, Lake District
National Park, Cumbria

Parking lots at Grasmere village. Seek out the path along the south side of these two lakes: walk past Grasmere Church on your right, take the left fork of the road to reach the lakeside path, which leaves the road near a boathouse. After a short wooded section, climb up to the level path along Loughrigg Terrace on your right for grandstand views of Wordsworth's valley. Either continue on around Rydal Water or head back by dropping through woods, over a bridge and the A591 to take a minor road to Wordsworth's Dove Cottage at the edge of Grasmere village. (1.5 hours)

Monsal Dale and · 172B3
Chee Dale, Peak
National Park, Derbyshire

Parking lots at Miller's Dale (old station). Turn left along the railroad track (Monsal Trail) to enter Miller's Dale; the trail swings away from the train track as it passes through a tunnel. You pass the Wye's old textile mills, rejoin the train tracks and cross Monsal viaduct (2.5 hours). In the other direction from the parking lot, the trail soon leaves the railroad track for an exciting stepping-stone route along the Wye as it enters a gorge beneath Chee Tor, a popular haunt of rock climbers. (2 hours)

Ullswater, Lake District · 172E1
National Park, Cumbria

Parking lot at Glenridding. Begin this walk by taking the lake steamer from Glenridding across to Howtown and then follow the well-traveled lakeside path back (allow approximately 4 hours); it undulates delightfully and ducks in and out of woods with sudden vistas. An optional add-on is to climb Hallin Fell, close by Howtown, by a path up its southern side.

175

A Lake District scene between Rydal Water and Grasmere

Blackpool: roller-coaster by night

THE ISLE OF MAN
Ruled by Queen Elizabeth II but not part of the U.K. (it has its own parliament), the Isle of Man has a certain curiosity value. Its residents are called Manx, as is its almost extinct Celtic language. Manx cats are naturally tailless. Located in the Irish Sea, the island does not enjoy the greatest climate and its resorts are somewhat faded. Fish-and-chips is the rule, *haute cuisine* the exception. Yet to some the isle's charms are irresistible: its coastline, particularly in the south around the fishing port of Peel and the folk museum village of Port Erin, is of high, unspoiled cliffs, while inland the hills rise dramatically. A splendid legacy of historic railroads has been preserved and the T.T. Races, an annual motorcycle event since 1907, draws large crowds. Reach the island by ferry from Liverpool, Heysham, or Fleetwood, or by air.

176

► **Blackpool**   *172C1*
(*Tourist information center tel: 01253 478222*)
In Victorian times this seaside resort was the traditional day out for millworkers from the Lancashire cotton towns, and Blackpool is still going strong in its unique, brash way. The beach suffers from pollution, but the Blackpool Pleasure Beach amusement park is Britain's most visited attraction. From the huge Blackpool Tower views extend into the Lake District from the top. Trams travel along the seafront to Fleetwood, giving the best view of the famous Illuminations (September to November).

The Citadel, a prominent landmark at the center of Carlisle

► **Carlisle**   *172E1*
(*Tourist information center tel: 01288 625600*)
Cumbria's largest town has recently spruced itself up as a regional shopping center. It does not rank among the great cathedral cities, but there is enough here for an absorbing half-day in the compact historic center.
    For centuries, Carlisle was plagued by border skirmishes and the **castle►►** (E.H.), dating from 1092, was much attacked and rebuilt (the view from its walls is stomach-churning). The keep is 12th-century; inside, the story of the Border Regiment is told with uniforms and weapons. Don't miss the graffiti carved by captives in the prison.
    Tullie House►►, an outstanding city museum, is an absorbing evocation of Carlisle's past. Also in the center are some good Georgian and earlier streets and the medieval **cathedral►**, one of Britain's smallest, notable above all for its east window with its 14th-century glass. Also worth a brief look is the **Guildhall**, which is a striking timber-framed survival dating back to 1407.
    The scenic **Settle–Carlisle line►►**, part of the nation's railroad network, was saved in recent years by a campaign of volunteers. From Settle, in the Yorkshire Dales, the route

crosses the high Pennines in spectacular fashion, over the Ribblehead Viaduct in the shadow of Whernside and along the Eden Valley. Special steam trains sometimes run on the route. By far the most dramatic landscape is between Settle and Appleby-in-Westmorland, which has a fine castle.

▶▶▶ Chester   172B1

(Tourist information center tel: 01244 402111)

Founded as the Roman city of *Deva*, Chester was a major port until the River Dee silted up in medieval times. Its fortunes then slumped until a revival in the 18th century. Today, it has plenty to show for these three periods.

Foremost is the **city wall**▶▶▶, one of the finest in the country, which provides a fascinating 2-mile walk, raised above street level for much of the way. A number of its gateways are still in place and Roman masonry can be seen, although much of the wall is medieval. A superb set of Roman tombstones are exhibited at the **Grosvenor Museum**▶▶ (*Admission free*). By **Newgate**, on the east side, part of the **Roman amphitheater** (Britain's largest) can be seen near a park, but more evocative is the **Deva Roman Experience**▶▶, where Roman streets are reconstructed with sounds and smells, and there are displays of local finds and a hands-on section.

Of medieval Chester, the most famous feature is **The Rows**, which has an upper tier of shops with its own walkway above street level. Nobody quite knows why it developed this way, but today it is a thriving shopping area. The central streets harbor a pleasing mix of half-timbered Tudor, red-brick Georgian, and exuberantly elaborate 19th-century fake black-and-white buildings. Chester's Victoriana also includes a Gothic-style **town hall**, where the Council Chamber and Assembly Rooms are open to the public, on Northgate Street. The red sandstone **cathedral**▶▶ was restored in the 19th century, but its superbly carved 14th-century choir stalls are unaltered. Many of the abbey buildings survived the Reformation in the 16th century, including the chapter house and cloisters.

Chester Zoo▶▶ is 3 miles up the A41. Animals roam in enclosures that simulate natural environments.

A WALK ALONG CHESTER'S WALLS: PART 1
From Grosvenor Bridge (the largest single span in the world when erected in 1832), take a counter-clockwise tour of the walls, crossing Bridgegate with its pleasant boating scene a little east (boat rentals available). The walls now turn north, past Newgate and the Roman amphitheater, over Eastgate with its ornamental clock of 1897.

A WALK ALONG CHESTER'S WALLS: PART 2
Skirt the cathedral precincts (Abbey Square); the northeast tower is known as the King Charles Tower since that king watched from here the defeat of his army by the Parliamentarians on Rowton Heath in 1645. By Northgate the drop on the canal side plummets spectacularly; on the south side is the Bluecoat Hospital (1717) and the sideless Bridge of Sighs, which condemned felons had to cross on their way to prison. From the Water Tower (1322) are views of the Welsh hills. The west side of the walls (where you must follow the road) has less of interest.

Chester's Victorian mock-Tudor streetscape, as seen from The Rows

The Lake District National Park—Lakeland, the English Lakes, or just the Lakes, call it what you will—is a microcosm of breathtaking variety and scenic perfection. Its character wavers between windswept mountainous upland and dry-stone-walled, lowland pastures. It is outstanding for outdoor pursuits, particularly walking, climbing and sailing, but the climate can be fickle: benign-looking summer days have a habit of clouding over suddenly. Fortunately the area has plenty of indoor attractions, especially for those on a literary pilgrimage.

178

LITERARY LAKELAND
William Wordsworth was born in Cockermouth in 1770, and a happy childhood there was to influence his poetry in later life. His favorite home was Dove Cottage, in Grasmere, where he lived from 1799 to 1808. He loved the place deeply and wrote about the area; aptly, he is buried in Grasmere churchyard.

The Wordsworths were the center of a group of friends, among them poet Samuel Taylor Coleridge. Alfred, Lord Tennyson reputedly wrote *Idylls of the King* at Mirehouse, near Keswick; later, poet Matthew Arnold and critic John Ruskin both lived here.

Beatrix Potter wrote and illustrated her children's stories at Hill Top in Near Sawrey. Arthur Ransome set his *Swallows and Amazons* in the Lakes.

LAKELAND GEOLOGY
The district is formed out of a huge volcanic dome, pushed out from within the earth, subsequently overlain with rocks and sculpted by glaciers into valleys and corries. The Skiddaw Slates, found in northwest Lakeland, make up green slopes, while the volcanic Borrowdale rocks include rugged fells. Limestone predominates in the eastern tracts.

Lake District National Park tel: 01539 446604

THE NORTH AND WEST Keswick▶, the major center for the northern lakes, is a gray-slate Victorian town, full of walkers, tourists, bed-and-breakfast signs, and outdoor sport stores. Here are the traditional **Keswick Museum and Art Gallery** (with its "piano" of Cumberland slates), and a unique pencil museum. Just east is the prehistoric **Castlerigg Stone Circle▶**. The beauties of **Derwent Water▶▶** can be appreciated from a public boat or from a shoreside path past Friar's Crag.

Borrowdale appealed to early discoverers of the "picturesque"; Castle Crag is a good vantage point. The main road over **Honister Pass** skirts **Buttermere▶▶▶**, magnificently located and looking like a miniature Scottish loch. **Cockermouth▶**, outside the park, is a likeable market town of colorwashed terraces and odd corners.

North of Keswick, the fells flatten and the crowds disappear, but the moors have a quiet beauty of their own. **Hesket Newmarket**, with its green and its old market cross, is the prettiest village hereabouts. Southeast of Keswick, **Thirlmere▶**, a lake enlarged into a reservoir, is the most popular starting point for walks up Helvellyn (3,117 feet). The lake of **Ullswater▶▶▶** twists its way south from Pooley Bridge, the scenery getting better all the time; a steamer plies the length of the lake. By the A592, **Aira Force▶▶** is a popular waterfall, tumbling into a shady chasm at the side of Gowbarrow Park, the hill where Wordsworth saw that host of golden daffodils. East of Ullswater, **Askham▶** is a trim village of stone cottages.

The Lake District's western tracts are less accessible and are a great place to get away from it all. **Wast Water▶▶▶** is one of the great sights, looking to the heights of Great Gable, and Scafell Pike is the highest peak in England at 3,207 feet. **Eskdale▶** is mellow and broad; the narrow-gauge Ravenglass and Eskdale Railway runs along the valley to the tiny village of Boot with its restored grain mill. Just outside the coastal village of **Ravenglass** stands a Roman bathhouse known as Walls Castle. At the dale's east end, the **Hardknott Pass▶▶▶** is the great scenic drive of Lakeland; the Isle of Man may be visible from the remains of a Roman fort near the top. Drivers can continue along **Wrynose Pass** or into the **Duddon Valley**.

THE SOUTH AND EAST Windermere, England's longest lake, has wooded shores sprinkled with villas built by 19th-century industrialists; steamers serve most parts of the lake and from Lakeside at the southern end (near the Aquarium of the Lakes) a steam train runs to Haverthwaite. **Bowness-on-Windermere** is a tourist trap, clogged with traffic in summer; **Windermere town**, away from the lake, is railway-age suburbia. **Ambleside**, at the lake's northern end, is more attractive, particularly up the hill. On Windermere's shores are a number of gardens (**Holehird▶**, **Stagshaw▶**, and **Graythwaite▶**), the **Brockhole National Park Visitor Centre▶** and the **Windermere Steamboat Museum▶**.

West of Windermere, the landscape rolls gently, thickly cloaked in trees; in **Grizedale Forest** woodland paths are enhanced by modern sculptures. **Stott Park Bobbin Mill▶** (E.H.) demonstrates the process of bobbin making. Visit the village of **Hawkshead▶▶** out of season—or line up for the parking lot and join the crowds in its quaint little streets; its chief sights are the **Beatrix Potter Gallery** (N.T.), with a changing exhibition of Potter's sketches and paintings, and the **Old Grammar School**, housing the desk on which former pupil William Wordsworth carved his name. Just out of the village, **Tarn Hows▶** is a pretty, if too-visited, pair of tarns artificially merged into one as a landscape feature. Above the village of Coniston, beneath the summit of the Old Man of Coniston, are spectacular relics of its bygone copper-mining industry. Glide silently over **Coniston Water** on the National Trust's antique steam yacht, *Gondola*▶▶.

North of Ambleside, the A591 enters more mountainous terrain; **Grasmere▶▶** and its surroundings are immortalized by the works of Wordsworth (see panel, page 178). Westwards loom the craggy **Langdale Pikes**.

Further south, **Cartmel▶▶** is a handsome village, less overrun than Hawkshead, with a fine priory church. Find out about the life and industry of the Lakes at the outstanding **Museum of Lakeland Life▶▶** at Kendal (just outside the national park).

Far left: the Windermere Steamboat Museum

Bliss was it in that dawn
  to be alive,
But to be young was
  very heaven.
—*The Prelude*, William Wordsworth (1770–1850).

KNOW YOUR LAKELAND TERMS
Small lakes are called *tarns*, mountains are always *fells* (from the Nordic *fjaell*), streams are known as *becks*, spotted black-faced sheep are *Swaledales*, white-faced ones are *Herdwicks*, loose stones created by freeze-thaw weathering are termed scree. *Force* means waterfall. Bassenthwaite Lake is the only lake in Lakeland termed as such: all the others are *meres* or *waters*. "Lake Windermere" is a useful term to avoid confusion with the town of Windermere, but Lake District purists will shudder if they hear you say it!

179

Grasmere, beloved of William Wordsworth

Drive

Lake District

The best of the Lakes (approx 80 miles), taking in Wordsworth's Grasmere, spectacular high passes and the less-visited western areas.

From **Keswick** (tel: 017687 72645) the route heads south along the A591 past **Thirlmere►**, beneath the shadow of Helvellyn, and past the Wordsworths' former houses, Dove Cottage at **Grasmere►►** and Rydal Mount, **Rydal**. Turning west at the resort town of **Ambleside**, you soon enter **Langdale**, passing beneath the impressive forms of the Langdale Fells, whose slopes were once home to a neolithic axe factory. A minor road loops around the end of the dale, above Blea Tarn, to turn right onto the **Wrynose Pass**. This leads to the magnificent **Hardknott Pass►►►**, passing the substantial remains of a Roman fort on the right after the summit; drop into **Eskdale**, with glimpses of its narrow-gauge railway. Fork right to **Santon Bridge** (from where you can detour to majestic **Wast Water►►►**) and continue to **Gosforth**, with its renowned **Celtic cross►** in the churchyard. Take the A595 to **Calder Bridge**, then fork right to **Ennerdale Bridge** via a high-level road with views of the coast and **Sellafield nuclear reprocessing plant** (its visitor center is now a major draw). Beyond **Lamplugh** bear right and right again on minor roads to **Loweswater** and the B5289, where you turn right for a superb finale past **Buttermere►►►**, up the **Honister Pass**, along Borrowdale and beside **Derwent Water►►►**.

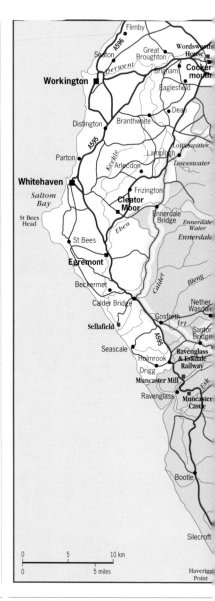

❏ Houses open to the public:
Brantwood, east side of Coniston Water: home of critic/artist John Ruskin.
Dalemain, near Penrith: Norman pele tower, Elizabethan rooms, priest's hole.
Dove Cottage, Grasmere: Wordsworth's home during his most productive period.
Hill Top (N.T.), Near Sawrey: Beatrix Potter's farmhouse.
Holker Hall, near Cartmel: flamboyant Victorian house in Elizabethan style.
Levens Hall, near Levens: Elizabethan manor, gardens. Superb topiary.

THE LAKE DISTRICT

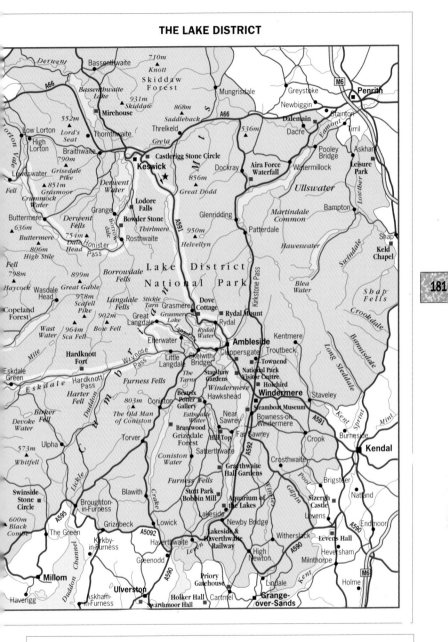

❏ Houses open to the public (continued):

Mirehouse, near Keswick: manuscripts of Tennyson, Wordsworth, etc.

Muncaster Castle, Eskdale: built around pele tower; owl center, woodland.

Rydal Mount, Rydal: Wordsworth's last house; grander than Dove Cottage.

Sizergh Castle (N.T.), near Levens: Elizabethan paneling, carvings; gardens.

Townend (N.T.), Troutbeck: traditional Cumbrian farmhouse.

Wordsworth House (N.T.), Cockermouth: birthplace of William Wordsworth. ❏

In the rejuvenated docklands

MUSEUMS AND GALLERIES IN ALBERT DOCK

(The Eight Pass covers entrance fees for eight Merseyside museums and galleries for 12 months.)

Beatles Story The Fab Four, who immortalized Penny Lane and the Cavern Club, are the focus for this sight-and-sound experience of the music of the 1960s.

Merseyside Maritime Museum An ambitious museum tracing the history of the port: pier-master's house, pilotage building, boat hall, ship-building, and a display on European emigrants.

Museum of Liverpool Life Social history: culture, making a living, voting and much more.

Tate Liverpool (*Admission free*) A branch of the great London establishment; modern art.

OTHER MUSEUMS AND GALLERIES IN LIVERPOOL

Conservation Centre, Whitechapel. Shows how all types of objects (including textiles, paintings, and stuffed animals) are conserved.

Liverpool Football Club Visitors Centre, Anfield Road: trophies, memorabilia, videos, and a look at the pitch.

Liverpool Museum and Planetarium, William Brown Street: science and natural history.

Speke Hall (N.T.) Fine half-timbered house, dating from 1490. Minibuses from here to **20 Forthlin Road** (N.T.; no cars allowed; reservation essential on 0151 486 4006), the 1950s house where Paul McCartney lived and where the Beatles rehearsed.

Walker Art Gallery, William Brown Street: among Britain's finest provincial art galleries.

▶▶ **Liverpool**   *172B1*
(Tourist information center tel: 0906 680 6866—25p/minute)
Industrial activity on the River Mersey (Merseyside) has declined and the city's population is less than it was in the early 1900s; out of the center, run-down streetscapes are testimony to some of the worst urban problem areas in Britain. Yet despite the long economic slump, Liverpool has a strong sense of place, recalling its 19th-century hey-day as England's second greatest port. After the silting up of Chester's port, Liverpool took over; it flourished in the late 18th century in its trade with the West Indies.

The ocean-going liners of the 19th and early 20th centuries have gone—to get a hint of what it was like to arrive by sea, you should take the **ferry** to Birkenhead and back. The **Royal Liver Building** (1911) and **Cunard Building** (1917) stand sentinel by the Mersey waterfront. Architecture in the city displays a legacy of wealth and civic pride, at its best around **Dale Street**, **Water Street**, and **William Brown Street**, and around classical **St. George's Hall** (1854). Now revamped, **Albert Dock**▶▶ (1846) has stores, cafés, and a branch of the Tate Gallery in the rejuvenated warehouses.

At either end of the plum-brick Georgian townhouses of **Hope Street** stand the city's cathedrals. The **Anglican cathedral**▶▶, the largest of its denomination in the world, is a mightily proportioned Gothic edifice, built between 1906 and 1980 to the design of 21-year-old Giles Gilbert Scott. To make the most of its hillside setting, the conventional east–west orientation was not used. An elevator, followed by a flight of more than a hundred steps, will take you to the top of the tower for a superb view. By contrast, the **Metropolitan Roman Catholic Cathedral of Christ the King**▶ is a squat, tent-like affair set beneath a pinnacled lantern. This design by Frederick Gibberd was adopted after it became apparent that the original plan of Sir Edwin Lutyens was too costly. Of Lutyens' vast building, the foundation stone (1933) and the crypt exist.

► Manchester
172B2

(tel: 0161 234 3157)

Manchester was the great commercial center for the Lancashire cotton industry. It has suffered some dreary post-war development, but there are several glimpses of 19th-century grandeur and enjoyable museums. The **town hall►** is a Gothic creation with a marble interior by Alfred Waterhouse that fills one side of Albert Square. Just north of this are the classical **Royal Exchange**, with its lunar-module-style theater; **Barton Arcade**, a Victorian shopping arcade of iron and glass; and at the city's heart the cathedral (originally a medieval church).

Further south around **Peter Street** imposing buildings include the Athenaeum (1837), the Theatre Royal (1845) and the Free Trade Hall (1856); just behind, in the former Central Station, is the modern G-Mex exhibition center. On Deansgate, the Gothic Revival **Rylands Library**, with its richly ornamental facade was founded as a memorial to Manchester cotton magnate John Ryland, while just off Deansgate, **St. John Street** is the finest Georgian street in the city. The **City Art Gallery►** is also in Deansgate.

The revived area of Castlefield includes a reconstruction of a Roman fort that once stood here. The canal basin, where the Bridgewater and Rochdale canals meet, has atmosphere; the walk along the Rochdale Canal passes Victorian warehouses. The outstanding **Museum of Science and Industry►►** occupies the world's oldest passenger train

183

station; displays include stationary steam engines, a reconstructed Victorian sewer you can walk through, and Xperiment, a hands-on science center. The **Gallery of Costume►►** in Platt Hall exhibits 400 years of fashion.

Football fans should head for **Old Trafford** to see the Manchester United Museum, the first purpose-built British football museum, and for the tour. The **Millennium Quarter** project (see page 185) includes a cathedral center, a city park, and the Urbis cultural center.

Trams have made a comeback on the city's streets

L. S. LOWRY (1887–1976)
Manchester-born Laurence Stephen Lowry studied art in Manchester and Salford, and around 1916 developed an interest in painting the bleak landscapes of industrial Lancashire's mill towns. The naïve style of his matchstick figures has been much copied, but at the time his choice of subject was quite apart from the mainstream; many of his works had touches of darkness and satire, and an element of the grotesque. A selection of his work is on display at the gallery in the Lowry, a waterfront complex in Salford, which will be linked by footbridge to the new Imperial War Museum for the North (opening 2002).

The largest cities in Britain were once its great manufacturing, engineering, and trading hubs. Their centers are packed with historical interest and cultural attractions. Yet with the demise of their original industries, many of their inner areas have become run-down, presenting policy challenges for governments since 1945. Many of the problems are now being tackled anew.

"The peculiar character of these streets and the close resemblance each one bears to its neighbour, by no means tends to decrease the bewilderment in which the un-experienced wayfarer through "the Dials" finds himself involved. He traverses streets of dirty, straggling houses, with now and then an unexpected court composed of buildings as ill-proportioned and deformed as the half-naked children that wallow in the kennels. Brokers' shops, which would seem to have been established by humane individuals as refuges for destitute bugs…are its cheerful accompaniments."
—Description of Seven Dials, London, from *Sketches by Boz* (1850) by Charles Dickens

Narrow boats in Birmingham's Gas Street Basin

For many centuries, a town was virtually all center. With its houses and churches, stores and inns huddled tightly together, the typical town was snugly protected from the outside world by its surrounding wall. The Industrial Revolution caused towns to swell out over the neighboring countryside and many became cities, their centers transformed by grandiose public buildings endowed by proud and philanthropic local entrepreneurs.

Community spirit Despite this vast expansion, the areas around the city's core still enjoyed a strong sense of identity: people lived near their work and often close to their extended families. The tiny back-to-back houses sheltered large families who shared a water tap and latrine at the end of the terrace with neighbors, but community spirit was strong even in the most overcrowded streets.

No-go areas With the decline of heavy industry and the migration outward towards the suburbs, some of these inner-city areas became deprived pockets of high unemployment and poor housing, isolated from the country's trend of increasing affluence. A wave of riots in the summer of 1981—in Brixton, Toxteth, and Bristol—led to them being portrayed by the media as "no-go areas" and caused the government to look urgently at making inner-city areas better places in which to live, work, and do business.

Upwardly mobile Birmingham Visitors to industrial cities some 20 years ago would have seen much dereliction round the centers, but there have been some big changes for the better. Long considered England's unglamorous second city, Birmingham has witnessed a remarkable renaissance, has become a major convention

destination—boosted by its geographical centrality—and now takes its heritage seriously. The Jewellery Quarter is once again flourishing after the recession-hit 1980s and visitors flock in great numbers to such attractions as Cadbury World at the headquarters of one of the foremost chocolate manufacturers. Neglected canals have been cleaned up, new cobbles laid, towpaths sign-posted and the waterfront developed with pubs, places to eat, nice stores, and gleaming offices. Much of the city center is now traffic-free. The year 2000 saw the start of the much-awaited redevelopment of the much-hated Bullring, a massive 1960s brutalist building adjoining New Street Station and housing a labyrinthine shopping center and market.

Manchester's Millennium Quarter Manchester is an example of revitalization for the third millennium, funded by the Millennium Commission (set up to assist public projects with revenues from the National Lottery). In 1996 a huge terrorist bomb devastated the Arndale Centre, Manchester's vast and drab-looking shopping center. Fortunately there were no fatalities and this event provided the catalyst for upgrading this area and its surroundings. The medieval town center around the cathedral has been a neglected backwater since World War I; the design links this area to the city center by means of a City Park—providing much-needed greenery—and a traffic-free street has been created giving a vista of the cathedral from the main part of the city. Meanwhile Manchester has gained a cathedral visitor center, encompassing the long-buried medieval bridge that originally served Manchester, and a new cultural attraction called Urbis (open spring 2002). The Arndale Centre has been totally refurbished.

Prosperity and pride Environmental pressure on the countryside and congestion on the roads has further led to a revival in the inner cities. In London, the once-neglected warehouse districts around London Bridge, for instance, have become distinctly yuppified, while previously unfashionable Hackney has become the city's major artists' community. The Docklands area virtually died after the end of London as a port, but has been rebuilt with futuristic office blocks and waterside housing, much of it extremely desirable real estate. It is in the inner cities' refurbished buildings, new concert halls, swathes of parkland and new architecture that future visitors should become aware of a reviving sense of civic pride.

Demonstrating a new spirit of enterprise: Manchester's MetroLink trams

THE SECOND BLITZ
Prince Charles once remarked that far more damage had been inflicted on London by developers after World War II than the entire might of Hitler's *Luftwaffe* had achieved during it. The same, unfortunately, is true of many other British cities and towns, devastated by a postwar alliance of urban planners and architects, but the emergence of civic societies and the designation of preservation areas has saved many centers in the past 30 years. There is increasing recognition of heritage; even Victorian warehouses that might have been torn down in the 1970s are now being carefully preserved.

London's Docklands: the redevelopment made use of the waterside

185

Monsal Dale: the old viaduct now carries the 8.5 mile Monsal Trail

WELL DRESSING
A visit to the Peak District between May and September will coincide with the decoration, or "dressing" of many village wells with mosaics of churches or biblical scenes, formed of petals, mosses, leaves, stones, and other natural materials. No one knows how far back the custom of well dressing goes, though it likely originated as a pagan ritual as a thanksgiving for water later taken over by the Church.

On the High Peak Trail

▶▶ **Peak National Park**   *172B3*
(tel: 01629 816200)

Britain's first national park, created in 1951, is encircled by large industrial cities. Though there are no major peaks as such—the district is essentially one of rolling hillscapes—the feeling of escape is exhilarating. The Peak forms the southern part of the Pennine chain which, in turn, forms the backbone of northern England.

THE WHITE PEAK Most of the southern park comprises the limestone landscapes of the White Peak, where rivers cut deep-grooved gorges, or "dales," beneath a plateau of stone-walled farmland. Most spectacular of all are **Dove Dale**▶▶ and its continuation, **Beresford Dale** (despite the crowds), **Monsal Dale**▶▶ (with its famous viaduct), the **Manifold Valley**▶ just below Wetton and wooded **Lathkill Dale**▶ near Youlgreave. Rewarding villages include **Winster, Alstonefield, Tideswell, Ilam, Ashford in the Water**, and **Eyam**▶, whose villagers were ravaged by the plague in 1665 when, following their vicar's lead, they confined themselves to their village after an infected box of cloth arrived from London. **Tissington**▶ has perhaps the loveliest of all Peak village streets, with wide grassy borders and a Jacobean hall. Equally absorbing is the industrial village of **Cromford**▶, where Richard Arkwright set up the world's first water-powered cotton mill in 1771 (now a museum). The Peak's finest prehistoric monument is **Arbor Low**▶, south of Monyash, a 4,000-year-old stone circle. **Castleton**▶▶ is the hub of the Peak's caving district (see panel): north of the village, a ridge ends at Mam Tor, known as "Shivering Mountain" because of frequent landslips; Cave Dale looks up to the Norman keep of Peveril Castle, holding its head high above the village.

The national park boundary excludes all the local towns except for **Bakewell**, home of Bakewell puddings (made of almond, jam, and puff pastry). The center is ruined by traffic, but it is more pleasant up the hill around the church and the delightful Old House Museum of relics of the past. Out of town are the Peak's two great houses.

Haddon Hall▶▶ is a wonderfully preserved medieval house with a paneled gallery, a chapel, and walled garden; palatial **Chatsworth House▶▶▶**, home of the dukes of Devonshire, has a breathtaking collection of art and furniture. Its grounds were landscaped by Capability Brown and Joseph Paxton (see page 17). Paxton also designed the quaint estate workers' village, **Edensor**.

Buxton▶▶, an elegant former spa, is the *de facto* Peak capital. Its classically inspired 18th-century Crescent, the Buxton Opera House, pavilion gardens, and town hall all contribute to the distinguished air. An excellent town museum features a Wonders of the Peak exhibition. **Matlock Bath**, another former spa, occupies an extraordinary site in the Derwent Gorge. Cable cars make it easy to explore the **Heights of Abraham**, a park with woodland walks, views, and caves. Nearby at Crich is the wonderful **National Tramway Museum▶▶**, which offers tram rides and a host of exhibits related to this mode of transport. **Wirksworth▶** is a characterful old town amid limestone quarries; the church has a superb 8th-century lead carved coffin lid known as the Wirksworth Stone.

THE DARK PEAK Millstone grit is the underlying rock in the northern Peak. The moors and grassland really are dark; the scenery is bleaker and more rugged. Millstones, for grinding grain, were once a major industry—workings litter abandoned quarries and the stone disks now stand on plinths to mark the national park boundary. The one-street village of **Edale** lies below the massive peat bog plateau of Kinder

Scout, the highest terrain in the Peak (2,087 feet). The A57 heads over the **Snake Pass**, displaying the austerity of the northern moors, while the **Derwent Reservoirs▶** near Hope are the most attractive of many manmade lakes. Old cotton-mill towns have a 19th-century workaday character: **New Mills** is one of the most rewarding, with a gorge beneath the Torrs Aerial Walkway. **Lyme Park▶** (N.T.) has a Palladian hall with Grinling Gibbons woodcarving. The gritstone edges such as **Stanage Edge** provide dramatic level tops, with easy paths and challenging rock climbs.

CAVES
Of the five limestone caverns near Castleton that are open to the public, Treak Cliff has some fine stalactites and displays of Blue John (a crystalline fluorspar, worked into jewelry and souvenirs, and sold locally), Speedwell Cavern features an underground boat trip along a tunnel that forms part of an old lead mine, and Bagshawe Cavern near Bradwell may appeal to those wanting to try adventure caving. Peak Cavern on the edge of Castleton has a magnificent entrance and is the largest cave in Derbyshire. The Blue John Cavern has Blue John but no stalactites. On the edge of Buxton, Poole's Cavern has the finest formations.

187

"Bakewell pudding" started life at the White Horse Inn, when a cook attempting to make a strawberry tart put the jam in first and poured the egg mixture on top

LEAD MINING
Lead mining was big in the White Peak until the last century—the Manifold Valley and Lathkill Dale have traces of past mining activity, Magpie Mine near Sheldon being the most conspicuous relic. Many villages expanded for the purpose; today these stone-built settlements are surprisingly rural and merge into the scenery along with their agricultural neighbors. At Matlock Bath an excellent mining museum lies close to the reopened Temple Mine, which non-claustrophobics may like to walk around.

This most famous of factory workers' villages looked forward to a new age of cities: of greenery, clean air, and sanitation. It was conceived as a place in which, in the words of its founder, the inhabitants "will be able to know more about the science of life than they can in a back slum and in which they will learn that there is more in life than the mere going to and returning from work and looking forward to Saturday night to draw their wages."

VILLAGE TRAIL

The Port Sunlight Heritage Centre tells the story of Port Sunlight and a village trail leads visitors around the garden village, taking in the Lady Lever Art Gallery. Set up by Lever after the death of his wife, the gallery contains a surprising wealth of art, including Pre-Raphaelite paintings and Wedgwood ceramics.

188

Fair deals for the workers Port Sunlight was in fact one of several 19th-century innovations in the Wirral (the peninsula between the River Mersey and Liverpool on one side, and the River Dee and Wales on the other). In 1842 Joseph Paxton's Birkenhead Park had been Britain's first public park and in 1853 Prices Patent Candle Company had created Bromborough Pool Village for its workers.

The soap king The industrialist William Hesketh Lever, the first Viscount Leverhulme, was a Liberal Member of Parliament and philanthropist with an interest in the arts and landscape design. He co-owned a soap factory in Warrington; the success of Sunlight Soap spiraled and in 1887 he came to the Wirral to set up a new factory. He acquired Thornton Manor and transformed Thornton Hough into a mock-Tudor village for his estate workers.

A vision of the future The factory village of Port Sunlight was to be a haven of peace and cleanliness. Cottages were built to a high standard in half-timbered Tudor and bricky Queen Anne and Elizabethan styles (no two groups of cottages are the same); gardens and parks were liberally provided. The village's visionary design was a predecessor of the garden cities of Ebenezer Howard, which in turn influenced the growth of the garden suburb and of the first "New Towns."

▶▶ Quarry Bank Mill   172B2
(tel: 01625 527468)

The centerpiece of Styal Country Park—a swath of green on the fringes of Manchester—is this water-powered cotton mill, built in 1784 and now maintained by the National Trust. It gives an excellent idea of how a weaving mill worked, complete with the deafening clatter of the looms. Exhibits explain cotton processing, the working conditions of the time, and the role of the mill owners as factory pioneers. Spinning and weaving demonstrations take place. Visitors can also see living conditions of the 1830s inside the Apprentice House. An 1840 beam engine is in steam in the **Steam Power Galleries**.

▶▶ Stoke-on-Trent (The Potteries)   172B2
(tel: 01782 236000)

Stoke is a conurbation of six towns—Burslem, Fenton, Hanley, Longton, Stoke, and Tunstall—but only locals can tell where one ends and the next begins. At first glance the industrial and residential sprawl is unappetizing; but this is the heart of pottery country and anyone interested in the craft should certainly make a visit.

The **Gladstone Pottery Museum▶▶▶** is a preserved 19th-century pottery with massive bottle-shaped brick kilns (once a common feature of Stoke-on-Trent, now all but vanished). It has pottery demonstrations, informative displays, and fine ceramics ranging from high-class ornaments to Victorian lavatories. The **Etruria Industrial Museum▶** features the last steam-powered potter's mill in Britain (where bone and flint were crushed to supply the potteries; the engines are usually in steam the first weekend of the month, Apr–Dec). **The Potteries Museum and Art Gallery▶▶** has a fine collection of Staffordshire pottery. Also open to the public and each with museums are the visitor centers for **Spode▶▶**, **Royal Doulton▶▶** and **Wedgwood▶▶** (see panel).

Around a courtyard and built in the 15th and 16th centuries, **Little Moreton Hall▶▶** (N.T.), 9 miles north of Stoke, is the best example of the half-timbered "vernacular," with a wainscoted gallery, great hall, chapel, as well as a knot garden.

About 15 miles east of Stoke-on-Trent is **Alton Towers**. Here the extensive parkland surrounding the ruined home of the Earl of Shrewsbury is today full of the sounds of Britain's most famous amusement park.

VISITING THE POTTERIES
Aim to see the **Gladstone Pottery Museum** (tel: 01782 319232) and some of Stoke's many bargain-price factory stores. Then visit one of the potteries (reserve ahead for factory tours, available Mon–Fri). The main ones (with visitor centers/craft demonstrations year-round) are **Wedgwood**, famous for its Jasper Ware, (tel: 01782 204218); **Spode**, specializing in blue and white bone china and still on its original 1770 site (tel: 01782 744011); and **Royal Doulton** (tel: 01782 292434), famous for its intricate figurines. There is also a visitor center at Etruria.

Stoke-on-Trent is the home of British pottery

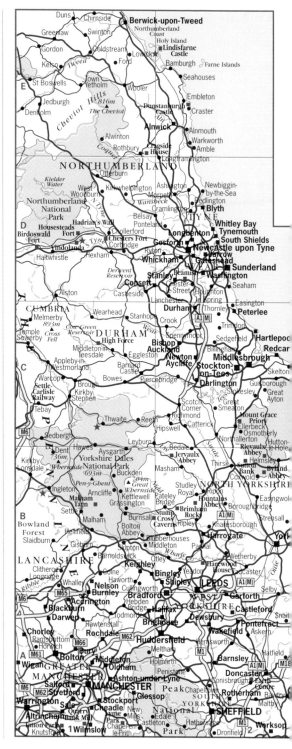

NORTHEAST ENGLAND This region includes most of the **Pennines**, the chain of hills that forms the backbone of upland England, from the Peak District in the south to the Scottish borders in the north. It also encompasses **Yorkshire**, the largest county in Britain, divided into North, South, East, and West for administrative purposes. It has a reputation for friendliness, with the finest of Britain's medieval cities in York itself, and a magnificent heritage of abbey ruins and ecclesiastical architecture.

INDUSTRIAL YORKSHIRE The industrial parts of **West Yorkshire** should not be overlooked. The moorland and the scenically sited, 19th-century stone-built mill towns around Calderdale have a strong and unique personality; you can explore canals and hills and the adjacent Brontë country at Haworth. Industrial heritage is the big theme here. Leeds recalls its mill days in the Armley Mills

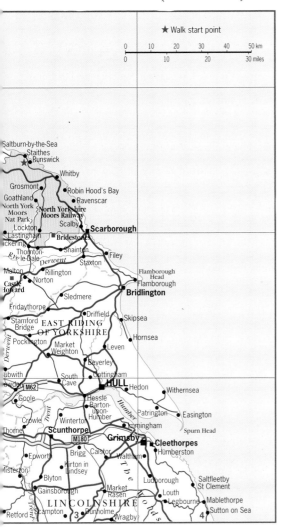

★ Walk start point

0　10　20　30　40　50 km
0　　　10　　　20　　　30 miles

▶▶▶ **REGION HIGHLIGHTS**

Beverley *page 194*
Castle Howard *page 195*
Durham *page 196*
Fountains Abbey *page 197*
Hadrian's Wall *page 201*
National Museum of Photography, Film and Television *page 194*
Northumberland Coast *pages 199–200*
North York Moors National Park *pages 202–203*
York *pages 204–206*
Yorkshire Dales National Park *pages 207–209*

The Swaledale tup, the Yorkshire Dales National Park emblem

192

RECOMMENDED HISTORIC TOWNS AND CITIES
County Durham: Barnard Castle, Durham.
East Riding of Yorkshire: Beverley.
North Yorkshire: Harrogate, Helmsley, Knaresborough, Middleham, Richmond, Ripon, Scarborough, York.
Northumberland: Alnwick, Hexham.
Tyne and Wear: Newcastle-upon-Tyne.
INDUSTRIAL HERITAGE
Abbeydale Industrial Hamlet, Beamish, Bradford, Halifax, Hebden Bridge, Hull, Saltaire.
SCENERY
North York Moors, Northumberland, South Pennines (Calderdale and Haworth areas), Yorkshire Dales.
COASTAL TOWNS AND VILLAGES
North Yorkshire: Robin Hood's Bay, Runswick Bay, Staithes, Whitby.
Northumberland: Bamburgh, Berwick-upon-Tweed.
HISTORIC SITES AND REMAINS
Fountains Abbey, Hadrian's Wall, Holy Island, Rievaulx Abbey.

Museum, and is home to the magnificent Royal Armouries Museum. Bradford is still impressive for its vibrant museums, while on its peripheries Saltaire is an outstanding example of a factory village built by a philanthropic industrialist to improve the lifestyle of his workforce. At Sheffield, in **South Yorkshire**, Abbeydale Industrial Hamlet is a fitting tribute to the city's steel manufacturing days.

THE DALES, THE MOORS, AND THE VALE OF YORK The **Yorkshire Dales** are for lovers of the great outdoors—an excellent area for car touring, walking, and caving. East of the Pennines in the **Vale of York** are York itself, the spa town of Harrogate, and the enchanting ruins of Fountains Abbey. Southeast Yorkshire is less visited: the flat agricultural scenery may be humdrum, but Selby and Beverley (the latter in the **East Riding of Yorkshire**) each have splendid churches; Hull has a range of sights, including the Town Docks Museum, which celebrates its nautical past; a huge suspension bridge spans the Humber. The **North York Moors** are detached from the Pennine chain and have quite a different character. The coast, with its high cliffs and fishing villages, is a joy. Further south along the coast are the scalloped chalk cliffs of **Flamborough Head** and the narrow spit of **Spurn Head**.

COUNTY DURHAM, NORTHUMBERLAND, TYNE AND WEAR The **Pennine** landscape becomes bleaker and more lonely as one proceeds towards Scotland, through Teesdale, in **County Durham**, and the Cheviot Hills, in Northumberland. Elsewhere much of County Durham has an industrial face and, like Middlesbrough (in North Yorkshire), is economically depressed. The open-air museum at Beamish is a splendid re-creation of an early 20th-century industrial village, while Durham has a great Norman cathedral. **Tyne and Wear** incorporates a conurbation centered on Newcastle-upon-Tyne; locals here are nicknamed Geordies and are known for their quickfire humor and guttural accent. On its back doorstep, **Northumberland**, in total contrast, has wide open spaces, the great Roman structure of Hadrian's Wall, and a long and quiet coastline punctuated by imposing castles.

Walks

Hadrian's Wall, 190D1
Northumberland National Park
Nearly all the interest is along the wall itself, with its host of Roman features. There is not much reason to go far afield. Simply walking along the wall is a great experience, with views from the ridge of the Great Whin Sill across lonely Northumberland. For a sample, start at Housesteads Fort and walk west, past Crag Lough to Twice Brewed youth hostel and back (2.5 hours). In summer you can use the bus service along the B6318 to take you back.

Holy Island, 190E2
Northumberland
Use main parking lot in village (note tide times). The island's best circular walk is three-quarters coastal, all of it level. Follow Sandham Lane north (turn left and left again out of the parking lot), turn right beyond the dunes and follow the coast around, past Emanuel Head, where an obelisk looks along the coast into Scotland. Then pass Lindisfarne Castle to finish in the village by Lindisfarne Priory . (1.5 hours)

Ingleton Waterfalls, 190B1
Yorkshire Dales National Park
Parking lot by main entrance to falls. Also known as Ingleton Glen, this

Lindisfarne Castle, Holy Island

splendid gorge is well worth the entrance fee. A circular trail takes in a series of falls of considerable individuality; the most dramatic are the first two, Pecka Fall and Thornton Force. Beyond lies a handily placed refreshment stand, then the path leads into more open country with views of surrounding hills before a finale along the Doe Gorge (2 hours). A booklet available locally explains the geology.

Runswick Bay and 191C3
Staithes, North York
Moors National Park
Park just above Runswick Bay village. This walk along the clifftops (part of the Cleveland Way) links two captivating coastal villages. From Runswick Bay village, walk up the road; at the top follow the Cleveland Way as it branches off on the right, soon reaching the clifftop for an easy walk past Port Mulgrave and reaching Staithes harbor. Return the same way. (2.5 hours)

Upper Swaledale, 190C1
Yorkshire Dales National Park
Roadside parking, Muker village. This walk from Muker enjoys a magnificent steep-sided section of the dale. Walk into the village and find a path out of its north end that leads to a bridge over the Swale; continue north up the dale for 1.75 miles to the next bridge (close by Keld). Cross and turn left on the Pennine Way (fork left soon for a short detour to Kisdon Force waterfall). The Way rises slightly, offering fine views. Finally leave it for a farm track that drops to Muker. (2.5 hours)

193

MISERICORDS

The folding seats in the choirstalls of many cathedrals and major churches have a carved under-bracket known as a misericord. When the seats were turned up, the misericords made ledges for the monks to rest on during the long periods of standing in their services. Frequently carved in fanciful designs, the misericords were deliberately made so narrow that there was no chance of dozing off.

Sundial (below) and open-top omnibus (right), Beamish

SALTAIRE

This famous example of a "factory village" dates from the 1850s, when Titus Salt, an enlightened industrialist of liberal views and temperance ideals, decided to house his workforce in this garden village of parks and spacious streets, free from Bradford's smog. The place has scarcely changed, though the houses are now mostly privately owned. The mill itself is used for a variety of purposes. Paintings by native son artist David Hockney are on display in the 1853 Gallery. Other sections are released for commercial use.

▶▶ Beamish: North of England Open Air Museum   190D2
(tel: 0191 370 4000)

Life in northern England in the early 1900s is re-created in meticulous detail at this ambitious museum. It is divided into five sections: the colliery village, the town with its stores and houses, the manor house, the railroad, and the farm. Costumed actors play roles within the museum.

▶▶ Beverley   191B3
(Tourist information center tel: 01482 867430)

Beverley has pleasing Georgian brickwork, the North Bar (the only survivor of five town gates), a Saturday market and, above all, two gems of church architecture. Begun in Norman times, the **Minster▶▶** is famed for its Gothic stone-carving, its 68 misericords (see panel) made by the Ripon school of woodcarvers and its fine-towered west front. **St. Mary's Church▶** has a 15th-century west facade and a paneled chancel ceiling depicting early kings, all cloaked and crowned against a gold background.

▶ Bradford   190A2
(Tourist information center tel: 01274 753678)

A patchily impressive Victorian city (knocked around by postwar planning), Bradford is the fruit of the textile-mill age; the Gothic Revival **town hall** and the spectacular tombs of **Undercliffe Cemetery▶** are monuments of past achievement. The entertaining **National Museum of Photography, Film and Television▶▶▶** (*Admission free*) has put Bradford on the map: encounter the animator's world, the story of British TV, the Kodak Gallery of still photography, and the power of advertising. The museum (*closed* Mon except bank holidays) is attached to an IMAX cinema (reservations tel: 01274 203395). The **Colour Museum▶** explores the use of color chemistry and the **Bradford Industrial Museum▶**

with rebuilt back-to-back houses, has a tour through the world of textile production. The **Cartwright Hall Art Gallery** (*Admission free*) has a good display of 19th- and early 20th-century paintings. Recommended visits (easy by rail) are **Saltaire**►► (see panel) and **Leeds**►► (see page 197).

►► Calderdale   190A1

(*Halifax tourist information center tel: 01422 368725*)

A former textile valley in the heart of the Pennines, Calderdale is rich with local color. Sturdy rows of stone cottages and the geometry of stone-walled fields stripe the sides of the valley. The largest settlement, **Halifax**►, is unjustifiably ignored by many visitors; in fact it is the best-preserved of West Yorkshire's industrial towns, with the splendid galleried **Piece Hall**►►, the former cloth market built around a courtyard. The town hall was designed by Charles Barry (one of the architects of the Houses of Parliament in London). **Eureka!** on Discovery Road, is a hands-on museum for children.

   Hebden Bridge►, near the site of the last clog mill in England, is magnificently set at the meeting of two valleys, its grey houses rising row by row up the hillside. From the original Hebden Bridge a cobbled path rises steeply to the hilltop village of **Heptonstall**►►, a fascinating place with cobbled streets, a ruined church, and the world's oldest Methodist chapel in continuous use (since 1764). The village was a busy hand-weaving center until eclipsed by the mills in Hebden Bridge.

►►► Castle Howard   191B3

(*tel: 01653 648444*)

In the gentle Howardian Hills, this early 18th-century house stands surrounded by a park adorned with ornamental lakes, a colonnaded mausoleum, and a "temple" designed by Vanbrugh. He is commonly attributed with the design of the house, yet he was then a man of no architectural experience; it seems extremely likely that his clerk of works, architect Nicholas Hawksmoor, lent a helping hand. The house has portraits by Holbein, statues, tapestries, porcelain, furniture, and a costume collection. It was also the setting for the popular TV dramatization of *Brideshead Revisited*.

WALKS IN CALDERDALE
Calderdale is an excellent walking center, with a dense network of footpaths, including the Pennine Way and Calderdale Way. From Hebden Bridge, walk along the Rochdale Canal towpath in either direction for glimpses of typical Pennine features, such as back-to-back cottages and old mills. Combine this with a walk up to Heptonstall, which abuts the top of a dramatic gorge known as Colden Clough. The area just north of Hebden Bridge offers riverside strolls through a densely wooded valley, or up to Hardcastle Crags.

195

The handsome mill at Saltaire, pre-eminent in its day

CATHEDRAL FIRSTS
Durham Cathedral represents the highest achievement of the Norman style. In addition to the characteristic use of rounded arches, the building has what are thought to be the earliest transverse Gothic-style pointed arches in English architecture: since the cathedral was largely built during a single period, this really shows a transition between the two building techniques. The sense of scale is created by the hitherto unprecedented use of rib-vaulting, which creates greater space between load-bearing columns.

Durham Cathedral stands high above the Wear

ST. CUTHBERT
The Chapel of the Nine Altars in the cathedral contains the relics of St. Cuthbert, brought here by Lindisfarne monks who escaped from Holy Island (see page 199) when Danish raiders arrived in 875. Cuthbert was a shepherd boy from the Lammermuir Hills who decided to dedicate his life to God, living on Holy Island and later the Farne Islands. He remained a lover of all animals.

▶▶▶ Durham   *190C2*
(Tourist information center tel: 0191 384 3720)

Few places in Britain can rival the drama of Durham's setting, its majestic cathedral soaring high over sandstone cliffs and woodlands ribboning the tight curve of the River Wear. The historic center is compact and largely traffic-free. **Durham Heritage Centre** in St. Mary le Bow Church chronicles the city's history.

The nave, chancel, and transepts of the **cathedral▶▶▶** were built over a single period (1070–1140). The sense of balanced might and soaring space is enthralling—it is Britain's finest Norman church architecture. In the cathedral precincts is College Green, the most complete example of a Benedictine monastery in England. Durham was until 1836 a "palatinate," enjoying royal rights and ruled by prince bishops, who were secular and religious leaders.

The main entrance to the cathedral is via **Palace Green**, where other buildings belong to the **university**, England's third oldest. The **castle▶▶** (*Guided tours*), erected to serve as the palace of the prince bishops for almost 800 years, dates from the 1070s. The university rebuilt the octagonal keep in 1840 but several early features survive, including the Great Hall (1284) and the Black Staircase (1662). For the best views, follow the **riverside path▶▶**, cross over **Prebends Bridge**, beside weirs and old mills (one houses an **archaeological museum**), up to **South Street**. To the north, **Crook Hall and Garden▶** is a 14th-century manor house with attractive gardens. In the university the **Oriental Museum▶**, Elvet Hill, is a treasure house of exotica, including Egyptian mummies and jade.

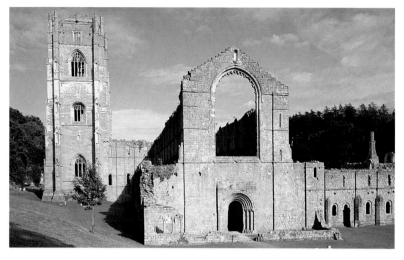

▶▶▶ **Fountains Abbey and Studley Royal** *190B2*
(tel: 01765 600888)
In medieval times, **Fountains Abbey** (N.T.) had grange farms and lands across much of northern England and was a major wool producer. Its former prosperity is evident in what are regarded as Britain's greatest abbey ruins. Founded for 12 Benedictine monks who later changed to Cistercian rule, the abbey still has a 12th-century nave and transepts, a tower completed shortly before the Dissolution, and buildings where the monks lived and worked. The **Studley Royal** estate has an 18th-century park with follies, deer park, and vistas of the abbey. St. Mary's Church is mock-medieval, with painted roof and walls of Egyptian alabaster.

▶ **Haworth** *190B1*
(tel: 01535 642329)
The Brontë Parsonage Museum (see page 198) and a walk to the Brontë Waterfalls and Top Withins justify a literary pilgrimage to this popular Pennine village. The village is a stop on the **Keighley and Worth Valley Railway**▶, which steams along between Keighley and Oxenhope.

▶ **Leeds**
(Tourist information center tel: 0113 242 5242)
Victorian municipal swagger does not come much stronger than Leeds Town Hall and the splendid covered shopping arcades. Industry and commerce is writ large over the city —the glass-roofed market is Yorkshire's biggest, and the former Corn Exchange has become a cheerful hall of stores and places to eat. In the rejuvenated docks, the hi-tech **Royal Armouries Museum**▶▶▶ contains arms and armor previously displayed in the Tower of London. The heady days of textile making are evoked in the **Armley Mills Museum**▶, a former woollen mill crammed with machinery and memories. The excellently presented **Thackray Medical Museum**▶ delves into all things medical, including social history, and the grisly world of the pre-anaesthetic era.

Trips out of the city northwards include **Harewood House**▶▶ (see panel) and the spa town of **Harrogate**▶.

Fountains Abbey

197

RIPON AND ITS CATHEDRAL
From the park road in the Studley Royal estate, there is a contrived vista of nearby Ripon Cathedral. This mostly medieval building is notable for its west front, misericords, and Saxon crypt. The daily blowing of the nightwatch horn at 9 PM in the spacious market square of this appealing town is a tradition dating back to 886.

HAREWOOD HOUSE
Completed in 1771, the seat of the Earls of Harewood boasts an impressive list of credits: interiors and furniture by Robert Adam, exterior by John Carr, murals by Angelica Kauffman, gardens by Charles Barry, and parkland by Capability Brown. Painted ceilings, porcelain, and intricate plasterwork further grace the building, and there is an aviary of exotic birds.

Charlotte (1816–1855), Emily (1818–1848) and Anne (1820–1849) Brontë were the daughters of an Irish clergyman. The Brontës' lives were constantly beset by ill health and unfortunate circumstance. Charlotte had an unhappy love affair in Brussels, Emily had no close friends, and Anne had a tendency towards religious melancholy. Meanwhile, their brother Branwell, disillusioned with his attempts to be a writer and artist, took to drink and opium.

"My sister Emily loved the moors. Flowers brighter than the rose bloomed in the blackest heath for her; out of a sullen hollow in a livid hillside her mind would make an Eden. She found in the bleak solitude many and dear delights; and not the least and best loved was—liberty."
—Charlotte Brontë (1816–1855)

198

Haworth's cobbled main street is today lined with gift shops

THE BRONTË NAME
The family name was originally Brunty or Prunty but the form Brontë was adopted after Lord Nelson was given the title Duke of Brontë by the King of Naples after the Battle of the Nile in 1798.

The Brontës lived in the bleak parsonage (now a museum) in Haworth, overlooking a graveyard that polluted the water supply, severely reducing villagers' life expectancy. The girls consequently escaped into fantasy worlds. It was Charlotte's determination that got the Brontës into print, after she had chanced upon some secret poetry of Emily's and had been convinced of its worth; the three contributed works to a volume published in 1846 under the pen names of Acton (Anne), Currer (Charlotte) and Ellis (Emily) Bell; the sales were dismal (two books in the first month), but with Charlotte's drive, the sisters each submitted novels. Emily's *Wuthering Heights*, probably set in the now-ruined farmhouse of Top Withins, and Anne's *Agnes Grey* were published in 1847. Charlotte failed to get *The Professor* published, but the constructive comments of one publisher gave her encouragement: she completed *Jane Eyre* soon after and it won immediate acclaim—Thackeray read it in a single sitting.

Hard times But the sisters had to spend much time nursing their brother Branwell and the money from the books went to paying off his debts; after his death in September 1848, Emily contracted tuberculosis ("consumption") and died three months later. Anne also fell ill and died the next year at Scarborough, after writing *The Tenant of Wildfell Hall*.

Charlotte was brought to London as a literary celebrity; here she made friends with the successful novelist Mrs. Gaskell, who later wrote a biography of Charlotte. Meanwhile, Charlotte worked on *Villette*, based on her time in Brussels and married Arthur Bell Nicholls, their curate, after two years of strong opposition from her father. She died nine months later in pregnancy.

IN MEMORY OF
EMILY JANE BRONTË
WHO DIED DEC. 19TH 1848,
AGED 30 YEARS.
AND OF
CHARLOTTE BRONTË
APRIL 21ST 1816
DIED MARCH 31ST 1855

►► Northumberland Coast   190E2
(Alnwick tourist information center tel: 01665 510665)

England's northeasternmost seaboard is low-lying and virtually unspoiled, characterized by expansive beaches, profuse birdlife, quiet resorts with golf courses and sands, and wind-haunted castle ruins.

Berwick-upon-Tweed►► changed hands 13 times between England and Scotland during the period 1100–1510. The Tweed, a salmon river which runs just south beneath a trio of bridges (including 17th-century Berwick Bridge with its 15 arches), would seem a natural border, but the town has been English since 1482. An excellent walk follows the 16th-century **walls**, the best-preserved fortification of its date in Britain, which encircle the town; you'll pass the restored quay, **Berwick Barracks►** of 1717 (E.H.; Britain's oldest purpose-built barracks; with an exhibition re-creating the life of British infantryman; plus a regimental museum and part of the Burrell art collection) and a church built in 1652.

BERWICK TRIVIA
● Although the town of Berwick is English, the old county of Berwickshire was in Scotland and Berwick Rangers play as a Scottish football team.
● With the coming of the railroad, Berwick's castle was torn down to make way for the station and much of its stone was used in Stephenson's railroad bridge.
● Berwick cockles are not molluscs but an old-fashioned peppermint.

199

The Farne Islands

Holy Island►► is accessible by car at low tide (times are given on noticeboards both on the island and mainland) via a causeway. It is excellent for walks (see page 193) and is regarded as the cradle of Christianity in England (see panel). Lindisfarne Castle, lone by the shore, was converted in the 1900s by architect Sir Edwin Lutyens and is open to the public. **Bamburgh►** close by has a Norman castle, revamped in the 18th and 19th centuries, with porcelain and armor collections. The Grace Darling Museum pays tribute to the woman who helped rescue nine shipwrecked marines in a gale in 1838. **Dunstanburgh Castle►** is an eerie ruin, the largest of the Northumbrian coastal strongholds, begun in 1313. It is an easy walk along the coast from the port of **Craster**, which has a working harbor and kipper smokeries. Inland lies **Alnwick►**, a dignified stone-built market town and a pleasant base for exploring the area. **Alnwick Castle►** dates from Norman times, but has a sumptuous Renaissance-style interior, fine Meissen china, and paintings

HOLY ISLAND
In 635, at the request of the king of Northumbria, a missionary landed here from the Scottish island of Iona. St. Aidan founded the Lindisfarne Priory on what is today known as Holy Island and from this spot Christianity spread across northeastern England. Lindisfarne became a Benedictine monastery in 1082. A museum tells the story. *The Lindisfarne Gospels*, an illuminated manuscript of ca700, is now in the British Library.

LINDISFARNE NATURE RESERVE
Home to wildfowl and waders, a major site for wigeon, and the only British wintering ground for pale-bellied Brent geese, the nature reserve includes mud flats and dunes around Holy Island, and the further-flung Farne Islands. The latter are an important habitat for seals and seabirds; April to September (inclusive) cruises depart from Seahouses (N.T. information center, tel: 01665 721099)—it is an exciting boat ride that offers really close encounters with the surprisingly tame wild birds.

by Reynolds and Titian; Anthony Salvin, the Victorian architect, was responsible for much of the building and a century earlier the parkland was landscaped by Capability Brown. Adjacent Hulne Park is open for walks on weekends; there is a Carmelite priory and an 18th-century folly tower. At the mouth of the River Coquet, **Warkworth▶** has a medieval castle and 14th-century hermitage chapel (both E.H.) cut out of the cliffs, with the hermit's living quarters still intact (walk along the river and take a ferry across).

In complete contrast, **Newcastle-upon-Tyne▶** is a sprawling industrial conurbation, definitely not pretty at first sight, but with plenty of atmosphere. For the new millennium, an innovative footbridge and cycleway has been built across the Tyne, bringing the total number of bridges up to seven. A cluster of medieval quayside buildings, the 17th-century guildhall and the castle are pre-industrial survivals, while Grey Street and Eldon Square are fine examples of early 19th-century townscaping. Newcastle's big three museums are the **Laing Art Gallery** (*Admission free*), the region's premier art collection; **Discovery Museum** (*Admission free*), with interactive science, plus costumes, displays on Tyneside inventors, the 100 foot vessel *Turbinia* and a hands-on social history of the city; and the **Hancock Museum**, with natural history, a Living Planet environmental gallery, and Egyptian artifacts.

▶▶ Northumberland National Park   190D1
(*tel: 01434 344396*)

Because of its remote location and lack of facilities, this is one of the least visited national parks. Villages are modest and scattered, the grassy hills are quiet and strikingly empty—even at the height of summer you often have only Cheviot sheep for company. It is a great place for solitary walks, although the variety is not immense. Vast Kielder Forest spreads its seemingly endless evergreen plantations, home to red squirrels and deer, over western Northumberland. Kielder Water and the forest trails offer

Man-made beauty: the huge Kielder Water amid the conifers of Kielder Forest

a retreat from the elements and there is an 12 mile forest drive. You can also rent boats and canoes.

The **Cheviot Hills** reach to the Scottish border. The best of the walks involve treks along solitary sheep-drovers' roads, now quiet grassy tracks, to the ridge which forms the border, taking in the summits of Windy Gyle (2,031 feet) and The Cheviot (2,677 feet). The scenic drives tend to be of the there-and-back variety as no roads lead right across the massif apart from the A68; notable among these is the road along **Coquetdale** from Rothbury, past the craggy Simonside Hills, to Alwinton and beyond. **Rothbury** itself is an attractive sandstone town with a sloping green and a spacious main street; **Cragside▶** (N.T.) on the edge of the town was built by the 19th-century architect Norman Shaw and was the first house in the world to be lit by hydroelectric power. The wooded grounds here are laced with trails and have lakes, a formal garden, and a fine show of rhododendrons. **Chillingham Castle** has for more than 700 years been home to Wild White cattle, a breed that was kept by ancient Britons. **Ford** is a model estate village for Ford Castle and has craft workshops.

The southern part of the national park holds the finest surviving stretch of **Hadrian's Wall▶ ▶ ▶** (E.H.), the largest Roman monument in Britain (see panel). Of its 74 mile length, remains can be seen along 10 miles, the best sections being between points north of Haltwhistle and Hexham. Walkers may like to make use of a summer bus service which runs along the main road parallel to the wall.

Housesteads Fort, which still has a hospital and latrines, and Chesters, a cavalry fort, are particularly well preserved. At Vindolanda Fort a section of wall is reconstructed as it would have been at the time of the Roman occupation, while at Corbridge are the remains of the garrison town of *Corstopitum* and a museum of finds. Also try to take in Birdoswald Fort, situated over the border in Cumbria, and the national park information center at Once Brewed.

Hexham▶ makes an attractive base. It has a superb abbey church; both its crypt and bishop's throne are Anglo-Saxon—before destruction by Danish marauders in 875 it was the largest church in northern Europe. Local history features at the Border History Museum (in an old prison).

The Roman ruins of Housesteads Fort, on Hadrian's Wall

HADRIAN'S WALL
This great fortification at the northernmost point of the Roman empire was planned in AD 122 by Emperor Hadrian from Newcastle to the Solway Firth on the Cumbrian coast. The natural feature of the Great Whin Sill, a ridge of hard rock, made an ideal base to the construction for much of its length. To the north lay wilderness and the Picts and it still feels primevally wild on the wall today. Structures known as milecastles were placed at intervals of Roman miles; the Vallum, or southern rampart, was below the wall and is visible in places. Seventeen forts, housing 13,000 infantrymen and 5,500 cavalrymen, were connected by a military road. The best preserved is Housesteads (N.T.). At Wallsend (just east of Newcastle-upon-Tyne) a museum and reconstructed bath house stand beside the remains of Segedunum Fort.

MORE NORTH YORKSHIRE PRIORIES AND ABBEYS

Byland Abbey, near Coxwold, had the largest priory church in England—the shattered rose window gives a scant idea of its glory. Mount Grace Priory, near the attractive village of Osmotherley, was a Carthusian house; the lifestyle was austere, with vows of silence and prison-like confinement; one cell has been reconstructed. Guisborough Priory, an Augustinian foundation at the edge of Guisborough in Cleveland, is now largely razed but retains a huge east window. The substantial ruins of Whitby Abbey overlook the sea; an inscription on a stone cross commemorates the Creation Hymn, one of the first poems in the English language, penned by Caedmon, an Anglo-Saxon herdsman.

The ruins of Rievaulx (pronounced "reevo") Abbey, desolate and still in sheltered Ryedale

RIEVAULX ABBEY

Before Henry VIII started his Dissolution of the monasteries in 1536, there were more monasteries in Yorkshire than in any other county in England. In North Yorkshire Rievaulx Abbey is the undoubted star. Founded in 1131, it became very prosperous, rich in sheep and by the 1160s there were 140 monks and 500 lay brothers. By the Dissolution numbers had dropped to 22. The ruins occupy a site of remote beauty in Ryedale.

▶▶ North York Moors National Park   *191C3*

(tel: 01287 660654)

This distinctive massif, tucked into Yorkshire's northeast corner, is England's largest tract of heather moor, a plateau dotted with ancient stone crosses and interrupted by contrasting green dales (valleys) scattered with red-roofed, yellow-stone farms and hamlets. The most dramatic scenery is at the point where the high terrain dips abruptly to the plain, as well as the sublime stretch of coast, absorbing villages, beaches, and walks along the east coast's highest cliffs. This variety of moods is perhaps the key to the area's enduring appeal.

THE MOORS AND DALES Farndale, celebrated for its wild daffodils, and **Rosedale**, once an ironstone-mining center, typify the contrasts of moorland plateau and lush vales. **Helmsley▶** is a small market town with craftstores, bookstores, and a handsome market square; close by are the east tower of the Norman castle and Duncombe Park, a revamped Palladian mansion memorable for its fine classical entrance hall and paneled saloon, and for its grass terrace complete with temples.

The village street of **Coxwold▶** is without blemish, all trim grass-edged lanes and stone cottages; Laurence Sterne lived and wrote *The Life and Times of Tristram Shandy* at what is now known as Shandy Hall (house open). Lonely St. Gregory's Minster in **Kirkdale** has a remarkably preserved Anglo-Saxon sundial from 1060. **Hutton-le-Hole▶▶**, with its sloping, sheep-nibbled green, is home to the Ryedale Folk Museum, where rural buildings have been rebuilt to give an insight into the life of yesteryear. **Lastingham Church▶** is built over a remarkable Norman crypt and the touristy village of **Thornton-le-Dale▶** has some pretty corners by its brook.

The area's major tourist attraction, the **North Yorkshire Moors Railway▶▶** runs from Pickering to Grosmont along unspoiled dale scenery (journey takes about an hour).

Enthusiasts reopened this line as the North Yorkshire Moors Railway in 1973; it had closed eight years earlier

Pickering▶ itself is a bustling market town with a lively local museum and the remains of a Norman castle (E.H.); look around the church for the set of 15th-century murals, one of the most complete in all of England. **Goathland** has a long green and sheep are everywhere; from the Mallyan Spout Hotel a path drops down to **Mallyan Spout**, a waterfall, while south of the village you can walk along a section of Roman road, **Wade's Causeway▶**. At **Grosmont** you can peer into the locomotive shed or take a train into **Eskdale**.

Much of the eastern moors is dominated by commercial forestry, including **Dalby Forest**, laid out with trails, picnic sites, and a drive; it abuts **Bridestones Nature Reserve**, where mushroom-shaped rocks are clustered on the moor. The western and northern escarpments, followed by the long-distance **Cleveland Way** footpath, offer grandstand views towards the Pennines and over industrial Teesside respectively; **Sutton Bank▶**, by the A170, is an inland cliff with a dizzying view across the Vale of York to the Pennines; at its southern end is the Kilburn White Horse, a 314 foot-tall hill carving created by local schoolchildren and their teacher in 1857.

ALONG THE COAST A footpath (the end of the Cleveland Way) follows the coast continuously; roads reach the coast in only a few places. **Staithes▶▶** is an authentic-looking fishing village, not too prettified; **Runswick Bay▶** is smaller and neater, picturesquely huddled beneath the cliff. **Whitby▶▶** was once a famous whaling center, hence the whalebone arch above town from which you can look across to the ruined abbey and St. Mary's Church. The town has expanded as a resort but kept its character in a maze of old streets around the harbor; a few shops still specialize in Whitby jet ornaments. The densely stocked Whitby Museum displays some impressive local fossils. A beach extends north to Sandsend.

Red-roofed **Robin Hood's Bay▶▶**, one of the most famous of all English fishing villages, clings to steep slopes that drop to the shore, where low tide reveals tide pools and fossils; tales of smuggling haunt the quaint hodgepodge of lanes. **Scarborough▶**, just outside the Park, is both a Regency spa and a Victorian resort with sandy bays. Wood End Museum displays natural history and has a section on the ultra literary Sitwell family, which used to live in this house. The Rotunda, a purpose built museum of 1828, features a Bronze Age tree trunk burial and displays on Victorian Scarborough.

CAPTAIN JAMES COOK
The great explorer was born in 1728 at Marton (now part of Middlesbrough, Cleveland), where a museum charts his life and travels. The site of the Cooks' house at Great Ayton is marked by an obelisk, and the school James attended is a modest museum. After being a shop apprentice in Staithes, he was apprenticed to a Quaker shipowner in Whitby (the house where he lived with his master is a museum of Cook's life). From 1768 onwards he undertook his voyages of discovery to New Zealand, the east coast of Australia, and the Pacific Isles. He was killed by natives in Hawaii in 1799.

The Laurel Inn, Robin Hood's Bay

York Minster, one of the wonders of Gothic architecture, as seen from the north corner of the city wall

▶▶▶ York

190B2

(tel: 01904 621756)

York is England's unrivaled showpiece cathedral city: nowhere else has such a concentration of medieval and other historic treasures. There are far more museums than can be visited in a single day (see page 206): the Castle Museum, the National Railway Museum, and the Jorvik Viking Centre are the top three. Around every corner are examples of buildings of every period, including medieval churches and time-warp streets like the Shambles, with its overhanging upper floors. Shoppers, sightseers, and street performers throng the center; much of it is pedestrianized and a pleasure to explore on foot. York prospered as a center of the wool trade in medieval times, when it was second only to London in importance.

THE CITY WALL▶▶▶ The Romans built the original defensive wall around the settlement of *Eboracum*, at the confluence of the rivers Ouse and Foss; in Viking times the city was known as Jorvik, later corrupted to "York". Today's wall is largely medieval. It can be followed along its top for much of its 2.75 mile length and provides a splendid city overview (see Walk, page 205); west of the river, the wall skirts a largely railroad-age residential area. The wall's gateways are known as bars; on Micklegate Bar during the Wars of the Roses, the heads of enemies would be exhibited on spikes.

THE MINSTER▶▶▶ Built 1220–1475, this is the largest medieval cathedral in Britain and the city's crowning glory. Its magnificent glass dates from 1150—look for the depictions of Genesis and Revelations in the east window, as well as the "Five Sisters" windows within a quintet of lancets. Look too for the rich interior of the chapter house, the painted roof of the nave, the carved rood screen, the undercroft display, and the Treasury.

THREATS FROM BELOW AND ABOVE

In the 1960s York Minster's lantern tower was threatened with imminent collapse. Only a major project, with supports erected between 1967 and 1972, saved the day; the undercroft exhibition gives a view of this repair operation. In 1984 the Minster was struck by lightning and was badly damaged by the fire that ensued. Some people interpreted this as an act of God after the Bishop of Durham, one of the Church of England's less traditional bishops, had made outspoken remarks that revealed his doubts about the literal truth of the Virgin Birth.

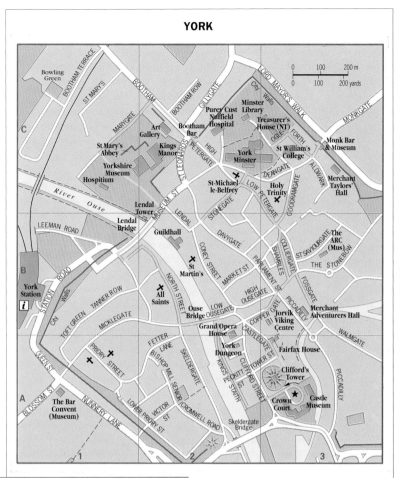

YORK

City highlights

Outside **Castle Museum▶▶▶**, face **Clifford's Tower▶**, turn left to take a path to the near side of the tower; beyond Ouse Bridge view the city from the north riverbank; recross by Lendal Bridge. Enter the **Museum Gardens**, pass fragments of medieval **St. Leonard's Hospital**; **Multangular Tower**, a Roman relic beside a section of Roman wall; and the ruins of **St. Mary's Abbey**. The **Yorkshire Museum▶▶** is also in this park.

Find a gate into Marygate and go to **Bootham Bar**; join the walkway along the top of the wall, with superb views of the Minster. Leave the wall at Monk Bar; the **Treasurer's House▶** (N.T.) is filled with 17th- and 18th-century décor, while **St. William's College** has an exhibition on the **Minster**. Skirt the **Minster▶▶▶** to its main entrance. Pass **St. Michael-le-Belfrey Church** (fine 15th- and 16th-century glass), detour to Stonegate for its store-fronts; go on along Low Petergate, detour left to Goodramgate for **Holy Trinity Church▶**. Find the **Shambles▶▶** York's most famous street. From Fossgate visit the **Merchant Adventurers' Hall▶▶**; beyond Coppergate are the **Jorvik Viking Centre▶▶▶** and the elegantly Georgian **Fairfax House▶**.

The Shambles, originally a street of butcher shops

York's museums

If you are visiting the city out of the summer months, check with the tourist office on special offers for rail travelers on accommodations and half-price entry to many attractions.

ARC▶ St. Saviourgate: hands-on archaeology for all; learn how to sort and label real Roman finds, and weave on a reproduction Viking warp-weighted loom.

Bar Convent Blossom Street: still a convent, but housing a museum on early Christianity in northern England.

Castle Museum▶▶▶ Eye of York: this alone justifies a visit to York. Collections include a full-scale cobbled street of stores, re-creations of domestic interiors over the centuries, and a working water mill by the river.

City Art Gallery Exhibition Square: includes nudes by local artist William Etty.

Clifford's Tower▶▶ (E.H.) Tower Street: this medieval keep was the site of the most horrifying event in English Jewry's history. In 1190, York's small Jewish community gathered inside the tower for protection from a violent mob. Many of the Jews took their own lives; others died when the tower was set alight, and any who surrendered were massacred.

Fairfax House▶ Castlegate: a Georgian town house with late 17th-century furniture, clocks, and paintings, mostly from Joseph Terry, a Quaker confectionery magnate.

Guildhall St. Helen's Square: a painstaking re-creation of the original 15th-century building, destroyed in an air raid.

Jorvik Viking Centre▶▶▶ Coppergate: entertaining and realistic time-travel journey into 10th-century Viking York. Go early or late when it is likely to be less busy.

Merchant Adventurers' Hall▶▶ Fossgate: the most impressive half-timbered building in the city; the 14th-century hall of a city merchants' guild, still in use.

National Railway Museum▶▶▶ Leeman Road: Britain's finest selection of historic locomotives and carriages. With working demonstrations and hands-on exhibits.

Richard III Museum Monk Bar: the medieval monarch on trial—guilty or not guilty?

York Dungeon Clifford Street: a chilling glimpse into a world of punishment and death.

Yorkshire Museum▶▶ Museum Gardens: Roman, Saxon, Viking and medieval treasures and finds, including a Viking ship and the Middleham Jewel.

The Castle Museum's re-created cobbled street, Kirkgate, takes its name from Dr. John Kirk, who started the museum with his collection of everyday miscellanea

Drive

This tour (approx 55 miles) takes in waterfalls, Castle Bolton, unspoiled dales, and lonely moors.

From the busy little town of **Hawes** at the heart of Wensleydale, take the

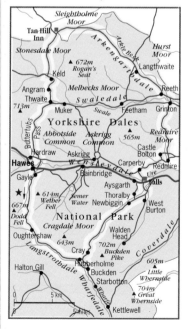

The Yorkshire Dales (see also pages 208–209)

A684 Sedbergh road, turning off very soon for an unclassified road leading to Kettlewell. Here you'll enter the northern end of **Wharfedale** at **Hubberholme** (with its charming church). The B6160 leads over into Bishopdale and **West Burton▶**, with its long village green. Proceed past **Aysgarth Falls**, taking the road rising up to the formidable fortress of **Castle Bolton▶▶**.

Beyond this, the road rises onto Redmire Moor; pause to admire the views at the top and drop down into **Swaledale** at **Grinton**. The odd castellated structure on the right as you descend is a former shooting lodge and now a youth hostel.

Grinton Church, grandiosely dubbed "Cathedral of the Dales," is worth a short pause, while **Reeth▶**, with its inns ranged around a sloping green, makes a good halfway stopping point.

The route goes along bleak **Arkengarthdale**, rising to the incredibly remote **Tan Hill Inn**, England's highest pub, near the meeting of Cumbria, North Yorkshire, and County Durham.

Re-enter **Swaledale** at **Keld**; beyond **Thwaite** the road to Hawes is known as the **Buttertubs Pass**, so-called because of the natural limestone "sinks" into which farmers used to place their butter to keep it cool on long journeys.

*Grassington, in
Wharfedale*

NIDDERDALE AND TEESDALE

Although outside the national park, Nidderdale's scenery matches the best of the Dales; but access is limited by grouse shooting (season: Aug 12–Dec 10) and reservoirs. How Stean Gorge has small cliffs; near Pateley Bridge (fine folk museum) are Brimham Rocks, a weird, naturally sculpted landscape of tors. Stump Cross Caverns are a tour-it-yourself show cave. North of the park, within County Durham, lies Teesdale in the midst of the wildest and emptiest tracts of the Pennines. High Force is the mightiest waterfall in England. With its harsh climate and unusual soils, the official nature reserve harbors Arctic and alpine species, including the rare Teesdale violet.

▶▶▶ Yorkshire Dales National Park 190B1
(tel: 01756 752774)

The great Pennine mass that forms the backbone of England has its proudest moments here, in the limestone dales and gritstone moors of the Yorkshire Dales National Park, where villages and field walls are almost universally grey stone. Spend a few days in the area and you will see the subtle differences between one dale and another.

WHARFEDALE This is a long dale, with several moods. Around **Bolton Abbey**▶, all is pastel-shaded and gentle, graced by the ruined Augustinian priory and the functioning priory church; upriver the Wharfe swirls through a chasm in Strid Wood. **Burnsall**, with its old bridge and green, and **Arncliffe** are two idyllic villages; **Grassington** is larger and busier, with a range of stores and places to eat around its central square. Looming over the dale is **Kilnsey Crag**, England's largest overhang, quite a challenge for rock climbers. Like many Dales places, **Buckden** and **Kettlewell** grew up around the lead-mining industry; relics litter the moors. Tiny **Hubberholme** has a gem of a church, with a rare musicians' gallery of 1558.

AIREDALE England's most famous limestone scenery is concentrated in the area around **Malham**▶▶▶, where the subterranean River Aire reappears at the base of Malham Cove, a great inland cliff. A short walk away, formidable Gordale Scar waterfall impressed the early Romantics. Other local walks include to Janet's Foss waterfall and Malham Tarn, with its rich plant and bird life. Downstream lies **Skipton**, a market town with a rewarding castle restored by the indefatigable Lady Anne Clifford after Civil War damage; a steam railroad heads into Wharfedale.

SWALEDALE Stone barns, abandoned lead mines (notably in Gunnerside Gill) and Swaledale sheep are features of the landscape along with the Swale itself. **Reeth**▶, ranged around a spacious green, is a charming large village and well placed for walks into neighboring Arkengarthdale.

The enchanting market town of **Richmond**▶▶▶ crowns a hilltop site, its mighty Norman **castle**▶▶ (E.H.) staring down to the Swale and over the marketplace. There are

*A traditional landscape:
Swaledale has 750 stone
barns and numerous
drystone walls*

One of the deep limestone shafts on Buttertubs Pass, a high route between Swaledale and Wensleydale

BARNARD CASTLE
Just beyond the park's northeastern boundary, in County Durham is the town of Barnard Castle, whose namesake castle (E.H.) perches above the Tees. The Bowes Museum here, built in opulent French château style, houses a splendid collection of fine arts.

THE DRUID'S TEMPLE
Lying outside the Dales national park's eastern boundary and tucked away in the woods at the end of a road west of Ilton, the Druid's Temple is one of Yorkshire's great surprises. At first sight it appears perfectly preserved prehistoric monument, but almost too perfect to be true: in fact it is a scaled down replica of Stonehenge (with additions), created in the early 19th century by a local landowner who wanted to give work to unemployed masons. The site is unstaffed and you need a good map to find it.

two museums (the Richmondshire Museum and the Green Howards regimental museum), and some choice streetscapes such as Frenchgate and Newbiggin Broad. Beyond one of two surviving town gateways, Cornforth Hill leads to a view of Culloden Tower, a fetching Georgian folly. Richmond's **Georgian Theatre Royal ▶ ▶** (1788), the oldest in its original form in England, is concealed by a barnlike exterior (*Open* for tours). There are tempting strolls beside the Swale, through Hudswell Woods or to the ruins of **Easby Abbey**.

WENSLEYDALE Cheese-making heritage is illustrated by rural relics in the Dales Countryside Museum in **Hawes** and shops sell the crumbly Wensleydale cheese. Villages such as **Askrigg**, **Bainbridge**, and **West Burton▶** have more appeal, while **Middleham▶ ▶** has a pretty square (around which horses from the nearby racing stables are paraded) and a 12th-century castle (E.H.), former home of Richard III. Of the dale's many waterfalls, **Aysgarth Falls** are the most well-known, with the best view a short walk downstream from the bridge. Look into Aysgarth Church, with its superb screen brought from **Jervaulx Abbey▶**, whose ruins can be seen further east. **Hardraw Force▶**, the tallest single-drop waterfall in England, is reached through the pub at Hardraw. **Castle Bolton▶ ▶** is an impregnable-looking bulk, little altered since the 14th century; Mary, Queen of Scots was imprisoned here between 1568–1569. **Masham▶** is attractively set around its large cobbled marketplace.

RIBBLESDALE AND DENTDALE Settle is a likeable market town, if noisy with quarry traffic; the train ride to Carlisle gives great views (see page 176). The "Three Peaks"— **Whernside** (2,414 feet), **Ingleborough** (2,372 feet) and **Pen-y-ghent** (2,277 feet)—are nearby; a popular challenge walk, often started from Horton-in-Ribblesdale, takes in all three. Ingleborough is dotted with potholes and caves, including **Ingleborough▶** and **White Scar▶** caverns (both *Open* to the public) and Gaping Gill, big enough to hold London's St. Paul's. Ingleton is the base for walks into **Ingleton Glen▶ ▶** (see page 193). Dentdale, in Cumbria, lies below Whernside; don't miss **Dent▶ ▶** with its cobbled streets, the epitome of the rural Pennines.

Limestone pavement above Malham Cove

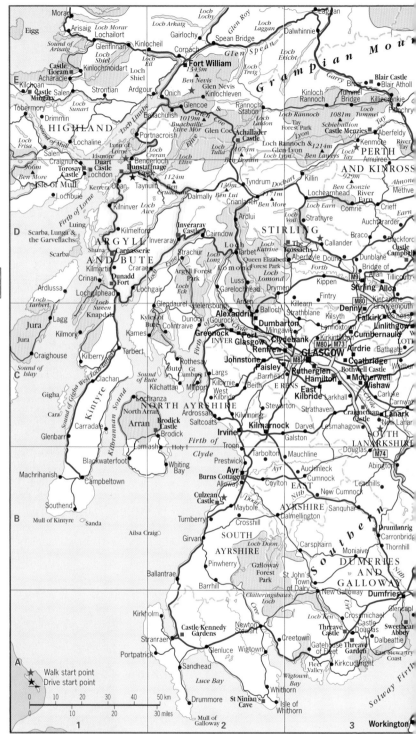

Braemar
Balmoral Castle
Linn o'Dee
Lochnagar
1154m
Lochnagar
North Esk
Strachan
Stonehaven

Deeside & Lochnagar
Clova
Spittal of Glenshee
Fettercairn
Inverbervie
Laurencekirk
Johnshaven

Kirkmichael
Edzell Castle
ANGUS
South Esk
Brechin
Abernethy
Montrose

Bridge of Cally
Kirriemuir
Forfar
Friockheim
Inverkeilor

Blairgowrie
Alyth
Isla
Glamis
Glamis Castle

Dunkeld
Birnam
Coupar Angus
Stanley
Muirhead
Dundee
Carnoustie

Perth
Scone Palace
Balbeggie
Monifieth
Newport-on-Tay
Firth of Tay

Glencarse
Newburgh
Leuchars

Echo Castle
Newburgh
St Andrews
Craigtoun

Auchtermuchty
Cupar
Ceres
Fife Ness
Crail

Falkland
Falkland Palace
Ladybank
FIFE
Pittenweem
Anstruther

Glenrothes
Kinross
Loch Leven
Leven
Elie
Earlsferry

Cowdenbeath
Buckhaven

Dunfermline
Kirkcaldy

Burntisland

South Queensferry
Inverkeithing
Firth of Forth
North Berwick

Hopetoun House
Gullane
Dunbar

EDINBURGH
East Linton

Musselburgh
Haddington
Cockburnspath
St Abb's Head

Livingston
Dalkeith
EAST LOTHIAN
Gifford
Grantshouse
St Abbs
Eyemouth

Loanhead
Bonnyrigg
Newtongrange
Lammermuir Hills

Penicuik
MIDLOTHIAN
Duns
Chirnside
Berwick-upon-Tweed

West Linton
Lauder
Greenlaw
Swinton

Dolphinton
Eddleston
Gordon
Coldstream
Ford

Peebles
Eildon & Leaderfoot
Galashiels
Kelso

Biggar
Traquair House
Abbotsford House
Melrose

Drumelzier
Upper Tweeddale
Selkirk
St Boswells
Town Yetholm
Wooler

Tweedsmuir
BORDERS (SCOTTISH)
Jedburgh
Cheviot Hills
816m
The Cheviot

Grey Mare's Tail
Hawick
Denholm

Moffat
Teviothead
Alwinton
Rothbury

Beattock
Eskdalemuir
Coquet

Hermitage
NORTHUMBERLAND
Otterburn

A74(M)
Kielder Water
West Woodburn

Langholm
Border Forest Park
Northumberland National Park
Kirkwhelpington

Lockerbie
Hadrian's Wall
Chollerford

Housesteads Fort
Chesters Fort

Gretna Green
Birdoswald Fort
Vindolanda

Caerlaverock Castle
Annan
Brampton
Haltwhistle
Hexham
Corbridge

Bowness-on-Solway
Carlisle
Crosby
Wetheral

Silloth
Wigton
Thursby
Alston
Castleside

Aspatria
CUMBRIA
Lazonby
Stanhope

Maryport
Bothel
Caldbeck
Langwathby
Melmerby
893m
Cross Fell
Wearhead
DURHAM

Cockermouth
931m
Skiddaw
Greystoke
Penrith
Cow Green Reservoir
High Force

Bassenthwaite

The miniature Highland scenery of the Trossachs: Loch Arklet

RECOMMENDED
CITIES Edinburgh, Glasgow.
INLAND TOWNS AND VILLAGES
Scottish Borders: Peebles.
Stirling: Stirling.
COASTAL TOWNS/VILLAGES
Angus: Arbroath, Montrose.
Fife: Anstruther, Crail, Culross, St. Andrews.
GREAT HOUSES
Angus: Glamis
Argyll and Bute: Hill House
Dumfries and Galloway: Culzean, Drumlanrig.
Perth and Kinross: Scone.
Scottish Borders: Abbotsford, Bowhill, Mellerstain, Traquair.
West Lothian: Hopetoun.
CASTLES
Argyll and Bute: Bothwell, Rothesay (Bute).
City of Edinburgh: Edinburgh.
Dumfries and Galloway: Caerlaverock.
Fife: Kellie, St. Andrews.
Stirling: Doune, Stirling.
West Lothian: Linlithgow. Craignethan.
RUINED ABBEYS AND CATHEDRALS
Dumfries and Galloway: Sweetheart.
Fife: St. Andrews.
Scottish Borders: Dryburgh, Jedburgh, Melrose.
Angus: Arbroath.
PALACES AND GARDENS
Stirling: Stirling.
Fife: Falkland.
West Lothian Linlithgow. Gardens
Dumfries and Galloway: Castle Kennedy, Threave.
City of Edinburgh: Edinburgh Royal Botanic Garden.

THE SCOTTISH NATION Scotland is now part of the U.K., but has a long history as an independent state. After having fought hard to maintain its sovereignty, Scotland surrendered its independence in an act of Parliamentary Union with England and Wales in 1707. Scotland's parliament was abolished and since then it has been ruled from London by a British parliament in Westminster. However, it was allowed to keep its church, legal and educational systems distinctive and separate. In 1997, the Scots voted to have their own parliament once again. The first elections for the Scottish Parliament were held in 1999, and a new Parliament building is being erected near the Royal Mile in Edinburgh; however, Scotland still retains Members of Parliament representing its views in Westminster.

THE LIE OF THE LAND Southern Scotland is composed of the Central Lowlands and the Southern Uplands, a wide band of hills that stretches from coast to coast. In the west this latter, wild area is known as **Dumfries and Galloway** while the eastern part is known as the **(Scottish) Borders**, though in fact both parts have acted since time immemorial as a war-torn border country, a self-governing shield between England and Scotland. The Lowlands occupy a rift valley, comprising the westward flowing River Clyde and the long eastern intrusion of the Firth of Forth. This is the heart of Scotland, studded with ancient Christian sanctuaries, sturdy medieval burghs, royal palaces, baronial seats, thickly populated manufacturing towns, and its great rival cities of Glasgow and Edinburgh. The Central Lowlands, encompassing **Argyll and Bute**; **West**, **mid-** and **East Lothian**; **Stirling**; **Fife** and part of the **Perth and Kinross** and **Angus** regions, are by no means uniformly low-lying. The handsome capital city of **Edinburgh** is perched among volcanic hills, Glasgow—Scotland's most populous city—is overlooked by the Campsie Fells, Dundee is fringed by the Sidlaw Hills, and the Kingdom of Fife is given a backbone by the Ochil Hills. The northern frontier of the Lowlands is the Highland Boundary

Fault. This is strikingly prominent feature cuts Scotland in two, with land rising abruptly on its northern side. The Fault divides the island of Arran in half, continues north-east through Helensburgh to Loch Lomond and skirts through old market towns such as Crieff and Dunkeld to reach Stonehaven on the east coast.

THE HERITAGE Most of the great prehistoric monuments of Scotland are found in the north, but there are good collections of Pictish and early Christian carved stones to be seen in Angus and St. Andrews. Viking invasions in the 9th century destroyed much of the evidence of Celtic Christianity except for the distinctive round towers at Brechin in Angus and Abernethy in Perth and Kinross. Dunfermline Abbey and the famous Norman church in Leuchars, near St. Andrews in Fife, are good examples of the Romanesque influence, which came to Scotland in the late 11th century. This was followed by the Gothic period, well represented by the ruined Border abbeys as well as the surviving cathedrals of Dunblane and Glasgow.

The 15th century is the most distinctively Scottish period: the simpler collegiate church developed then, with battlemented towers and stone-slabbed roofs and spires. This period also saw the birth of the tower house with its thick, vertical stone walls, a concept gradually enriched by combining towers into L, T and Z plans; the roofs budded a playful array of corner turrets, crow-stepped gable ends, and balconies. The neat burghs, or market towns, are dominated by a broad high street, typically with a mercat cross and the Tolbooth, which served as both jail and town hall. The 16th-century royal palaces at Linlithgow, Falkirk, and Stirling reveal the influence of the Renaissance, but it was not before the more peaceful politics of the late 17th century that Scotland produced a truly classical style. Sir William Bruce ushered in this period, but it was dominated by two generations of the Adam family (William and sons—Robert, James and John), who gave the term Adamesque to their Palladian vision of 18th-century Britain. Mellerstain, Culzean, and Charlotte Square in the New Town of Edinburgh are among the family's great works.

In the early 19th century the Romantic movement encouraged a return to a native Scottish spirit, leading to the Gothic-Baronial style of the high Victorian era, which still dominates the land.

By contrast the unrivaled modernist architect Charles Rennie Mackintosh created an idiosyncratic version of Art Nouveau in such buildings as Hill House and the Glasgow School of Art, among many others.

O Caledonia! stern and wild,
Meet nurse for a poetic child!
Land of brown heath and shaggy wood,
Land of the mountain and the flood,
Land of my sires! what mortal hand
Can e'er untie the filial band
That knits me to thy rugged strand?
—Sir Walter Scott, *The Lay of the Last Minstrel* (1805)

▶▶▶ **REGION HIGHLIGHTS**

The (Scottish) Borders *pages 217, and 218–219*

Caerlaverock Castle *page 221*

Culross *pages 226–227*

Culzean Castle *page 216*

Edinburgh *pages 223–225*

Glasgow *pages 228–229*

New Lanark *page 220*

St. Andrews *page 230*

Stirling Castle *page 231*

Threave Castle and Gardens *page 221*

213

SCOTS GLOSSARY
Some of the Gaelic and local terms you might come across:
Ben Mountain
Broch Circular stone defensive tower
Burn Stream
Ceilidh Impromptu gathering with singing and storytelling
Croft Small farm, often tenanted
Firth Narrow sea inlet
Glen Valley
Law Isolated hill
Linn Waterfall
Loch Lake
Lochan Small lake
Machair Coarse grass beside the sea, often used for grazing
Mull Promontory

Walks

Callander Crags, Stirling *210D3*
Parking lot on west side of Callander.
A marked path from Tulipan Crescent,
by the tennis courts, leads into
woods. A steep climb is rewarded by
splendid views of the Trossachs from
the top of the Crags, which form the
edge of an abrupt escarpment.
(1.5 hours)

Culzean Country Park, *210B2*
South Ayrshire
Parking lot by Culzean Castle. The
park is laced with trails; a detailed
map is available on site. Aim to visit
the castle, Happy Valley (with its
exotic trees), the walled garden, and
Swan Pond. Maidens village to the
south is an alternative starting point,
where you can walk along the shore to
the estate gates. (1–2 hours)

Grey Mare's Tail, *211B4*
Dumfries and Galloway
*Parking lot by A708 between Selkirk
and Moffat.* A fine waterfall, visible
from the road, but worth taking either
of the marked trails for close-up
views. The longer trail climbs to the
top of the fall and heads for lonely
Loch Skeen. (1–2.5 hours)

*St. Abb's Head: the view of the cliffs
at White Heugh, where guillemots and
kittiwakes may be seen*

New Lanark, *210C3*
South Lanarkshire
Parking lot in New Lanark. This "model"
village is quite remarkable, and is the
starting point for walks along the Clyde
Gorge, with its dramatic waterfalls.
Walk south, parallel with the river,
through the village, then fork right onto
a track, and right again onto a path
above the river. Cross the river at a
sluice bridge and turn right for further
views to ruined Corra Castle. Return
the same way. (2 hours)

St. Abb's Head, *211C5*
(Scottish) Borders
*Parking lot by nature reserve visitor
center just west of St. Abb's village.* A
short path leads towards the village,
then turns north parallel with the
coast for bracing cliff views to the
lighthouse at St. Abb's Head, where
there are nesting sites for 50,000
birds, including puffins. Either return
along the cliffs or take the easier lighthouse access road, with spectacular
views of the coast. (1 hour)

▶ **Angus** *211E5*

(Angus and City of Dundee Tourist Board tel: 01382 527527)

The county of Angus extends westwards from the North Sea across prosperous farmland (renowned for its black cattle) to the Grampians. The best scenery is to be found in the "Braes of Angus"—beautiful glens such as Glen Isla, Glen Prosen, Glen Clova, and Glen Esk—and on the rocky coast between **Montrose▶** and **Arbroath▶**. Montrose is a delightful summer resort whose Flemish-style architecture reflects centuries of trading with the Low Countries. **Montrose Basin**, the adjacent brackish tidal inlet, is the haunt of thousands of birds, including oystercatchers, curlews and pink-footed geese; there is a wildlife center on the A934. The fishing and market town of Arbroath, too, has something of a resort air in the summer. Its most famous monument is the 12th-century, red-stone abbey—a picturesque ruin which is surrounded by tombstones.

Inland and north of Arbroath by 14 miles is **Brechin**, a red-stone market town on the banks of the River South Esk. Standing proud beside the small cathedral is Scotland's finest **round tower▶**. Only three such tall towers are known outside Ireland; they date from the 10th century and were used as the refuge and watchtower of the independent monasteries of the Celtic Church. At **Aberlemno**, 5 miles southwest along the back road to Forfar, are some fine carved Pictish stones.

Due north of Brechin is **Edzell▶ ▶** (H.S.). The ruins of its castle are handsome enough, but it is the Pleasance, the walled garden laid out by the scholar Sir David Lindsay in 1604, that makes the place exceptional.

In the fertile Vale of Strathmore, a little southwest of Forfar, is **Glamis Castle▶ ▶** (as in Shakespeare's *Macbeth*), its brooding bulk standing quiet and solemn in the spacious acres of its deer park. Near the castle, a row of stone-roofed cottages houses the **Angus Folk Museum ▶** (N.T.S.) of reconstructed interiors and domestic bygones.

▶▶ **Arran** *210C1/C2*

(Ayrshire and Arran Tourist Board tel: 01292 288688)

The largest of the Clyde Islands, Arran is a traditional vacation island, easily and quickly reached from Glasgow by train and ferry. Sheltered by the Kintyre Peninsula, it enjoys unusually warm weather and has dramatic mountains (Goat Fell rises to 2,867 feet), deep valleys, and sandy and rocky bays. As you approach the island on the ferry from Ardrossan, **Brodick Castle▶** (N.T.S.), an ancient stronghold of the Stuarts and from 1503 the Hamilton family, dominates the shoreline. Its gardens include one of the finest rhododendron collections in Scotland. Arran is studded with prehistoric stones and is a paradise both for hikers and birdwatchers, and for geologists, who come by the busload because virtually every rock type is represented on the island.

North lies the flatter, fertile island of **Bute**. Another important Clyde resort, the capital town of Rothesay is reached by ferry from Wemyss Bay. Ruined Rothesay Castle, like Arran's, was once the property of the Stuart kings: Cromwell destroyed it in the 17th century. Following a minor road to the south of the island and then a footpath across a field, you can walk among the ruins of St. Blane's monastery with views of the Firth of Clyde.

ANGUS TRIVIA
● The Angus market towns proudly boast more fish-and-chip shops per head of population than anywhere else in the world.
● Arbroath has its own, separate culinary status as the home of "Arbroath Smokies", split smoked haddock on the skin.
● In 1885 Arbroath entered a team in the Scottish Cup that recorded the highest score in British football history. They beat Bon Accord 36–0. The score might have been even greater: much time was spent retrieving the ball when a goal was scored, as the goalposts then had no nets and seven further goals were disallowed for offside. The Arbroath goalkeeper was said to have smoked a pipe throughout the match.
● The Declaration of Arbroath was an open letter presented by the abbot of Arbroath in 1320, signed by all the dignitaries of the land and addressed to the Pope. It summarised the case for an independent Scotland.

Brodick Castle and Garden, Isle of Arran

ROBERT BURNS

Often described as Scotland's ploughman poet, Robert Burns (1759–1796) was well educated for his time. Though his amorous exploits have gained notoriety, his contribution to literature was through poetry that shrewdly observes the foibles of his fellow men. He also wrote numerous sentimental, lyrical and narrative pieces and was an avid "improver" of Scottish traditional songs. A major theme running through his work was a belief in the universal brotherhood of man.

MORE BURNS SITES

Near the birthplace and Burns Museum in Alloway are the Brig o'Doon and 17th-century Alloway Kirk; both feature in Burns's poem *Tam o'Shanter* and Burns was baptized in the Kirk itself. The imposing Burns Monument was erected in 1823 and bears figures (added five years later) of Tam o'Shanter and his drinking companion, Souter Johnny.

▶ **Ayr** *210B2*

(Tourist information center tel: 01292 288688)

Admirers of Scotland's national poet, Robert Burns, will need no encouragement to visit his birthplace at **Alloway**▶▶ on the southern outskirts of the coastal resort of Ayr. Burns, who was one of the few European poets to rival Shakespeare for wit and vigor, spent his first seven years at the humble cottage next to what is now the **Burns Museum**. Close by, the **Tam o'Shanter Experience** is an audiovisual show recounting his famous poem. To the south is the **Burns Monument** of 1823.

High on a clifftop 12 miles down the coast road from Ayr, **Culzean Castle**▶▶▶ (N.T.S.), built 1772–1790 and the ancient seat of the Kennedys, hides behind its battlemented exterior a supremely elegant classical interior by Scottish architect Robert Adam, one of his finest Scottish creations. The celebrated oval staircase rises through three tiers of columns to an exceptional second-floor salon. Culzean Country Park, with its walled summer garden, woodland walks, lake, and camellia greenhouses, is the most popular of the National Trust for Scotland's properties. Laid out on the dunes a little south of Culzean is the famous **Turnberry Golf Course**.

Culzean Castle, Robert Adam's elegant creation

THE (SCOTTISH) BORDERS

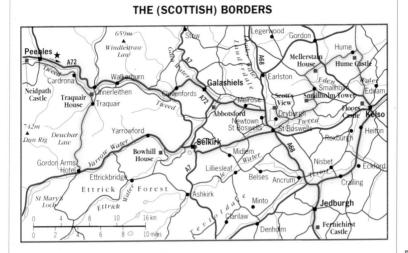

Drive

The (Scottish) Borders towns, abbeys, and houses to visit

A 100 mile tour of the best of the (Scottish) Borders towns, abbeys, and uplands. See also pages 218–219.

Start from **Peebles** and take the A72 east, following the Tweed, to **Traquair House**▶▶ outside Innerleithen. Continue along the A72 (passing the Scottish Museum of Woollen Textiles in Walkerburn) to reach Galashiels. Here, look for the turning to Walter Scott's house, **Abbotsford**▶. From Abbotsford join the A72, but turn off into **Melrose** for the ruined **abbey**▶▶ (H.S.). Head back onto the A72 then the A68 for St. Boswells and **Dryburgh Abbey**▶▶ (H.S.). Detour north on the B6356 to Scott's View. Take the B6404 for a look at **Smailholm Tower**▶ (H.S.) on your way north to **Mellerstain House**▶▶. From here cross to **Hume Castle** and join the B6364 to Kelso to see its ruined abbey and, to the west of town, **Floors Castle**▶▶.

Follow the A698 south along the Teviot Valley to **Jedburgh**▶▶ with its ruined **abbey**▶▶ (H.S.), Jail Museum and Mary, Queen of Scots House. You can detour south of the town to Ferniehirst Castle Centre and the Capon Tree. From Jedburgh take the A68 north to St. Boswells and turn west onto the A699 to **Bowhill House**, west of Selkirk.

Follow Yarrow Water upstream, along the A708, turning north at Mountbenger onto the B709 for the lonely crossing of Deuchar Law to Traquair House. From here a small road on the south bank of the Tweed passes **Kailzie Gardens**, near Cardrona, on the return to Peebles.

Dryburgh Abbey, founded in 1150

Young Walter Scott, in Smailholm Tower

THE EILDON HILLS AND WALTER SCOTT

Legend has it that these pink hills that rise prominently out of the valley near Melrose were cleft in three one night by the 13th-century wizard Michael Scott (Michele Scot in Dante's *Inferno*), to settle a dispute with the devil (the wizard's spellbook is said to be buried in Melrose Abbey). Geologists insist they are the relics of old volcanoes. Either way, they make excellent walking territory for those staying in Melrose and were a favorite of Sir Walter Scott. Visit Scott's View, beside the B6356 north of St. Boswells, for the view of them he so enjoyed.

▶▶ The (Scottish) Borders 211B4

(Scottish Borders Tourist Board tel: 01750 20055)

As famous for its salmon as for its tweed, the (Scottish) Borders is a land scarred by centuries of turbulence. Fought over since the days of the Romans, it has many sites that bear silent testimony to this past—tower houses built to ward off border raiders, skeletons of abbeys vengefully destroyed by England's Henry VIII. It is also Sir Walter Scott country, the countryside that inspired Scotland's most celebrated novelist. There is nowhere else quite like it in Scotland—a pleasant coast, no big mountains but lonely, rounded hills, good for bracing moorland walks. Even in the vacation season, there are no tourist jams.

The town of **Jedburgh▶▶** is best known for its **abbey▶▶** (H.S.) and anyone planning to visit the four great Borders abbeys—Jedburgh, Dryburgh, Melrose, and Kelso—should visit the Abbey visitor center here, which admirably explains their role. Jedburgh Abbey holds the record for raids—destroyed and rebuilt eight times in its 400-year working life. Its finest features are the two late Norman doorways and the excellent tracery window in the north transept. Also in the town are **Mary, Queen of Scots House**, which tells the story of the queen who stayed here in 1556, and the **Castle Jail Museum**.

Selkirk is a tweed-manufacturing town and a good base. **Bowhill House▶** is 4 miles west, set in the high ground between two tributaries of the Tweed. Its many magnificent works of art include the last Leonardo da Vinci in private hands in Britain. The house is surrounded by beautiful grounds.

Just outside Innerleithen, is **Traquair House▶▶**, one of Scotland's oldest inhabited houses, dating from about 1,000 years ago, although most of the structure is 17th century. Its forbidding outline is softened by the pale harling of its walls, but it remains dark and chilly inside. In the gardens the excellent maze is popular with children. The house includes an 18th-century brewery, which produces the excellent Traquair House beers. **Peebles**, a pleasant town set on the River Tweed, is popular for outdoor pursuits, such as walking, golf, fishing, and cycling. The 90-mile long Tweed Cycleway starts at nearby Biggar.

Children's playthings on display in Traquair House

Between Galashiels and Melrose is **Abbotsford▶▶**, the imposing turreted mansion that the great novelist Sir Walter Scott had built on the banks of the Tweed. It is still inhabited by his descendants and houses his extraordinary collection of assorted Scottish curiosities.

Melrose is an appealing town. Close by the compact main square stands **Melrose Abbey▶▶** (H.S.), its remains being the finest example of the golden age of Scottish ecclesiastical architecture. Its soft pink stone is warm, forgiving, and kind, and a magical atmosphere pervades the site. Robert the Bruce's heart is said to be buried here. From the town there are delightful walks up to the Eildon Hills (see panel, page 218) and along the River Tweed.

Dryburgh Abbey▶▶ (H.S.), set peacefully in an exquisite bend of the graceful River Tweed near St. Boswells, is the most moving of the four Borders abbeys. Large sections stand astonishingly well preserved, especially the cloisters. If you walk nowhere else, walk here; it's the best way to enjoy the peace and tranquillity of Scotland's most serene ruin. Leave your car and cross the Tweed by the footbridge.

A little way northeast is **Smailholm Tower▶** (H.S.), a classic pele tower (see panel). **Mellerstain House▶▶** is found 6 miles northwest of Kelso. This breathtaking Georgian house, built by William and Robert Adam in the

mid-18th century (see panel page 51), is the perfect example of the Adams' skill in combining stateliness with domestic ease and comfort. Inside, the large, wide, light rooms, in their pale Adam colors, are as perfect as the day they were finished. A museum contains a wonderful portrait of Bonnie Prince Charlie disguised as Flora MacDonald's Irish maid, Betty Burke (see page 246).

Kelso is a proud town, but the abbey ruins are the least captivating of the Borders' abbeys, the square tower resembling a fortress. To the west of Kelso stands **Floors Castle▶▶**, its William Adam and William Playfair exterior one of the stateliest of all the Border palaces. On a sunny day its pinnacled façade gleams above its terraced riverside grounds. Only the hall retains its original Adam interior, but in the state rooms are many treasures. The 19th-century Gothick bird room is a popular curiosity.

The coast at **St. Abb's Head▶** (see Walks, page 214) is a prime site for naturalists and birdwatchers.

PELE TOWERS
The word "pele" or "peel" is derived from the Latin *palus* or palisade and was the name given to the tower houses built around the Scotland-England border against the raiding enemy. Smailholm Tower, near St. Boswells, is a well-preserved example from the 16th century. Then it housed a continuous day and night watch; now it stands square and stern and stark on a moorland crag, overhanging a sullen pool. The 15th-century tower house at Cranshaws in the Lammermuir Hills features in Scott's *The Bride of Lammermuir*.

Founded in the 12th century, Jedburgh Abbey was used as a place of worship until 1875

TWEED MAKING
For countless centuries Borderers have made tweed, a practical, hard-wearing woollen cloth that was formerly known as "Galashiels Grey." In the 1820s Sir Walter Scott brought the material to the attention of fashionable London society by making a sensational appearance in black-and-white checked trousers and later tweed enjoyed the patronage of Queen Victoria and Prince Albert. The styles and colours have become more sophisticated and today many spinners, weavers, designers, and tapestry makers work in the Borders. In Galashiels, the **Scottish College of Textiles** is a renowned center, while the **Lochcarron of Scotland Visitor Centre**, Waverley Mill (*Open for tours*) is the producer of the world's largest range of wool worsted tartans.

THE COVENANTERS

The Covenanters were a leading faction of Scottish society in the 17th century that supported a Presbyterian system of church government. The National Covenant was signed in 1638 and the bishops, appointed by the Crown, were abolished the same year. Under the leadership of Archibald Campbell, 8th Earl of Argyll, the Covenanters successfully opposed an army sent north by Charles I. This campaign, known as the First Bishops War, led directly into the greater engagement of the Civil War. Sir Walter Scott's novel *Old Mortality* tells the story of the Lowland Covenanters and the extremes to which their religious fervor led them.

The Falls of Clyde run through a gorge just below New Lanark

MARY, QUEEN OF SCOTS' LOVER

James Hepburn, Earl of Bothwell, is one of history's more exciting characters. He was the lover of Mary, Queen of Scots, the possible father of James VI and certainly the murderer of Darnley, the queen's second husband, whose body was found strangled outside the bombed-out house of Kirk O'Field. He then divorced his wife and rushed the queen out to a secret marriage at Dunbar Castle in 1567. Hounded by their enemies, the lovers were, however, forced to part and Bothwell was eventually imprisoned in the Danish Castle of Dragsholm, where he died insane.

▶ The Clyde Valley   210C3

(Greater Glasgow and Clyde Valley Tourist Board tel: 0141 204 4400)

Deep in the wooded Clyde Valley near Lanark (see Walks, page 214) is the 18th-century model mill town of **New Lanark**▶▶. It is linked with such key figures of the Industrial Revolution as the inventor Richard Arkwright and Robert Owen (1771–1858), the social reformer, who attempted through enlightened programs to create a cooperative industrial community here; Owen believed that such ideas would one day replace private ownership. His Nursery building, the Institute for the Formation of Character, the school, and apartments housing the workers have all been restored. You can take in a short introductory history "ride" in the award-winning visitor center before looking in at Robert Owen's House, the Millworker's House, and the period-style village store.

Some 5 miles west of Lanark, **Craignethan Castle**▶▶ (H.S.) is a fine example of a 16th-century stronghold. The most exciting feature is the caponier, a vaulted gallery built onto the floor of the moat providing protection from artillery fire (though it nearly suffocated the defenders in smoke); this one is thought to be the earliest in Britain.

Bothwell▶▶, southeast of Glasgow, boasts a pretty 14th-century church and a monument, which commemorates the defeat of the Covenanters (see panel) in 1679. The town is chiefly renowned for its 13th-century castle, set high above the Clyde, its walls studded with round towers. This strategic castle was much damaged in the Wars of Independence of 1296–1330 against England.

▶ Dumfries and Galloway · 210B3

(tel: 01387 253862)

The western hills are wilder and more expansive than those of the better-known (Scottish) Borders district to the east. The character of the region is also more solemn, though it is enlivened by some interesting archeological sites, some haunting ruins, and some splendid castles. While much of the countryside inland is humdrum, the southern coast is a pleasant place to wander around, with an occasional surprising view of the English Lake District (best from the top of Criffel, south of Dumfries). The area is never crowded; some of the wildest parts of the Southern Uplands are in Galloway Forest Park (parts of which are tediously blanketed in evergreen plantations), and some of the Lowlands' most beautiful countryside is in the hills and valleys of the Rivers Nith, Annan, and Esk, to the north and east of the gray-stone town of Dumfries.

Standing beside the Solway Firth 9 miles south of Dumfries is **Caerlaverock Castle▶▶** (H.S.). Its unusual triangular plan, its full moat, and the green serenity of its site make this, "the lark's nest" castle, one of the most memorable in the country. It has been much fought over, and the outer walls were beseiged by King Edward I in 1300 less than a decade after the foundations had been laid. The interior bears a very fine Renaissance facade added by the enlightened Lord Nithsdale, head of the Maxwell clan, in the 17th century. Not far away at Ruthwell is the particularly fine carved Anglo-Saxon **Ruthwell Cross▶**. Over 16 feet high and dated to the 7th century, it is one of the most important monuments of the Dark Ages.

Threave Castle and Threave Gardens (N.T.S.)▶▶, a grim castle and a delightful garden, lie a few miles apart near Castle Douglas, 10 miles northeast of Kirkcudbright. Threave Castle was built by Archibald the Grim, who boasted how the awful gallows' knob that sticks out over the entrance "never wanted a tassel." Threave Castle was a 14th-century stronghold of the notorious Black Douglases, so called because of their merciless pillaging, and was besieged unsuccessfully by the royal forces of James II (of Scotland) in 1455. South of the ruined castle is the Threave Wildfowl Refuge, where wintering birds include wild geese and teal.

CURLING
For at least 350 years this team game, played on ice, has been enjoyed all over Scotland. The curling stones are made from granite and have handles sunken into the top. The object is to slide the stones along the ice into a tee, the team with the most stones at the center of the tee being the winner. The best stones are reputed to be from Ailsa Craig, a 1,100 foot-high volcanic plug of rock 10 miles off Girvan that persistently pops up into view as you drive around the Ayrshire coast.

221

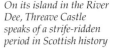
On its island in the River Dee, Threave Castle speaks of a strife-ridden period in Scottish history

DULCE COR
The beautiful ruined red walls of Sweetheart Abbey, south of Dumfries on the A710, have a romantic tale to tell. The abbey was founded in 1273 by Lady Dervorgilla after her husband John Balliol was killed by Robert the Bruce (she also founded Balliol College, Oxford, in his honor). She kept her husband's embalmed heart close to her until her death at the age of 90. Both were then interred in the church, which became known as Dulce Cor ("sweet heart").

Drumlanrig Castle, ringed by forests and rolling hills

The nearby (but separately administered) Threave Gardens are where the National Trust for Scotland trains its budding young horticulturalists. Every type of terrain and condition they are likely to encounter is authentically re-created here, from rose to heather garden, from rock to wood; there are herbaceous borders, a walled garden, and fabulous glasshouses in which exotic flowers and fruits grow. In spring there is a display of some 200 different types of daffodil.

The town of **Kirkcudbright▶** is set sweetly on the River Dee around MacLellan's Castle. With its typical pastel-painted housefronts, it has long been beloved of Scottish artists; Edward Atkinson Hornel was a member of the artists' colony founded here in the early years of the 20th century. There are several art galleries in the town today. It is a tranquil place to spend a day wandering around. Visit the ancient tollbooth, with its curious and beautiful spire, or the Stewartry Museum with its many local antiquities and curios; a display explains the strange and ancient Scottish pastime of curling (see panel, page 221). In Gatehouse of Fleet, 8 miles northwest, is the **Mill on the Fleet▶**, a visitor center based on a restored 18th-century cotton mill that portrays the town's industrial past.

Whithorn, 18 miles south of Newton Stewart, is one of the oldest Christian centers in Britain; here, in 397, St. Ninian built the first Christian church in Scotland, although the present ruin dates from the 13th century. The Whithorn Museum (H.S.) has finds related to the saint.

The southwesternmost corner of this region is the strange spit of land known as the Rhinns of Galloway (from which there are views of the Mourne Mountains across the water in Northern Ireland). Here is the **Logan Botanic Garden▶**, where plants from the temperate regions of the southern hemisphere thrive in a walled garden. **Castle Kennedy Gardens▶**, near Stranraer, were laid out on a grand scale by the 18th-century Earl of Stair, with ruins, lakes, and wooded walks. It is at its most majestic when the rhododendrons and azaleas are in bloom in early summer.

In the northern part of Dumfries and Galloway, set beside the River Nith near Thornhill, is **Drumlanrig▶▶**. No building looks more solid or more imposingly rooted in Scotland than this pink 17th-century palace. Within its massive walls are the region's finest collections of Old Masters, including a Rembrandt and exquisite French furniture of the 18th century. Rural craftsmen, with work for sale, operate in the grounds.

▶▶▶ Edinburgh

(tel: 0131 473 3800)

211C4

The capital of Scotland is an outstanding city. It is rich in open spaces, museums, beautiful buildings, and elegant streets, all lit by the clear Lothian light. The dark courts, cobbled streets, and steep steps of the medieval Old Town contrast with the gracious squares, circuses, and crescents of the Georgian New Town. It is at its most exhilarating during the International Festival and Fringe in August.

The Royal Mile▶▶▶ is the original and chief street of the city. At its western end lies the **castle**▶▶ (H.S.), on the site of an ancient fortress and home to the Scottish Crown Jewels; at the other end are the Abbey and **Palace of Holyroodhouse**▶, the official Scottish residence of the Queen (open to the public when the Royal Family is not here). The Royal Mile is the heart of the Old Town; many of the city's most historic landmarks are on it, and there are numerous museums and houses to visit (see panel).

St. Giles' Cathedral▶, the High Kirk of Edinburgh, was originally built in the traditional shape of a cross, though later additions have given it an unusual square design. **Canongate Kirk**▶ is a dignified example of a Presbyterian church, with typical white-painted walls and wooden box pews. **The Royal Museum of Scotland**▶▶ on Chambers Street is a worldwide collection with decorative art and archeology galleries, a natural history section, a geology department, and (most popular with the young) technology galleries. Admission covers the adjacent **Museum of Scotland**, which concentrates on all things Scottish. In Holyrood Road, **Our Dynamic Earth**▶▶ (a funded Millennium project) uses state-of-the-art technology in a voyage of discovery around our planet. **The Grassmarket**▶▶ is for many the most pleasant part of the Old Town, with its plentiful antiques stores and bistros.

The Mound is a causeway between the Old and New Towns. There are views across to breezy **Calton Hill**▶▶ where the **National Monument**▶ stands, modeled on the Parthenon in Greece to commemorate the Scots who fell in the Napoleonic Wars. Though never completed, it is

Princes Street and Edinburgh Castle, dramatically perched on a volcanic crag, as seen from Calton Hill

THE ROYAL MILE
The Camera Obscura, near the castle in the Outlook Tower, gives a "living image" of the city projected via lenses (best on a bright day). Opposite, **The Scotch Whisky Heritage Centre** tells all there is to know about whisky. **Gladstone's Land** (N.T.S.), on the Lawnmarket, is a re-creation of a typical Old Town, six-story tenement house. **The Writers' Museum** contains memorabilia of Scottish writers, including Robert Burns, Sir Walter Scott, and Robert Louis Stevenson. **The People's Story Museum** tells the story of ordinary folk from the 18th century on. **John Knox House** displays interesting artifacts from the life of this pivotal figure of the Scottish Reformation. Opposite is the absorbing **Museum of Childhood. Huntly House,** a striking 16th-century mansion, houses the city's excellent museum of its own history.

THE FORMER ROYAL YACHT *BRITANNIA*
The Queen's famous royal yacht, built in Clydebank near Glasgow and launched in 1953, is now a museum berthed at Leith, on the edge of Edinburgh. Britannia buses run by Guide Friday depart from Waverley Bridge, or you can take a less expensive city bus number 10 or 17 from the store side of Princes Street. Leith has pleasant waterfront restaurants.

THE NATIONAL GALLERY OF SCOTLAND
The collection includes Rembrandt's self-portrait at the age of 51, Poussin's sequence of *The Seven Sacraments* (now set in a room whose details are taken from the pictures), Velasquez's *Old Woman Cooking Eggs*, El Greco's *Savior of the World*, and many works by Scotland's own painters. *The Reverend Robert Walker Skating on Duddingston Loch* by Sir Henry Raeburn (1756–1823) is one of Scotland's favorite paintings. An excellent cross-section of modern works are on show at the Scottish National Gallery of Modern Art in Belford Road, west of the New Town.

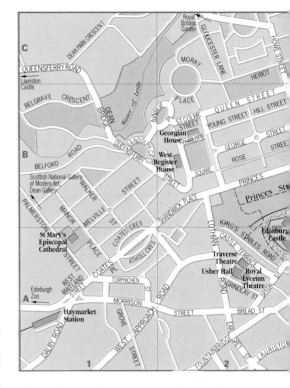

evidence of the 18th-century boast that Edinburgh had become the Athens of the North. Beside the Mound is the **National Gallery of Scotland▶▶▶**, a classical building housing the national art collection (see panel).

Princes Street▶ is the principal shopping street. Running along one side are Princes Street Gardens; the **Scott Monument** is the most striking, if endearingly excessive, landmark, covered with statuettes depicting characters from Sir Walter Scott's novels and poems; you can climb steps to the top.

In Queen Street, in the New Town, a distinctive red-brick Venetian palace houses the **Scottish National Portrait Gallery▶**. There is not one second-rate picture in the portrait gallery, and no shortage of famous subjects. Especially striking is the wonderful Allan Ramsay portrait of the great 18th-century Edinburgh philosopher David Hume. In 1791 Robert Adam was commissioned to design one superb square to enhance the quality of the New Town. Grand, spacious and elegant, his **Charlotte Square▶** is the quintessence of the New Town. No. 7, the **Georgian House** (N.T.S.), has been restored as a typical Georgian New Town home, giving a glimpse of an interior of about 1800.

The **Royal Botanic Garden▶**, beyond the New Town, has superb tropical greenhouses. Good walks are to be had on **Arthur's Seat**, a volcanic hill in Holyrood Park and along the **Water of Leith**, to the west of the New Town.

EDINBURGH

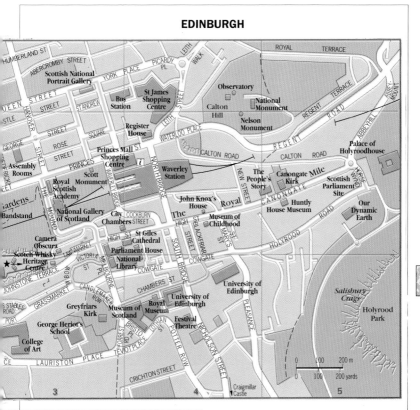

From the Castle to Charlotte Square

Start at the **Castle**▶▶, then enter the **Royal Mile**▶▶ at Lawn Market to visit the **Scotch Whisky Heritage Centre**▶, **Camera Obscura**▶ and **Gladstone's Land**▶ (N.T.S.). Continue along High Street past Parliament House, the Tron Kirk, **St. Giles Cathedral**▶, and the City Chambers. Go on past the **Museum of Childhood**▶ and **John Knox House** along Canongate, to the **People's Story Museum**▶, **Huntly House Museum**, and the **Canongate Kirk**▶, to the **Palace of Holyroodhouse**▶.

Return up Holyrood Road and along the Cowgate to pass the University, the **Royal Museum of Scotland**▶▶, **Greyfriars Church**▶ (and statue of the loyal little dog, Greyfriars Bobby) and then the **Grassmarket**▶▶. Turn up Victoria Street, left down Bank Street to **Lady Stair's House**▶ and then down the Mound to the **Scottish National Gallery**▶▶▶ and the **Royal Scottish Academy** (catch the views towards the National Monument on Calton Hill). Turn right onto **Princes Street**▶ to the **Scott Monument**, across and onto St. Andrew Square and Queen Street for the **Scottish National Portrait Gallery**▶ and **Museum of Antiquities**▶.

Follow George Street as far as Frederick Street, turn left, then right on Rose Street, and continue to Robert Adam's **Charlotte Square**▶ to visit the **Georgian House** (N.T.S.).

The Cramond ferry leaving the Dalmeny side of the river

END OF AN ERA
With the opening of the Forth road bridge, the villages that stand on either side of the Firth—known as North and South Queensferry—lost the ferry service that had existed for some 900 years. Among the earliest travelers here was Queen Margaret, wife of Malcolm Canmore, who used this route in the 11th century between her palace and her abbey near Dunfermline—hence the name "queen's ferry."

THE FORTH BRIDGES
The Forth train bridge, built between 1882 and 1889 and illuminated since its centennial, still wins the admiration of young engineers. For most of its life it was the longest bridge in the world. A little west is the fabulous modern suspension road bridge (1964), much lighter and a superb feat of modern engineering. A visitor center at South Queensferry explains the structures.

►► **The Firth of Forth**   211D4
(Edinburgh tourist information center tel: 0131 473 3800; Kingdom of Fife Tourist Board tel: 01592 750066)

The Firth of Forth is a wide tidal inlet that bites deep into the east coast of the country. From a first glance at a map it appears to have almost severed Scotland into two. It has functioned more as a trading canal than as a frontier moat. The long tidal shores are dotted with merchant towns whose markets and privileges are established in ancient royal charters. The old local adage says that a farm by the Forth is better than an earldom in the north—expressing the realities of this land that formed the heartland of the medieval kingdom of Scotland.

Four miles west of the Forth rail and road bridges is **Hopetoun House►**, the beautiful stately home of the Marquis of Linlithgow. Begun in 1699 by Sir William Bruce and completed by William Adam and his sons, it houses a sumptuous collection of paintings, tapestries, and furniture. An equal distance east of the bridges, near South Queensferry, is **Dalmeny►**, a large 19th-century house set in a fine park. It's home to one of Britain's outstanding Rothschild Mentmore collections of 17th-century French furniture, tapestries, and Sèvres porcelain. Dalmeny can be reached on foot along the estuary from Cramond, a lovely walk. **Cramond►** is a pretty village of whitewashed cottages and old mills at the mouth of the River Almond, on the outskirts of Edinburgh. A little ferry takes you across to the Dalmeny estates, and there are delightful walks up the riverbank.

Further west, still on the southern side of the Firth, **Linlithgow Palace►►**(H.S.) stands above the town of Linlithgow. At the time of Mary, Queen of Scots' birth here in 1542 it was a magnificent structure, but a fire in 1746 left it a ruin. Its enormous roofless red body survives and there is a fine octagonal fountain in the courtyard, a vast Great Hall, and a swath of grass around the outer walls on which to picnic.

Across the Firth, on the western edge of Fife, the small coastal town of **Culross►►►** (pronounced Coo-ross) is

set in an unpromising landscape of former coal mines with a distant view of the Grangemouth refinery. Persevere, however, for Culross is one of the jewels of the National Trust for Scotland. This perfectly preserved example of an early 17th-century trading burgh made its way in the world by digging coal from under the Forth, smelting iron to be hammered out into girdles, and boiling up seawater to extract salt. The cobbled streets are lined with traditional corbeled houses, roofed with the distinctive terracotta pantiles of Fife. You can inspect three period interiors: start at the town's Tolbooth where free video shows on local history are shown alongside the jail chamber in the basement. Next door is the restored palace of Sir George Bruce, the local entrepreneurial landowner, with its painted ceilings, tiled kitchen, and paneled rooms. Bishop Leighton's Study, also carefully restored, is the traditional name for the tall corbeled town house that overlooks the Mercat Cross. From there a short walk up steep Kirk Street leads to the slight ruins of a Cistercian monastery standing immediately beside the old abbey chapel, which has functioned, with later additions, as the parish church since the Reformation.

Dunfermline Abbey▶▶(H.S.) stands above the wooded glen of Pittencrieff Park in Dunfermline. The abbey was founded as a Benedictine house in the 11th century. Its tower and the eastern end were rebuilt in the 19th century to serve as a parish church, but the sturdy 12th-century nave with its solid pale stone columns, strong round arches, and the zigzag chevrons so characteristic of the Romanesque is more interesting. The visitor center has a good range of display material.

A more recent attraction at North Queensferry is **Deep Sea World**▶▶, an elaborate and innovative aquarium, with the world's largest viewing tunnel, as long as a football field. In summer, boat trips can be taken from South Queensferry, by the Forth bridges, to Inchcolm Island, to see the well-preserved abbey and a colony of seals.

See page 230 for more information on the fishing villages of the East Neuk of Fife.

Dunfermline Abbey, burial place of King Robert the Bruce

The Forth train bridge, which needs continuous repainting on a four-year cycle

ROYAL TENNIS
The 16th-century Falkland Palace (N.T.S.), inland from Kirkcaldy, was a favorite hunting seat of the Scottish kings until James VI died in 1625. The royal tennis court was built in 1539 and is still in use. Sir Walter Scott used the palace as the setting for part of his novel *The Fair Maid of Perth*, which was made into an opera by Bizet.

GLASGOW SCIENCE CENTRE

Opened in 2001 as a major Millennium project funded by revenue from the National Lottery, this development on the south bank of the Clyde in the Govan area has a range of hands-on activities. Exhibits include virtual volleyball, animatronic figures, space, the human body, and the environment, including monitoring the Clyde.

FOR A DIFFERENT PERSPECTIVE

To see another side of Glasgow, visit The Barras, the extensive and world-famous weekend flea market. It was established 100 years ago and now has 800 covered stalls. With street musicians, cafés, and even childcare, it makes for a lively visit, even if you don't find a bargain. The market is reached via London Road or Gallowgate in the East End (just north of the People's Palace).

The great shipbuilding yards on the Clyde were born in the 19th-century steam era when Clyde-built vessels acquired a high reputation worldwide

▶ ▶ ▶ **Glasgow** *210C3*

(Tourist information center tel: 0141 204 4400)

Glasgow's skyline of chimneys, factories, and high-rises offers a prospect of almost grotesque beauty. These outskirts are a reminder of Scotland's 19th-century industrial core, but the middle of Glasgow is today a place of captivating charm and a vibrant center. The city's merchant dynasties bequeathed it an extraordinary legacy of art and architecture—and most of the museums and galleries are free. The grid plan of the streets makes it easy to explore.

The city has three distinct areas: the original medieval center, the Merchant City, and the West End. The **cathedral▶**, a dark-hued, heavy Gothic glory begun in the 13th century, is one of the two surviving buildings of the medieval town, on the eastern side of the city. St. Mungo (or Kentigern) founded a missionary chapel here in the 6th century, around which the trading burgh of Glasgow later grew. Opposite the cathedral, the unique **St. Mungo's Museum of Religious Life and Art▶** explores the religions of the world. In High Street, is **Provand's Lordship**, built in 1471 for a canon of the cathedral and now displaying period artifacts and furnishings; it is the city's oldest house.

The Merchant City district has its origins in the heyday of the "tobacco lords." Glasgow was well placed for trade with the New World, and the 18th century saw a period of glory as an international trading city. By the 19th century Glasgow was one of the world's greatest shipbuilding centers and, in an expression of bursting civic pride, money was poured into the Merchant City district to create some of the best Victorian streets in Britain, with some of the most innovative architecture of the day. The great rectangular **George Square▶** is the center of Glasgow today, flanked on one side by the splendidly overblown facade of the **City Chambers▶ ▶** (*Free guided tours* of the marbled interior, 10:30 AM, 2:30 PM), built 1883–1888. Immediately to the north is Queen Street station; Central station, with its even more impressive 19th-century interior, is just a few blocks west. **Trades House** with its Adam facade dates from 1791, while **Hutchesons' Hall** and **Stirling Library** are early 19th-century. Glasgow Green is one of many city parks and here is the **People's Palace▶ ▶**, an excellent museum devoted to the social history of Glasgow, and its huge Winter Gardens conservatory. Nearby is the old Templeton's carpet factory (1889), an amazing replica of the Doge's Palace in Venice.

In the leafy area of the West End, with its fine early 19th-century town houses around Glasgow University, is the **Kelvingrove Art Gallery and Museum▶ ▶**, an enormous Victorian red sandstone building in Kelvingrove Park. It holds works of art from neolithic weapons to Cubist paintings; there is a strong emphasis on 17th-century Dutch and Flemish works. In Kelvin Hall, opposite, is an exciting **Museum of Transport▶ ▶**, with reconstructed Underground stations and stores, old trams, cars, and motorcycles. The **Hunterian Art Gallery▶ ▶** is renowned for its collection of works of James McNeill Whistler (1834–1903). Also strongly represented is 19th- and 20th-century Scottish art, including works of the Scottish colorists, the "Glasgow Boys," a group of painters who advocated realism in art instead of Victorian romanticism. The Mackintosh Wing is an elegant re-creation of the nearby house (now

The interior of the City Chambers

CHARLES RENNIE MACKINTOSH (1868–1928)

Mackintosh was prominent in the Arts and Crafts Movement and was the first Scottish architect since the 18th century to achieve international fame. While his stained glass and metalwork used the art nouveau motifs of intertwining tendrils, his buildings have a taut quality of geometric simplicity; his furniture design is typified by the tall, starkly simple ladder-chair. The Glasgow School of Art (1896–1909) is his masterpiece, designed when he was only 28; other notable buildings include Scotland Street School, the Willow Tea Rooms on Sauchiehall Street, and the Lighthouse (the former *Glasgow Herald* Building) in Mitchell Street—now a center of architecture and design including a Mackintosh Interpretation Centre. In Bellahouston Park, *House for an Art Lover* was built in 1996 using Mackintosh's plans of 1901. At Helensburgh, west of Glasgow, Hill House (N.T.S.) is an outstanding example of his domestic style.

Façade of the Glasgow School of Art

demolished) occupied and furnished by Glasgow architect Charles Rennie Mackintosh (see panel). Within the Botanic Gardens is a beautiful 19th-century glasshouse, **Kibble Palace▶▶**, where tree ferns grow amid white statuary.

The **Glasgow School of Art▶▶▶** (*Guided tours* Mon–Fri 11 AM and 2 PM, Sat 10.30 AM and 11:30 AM; plus Sat 1 PM and Sun 10:30 AM, 11:30 AM and 1 PM July–Aug), in Renfrew Street, is the finest completed example of Mackintosh's vision. It houses a comprehensive collection of his paintings and his designs for furniture, metalwork, light fittings, and stained glass. **The Tenement House▶▶** (N.T.S.) on nearby Buccleuch Street is the ordinary city apartment of Miss Agnes Towards, preserved as she left it in 1965, having changed virtually nothing in over half a century. The simple dignity of her four-roomed home and belongings tell a visitor more about the realities of Scottish life than a dozen palaces.

A short drive out (or take a bus or train from Glasgow Central station; courtesy bus from Pollokshaws West rail station) is a fantastically light, glass-walled building, constructed in 1983 in the grounds of Pollock House. It houses the extraordinary art collection of shipping magnate Sir William Burrell. Though vast, the **Burrell Collection▶▶▶** (*Admission free*) is well worth a visit. Everything is of the best, be it Egyptian alabaster, Chinese ceramics or jade, Persian rugs, tapestries, stained glass, medieval illuminated manuscripts, or carved doorways.

St. Andrews, Scotland's first university town, seen from St. Rule's Tower

GOLF IN ST. ANDREWS
To many St. Andrews is synonymous with golf, a sport that has been played there since the 15th century. In 1754 local dignitaries set up the Society of St. Andrews Golfers, which had the title Royal and Ancient ("R & A") conferred upon it in 1834. New courses have been added around the Old Course, where the 18th hole is named after the great Tom Morris. There are more than 500 courses in Scotland, and "round" and day tickets are available at most (including St. Andrews, except for the Old Course); discounted golf passes cover some areas. For a Golf Map of all the courses, contact the Scottish Tourist Board (see page 274).

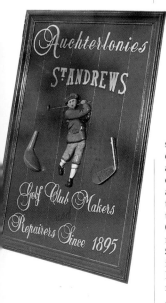

▶▶▶ St. Andrews   211D4
(tel: 01334 472021)

Scotland's oldest university, its first golf course, and the ruins of its principal pre-Reformation cathedral mingle with the everyday business of an old Fife market town and summer resort. It was already a holy place for the southern Picts when a shrine to St. Andrew, patron saint of Scotland, was established on the eastern clifftops in the 8th century. Within a century St. Andrews had become the administrative center of Christianity in Scotland. The top of 12th-century St. Rule's church tower gives a bird's-eye view over the enormous ruined nave of the adjoining 14th-century **cathedral▶▶**(H.S.) and of the town's little harbor with its long pier, known as a mole. Westwards along the coast are the ruins of the bishop's **castle▶** with its bottle dungeon, from which no one ever escaped, and 16th-century mine and counter mine (a defensive tunnel). Below the Martyrs' Memorial, the handsome **Royal and Ancient Club House** (home of the ruling body for golf the world over) overlooks the oldest course in the world and the **British Golf Museum**. Nearby a Sea Life Centre stands by the long West Sands. On the three converging streets that comprise the "auld grey toun" are lesser but impressive buildings such as the university's 15th- and 16th-century colleges and the West Port gate, all among town houses and secret "wynds," or alleyways.

The East Neuk A road south leads to **Anstruther▶**, one of several old fishing villages dotted along the southern coast of Fife's East Neuk. Here is the Scottish Fisheries Museum and an aquarium. There are boat trips in summer to the Isle of May. Fishermen's cottages in **Crail▶▶** are now home to artists and vacationers. To see a fishing fleet in action go to the harbor at **Pittenweem▶**. Flemish gables reflect former trading links with the Low Countries. Inland is **Kellie Castle▶▶** (N.T.S.), a good example of the 16th-century round tower houses typical of the Lowlands; another is **Scotstarvit Tower▶** (N.T.S.), near Ceres. Also in the vicinity is the **Hill of Tarvit Mansion-house** (N.T.S.), rebuilt by Sir Robert Lorimer in 1906 to house the art collection of a jute magnate; there are paintings by Sir Henry Raeburn and Allan Ramsay, fine furniture, Chinese porcelain, and an Edwardian laundry evocative of life "downstairs."

▶▶ Stirling   *210D3*

(tel: 01786 479901)

Stirling Castle▶▶ (H.S.) stands in a strategically commanding position on a volcanic crag, the symbolic key to Scotland, at the geographical and historical center of the country. Nearby, the **Old Town Gaol**, St. John's Street, recaptures the feel of prison life, with the actor-guide playing the role of both guard and prisoner.

On the other side of town, the **Bannockburn Heritage Centre** tells the story of the most famous battle in Scottish history (see panel). Midway between them on the banks of the Forth are the restored Gothic ruins of **Cambuskenneth Abbey**. Walk up to the old town to see the **Church of Holy Rood** where in 1543 Mary, Queen of Scots was crowned at the age of nine months. The **Guildhall**, the shell of **Mar's Wark**—built in 1570 as the town house of the 1st Earl of Mar, Regent of Scotland—as well as **Argyll's Lodging** (H.S.), are all notable buildings in this vicinity (all *open*). Within the grey castle walls are 18th-century artillery batteries, gardens, a royal chapel, and the Renaissance palace of the Stuart kings. Also here is the Argyll and Sutherland Highlanders regimental museum.

The **Wallace Monument▶▶**, on the northeastern edge of the town, commemorates Scotland's first freedom fighter, William Wallace; Wallace rose from obscurity to lead the national resistance to the advancing English king, Edward I, winning a victory at the Battle of Stirling in 1297.

Dunblane▶ is a small residential town beside the meandering River Allan. Although its name is now indelibly associated with the 1996 massacre, when a gunman opened fire on children at school, Dunblane does have one of Scotland's finer Gothic cathedrals. The tower is 12th-century, but the splendid interior, one long soaring 207-foot nave, is mid-13th century. The town is also a good base for touring the Ochil Hills to the east. At the foot of the Ochils near Dollar, 10 miles east of Stirling, **Castle Campbell▶** (N.T.S.), built at the end of the 15th century, stands perched on a huge crag. Do take the short trail around its base through Dollar Glen, part of it hewn out of rock, over catwalks and past cascades and drippy ferns. A little west of Dunblane, **Doune** is worth a visit for a fine 14th-century royal **fortress▶** (H.S.) and **motor museum**.

ROBERT THE BRUCE

The Battle of Bannockburn was one of the most decisive in Scottish history. For several years Robert the Bruce (1274–1329) had been successfully waging a guerilla war against the English—and those of the Scottish nobility whom he had alienated. In 1314 he was forced into a pitched battle over the vital control of Stirling Castle; with a mere 5,000 men but great cunning, he destroyed an English force of some 20,000. Stirling surrendered and Edward II fled to Dunbar; Scotland later won independence for 400 years, and Bruce was acknowledged as king of Scotland.

231

Castle Campbell towers above the Burn of Sorrow and the Burn of Care

TROSSACHS WALKS

The area's most energetic hikes are the main peaks such as Ben Ledi, Ben Lomond, and Ben Venue, but numerous lesser summits have fine views, among them Ben An (climb up from the Trossachs Hotel north of Loch Achray on the A821) and Conic Hill, near the southeast corner of Loch Lomond. For lower-level walks try the forest around David Marshal Lodge near Aberfoyle, where there is an old tramway to explore, or the wooded glen north of Rob Roy's Grave at Balquhidder. (See also Walks on page 214.)

ROB ROY MACGREGOR

Robert MacGregor, known because of his red hair as Rob Roy (Red Robert), was a colourful and free-booting cattle thief whose exploits frequently involved robbing the rich for the benefit of the poor. He was forced to become an outlaw in about 1712, but having successfully outwitted all attempts to bring him under control, he gradually returned to living openly among his own people. In 1725 he was given a formal pardon. The full story of this Scottish folk hero is told in the Rob Roy and Trossachs Visitor Centre in Callander.

▶▶ The Trossachs
210D3

(Argyll, the Isles, Loch Lomond, Stirling and the Trossachs Tourist Board tel: 01786 475019)

The Trossachs is an area of rugged hills, tumbling streams, and picturesque lochs. It may lack the drama of the true Highlands, but its accessibility from central Scotland has made it popular. Strictly speaking, the Trossachs is a narrow strip of country between **Loch Katrine** and **Loch Achray**, but in effect it is considered to stretch west from the busy town of **Callander** to the shores of Loch Lomond, with the somewhat commercialized **Aberfoyle** as its heart. Undeniably beautiful, it is also one of the most visited areas in Scotland, and is particularly popular in high summer.

The area became fashionable with the 18th-century Romantics in their cult of the picturesque—it was wild, but not too wild, and it was also easy to reach. Sir Walter Scott also helped to popularize the area, using the Trossachs as the setting for his poem *Lady of the Lake* and his novel *Rob Roy*. For this was the territory of Rob Roy's Clan Gregor, a near-criminal band touched by a spirit of romantic lawlessness (see panel). The Trossachs was also the favorite sketching ground of the Glasgow Boys (see page 228), and with Loch Lomond became Scotland's first National Park in 2002.

The 23 mile-long, **Loch Lomond▶**, Scotland's largest inland loch (in terms of surface area), stretches from the suburbs of Glasgow to the fringes of the Highlands. It is surrounded by a dramatic variety of wooded farmland, empty hills, and rocky shores, but traffic along the road up its western shore is sometimes so busy it can be hard to enjoy its beauty.

There are several pleasant summer **boat trips** (but get there early to avoid lines): along the length of Loch Katrine on the SS *Walter Scott*; on Loch Lomond from Balloch, Ardlui, and Tarbet, on the western shore and from Balmaha or the Inversnaid Hotel pier on the quieter eastern shore; a more modest excursion goes out to the ruins of **Inchmahome Priory** (H.S.) on an island in the Lake of Menteith. Activities such as "pony trekking" (riding), cycling, fishing, and golfing are available. Walkers can choose between numerous forest trails or hill walks. The area's scenic drives can be combined with short walks from the road, to beauty spots such as the Falls of Leny, off the A84 northwest of Callander and the Trossachs viewpoint at the top of the A821 north of Aberfoyle.

Still waters: Loch Ard

The Highland clans in their 15th-century heyday formed a tribal system strong enough to threaten the authority of the Stuart monarchs. The aftermath of the last Jacobite rebellion of 1745 brought about the final dismantling of their distinctive way of life. However, the dress and tartan of the Highlands of former times then became fashionable—and the scene was set for the once outlawed cloth of a tribal minority to become the most potent symbol for the whole of Scotland.

Life beyond the Highland Line In Gaelic the word "clann" means family. By the 13th century, clans had evolved into self-governing tribal units at whose head was a chief or "father" to whom lesser chieftains and ordinary clansmen gave allegiance. The clan, at least in earlier times, counted its wealth in cattle. Consequently, cattle-raiding was common, as were territorial disputes. However, not all of the clan's preoccupations were warlike. The more powerful chiefs kept extensive retinues, an important member being the clan bard, who was official record keeper as well as composer. By the 18th century, better communications meant that the clans came more into contact with southern or Saxon—hence "sasunnach"— ways. Some chiefs even sent their children to school in the Lowlands and developed a taste for fine wines or fashionable clothes. Thus the system was already in decline before the shock of Culloden (see page 246).

The dress of the clans The idea of a "clan tartan" was essentially a marketing device of 19th-century textile manufacturers. Tartan was banned after Culloden, though the Highland regiments of the British army were still per-mitted to wear it. Later, the fashion industry used the military as a source of inspiration and tartan became very fashionable. Then the visit of King George IV to Scotland in 1822 created an excuse for the new landowners and clan chiefs of Scotland to act the part and dress up in tartan costumes. The cloth has remained popular ever since, creating its own mythology and conventions.

HOW TO RECOGNIZE A FELLOW CLANSMAN
Contemporary evidence from the Battle of Culloden indicates a wide variety of tartans worn even by members of the same clan. The govern-ment forces were identifiable by the red or yellow tied badges on their bonnets, while the Jacobites had their famous "white cockades," inspired by the wild white rose said to have been plucked by Bonnie Prince Charlie as a symbol for the campaign. In fact, the British army was the first to define uniform tartans in the 18th century.

THE BLACK WATCH
One of General Wade's ways of policing the Highlands (see page 244) was to recruit local Highlanders. Six indepen-dent companies first enlisted in 1725 and from these was formed the 43rd, later the 42nd or Black Watch Regiment. By creating fighting units of this type, the martial spirit of the Highlands was harnessed for Britain's imperial wars of the 19th century.

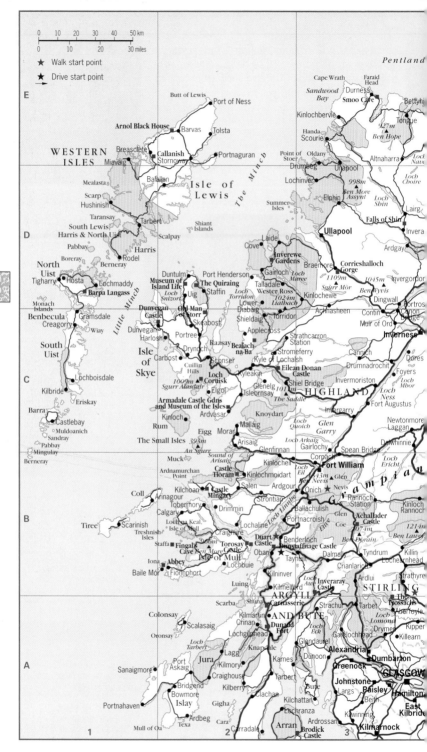

Northern Scotland

RECOMMENDED COASTAL TOWNS
Argyll and Bute: Inveraray, Oban.
Highland: Portree (Skye), Dornoch, Ullapool.
Orkney: Stromness.

COASTAL FEATURES
Highland: Cape Wrath, Handa Island, Stacks of Duncansby.
Orkney: Old Man of Hoy.

CASTLES
Aberdeenshire: Crathes.
Argyll and Bute: Duart (Mull), Kilchurn.
Highland: Dunvegan (Skye), Eilean Donan.

PALATIAL INTERIORS
Aberdeenshire: Haddo.
Argyll and Bute: Inveraray.
Highland: Cawdor.
Perth and Kinross: Blair.

MOUNTAIN WALKING
Cairngorms, Cuillins (Skye), Fort William area, Glen Coe, Torridon.

PREHISTORIC MONUMENTS
Orkney and Shetland: Maes Howe, Ring of Brogar, Skara Brae, Jarlshof, Mousa Broch.
Western Isles: Callanish Circle (Lewis).

ISLAND ESCAPES
Argyll and Bute: Jura.
Highland: Raasay, Rum.
Western Isles: Barra.

CHRISTIAN ARCHITECTURE
Aberdeenshire: St. Machars Aberdeen,
Argyll and Bute: Iona.
Moray: Elgin Cathedral.
Orkney: St. Magnus Kirkwall.

GARDENS
Aberdeenshire: Crathes.
Argyll and Bute: Crarae.
Highland: Inverewe.

Bagpipes and tartan show that Highland culture is still alive today

NORTHERN SCOTLAND The **Highlands and Islands**, with their awesome mountain and coastal scenery, have contributed much of what is now considered typical of Scotland. Malt whisky, bagpipes, tartans, clans, kilts, and Highland flings were all distinctive aspects of Highland culture that today are considered essentially Scottish. This would have amazed any 17th-century Scot, for one of the key facts of Scottish history was the marked division between the northern Highlands and the main body of Scotland. The Highlands and the Lowlands were as different as night and day, and they held each other in mutual scorn.

THE GREAT DIVIDE Though they might have traded cattle for grain at market towns, Highlanders and Lowlanders otherwise kept their distance. The Highlanders were Gaelic-speaking with a highly developed oral culture of bards, oaths, and undying loyalty to kinship groups; the Lowlanders were English-speaking, literate, and fond of lawsuits. The Highlanders were semi-nomads who counted their wealth in cattle and avoided towns, whereas the Lowlanders were firmly rooted in the farms and well-established towns that were evenly scattered over the coastal plains. The Highland Boundary Fault, running from southwest straight across to northeast Scotland, was not merely a geological divide: it was a linguistic, social, military, legal, and economic boundary.

A WAR-TORN TERRITORY Though the Highlands brought limited rewards back to the central government in Edinburgh, they provided a vital resource in times of danger. The mountain valleys could be relied upon to produce hardened troops for any military adventure that offered loot. The region also served as a bulwark against foreign conquest, most graphically in the 14th century when the

English occupied the Lowland towns for a generation but could make no effective headway into the Highlands. Even after the Act of Union between England and Scotland in 1707, the Highlands continued to supply manpower for Britain's imperial adventures and to this day there is a tradition of military service.

Jacobite rebellions broke out in 1715 and 1719 as part of a long history of dissidence, but this time the south responded differently. General Wade was commissioned to design and build a string of strategic forts and fortified barracks for the military occupation of the Highlands, all linked by roads and elegant bridges. Several examples survive in the old county of Inverness-shire, in what is now known as the **Highland** region. The Jacobite rising led by Bonnie Prince Charlie in 1745 (see page 246) had catastrophic effects, for the Hanoverian victory at Culloden Moor near **Inverness** was followed by the deliberate destruction of the military basis of Highland society. The legal powers of the clan chiefs were destroyed, the kilt and weapons were forbidden and a series of ruthless judicial commissions brought the gallows to every glen. This was followed, a generation later, by an economic crisis resulting in the Clearances—wholesale eviction of the tenant farmers to make space for sheep pastures (often run by English-speaking farmers from the Lowlands), particularly in **Sutherland** and the **Black Isle**, the **West Highlands**, and the **Western Isles**. Today, the shells of single-story cottages are the desolate reminders of more populous times.

THE HERITAGE The primitive stone castles of the Highland chiefs decayed into romantic ruin while the turf and stone round huts of the tenant crofters were reduced to lumps in the pasture. They were replaced by neat stone farmhouses, crisp neo-classical manses for the influential clergy, and the light plain halls of their Presbyterian churches. Ironically, at the same time as the Highland crofters were being packed off in emigrant boats, the fashion for things Highland got into full swing, intensified by Queen Victoria's patronage of **Deeside**. In the late 19th century a series of enormous and exclusive sporting estates were created for the summer recreation of Britain's wealthy, notably in **Angus**, **Perth and Kinross**, **Moray**, **Aberdeenshire**, **Sutherland**, and **Wester Ross**. A series of excessive Gothic Baronial lodges, hotels, and palaces still are the dominant architectural note of the Highlands, softened by modern bungalows and the older, stone-built dormer-windowed houses still seen all over the Highlands and Islands. The influx of English speakers helped make the Gaelic tongue obsolete, and, though its use is still widespread in the crofting population of the **Western Isles**, Gaelic is now rarely heard on the mainland.

▶ ▶ ▶ REGION HIGHLIGHTS

Blair Castle page 253
Deeside pages 240–241
Iona page 247
Inveraray page 248
Lochaber
pages 244–245
Orkney and Shetland ancient sites
pages 250–251
Scone Palace
page 252
Skye pages 254–255
Torridon area page 258
The Western Isles
pages 260–261

237

Quoth God to the Highlander,
"What will you do now?"
"I will down to the Lowland, Lord,
And there steal a cow."
—Anonymous

"THAD'S A DH' FHASAS FLUR AIR MACHAIR MAIRIDH CLIU NA H-AINNIR CHAOIMH. THE PRESERVER OF PRINCE CHARLES EDWARD STUART WILL BE MENTIONED IN HISTORY AND IF COURAGE AND FIDELITY BE VIRTUES, MENTIONED WITH HONOUR" JOHNSON

Walks

Beinn Lora, Argyll and Bute   *234B2*

Forestry Commission parking lot just south of Benderloch village (north of Oban). Beinn Lora is a 1,010 foot-high hill with magnificent views of Loch Linnhe. Follow a path through the forest; follow signs and eventually skirt an area of boggy pools; the summit then comes into view. Return the same way. (2.5 hours)

Findlater Castle, Aberdeenshire   *235D5*

From Cullen harbor follow the shore-level road eastwards; this dwindles to a coastal path. On a clear day the Caithness and Sutherland coastline can be seen across the Firth. Walk onto the 15th-century ruins of Findlater Castle, perched high on the cliff. Then return the same way. (2.5–4 hours)

Duncansby Head, Highland   *235E4*

Parking lot at Duncansby Head lighthouse. From the northeastern-most tip of the British mainland a fine coastal path heads south to the Stacks of Duncansby, a trio of natural pillars cut off from the mainland by erosion from the sea. Return the same way. (1.5 hours)

Glen Nevis, Highland   *234B3*

Parking lot at end of road in Glen Nevis, southeast of Fort William. There is a waterfall by the parkin lot. The path leads into a splendid gorge before entering more open terrain, passing further waterfalls and reaching ruins at Steall. Return the same way. (2 hours)

Kenmore, Perth, and Kinross   *235B4*

Start in Kenmore village square (east end of Loch Tay). Take the road northwest, cross the River Tay, then immediately take a riverside path on the right; a little later, turn right on a road, then left on a rising forest track, which soon levels out; 45 minutes' walking leads to a well-marked vantage point for views over the loch and over Taymouth Castle; return to the last track junction you reach and then turn right downhill to Kenmore. (2.5 hours)

The stacks at Duncansby Head

▶▶ Aberdeen 235C5
(Aberdeen and Grampian Tourist Board tel: 01224 632727)

The "Granite City" is the third largest in Scotland, but although the oil boom years of the 1970s gave rise to handsome new buildings on the waterfront and huge oil-rig vessels in the harbor, the town has managed to retain its Georgian roots and its 19th-century dignity. A major port, it has long been a bustling center of commerce and the grand sweep of Union Street reflects the city's rich history. Elegant floral displays soften the imposing Victorian buildings and the silver granite squares and terraces.

St. Machar's Cathedral▶ was founded in 1131; the main part was built in the mid-15th century. It dominates the part of the city known as **Old Aberdeen**, a calm haven of cobbled streets and houses that date from 1500. In this area too is **King's College**, founded 1500–1505 and part of the university, as well as the Cruickshank Botanic Gardens and Seaton Park. Further out, the **Brig o'Balgownie** across the River Don is the oldest medieval bridge in Scotland.

Central Aberdeen is more formal, with straight rows of granite town houses and spacious streets. Its numerous university buildings, markets, and museums are dotted on and around Broad Street and Union Street. The **Tolbooth**, on the corner of Broad Street, is the town jail, built in 1627 and open to the public. On Ship Row, the **Maritime Museum▶▶** brings the city's relationship with the North Sea to the fore, with absorbing exhibits on fishing, shipbuilding, and the oil industry; it also includes Provost Ross's House of 1593. **Provost Skene's House** has changing exhibits and period furnishings, while **Satrosphere** is a hands-on science and technology center. The **city library**, **St. Mark's Church**, and **His Majesty's Theatre** are known collectively as "Education, Salvation and Damnation." The **Art Gallery and Museum▶** has works by George Romney, Sir Joshua Reynolds, James McBey, Augustus John, and Scottish impressionist William McTaggart among others. The **Duthie Park Winter Gardens** are the largest glassed gardens in Europe.

Haddo House▶ (N.T.S.) is a half-hour's drive north, near Pitmedden, a handsome house designed by William Adam in 1731 and relatively unchanged. In Viewfield Road, the **Gordon Highlanders Museum** pays tribute to what Churchill called "the finest regiment in the world."

In the tropical hot houses of Duthie Park

NORTH SEA FLIER
Cruden Bay, north of Aberdeen, witnessed the takeoff of the first flight across the North Sea back in 1914, when solo pilot Tryggve Gran flew 300 miles to Stavanger in Norway. But with the advent of World War I, his achievement went almost unnoticed. There is a monument to Gran close to the sinister ruin of Slains Castle, which Bram Stoker saw on a visit in 1895, inspiring him to write *Dracula*.

THE BUCHAN COAST
Aberdeen is the gateway to some of the country's most pristine coastline. Northwards to Cruden Bay and on to the busy fishing ports of Peterhead (the biggest whitefish port in Western Europe) and Fraserburgh stretch glorious miles of untouched sandy beaches. Along the north-facing coast of this far corner of Scotland little fishing villages such as Pennan and Gardenstown, west of Rosehearty, hide under spectacular cliffs.

HIGHLAND GAMES

Athletes compete at these traditional Highland gatherings, held all over Scotland in summer. Venues include Inverness, Stirling and Callander, with the most famous being the **Royal Highland Gathering** in Braemar (September), usually attended by the Royal Family. Events include throwing the hammer, hill races, putting the stone and tossing the caber (a long wooden pole). Braemar's caber weighs in at 132 pounds, claims to be the longest at 19.75 feet and has been thrown successfully (absolutely straight and from end to end) fewer than five times. There are also bagpipe and dancing competitions. The games originated in martial contests held by King Malcolm Canmore back in the 11th century, to find the toughest men to fight the Normans. The tradition was revived in the 19th century.

The River Dee near Braemar

MALT WHISKY

Single malts, as distinct from blended whiskies, have their origins in more than a hundred distilleries, whose whitewashed buildings and barley-drying kilns are a component of the Highlands landscape. Many offer guided tours and in Speyside is the signposted Malt Whisky Trail (see panel, page 257), a road touring route. Malt whisky varies greatly in taste; in Islay, for example, the peat burned for drying out the barley gives a highly distinctive flavor. For an overview of the whisky industry, visit the Scotch Whisky Heritage Centre in Edinburgh's Royal Mile.

▶▶▶ Deeside   235C4

(Aberdeen and Grampian Tourist Board tel: 01224 632727)

The River Dee drains the eastern slopes of the Cairngorms and flows almost 80 miles east to Aberdeen and the North Sea, passing on its way through a classic Scottish landscape of blue hills and heather moors, woods of larch, juniper, and birch, rocky riverbeds and rippling waters.

The village of **Braemar**, 1,083 feet up and circled by layers of hills, is at the heart of the most beautiful stretch of the Dee and a popular summer holiday area. Braemar is famous for its round-towered, L-plan castle, which was built as a hunting lodge by the 2nd Earl of Mar in 1628 and buffeted by the Jacobites in 1689, as well as for the Braemar Gathering held on the first Saturday in September. The Royal Family usually pays a visit to these Highland Games (see panel), which may account for the crowds of around 50,000 people. Robert Louis Stevenson wrote *Treasure Island* while staying in Braemar in 1881. To the west of the village, at the head of the valley just beyond Inverey, is the **Linn o'Dee▶**, where the river waters cascade down into a series of rocky pools. The minor road from Braemar to this beauty spot, often reproduced in Victorian engravings and contemporary postcards, is an attractive drive. From the road, you can set off for some beautiful walks in the Mar Forest and the foothills of Ben Macdhui (4,301 feet).

Balmoral Castle, some 9 miles east of Braemar, was bought by Queen Victoria and her husband Prince Albert in 1852. The old castle was too small and today's mansion, typically Scottish baronial in style, was commissioned by Prince Albert. The Royal Family still spends vacations here; the grounds and exhibitions are open to the public from May 1 to July 31. The peak of Lochnagar (3,786 feet), which towers over Balmoral, was featured in Prince Charles's first book, *The Old Man of Lochnagar*, an illustrated children's story written to amuse his younger brothers. Across the main road is the granite Crathie Church, attended by members of the Royal Family when staying in Balmoral. Queen Victoria's favorite dram was Lochnagar malt whisky; the Royal Lochnagar Distillery today has a visitor center and store, and offers visitors a tour of the distillery.

Continuing east along the banks of the boulder-strewn Dee, the A93 passes through the granite village of **Ballater**, built at the end of the 18th century to accommodate visitors taking the spa waters of nearby Pannanich Wells. With its hotels and guest houses, it makes a good base for walking around on the hills of Craigendarroch, Craig Coillich, and Glen Muick.

The main road stays close to the river, pausing at **Aboyne**, a town neatly planned around a large level green where the Highland Gathering takes place in September. The valley then opens out to **Banchory**, where the Water of Feugh joins the Dee from the Forest of Birse. Watch the salmon leaping up the rapids from the Bridge of Feugh. Like most of these Deeside resorts, Banchory has a golf course.

North from Banchory about 15 miles, near Kemnay, **Castle Fraser▶** (N.T.S.) is a massive Z-plan castle. It is an excellent example of the Scottish baronial style, notable for its turrets. East along the Dee from Banchory, **Crathes Castle▶ ▶** (N.T.S.) is a celebrated L-shaped tower house dating to 1553, one of the finest Jacobean houses in the country. Inside, the Room of the Nine Nobles, the Room of the Muses, and the Room of the Green Lady are renowned for their remarkable, highly decorative ceilings. The ghost of the Green Lady, carrying a baby and, of course, dressed in green, is thought to haunt certain rooms. The grounds too are special, a labyrinth of color enclosed within the dark green walls of a 300-year-old yew hedge. Don't look at the map; just be lured on by the skilfully contrived arches, avenues, and enticing prospects.

About 6 miles down the glen, in the midst of a surviving section of the Caledonian Forest called the Old Wood of Drum, stands **Drum Castle▶** (N.T.S.). A cold, solid 13th-century keep, thick-walled and 66 feet-high, adjoins a crow-stepped gabled Jacobean mansion. It houses a fine collection of portraits, silver, and furniture, and has pleasant grounds with a café and an adventure playground for children.

RAISING THE OLD PRETENDER'S STANDARD
Only the Highland chiefs were able to raise the men needed to fight the cause of Britain's exiled Stuart king. When George of Hanover became king of Britain in 1714, it was in Braemar, on the spot where the Invercauld Arms Hotel now stands, that the 6th Earl of Mar raised the standard in 1715 to launch the Jacobite Rising, proclaiming the Old Pretender, James VIII of Scotland (and III of England) as king.

241

THE LOCH NESS MONSTER

The alleged appearances of this supposedly dinosaur-like beast lend a hypnotic lure to the loch. The Loch Ness Monster Exhibition at Drumnadrochit has photographs of "Nessie," together with scientific explanations and demonstrations of the latest techniques being used to solve the mystery.

DOLPHIN CRUISES

Dolphin Ecosse run boat trips from Cromarty into the Moray Firth to see bottlenose dolphins (all year, weather allowing) and harbor porpoises and, in summer, minke whales (for reservations, call 01381 600323).

Loch Ness, seen near Drumnadrochit, lies in the Great Glen Fault, which runs across the Highlands

▶Inverness 234C3

(Tourist information center tel: 01463 234353)

Now, as ever, the Capital of the Highlands, Inverness has a strategic position at the head of the Great Glen. Its often violent history has left it with few historic buildings. The **Museum and Art Gallery** has good, original collections.

Less than 6 miles out of town, the vast depressing Drummossie moor, renamed **Culloden**, witnessed the last battle fought on British soil, on April 18, 1746. This was the last gasp of Prince Charles Edward Stuart's attempt to gain the throne from George II (see page 246). There is a good **visitor center** (N.T.S.) that tells the story of that rainy day in which a thousand of Bonnie Prince Charlie's Highlanders met their deaths. A mile south lie the prehistoric **Clava Cairns** and standing stones. **Cawdor Castle▶**, a little to the east, was built by the thanes of Cawdor in the 14th century. The original keep remains and inside are Jacobean rooms. At the entrance to the Inverness and Beauly Firth sits **Fort George▶**, built between 1748–1769 in demonstration of the government's intent to keep the Jacobites at bay.

The largest loch in Scotland in terms of volume of water, **Loch Ness** relies more on the "Nessie" legend (see panel) than its beauty. Good views can be had from **Urquhart Castle** (H.S.), its ruins set on a rocky cliff.

Visit **Beauly▶** for the remains of its 13th-century priory and for Campbells, a good tweed, tartan, and woollen store. **Strathpeffer** is a Victorian spa town with several old hotels; walk from here to the Rogie Falls. The **Black Isle▶** is in fact a broad, fertile peninsula whose shores are the haunt of wading birds. In Cromarty look at the old port, the lighthouse and **Cromarty Courthouse▶** where you can tour the cells and courtroom. In **Rosemarkie** see the Pictish stone in the churchyard and Groam House Museum. In nearby **Fortrose** visit the Gothic cathedral ruins.

LOCH NESS AND THE BLACK ISLE

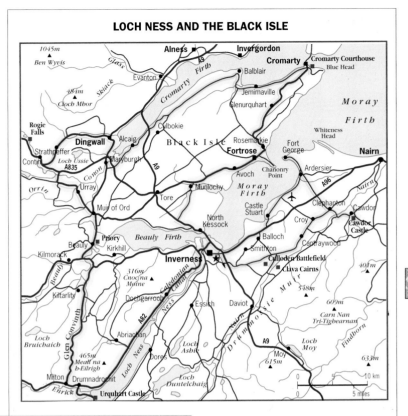

Loch Ness and the Black Isle

A 130 miles tour through varied mountain and coastal landscape.

Leave Inverness on the A9 towards the southeast, turn onto the B9006 to see **Culloden battlefield** and visitor center (N.T.S.) and nearby **Clava Cairns** prehistoric stones. Continue to **Cawdor Castle▶**, scene of Duncan's murder in Shakespeare's *Macbeth*.

Turn back and take the narrow B9006 to **Fort George▶** (H.S.) with its museum of period barrack rooms and weaponry. Follow the east coast of the **Moray Firth** into Inverness and out again on the A82 along the northern shore of **Loch Ness** to ruined **Urquhart Castle** and the Nessie Exhibition in **Drumnadrochit**.

From here return northwards over the hills to the remains of **Beauly Priory**. At Muir of Ord take the A832 northwest to reach **Strathpeffer**. Head east to **Dingwall** and follow the Black Isle shore to reach the old sea-port of **Cromarty**. Head south along the A832 to the charming little resorts of **Rosemarkie** and nearby **Fortrose**. Continue southwest to rejoin the A9, crossing over the Moray Firth on the Kessock suspension bridge (1982), which leads back into Inverness.

A sgian dubh (Gaelic dagger) in Inverness Museum and Art Gallery

WADE'S ROADS

In an attempt to disarm the Jacobite supporters of the exiled Stuarts, concentrated in the Highlands, General Wade stationed his government troops, the Redcoats, in forts which he built at Fort William, Fort Augustus, and Fort George. He linked these forts with military roads and connected them to the Lowlands. From Fort Augustus one of Wade's roads runs over the Corrieyairack Pass; it was used by Bonnie Prince Charlie's army on its 1745 march to Edinburgh.

244

Ben Nevis and Carn Mor Dearg

The Caledonian Canal

▶▶▶ Lochaber 234C3

(Highlands of Scotland Tourist Board tel: 01997 421160)

This region, known as the West Highlands, is an area of archetypal highland landscape—bleak moorlands set against soft valley meadows and the long reach of still lochs. It is the land of the Camerons and the Macdonnels, clans that provided the core support for the '45 Rebellion (see page 246) and that, a year later, dumped the Jacobite treasure into Loch Arkaig rather than see it in the hands of the Hanoverians.

At the southern end of Loch Ness (see page 242) the little town of **Fort Augustus** sits around the Caledonian Canal, a splendid waterway, with several staircase locks, designed by Thomas Telford. By linking the lochs of the Great Glen the canal joins Fort William on Loch Linnhe with Inverness on the Moray Firth. Fort Augustus has long since lost the fort built by General Wade (see panel).

The resort and aluminum-smelting town of **Fort William** stands in the shadow of **Ben Nevis▶**, Britain's highest mountain at 4,406 feet. It is not the best in the Highlands for walking, but if you do wish to climb it, allow five hours to get to the top and three hours to pick your way back down (it looks deceptively small because it lacks a definitive peak). It is of course essential to be properly equipped and take all safety precautions. Low-level walks with superb views of the mountains include Glen Nevis (see Walks, page 238), the towpath of the Caledonian Canal (notably Neptune's Staircase, a flight of locks north of Fort William) and Glen Leven (east of Kinlochleven), which threads its way up to the vast Blackwater Reservoir. Fort William is a modern, commercialized place, but makes a convenient base. Its story began in 1655 when General Monk built an earthwork fort here. This was later replaced by General Wade's stone construction in the reign of William III, which was torn down in the 19th century. The **West Highland Museum** on Cameron Square provides a good introduction to the region and its natural history.

South from Fort William the main road passes through **Glen Coe▶▶**, the scene, in the early hours of February 13, 1692, of Scotland's most infamous massacre. Acting under government orders, members of the Campbell militia

Fishing boats in Mallaig harbor: the catch is auctioned on the quay

THE WEST HIGHLAND LINE
The railroad that runs from Glasgow to Mallaig justly claims to be Britain's most scenic route. The construction of the line between Fort William and Mallaig in particular involved some major feats of engineering, with gradients of up to 1 in 48, several rock cuttings and dramatic bridges, viaducts, and tunnels. Some services are steam-hauled.

The monument to the '45 at Glenfinnan

who were billeted on members of the MacDonald clan, turned on their hosts—breaking the strict code of hospitality that existed between clans—and indiscriminately massacred them. An act, so the government thought, that would dissuade anyone from harboring doubts about the legitimacy of Queen Mary on the throne instead of her father James VII (James II to the English). There is a visitor center near the foot of the glen.

West of Fort William, at the head of Loch Shiel, the **Glenfinnan Monument▶** (N.T.S.) marks the spot where the Young Pretender, Prince Charles Edward (see page 246), raised his standard on August 19, 1745 and launched the campaign to see his father recognized as rightful king.

The songwriter's "Road to the Isles" from Fort William leads to **Arisaig** and **Mallaig▶▶** past the coral sandy beaches that featured in the movie *Local Hero*. Inland are the dark waters of Loch Morar, the deepest freshwater stretch of water in Britain, with its own lesser-known monster, Morag. On the wooded islands in the loch, the Jesuits maintained a secret seminary to keep the Roman Catholic faith alive. The busy fishing port of Mallaig is the departure point for ferries to the Inner Isles of Eigg, Muck, Rhum, Canna, Soay, and Armadale on Skye (see pages 254–255). All the islands are easy day-trips; only the Skye boat takes cars.

To the south is the untamed **Ardnamurchan Peninsula**, whose far point is the westernmost part of the British mainland. Isolated on a tide-washed island in Loch Moidart stands the empty keep of **Castle Tioram▶**, last used by the MacDonald chief of Clan Ranald, who burned it after the 1715 uprising failed, rather than let the Campbells take possession. A short walk from the hotel in the village of Kilchoan, **Castle Mingary▶** stands in one of the most impressive locations on the peninsula's southern shore, looking across the Sound of Mull to Tobermory.

The small Highland village of **Lochaline▶**, where ferries depart for Mull, sits on the picturesque Morvern Peninsula overlooking the tidal inlet of Loch Aline. The strong square keep of 14th-century Ardtornish Castle was one of the chief bases of the Lord of the Isles (see panel, page 254).

THE WEST HIGHLAND WAY
This 95 mile long-distance footpath starts from Milngavie, just north of Glasgow, and heads north of the eastern side of Loch Lomond, before passing Rannoch Moor, Glen Coe, Glen Nevis, and Ben Nevis to reach Fort William. As you get further north, the scenery is more and more magnificent. It is never really steep, but be prepared for plenty of up-and-down sections.

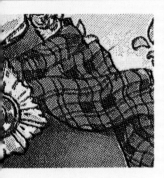

Seen by contemporary opponents as a political and military threat to 18th-century Britain's stability, the Jacobites and their hopeless quest to restore a Catholic monarch to the British throne was soon turned into a romantic lost cause. At its head was the most romantic figure of all: Italian-born Prince Charles Edward Louis Philip Casimir Stuart, know variously as the Young Pretender, the Young Chevalier, and, most familiarly, Bonnie Prince Charlie. He was in Scotland for only 14 months.

"Charles was the candle who lighted the bonfire, but they [his Highland supporters] were the timber that filled a dark sky with their splendid ardour."
—Eric Linklater, in *The Prince in the Heather*

246

Charles set off from St. Nazaire on his escapade with the blessing of a French government eager to see Britain de-stabilised. When the handsome young man landed on the island of Eriskay in the Western Isles, the local MacDonald chief told him to go home. Charles rather romantically replied that he had "come home" and, undaunted, went on to raise his standard at Glenfinnan in August 1745.

A persuasive personality The fatal charm of the Stuarts managed to persuade about one-sixth of the estimated 30,000 fighting men in the Highlands of Scotland to take up arms in his cause. The campaign met with early successes but was finally halted on Culloden Moor in April 1746. There the Jacobites were blown away by the superior artillery of the British army. Charles went into hiding and the government forces (which comprised a number of Scottish regiments) went on to commit numerous atrocities in its efforts to destroy the Highland way of life. This policy was implemented by a far-off government in Westminster, which perceived the Highlands as a hotbed of potential Jacobites, where clan chiefs were able to call on what were, in effect, private armies.

The romance of a lost cause From these bare facts sprang the legend of an irresistibly handsome young man on a lost cause. With the real threat out of the way, the Jacobites were soon reinterpreted in song and story. Bonnie Prince Charlie became the figurehead of Jacobite mythology and has been seen on shortbread boxes ever since. Flora MacDonald—whose dealings with the Prince covered only a few days and who had to be persuaded to have anything to do with the business at all—was quickly elevated to a romantic heroine. The notion that the Prince was never betrayed by a sympathetic Scottish people is a still current tale. In reality his supporters had to keep him well out of the way. But none of this matters. With Bonnie Prince Charlie, the romance is all.

OVER THE SEA TO SKYE
"Carry the lad born to be King over the sea to Skye" is perhaps the best-known line from the corpus of Jacobite songs and alludes to the perilous voyage from Benbecula to Skye which Charles took while disguised as Betty Burke, Flora MacDonald's maid. *The Skye Boat Song*, however, is a 19th-century fake: its famous lyrics date from 1884 and most of the melody from 1879.

▶▶ Mull 234B2

(Tobermory tourist information center tel: 01688 302182)

The beautiful "isle-of-the-cool-high-bends," 24 miles long and 26 miles wide, has many aspects—rocky cliffs, sandy beaches, quiet fishing coves, bleak moors, lone gray castles, and lofty mountains—but is dominated by treeless green terraces of grazing land skilfully managed by crofts and small farms. Mull is served by ferries from Oban, Lochaline and, in summer, Kilchoan.

Duart Castle, perched above the Sound of Mull 3 miles from Craignure, has its origins in the 13th century. It has been restored as the summer home of the chief of Clan Maclean. **Torosay Castle**, just outside Craignure, is a 19th-century baronial building (designed by David Bryce) with grounds laid out by Sir Robert Lorimer. A narrow-gauge railroad runs between the castle and Craignure.

Tobermory▶, named after a holy well dedicated to Our Lady, is the island's main town, its arc of brightly painted houses encircling a bay popular with yacht owners.

The Holy Island of **Iona▶▶▶**, the "Cradle of Christianity," is served by ferry from Fionnphort on the

ANCIENT BURIAL PLACE OF KINGS

St Oran's Cemetery on Iona is the oldest Christian cemetery in Scotland. Here are buried 48 Scottish kings, including Kenneth MacAlpin, who first united the Scots and Picts in 843 and Duncan, murdered by Macbeth in 1040. Eight Norwegian kings also have graves here, a reflection of the several hundred years of Norse occupation of Scotland from the 9th century on.

A prehistoric standing stone on the Ross of Mull

247

western tip of the Ross of Mull or by boat excursions from Oban via Mull. No cars are allowed on the island, but all sights can be easily reached on foot. In 563 St. Colomba and 12 companions landed here from Ireland, and established a monastery as a base for numerous missionary journeys among the pagan Picts. It became the mother-house of the Celtic church in Scotland and England. This era of great spiritual and creative achievement ended, however, with the Norse raid of 803, which killed 68 monks and persuaded those left alive to return to Ireland. Nothing of their monastery remains, but an astonishing collection of early Christian stone carvings recalls this heroic period. Apart from St. Oran's Chapel of 1080, the existing abbey buildings all date from the second foundation in the early 13th century, when a Benedictine monastery and nunnery were established. In the 20th century, the abbey buildings were restored and are now the home of the Iona Community. The island's sense of peace is a source of spiritual refreshment for many visitors.

FINGAL'S CAVE, STAFFA

The cathedral-like cave that inspired Felix Mendelssohn's *Hebrides Overture* is one of several on this tiny uninhabited island north of Iona. Smooth columns of black basalt, the result of volcanic action, rise out of the sea in what is known in Gaelic as "An Uamh Ehinn" (the musical cave), because of the echoing sounds that the sea makes within it. Boat trips leave from Oban throughout summer.

▶ Oban and Argyll 234B2

(Argyll, the Isles, Loch Lomond, Stirling, and the Trossachs Tourist Board tel: 01786 475019)

Oban is a popular family resort, accessible by bus and train from Glasgow. The harbor bustles with fishing vessels and ferries for the islands of Mull, Coll, Tiree, Colonsay, and the Western Isles. Stroll along the seafront, browse in the woollen mills, then head for Dunollie Castle where the Lords of Lorne used to preside. McCaig's Tower, an unfinished 19th-century folly modeled on Rome's Colosseum and built to give work to unemployed masons, overlooks the town with fine views across to the Inner Hebrides. Oban is not known for reliable weather, but there are a number of indoor attractions to enjoy when it rains, such as a glass factory, pottery, toy and model display, and the distillery, best known for its 12-year-old malt whisky. Just east of the town is the Oban Rare Breeds Farm Park. The road north passes the 13th-century MacDougall fortress of **Dunstaffnage** (H.S.) on its way to the Seal and Marine Centre on the shore of Loch Creran.

Just north of the village of Taynuilt is the **Bonawe Iron Furnace▶** (H.S.). Here you can see the restored remains of a charcoal furnace, founded in 1753, used for iron smelting. The village of Lochawe sits at the head of Loch Awe, the longest loch in Scotland, famous for its fishing. In summer the steamer *Lady Rowena* threads through the romantic burial islands of the MacNaughtons on Innis Fraoch and the MacArthurs on Innishail. The gaunt ruins of Kilchurn Castle, the original fortress home of the Campbells of Breadalbane, stands at the head of Kinloch Awe.

Inveraray▶▶, at the head of Loch Fyne, is a supremely elegant 18th-century town noted for its bridges, fishing harbor, gibbet pier, judges' lodgings, and central double church. Its chief attraction is the **Jail▶**, with its tableaux of jailers and wretched inmates. **Inveraray Castle▶▶**, home of the Campbell Dukes of Argyll, is a heavy gray-stone castellated mansion, but it has delightful 18th-century interiors and is stuffed with Highland weapons, portraits, and memorabilia. Walk through the grounds to the stone folly tower on the summit of Duniquaich for a panoramic view over the area.

THE CRINAN CANAL
In 1793 work started on the construction of this short 9 mile canal that would link Loch Fyne with the Sound of Jura, saving ships the long, hazardous journey around the Mull of Kintyre. The chief engineer, Scotsman John Rennie, met with financial and engineering problems (Thomas Telford was also called upon for his expertise) and it was never a commercial success. However, it passes via 15 locks through a beautiful landscape of wooded mountains, and its basin at Crinan is now popular with yachtsmen.

A "Cal Mac" ferry arrives in Oban from the islands

Crinan▶ is a tiny place at the western end of the Crinan Canal (see panel), its handful of houses and a hotel overlooking the yachting activity in the old basin. The village of **Kilmartin▶ ▶** is surrounded by prehistoric sites, including the Nether Largie Linear Cemetery—an alignment of Bronze Age burial mounds, including one you can climb into by ladder—and the Temple Wood stone circles; in the churchyard is a collection of medieval carved stones and in the church itself a Celtic cross. **Dunadd Fort** may have been the capital of the early Scots kingdom of Dalriada. On its rocky top are carved a footprint and a boar.

Across the Sound of Jura lies **Jura▶**, the rugged, barely populated island, home of red deer, where George Orwell wrote *1984*. Next door is the pretty, peaty isle of **Islay▶ ▶** (ferries from Kennacraig on the Kintyre Peninsula), where no fewer than six distilleries operate. Islay's sights include the superb 9th-century Kidalton Cross and the local history museum at Port Charlotte.

A carved stone at Kilmartin

The dazzling interior décor of Inveraray Castle

Drive

Oban and Argyll (see yellow route on map, page 234)

This tour takes in the beautiful Loch Etive, the dramatic Pass of Brander, and the shores of Loch Fyne, with its fine Inveraray Castle. Return through an area studded with prehistoric remains on a road past sea lochs with views of the Inner Hebridean islands (about 100 miles). There is an optional detour of about 40 miles down the Knapdale Peninsula.

Leave **Oban▶** going north on the A85 to pass Connel Bridge. Continue to Taynuilt for **Bonawe Iron Furnace▶** (H.S.) and then on the A85 through a narrow treeless defile, the Pass of Brander, to **Lochawe**. Take the A819 south to **Inveraray▶ ▶** with its splendid **castle▶ ▶** and then turn south on the A83, skirting the shores of Loch Fyne and passing Auchindrain open-air museum and Crarae Glen woodland gardens. Reach the market town of **Lochgilphead** and turn north up the A816. A detour may be taken on the B841 to **Crinan▶** at the end of the Crinan Canal and then south to Castle Sween and **Kilmory Knap** for its medieval carved stones.

Continue north on the A816 to **Dunadd Fort** and **Kilmartin▶ ▶**, center for some absorbing prehistoric sites. Pass **Carnasserie Castle** to the west end of Loch Awe and, twisting in and out of view of the Firth of Lorne, return to Oban.

WILDLIFE

Both island groups are renowned for their seabird colonies, which are among the most important in the world. On Shetland, visit the Island of Noss, accessible by small ferry (weather permitting). Here and at Hermaness on the north of Unst you get wonderful views of puffins, gannets, guillemots, razorbills, and many more species. As you explore the island, watch out for great skuas, arctic skuas, and whimbrels, which nest on the moorland. On Orkney, visit Yesnaby Cliffs on Mainland, both for their seabirds and for the rare and miniature Scottish primrose.

The relentless pounding of waves at Yesnaby, Orkney, has created a precarious pillar of rock, now detached from the rest of the island

▶▶▶ Orkney and Shetland   235A5/E5

(Orkney Tourist Board tel: 01856 872856; Shetland Tourist Board tel: 01595 693434)

These two groups of islands have such a different cultural atmosphere from the rest of Scotland that many visitors feel they have arrived in another country. For 600 years they were under Norse rule and even when this domination officially ended, in the 15th century, it was another 200 years before the Scottish throne became strong enough to exert any real authority over these remote islands. Both groups of islands are astonishingly bleak and treeless, but have splendid cliff and sea loch scenery and rare birdlife. Despite boasting what is arguably the finest collection of prehistoric sites in Britain, they receive comparatively few visitors.

ORKNEY ISLANDS▶▶▶ In Kirkwall on Mainland the unaltered pre-Reformation **Cathedral of St. Magnus▶▶** stands in proud dominance over the town. It was begun in the 12th century and the massive round pillars and arches of the arcades date from this time. In one of the pillars two skeletons were discovered early this century, one of which may be St. Magnus himself. In the cathedral precincts are the ruins of the Bishop's Palace and Earl's Palace and **Orkney Museum**, a 16th-century town house turned into a museum of Orkney. Around the precincts wind streets of crowstepped gabled houses, brightly painted.

Skara Brae▶▶▶ (H.S.), also on Mainland, is an entire neolithic settlement that lay perfectly preserved in sand dunes for 4,000 years until a storm first uncovered a corner of it in 1850. Inside the houses are beds, hearths, dressers, closets, even fish tanks. The inhabitants left pots, jewelry, clothes, and tools, which are displayed in the museum. **The Ring of Brodgar▶▶** is a wide circle of stones. When first constructed it was surely one of the most magnificent stone circles ever built by neolithic man. The scale is quite breathtaking and although only some of the stones remain, the original majesty is well preserved. Many of the stones reach a height of 14.75 feet. Nearby, **Maes Howe▶▶** (H.S.) is the finest chambered cairn, or burial chamber, in Europe, both for size and preservation. It was built around 2700 BC and so had been standing for at least a century before the first circle was marked out at Stonehenge in Wiltshire. It remained intact for nearly 4,000 years until the Vikings plundered it; their rude Norse inscriptions can still be seen on the walls.

A more modern curiosity is the **Italian Chapel►** at Lamb Holm, created from Nissen huts and scrap materials in 1943 by Italian prisoners of war who were building the Churchill Barriers in the bay of Scapa Flow. **The Pier Arts Centre►** is a delightful little gallery in the ferry port of Stromness. It has the best collection of modern British art in the north of Scotland. The masterpieces of Ben Nicholson and Barbara Hepworth admirably complement the island's ancient remains.

The famous **Old Man of Hoy► ►** is an enormous stack of rock rearing a tremendous 443 feet out of the sea off the island of Hoy. Like most of Orkney's cliff scenery, it is best seen from a boat (or the ferry from Scrabster, or you can walk the 2 mile path from Rackwick).

SHETLAND ISLANDS► ► These are the most northerly part of Great Britain (Shetland is about 60 miles north of Orkney) and the beauty of midsummer nights when there is little or no darkness has to be seen to be believed. The main industries are crofting, fishing, and knitting. The fine wool of the Shetland sheep is knitted in distinctive, traditional colors and patterns, often known as Fair Isle.

Some people travel to Shetland just to see **Mousa Broch► ► ►**, on a little island to the southeast of Mainland. The Iron Age fortress tower still stands over 39 feet high, all its distinctive features wonderfully preserved. Interestingly, when Shetland was covered with brochs (see panel), Mousa was acknowledged to be the smallest and least noble of them all. **Clickhimin►**, near Lerwick, is another well-preserved broch.

On the southernmost tip of Mainland is **Jarlshof► ► ►** (H.S.), one of the most remarkable prehistoric sites in Europe. Impressive remains, standing several feet high, can be seen of the Bronze Age courtyard settlements, the Iron Age "wheelhouses" (see panel) that succeeded them and the longhouses of the Viking settlers who came next. There is also a 16th-century laird's house, once home of the Earl of Orkney Patrick Stewart and linked with Walter Scott's novel *The Pirate*. The same earl, renowned for his cruelty, built **Scalloway Castle**. The **Shetland Museum** in Lerwick tells the islands' story.

BROCHS AND WHEELHOUSES

Brochs are round towers, shaped like modern cooling towers, that are found only in the north of Scotland, the Outer Hebrides, and Orkney and Shetland. Built by the Picts during the 2nd and 1st centuries BC as defensive structures, they have double stone walls, with an inner staircase giving access to upper galleries. In the middle was a courtyard. Wheelhouses were a speciality of prehistoric Scotland, round buildings with a thick outer wall and a slab or corbeled roof. A number of inner walls ran in from the outer wall to a central area, like spokes of a wheel, forming rooms.

251

This Iron Age wheelhouse is part of Jarlshof's remarkable legacy of 3,000 years of settlement

Sinuous Loch Tay, one of Scotland's great salmon-fishing spots

THE STONE OF SCONE
Also known as the Stone of Destiny, this is believed to be a druidic talisman, consecrated by St. Columba at Iona, that was used in the investiture of the Dalriadic princes. It was brought here in the 9th century by Kenneth MacAlpin, the man who united Scotland after his defeat of the Picts at Scone. In 1296 it was removed by King Edward I of England and placed under the coronation chair in London's Westminster Abbey; in the 1950s it was sensationally stolen and mysteriously reappeared in Arbroath Abbey. In 1996, the government announced that the Stone was to be returned to Scotland after 700 years, and now it can be seen in Edinburgh castle.

▶▶ Perth and Kinross 235B4
(Perthshire Tourist Board tel: 01738 627958)
At the center of Scotland, and rich in historical associations, Perth and Kinross (formerly Perthshire) is a county of contrasts. As you travel north the farmland of the south is transformed into the rounded heather-covered slopes of the Grampian Mountains. Cut through with great lochs, it is bound into one region by the waters of the Tay.

The town of **Perth▶** enjoys a pleasant position beside the River Tay. Despite its bridges, its Georgian terraces, and the Millais paintings in the **Perth Museum and Art Gallery**, and the distinctive watercolors of John Duncan Fergusson in the **Fergusson Gallery**, it does not quite live up to the expectations set by its long history. On the north edge of town, the **Caithness Glass Factory** gives the chance to see glassmaking in progress (it has a factory store), while above the town, Kinnoull Hill is graced with two 18th-century follies, imitations of Rhenish castles. **Branklyn Garden▶** (N.T.S.) is a small but delightful collection of rhododendrons, shrubs, and alpines. Balhousie Castle houses the regimental museum of the Black Watch.

Located just 2 miles upriver from Perth is **Scone Palace▶▶▶**, one of Scotland's great treasure houses. Scone (pronounced "Skoon") was the seat of Pictish government, and the site of the famous Stone of Scone (see panel). Until the time of James I all the Scottish kings were crowned here. The present palace was built over the foundations of the ancient abbey by William Atkinson, a pupil of James Wyatt, at the onset of the fashion for Gothick in the first decade of the 19th century. Its state rooms display the treasures from England and France, but it is chiefly loved for its lived-in, family atmosphere.

Pitlochry▶ is a Highland resort town, in a beautiful setting of loch, river, mountain, and wood. It was created in the Victorian era when the railroad station and the Hydro, the large (and originally strictly teetotal) hotel, offered healthy walking breaks away from the smog and sin of the big cities. It boasts a respected Festival Theatre with a broad summer program. Local beauty spots include the Queen's View up Loch Tummel and Loch Rannoch, beneath volcano-shaped Schiehallion (3,490 feet). Just outside town is the site of the Battle of Killiecrankie (an early Jacobite victory) with its visitor center (N.T.S.).

To the north of Perth the attractive "Little Houses" of **Dunkeld►** date from its rebuilding following a siege during the Jacobite rebellion of 1689, in which the vastly outnumbered Lowland Cameronians held out against the Highlanders; the nave of the ruined 14th-century cathedral was later restored to serve as the parish church.

To the northwest is **Blair Castle► ►►**, its white walls and turrets surrounded by the rugged beauty of the Atholl Hills. The province of Atholl has been ruled from this tower house since the 13th century. The castle is famous as the seat of the only duke to be permitted a private army, the 100-strong Atholl Highlanders, who are recruited from tenants and neighbors. They parade on the last Sunday of May; the tunics, worn with a distinctive white bow tie, enliven many a Highland Ball throughout the year. The castle has many rooms open to the public, packed with treasures, including some rare surviving examples of 17th-century Scottish furniture. In the model 18th-century village outside the castle gates there is a local folk museum. A 3 mile track leads to the gorge, bridges and waterfall of Bruar.

Each loch in Scotland has its own marked character, but **Loch Tay► ►**, overlooked to its north by the 3,983 foot summit of Ben Lawers, has a serenity which is totally out of keeping with the bloody clan feuds that went on around its shores. At its western end the village of **Killin** is noted for the **Falls of Dochart►**. Between the village and Loch Tay are the ruins of Finlarig, the murderous stronghold of Black Duncan of the Cowl, who was the acquisitive chief of the local Campbells. His wealthy descendants built the elegant bridge and model village of **Kenmore►** at the east end of the loch. The market town of **Aberfeldy**, 7 miles east, with its monumental Wade bridge (see panel, page 244), is a popular base for summer visitors. You can walk to such nearby attractions as **Castle Menzies►**, a classic 16th-century Z-plan tower house; the old **Kirk of Weem** with its pair of Celtic crosses; and the **Birks of Aberfeldy►**, a sylvan glen made famous by Burns's poem.

HIGHLAND GENEALOGY
Beware of trying to follow too closely the tangled web of Highland genealogies. Despite fearsome blood feuds, practically all the great chiefs and nobles were and are, interrelated. This allowed any one family to keep a finger in a number of pies, which was the best way to survive the mercurial and murderous politics of Scotland. The Murrays are a fine example: during the '45 Rebellion John Murray, the 1st Duke of Atholl, remained a fervent Hanoverian while his son George was in command of the Jacobite army.

253

Above: Perth city's coat of arms, on a lamppost
Below: Queen Victoria's bedroom at Scone Palace

THE LEGACY OF FORBES

In 1836 Professor James Forbes, a 23-year-old geologist, made what is believed to have been the first rock climb in the Cuillins. He later produced the first accurate map of the range, naming some summits himself, thus bringing the area to the public notice. Soon the sport of climbing for its own sake was born. Sheriff Alexander Nicolson became a leading exponent, and with the setting up in 1889 of the Scottish Mountaineering Club the sport spread to Ben Nevis and Glen Coe.

LORDS OF THE ISLES

The lordship of the Isles was an independent state that controlled the islands and much of the west coast of Scotland in the medieval period. The founder was Somerled, the progenitor of clan MacDonald, who used the conflict between his Norse overlords and the Scots kings to establish a near-autonomous state in the 12th century. When Norse overlordship ended, the MacDonald chiefs agreed to accept the rule of Donald of Islay, as Lord of the Isles. James IV managed to annex the title in 1493 (one still borne by the heir apparent to the British throne).

The path to Moonen bay and cliffs

▶▶▶ Skye   *234C2*
(Portree tourist information center tel: 01478 612137)

The most startlingly magnificent of the Hebridean islands, Skye is also the closest to the mainland. Since 1995, Skye has been joined by a bridge from Kyle of Lochalsh to Kyleakin. It is an island of extremely irregular shape, a sort of smudged handprint some 50 miles from end to end and varying from 6 miles to 25 miles in width. It consists of a central nexus—on which are **Portree**, the bustling capital (and hub of the island's bus network) and the Cuillin Hills; a number of long peninsular fingers stretch out from there, intersected by sea lochs. The landscape changes with disorienting ease from alpine peaks, to rolling farmland, bleak moorland, wooded valleys, coves of white coral sand, and cliffs dotted with secret caves.

Close to the ferry terminal at Armadale, **Armadale Castle Gardens and Museum of the Isles▶** feature displays telling the story of the clan Donald and its progenitor, Somerled, the first Lord of the Isles (see panel). The castle is a restored 19th-century castellated mansion.

The central chain of mountain peaks, the **Cuillins▶▶**, their jagged silhouette seldom seen without at least a wisp of cloud, provides some of the most splendid scenery and demanding climbing in Britain. Rising to 3,310 feet, they enclose Loch Coruisk, a great pool of water locked in an amphitheater of crags of the blackest gabbro; it is a scene of overpowering desolation and grandeur. You can reach it by boat trip from Elgol, or in a full day's walk from Elgol or Sligachan (it is not a walk, however, for the faint-hearted). An easier option is to walk the 4 miles along the coast from Elgol to Loch na Creitheach on the threshold of the Cuillins.

In Portree, the **Aros Experience▶** tells the island's story from the point of view of the ordinary people rather than the landowners. At Skeabost, a little way northwest of Portree, are the ruins of the tiny **Columban Chapel▶**, one of a number of the earliest Celtic churches known to have been built here.

Further west, **Dunvegan Castle▶▶** has been home to the MacLeods of Skye since the 12th century. Striking a magnificent attitude on this remote shore of the island, it contains treasures sacred to the clan such as the fairy flag, which when waved has the power to save the clan. Legend says it will only work three times and it has

already been used twice, with miraculous results. In the churchyard at **Kilmuir** lie the remains of Flora MacDonald, Hebridean heroine of the '45 Rebellion (see panel, page 246), beneath an imposing Celtic cross. Nearby, the **Museum of Island Life** uses four thatched cottages to recreate aspects of the simple yet heroic self-sufficiency of the island's crofters.

The **Trotternish peninsula▶▶▶** constitutes northeast Skye, a surreal terrain of geological oddities: sandstone and limestone layers have collapsed beneath volcanic basalt to form a moonscape. Beneath the peninsula's summit, the Storr, stands a precarious needle of rock, **The Old Man of Storr**. The **Meallt Falls** thunder into the sea near **Kilt Rock**, so named because of the pleated appearance of the rock strata. **The Quiraing** is one of the strangest and most fascinating hills in Scotland. Seldom seen without its raven guardians swirling around, it is a confused mass of cliffs, scree slopes, and towering pinnacles, including features named the Prison, the Needle, and the Table. On a wind-blown promontory at the northern end of Trotternish stand the ruins of **Duntulm Castle▶**, a historically impressive fortress built by the MacDonalds of Sleat when they were battling with the MacLeods of Dunvegan for the control of this region (see panel, page 254).

From Sconser a little ferry journeys across to the tranquil island of **Raasay▶▶**. A track follows the island's long spine of hills to end at the silhouetted ruins of medieval Brochel Castle.

Across the Cuillin Sound south of Skye lie the **Small Isles**, Rum, Eigg, Muck, and Canna, served by ferries from Mallaig on the mainland and Armadale on Skye. Each has a limited number of hotels. **Rum▶▶** is the largest of the group and has a volcanic mountain cluster, the highest peak being Askival (2,657 feet). The haunt of red deer, wild goats, golden eagles, and sea eagles, the island is a national nature reserve and has nature trails and a hotel owned by Scottish Natural Heritage.

Skye style: old croft house, traditionally maintained with white-washed walls, a central doorway, and a roof of heather thatch

MIGHT IS RIGHT?
The 1882 Battle of the Braes was a half-heroic, half-comical affair. A group of bailiffs who were attempting to evict crofters from the coastal strip just south of Portree were beaten off by a fierce band of Hebridean house-wives armed with stone-weighted stockings. The English government, used to sending gunboats all over the world to force their way, promptly sent one up to Skye but backed down in the face of universal hostility. Instead they sent a Commission whose report paved the way for the enlightened Crofting Acts.

The valley of the River Spey near Newtonmore

GORDONSTOUN SCHOOL
The school, near Elgin, is famous nowadays as the establishment where the Queen's three sons were educated, but its buildings have had a local notoriety since the 17th century, when they served as the residence of Sir Robert Gordon. Known as the Warlock Laird, he laid out the school's famous round square so that his diabolic familiars could never corner him. His accomplice, the local minister, was not so lucky and was found one morning horribly shreded by giant claws outside the kirk.

▶ **Spey Valley**   *235C4*
(Highlands of Scotland Tourist Board tel: 01997 421160)
One of the broad classifications of single-malt whiskies is the Speyside malts which take their name from the River Spey. It rises in the Monadliath (literally "the grey moors") and runs northeast, spreading through the wildlife-rich Insh Marshes with the Cairngorms as a spectacular backdrop. Beyond Grantown-on-Spey it reaches the whisky-distilling area stretching all the way to the Moray coast. The typical Strathspey view features a pleasing mix of woods and farmlands backed by moorland slopes and, inevitably, a plume of white steam jetting up from yet another distillery tucked into the landscape. Visit Glenfiddich at Dufftown for a wide-ranging and entertaining interpretation of malt whisky, though there are plenty of other famous names, some on the marked **Malt Whisky Trail** (see panel, page 257).

The resort town of **Aviemore** is a rather unattractive creation of the 1960s but it is a popular base for hill walking in the **Cairngorm Mountains**▶▶ in summer and skiing on them in winter. Cairn Gorm itself rises to 4,084 feet; take the ski lift (it operates all year round) for a wonderful view. Other activities might include a visit to the osprey reserve at Loch Garten, a ride on the Strathspey Steam Railway from Aviemore to Boat of Garten (good walks at either end), or a visit to the Landmark Highland Heritage visitor center. South along the A9 towards Kingussie is the Highland Wildlife Park.

Kingussie▶, pronounced "Kinusie," is a pleasing town of just one main street, with plenty of beautiful walks nearby. If you visit only one highland history museum in Scotland, visit the **Highland Folk Museum**▶▶ here. It is divided into indoor and outdoor exhibitions and includes a "black house" from the Outer Hebridean island of Lewis, a corn mill, a salmon smokehouse, and fascinating exhibits from farming and domestic life. Close by at Newtonmore, the **Highland Folk Park**▶▶ demonstrates the life and work of crofters in the early 1900s and has a turfhouse township evoking the 18th century. On a natural escarpment the other side of the Spey and the A9 stands the gaunt roofless ruin of the **Ruthven Barracks**, a sister to the one in Glenelg (see page 258). They were built to police the main Highland trade routes after the 1715 rebellion was suppressed, but a generation later, in 1746, they were blown up by retreating Jacobites.

Elgin▶ is the administrative center of Moray and the largest town in the favored Laigh of Moray. (Laigh means a sheltered low-lying area and, in this case, refers to its position in the "rain shadow" of the Grampians.) Elgin's cathedral, "the lantern of the North," founded in 1224, was burned in 1390 by the villainous Wolf of Badenoch. Though subsequently rebuilt, it is now a picturesque ruin. Beside it, the **Biblical Gardens** claim to incorporate every plant mentioned in the Bible, with paths laid out in the form of the Cross. The local museum features a display on Britain's oldest dinosaurs, found nearby. East of the town is the attractive community of **Fochabers**, with plenty of antiques stores to attract browsers, as well as another absorbing folk museum. On the coast, the otherwise workaday town of **Buckie** is enhanced by an interpretation of the development of the northeast fishery, the Buckie Drifter Heritage Centre. Summer boat trips from here provide the opportunity to watch bottle-nosed dolphins. At Macduff, the **Macduff Marine Aquarium**▶ displays the sealife of northeast Scotland in Britain's largest indoor tank.

Pluscarden Abbey▶ lies in a fertile valley 6 miles to the southwest of Elgin. Its atmosphere is memorably potent, with Benedictine monks going to and fro amid the Gothic ruins. Founded by Alexander II in the early 13th century, the abbey was damaged by the warfare of the region and fell into further decay after the Reformation. It was partly restored by the Marquis of Bute in the 19th century and in 1943 was bestowed by his son on a Benedictine community from Prinknash in Gloucestershire. The monks moved in five years later and are now rebuilding it.

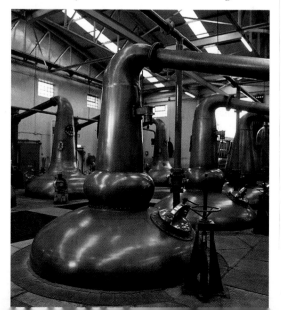

The copper stills at Glenfiddich Distillery; there are eight distilleries on the Malt Whisky Trail

THE MALT WHISKY TRAIL
Speyside is home to half of Scotland's malt distilleries, many of which are fascinating 19th-century time-warps. On the 68 mile Malt Whisky Trail are Cardhu (at Knockando), Dallas Dhu (Forres), Glenfarclas (Ballindalloch), Glenfiddich (Dufftown), Glen Grant (Rothes), Glenlivet (Glenlivet), Strathisla (Keith) and Tamnavulin (Tamnavulin). Of these, Glenfiddich, Glenlivet and Tamnavulin are free; otherwise admission covers a guided tour, and a voucher redeemable in the store. Children under 8 are not admitted to some production areas. At Speyside Cooperage (Craigellachie), Britain's only working cooperage open to the public, oak casks are repaired for reuse in whisky manufacturing.

257

THE SPEYSIDE WAY
The 47 mile long-distance path starts at Spey Bay where the River Spey flows into the North Sea and offers fairly easy walking as far as Ballindalloch before tackling the more challenging section through the hills to Tomintoul. The countryside is varied and the path passes near several whisky distilleries.

**THE SUTHERLAND
CLEARANCES**
Dominating the skyline
around the village of
Golspie is a statue of the
1st Duke of Sutherland.
He was the infamous
Leviathan of Wealth who
between 1810 and 1820
evicted 15,000 of his
tenants from their self-
sufficient crofts in order to
turn their small plots into
profitable sheep pasture.

▶▶▶ Sutherland, Caithness, and Wester Ross *234C2*

(Highlands of Scotland Tourist Board tel: 01997 421160)

The northernmost reach of mainland Scotland is often referred to as the last great wilderness of Europe. The eastern coast, a fertile strip backed by brown moorland, could not be in greater contrast to the green-grey mountains that overlook the sea lochs of the west coast of Ross.

In a remote and picturesque situation on the Sound of Sleat, **Glenelg▶** was once on the main cattle-droving route to Skye. Here are found the two best-preserved brochs (see panel, page 251) in mainland Scotland, a handsome, ruined Hanoverian barrack block and Sandaig Bay, site of Gavin Maxwell's otter refuge of "Camusfearna" so vividly described in *Ring of Bright Water*. In summer you can take a ferry across the surging Kylerhea tidal stream to Skye.

*Eilean Donan Castle, a
Mackenzie fortress, was
rebuilt early in the 20th
century by Colonel
Macrae after he suppos-
edly saw its original
appearance in a dream*

North, across Loch Duich, the stunning **Eilean Donan Castle▶▶** stands on an islet at the meeting of three lochs. On the northern shores of this peninsula are the stone-built houses and palm trees of the delightful coastal village of **Plockton▶**. West of Lochcarron, the adventurous should take an exhilaratingly twisty road (certainly not one for more timid drivers) over **Bealach Na Ba (The Pass of the Cattle)▶▶**. The glacier-scarred rocks on the summit of this pass offer a very fine view over Skye, especially at sunset. The road then leads down to the remote coastal village of **Applecross**. A carved Celtic cross beside the kirk marks the site of the once influential 7th-century monastery of St. Maelrubha.

Torridon▶▶ lies at the end of one of Wester Ross's wildest glens. The road along the southern shores of Upper Loch Torridon offers magnificent views of Beinn Alligin (3,232 feet). A National Trust for Scotland countryside center in Torridon has a deer museum and an audio-visual presentation on local wildlife. Further north, in one of the most beautiful corners of the west coast, lies the spectacular, world-famous **Inverewe Garden▶▶▶** (N.T.S.), a collection of some 2,500 species of tender and hardy shrubs and trees which flourish in the warmth of the Gulf Stream.

The port of **Ullapool**, placed amidst breathtaking scenery, doubles as a resort. The A835 eastward heads down Loch Broom to the Falls of Measeach in the dizzying

**DORNOCH'S CLAIMS TO
FAME**
Besides having the third
oldest golf links in the
world, considered as far
back as 1630 to be
superior to those of
St. Andrews, Dornoch also
claims the best sunshine
record in northern
Scotland and the dubious
distinction of being the
last place in Scotland to
burn a witch. The Witch's
Stone by the 17th hole of
the golf links commemo-
rates the country's last
judicial execution for
witchcraft, in 1722.

Himalayan lilies and other exotic species flourish in Inverewe Garden, formerly a peaty wasteland

Corrieshalloch Gorge►►. To the north the same road passes **Knockan Cliff►**, in the Inverpolly Nature Reserve and glimpses Stac Pollaidh and Suilven, two of the most striking mountain shapes in Scotland.

In the far north, you can take a ferry and minibus from Durness to **Cape Wrath►►** to see some stupendous coastal scenery. Britain's highest mainland cliffs are nearby Clo Mor, east of Cape Wrath. Just outside Durness itself is the Smoo Cave, which is in fact three vast caves in the limestone cliffs, with a waterfall. A boat trip can be taken right into the second and third caves.

Few people who come this far north fail to visit Britain's most northeasterly point, **John O'Groats**, named after the Dutchman Jan de Groot (Dunnet Head, nearby, is actually the northernmost point). It's basically an untidy collection of tourist shacks, disappointing to many visitors. Persevere instead to nearby Duncansby Head (see Walks, page 238): the three dramatic offshore stacks rise to over 197 feet.

South of Wick, near the village of Lybster, are two impressive ancient relics, the **Hill o' Many Stones** and the **Grey Cairns of Camster►►**. The former is a curious and attractive arrangement of 22 rows of stones in a fan shape, the latter two excellently preserved neolithic burial chambers. If you don't mind the idea of crawling into someone's grave, you can enter one of the handsomest in the country, 197 feet long and 59 feet wide with separate chambers inside.

North of Dornoch the fairy-tale towers of **Dunrobin Castle►►** stand on a coastal escarpment, the former seat of the earls and dukes of Sutherland, the largest landowners in Britain. Despite its fanciful 19th-century exterior, it is an ancient fortress with a medieval keep as its core. The collection of paintings inside includes a Reynolds and two Canalettos. **Dornoch►►** is a secluded and ancient royal burgh, a pretty little sandstone town with several miles of safe sandy beaches. The small cathedral of the Bishops of Caithness dates from the 12th century. The town is also renowned for its golf links.

GENERATING POWER
Standing on the clifftops 10 miles west of Thurso, the giant golf-ball shape of Dounreay nuclear power station can be seen for miles around. Elsewhere the waters of Scotland's mountains and reservoirs are harnessed to produce electricity: the great pipes of the hydroelectric plant at Kinlochleven can be seen on the hillsides south of Fort William and those of the Tay-Tummel system around Glen Affric. The pumped storage plant at Ben Cruachan in Argyll has a visitor center.

259

WILDLIFE
The flow or marsh country of Caithness and Sutherland is a vast stretch of plantations. It is home during the summer months to greenshanks, dunlins, golden plovers, and other wading birds. Dunnet Bay, near Wick, is an excellent birdwatching spot in winter. Look for great northern divers, long-tailed ducks and scoters. The flora of the Arctic species mingles with mountain species, almost at sea level. Handa Island, off Scourie, is another wonderful site for breeding seabirds. A private ferry often runs from Tarbert.

Scarista Bay, Harris, typifies the majestic remoteness of the Western Isles

A voice so thrilling ne'er
was heard,
In spring time from the
cuckoo-bird,
Breaking the silence of
the seas
Amongst the farthest
Hebrides.
—William Wordsworth,
The Solitary Reaper

THE LEWIS CHESSMEN

The chance discovery in the 19th century of the 12th-century chessmen on Lewis caused a storm of controversy. Their artistry was of a standard many found hard to attribute to the 12th century. Carved from walrus ivory, they are now divided between the British Museum in London and the Museum of Antiquities in Edinburgh. Replicas can be bought on Lewis.

►►► Western Isles   234D1

(Western Isles Tourist Board tel: 01851 703088)

Sail west across the Minch and you reach the Western Isles, or Outer Hebrides. For the most part the eastern side of the archipelago is barren, rocky, and steep. Its west coast is all silver-white beaches, long and empty and backed by the "machair," fertile peaty grassland enriched by white shell-sand—an almost unique habitat that supports a rich wildlife. Between the two lie watery, peaty, and totally treeless moors.

The Western Isles change their religion with their latitude: strict Presbyterianism in Lewis, Harris, Berneray, and North Uist; Roman Catholicism in South Uist, Eriskay, and Barra; with Benbecula in between a mixture of the two. The difference is readily apparent: strict observation of the Sabbath in the northern islands means people go out only to attend church services (stores and bars are closed), whereas Sundays in the south are livelier and more relaxed. Even the houses on the southern islands have a brighter look, often with colored roofs and painted walls.

It is a perfect place to get away from it all. The people are exceptionally friendly and welcome visitors, but you will not find organized facilities. The few "sights" are mostly archeological; what visitors will remember is the empty beaches, the lochs, the hills, the wildlife, the pure quality of the light, and the way of life.

LEWIS AND HARRIS Lewis and Harris are in fact one island, linked to the mainland and Skye by ferries from Stornoway and Tarbert. The world-famous Harris tweed is still produced here. The stone circle of **Callanish►►►** is one of the most haunting and eloquent places in Britain (there is an exhibition in the nearby visitor center). An open-air temple of the Bronze Age that seems to have related particularly to the moon, it is tucked onto a broad peninsula on the west coast of Lewis that protrudes into the sheltered waters of Loch Roag. The inner circle of 13 stones surrounds a central 16 foot, 5-ton menhir. In the central cairn, remains of a human cremation were discovered when the 5 foot-high banks of peat were removed in 1860. At Arnol, the squat **Black House►** (H.S.) is now a

museum (see panel, page 261); another museum evoking crofting life is found at nearby **Siabost**. To the west, **Dun Carloway▶** is one of the best brochs (Iron Age towers) in the Hebrides, dating from the 1st century BC and with walls rising to 20 feet; its interpretation center is open in summer. **Rodel Church▶ ▶**, a bold cruciform dating from 1500, stands on the southern tip of Harris. The cold bleak interior preserves a number of carvings.

NORTH AND SOUTH UIST On the road south from Lochmaddy is the finest chambered cairn in the Hebrides. **Barpa Langass▶** sits on the side of the hill, Ben Langass; a little tunnel leads into the communal burial chamber built by Bronze Age Beaker people.

The northwest coast of North Uist has several beautiful coves and beaches; the one near Hosta is, on a clear day, the best place to see **St. Kilda**, the most remote of the Hebrides 45 miles out in the Atlantic. Nearby **Balranald R.S.P.B. Reserve▶** harbors the rare corncrake and offers a trail across the flower- and bird-rich machair.

North Uist, Benbecula, and South Uist are linked by a causeway. At Milton a cairn stands on the site of the birthplace of Jacobite heroine Flora MacDonald (1722). At the island's southern tip a ferry goes to tiny **Eriskay**, celebrated in the Gaelic melody, the "Eriskay Love Lilt." It was here that Bonnie Prince Charlie first set foot in Scotland on his way from France.

Barra▶ ▶ is a microcosm of all the Western Isles with its rocky coastline on the east, sandy bays, and machair on the west. Small-scale farming is still the main occupation and Gaelic is still spoken. Ferries connect Castlebay with South Uist and the mainland.

Harris wool, here being sold locally; the tweed is sold worldwide

The standing stones at Callanish on the Isle of Lewis

CROFT HOUSES OLD AND NEW

The Arnol Black House on the west coast of Lewis is a traditional crofter's house that gives a fascinating insight into a way of life that was common until the 1970s. Inside the thick stone walls a peat fire smolders in the middle of the floor, the smoke filtering out through the oat-straw thatch held down by stone-weighted strands of rope. Many of these old croft houses can still be seen, some left in ruin, some given new roofs. The modern houses that replace them are similarly low buildings, usually with dormer windows.

Mountains, lochs, and glens make a magnificent landscape but a harsh environment in which to live and work. Traditionally the Highlands supported a sophisticated, martial society with its own code of conduct and social responsibilities. This was wilfully destroyed in the mid-18th century, and within a generation the infamous Clearances began, when the people were driven from the land.

PROPHET OF DOOM
The 17th-century poet Brahan Seer, born on Lewis in the Outer Hebrides, described how the glens would be emptied of their people by sheep, how the sheep would in turn be displaced by deer before the coming of the black rain that would clear all life from the land. The "black rain" has been widely identified with fallout from a nuclear war or a disaster at the Dounreay nuclear reactor. Too many of his prophecies have been fulfilled for his dark vision of the future of the Highlands not to cast a chill of apprehension.

Mass evictions and emigrations have left the landscape dotted with ruined crofters' houses

The rule of the Highland chieftain Up until the defeat of the Jacobite clans at Culloden Moor in 1746, the Highlands were divided into small communities by the dramatic landscape of mountains and sea lochs. It was primarily a cattle-breeding society that traded for grain grown in the Lowlands. The Highland cattle, small herds of sheep, goats, and chickens were highly mobile and every community required a strongly motivated fighting force to protect its wealth from "lifting." This was the economic basis of the closely knit and intensely martial Highland clans. There was a long tradition of paternalistic care, but it was a feudal society for the simple reason that a hundred strong men in times of crisis were of much greater use than a money rent.

The changing tide After their victory at the Battle of Culloden, the Hanoverian government, frightened by the partial success of the Highland army that rallied to Bonnie Prince Charlie, determined to control this militant society. They banned firearms, the martial kilt, and the strong legal powers of the clan chiefs—and they were undeniably thorough. Within a few years the Highlands were at peace and money rents began to replace feudal tenures. For a few decades everything seemed rosy—the potato provided a new cheap staple crop for the poor, grain prices stayed down, and livestock prices soared. Capitalists built iron foundries, fishing harbors, piers, linen and woollen mills, partly financed by enormous profits made by gathering kelp. The population quickly doubled, but the plots of farming land became ever smaller.

The Clearances The end of the Napoleonic wars brought a violent depression with the total collapse of fish, cattle, and kelp prices and the near-extinction of rural industries. Only sheep brought in a handsome profit. Sheep farming, however, was incompatible with thousands of tenants packed into the glens and coastal strips and many people began to be evicted from their land to make room for sheep paddocks. They were moved south to the slums of the industrial cities or packed off to Canada, Australia, New Zealand, and the U.S. Gladstone's Crofting Act of 1886 gave the surviving tenants a guaranteed claim on their smallholdings and allowed strong communities to survive in the Hebrides, but many big estates were turned over to deer hunting and grouse shooting. With forestry, fish farming, and tourism, these still play a major part in the Highlands' economy.

Travel Facts

Arriving and departing

By air London has five international airports. The largest is **Heathrow** (one of the largest in the world). Airbuses run to London Victoria, Heathrow Express trains to London Paddington (taking 15 minutes) and Underground trains (the cheapest option) take 45–60 minutes to central London. These services do not run all night.

The next largest airport, **Gatwick**, has a direct rail link to Victoria Station. **Luton** (north of London) has a bus link to Luton railroad station, and **Stansted** has trains to London Liverpool Street. **City Airport** is served by a shuttle bus from Liverpool Street and Canary Wharf, as well as overground trains. **Birmingham**, **Edinburgh**, **Glasgow**, **Leeds/ Bradford**, and **Manchester** also serve international flights.

264

By boat Numerous ports have cross-Channel services to the rest of Europe. Dover in Kent (71 miles from London) is the main cross-Channel port connecting with Belgium and France; if you get stuck here for the night, there are plenty of bed and breakfasts.

FOR TRAVEL DETAILS

Flight arrivals: see Ceefax (accessed through most TVs via BBc channels), page 440
Flight departures: contact individual airlines
European Rail Travel Centre, Rail Europe, tel: 0870 584 8848
Eurostar tel: 0870 518 6186

By rail Trains via the Eurotunnel run from the European mainland. Services from Brussels and Paris to London Waterloo take about 3 hours.

Camping

Campgrounds are abundant in Britain, ranging from small fields with just a single cold-water tap by way of facilities to large-scale grounds with showers and stores. Useful sources of information include the English Tourism Council/British Tourist Authority book *The Official Guide to Camping and*

Caravan Parks in Britain (on sale at major bookstores or by mail tel: 020-8563 3156, fax 020-8563 3048), and *The Big Sites Book* published for members of the Camping and Caravanning Club (Greenfields House, Westwood Way, Coventry CV4 8JH; tel: 024-766 9499, fax 024-7669 4886). Tourist information centers can help with lists of local campgrounds. If you want to try camping in the wilds, be aware of all that the British climate can throw at you, and remember that even open moorland is owned by someone—try to ask permission first.

Children

Child **discounts** are offered for many admission fees. On the rail network, up to two children under five years of age may travel free with each fare-paying adult, while children under 16 travel at half the full price. Anyone traveling by train with children should invest in a Family Railcard: up to four under-16-year-olds travel anywhere in the country for 20 percent of the adult fare, and up to two accompanying adults have a discount of 20 percent on most leisure fares.

Pubs Children under 14 are not allowed in the bar area. Some pubs allow accompanied children onto the premises (in the restaurant, for instance) and in the garden, but practice varies from one establishment to another. You have to be 18 years or over to buy or consume alcohol in a pub.

Theme parks and safari parks These include Alton Towers (Staffordshire), Camelot Theme Park (Preston, Lancashire), Chessington's World of Adventures (Surrey), Knowsley Safari Park (Prescot, Merseyside), Legoland (Berkshire), Lightwater Valley (Ripon, North Yorkshire), Lions of Longleat Safari Park (Warminster, Wiltshire), Thorpe Park (Chertsey, Surrey), West Midland Safari and Leisure Park (Bewdley, Herefordshire), and Woburn Wild Animal Kingdom and Leisure Park (Woburn, Bedfordshire). At Piccadilly Circus in London is the animatronic Rock Circus.

London, the South Coast (Devon, Dorset, and Sussex in particular), the North Yorkshire coast, and Cornwall

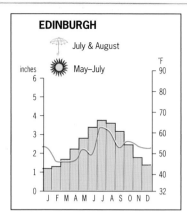

EDINBURGH

🌂 July & August

☀️ May–July

inches / °F

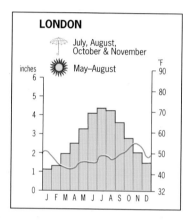

LONDON

🌂 July, August, October & November

☀️ May–August

inches / °F

are among the most appealing areas for families; older children may also enjoy the Lake District, Exmoor, Pembrokeshire, York, Edinburgh, as well as the Scottish Highlands.

Climate and seasonal considerations

Britain is a temperate country—the weather is seldom extremely hot or extremely cold and there is no prolonged rainy or dry season. The British climate is a fascinatingly fickle beast: the seasons are distinctive but fuse into each other; brilliant mornings often cloud over as they proceed. No wonder the umbrella seems like part of the national costume. Be prepared for sudden changes in temperature.

The prevailing wind comes from the west, bringing most rain to western Britain; a rain-shadow effect causes eastern areas to have consid-

erably lower rainfall. The south coast gets less rain than the far north, and the climate tends to get warmer the farther south you go. In mid-June it stays light until 10 PM (later in northern Scotland); but in winter it gets dark early, and the very far north stays gloomy all day.

Travel in spring and you could encounter blustery squalls or fragrant whiffs of nature reawakening in benign sunshine; May and June are excellent times to travel, with the long daylight hours and comparatively uncrowded roads and sights (except for three-day public holiday weekends). The colleges of Oxford and Cambridge are mostly closed in the weeks running up to examination time in late May and early June.

Schools' summer vacations make late July and all of August extremely busy in many areas, including

265

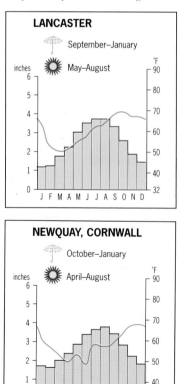

LANCASTER

🌂 September–January

☀️ May–August

inches / °F

NEWQUAY, CORNWALL

🌂 October–January

☀️ April–August

inches / °F

national parks and coastal areas—Devon, Cornwall, the Lake District, the South Coast, the Scottish Highlands (also infested with midges over this period), and Snowdonia are among the most crowded regions. Some historic cities fill almost to capacity, York, Chester, and Canterbury among them. But other places are still quite manageable, including the Welsh borderlands, Eastern England, East Anglia, and the Scottish borders.

September can have fine late-summer weather and is a good time to visit.

Visitor numbers drop along with the temperature in October and November (the West Country stays reasonably mild), but Christmas is busier, with many hotels offering special Christmas break deals. Many attractions close in the off-peak season from October or November to Easter (including most National Trust properties). Scottish winters get enough snow for skiing to be feasible in places, notably the Cairngorms.

Crime

Violent crime is still rare in Britain and city centers are mostly quite safe, but minor offenses against property have risen over recent years, particularly in some inner-city areas. Even in remote countryside, it is wise to be on guard against car theft, and keep all valuables locked out of sight. Be extra vigilant of your belongings at airports and major railroad stations: do not let them out of your sight. Because of the risk of terrorist bombs, unattended packages are likely to be removed.

Customs

Note the distinction between **duty-free** and **duty-paid** allowances. Duty-free goods (bought at duty-free shops in airports, ferry terminals, on ferries, and on airplanes, even those in the E.U.) have had no duty paid on them and do not entitle you to the higher allowances now set for duty-paid goods bought in the E.U. Duty-free allowances have been abolished for travel within E.U. countries. The countries of the E.U. are Austria, Belgium, Denmark, Finland, France, Germany, Greece, Italy, Luxembourg, the Netherlands, Portugal, the Republic of Ireland, Spain (not the Canary Islands), Sweden and the United Kingdom (not the Channel Islands).

Cycling

You need to be canny to explore Britain by bike, as many roads are too busy to be much fun, yet elsewhere you can explore some delightfully quiet countryside. Good areas include East Anglia, the Cotswolds, mid Wales and the Welsh borderlands, Northumberland and the Scottish Borders, the Isle of Wight and (off road) along the South Downs Way in Sussex. The 9,315 mile National Cycle Network is rapidly being developed, giving access to quiet roads and specially constructed cycle paths. It will pass within 2 miles of half the U.K. population. The Network has been established by the charity Sustrans, 35 King Street, Bristol BS1 4DZ, tel: 0117 929 0888 (website: www.sustrans.org.uk); excellent maps of the routes are on sale. The general organization for cycling matters is the Cyclists' Touring Club (CTC), 69 Meadrow, Godalming, Surrey GU7 3HS, UK, tel 01483 417217 (www.ctc.org.uk).

Disabilities, visitors with

The English Tourism Council grades hotel, farmhouse, inn, and guest house accommodations according to suitability for visitors with disabilities from Category 3 (suitable for a

A clock in Chester commemorates Queen Victoria's diamond jubilee

DUTY-FREE ALLOWANCES

Duty-free allowances (for goods bought outside the E.U.) and duty-paid allowances for goods bought outside the E.U.

Cigarettes	200
or cigarillos	100
or cigars	50
or tobacco	250 g
Still table wine	2 liters
Spirits, strong liquor over 22% volume	1 liter
or fortified or sparkling wine	2 liters
Perfume	60 cc/ml
Toilet water	250 cc/ml
All other goods including gifts and souvenirs	£145 worth, for travelers from outside the E.U.

wheelchair-user who is also able to walk short distances and up at least three steps) to Category 1 (accessible for a wheelchair-user traveling alone). You can get help finding suitable accommodations from the Holiday Care Service, 2nd Floor, Imperial Buildings, Victoria Road, Horley, Surrey RH6 7PZ, tel: 01293 774535 or Minicom (for hearing-impaired callers) 01293 776943, and from the Royal Association for Disability and Rehabilitation (RADAR), 12 City Forum, 250 City Road, London EC1V 8AF, tel: 020-7250 3222 (website: www.radar.org.uk). RADAR publishes the annual *Holidays in Britain and Ireland: A Guide for Disabled People,* as well as *Getting There,* a book-covering aspects of transport such as rail stations and airports from the point of view of travelers with disabilities. Some hotel chains have rooms adapted for use by disabled people.

Toilets for wheelchair-users are provided in many museums and tourist sites; a booklet showing them is available from RADAR.

Wheelchair-users planning train travel should first contact the rail network that they will be using—telephone numbers are in the *Yellow Pages,* or through directory enquiries

(192)—so that arrangements can be made for boarding and seating. RADAR has addresses of local disability associations.

Driving
Driving in Britain can be a delightful way to see the country, or diabolically frustrating. In many remote country areas it is the only way of getting around; for village-to-village wandering (such as the Cotswolds, the Weald, and Constable Country), where local public transportation is limited, a car is essential. The huge network of narrow, crooked lanes (many very ancient indeed) is a particular feature. Rural tourist areas such as the Lake District and the Cornish coastal towns and villages can get so busy in summer that finding somewhere to park requires ingenuity; consider using local buses (if there are any) or finding a footpath. In big cities, finding your way can be difficult; in central London (where parking is something of an ordeal) avoid driving if possible and use public transportation or taxis.

DUTY-PAID GUIDE LEVELS

People traveling within the E.U. are no longer entitled to import duty-free goods—these are the guide levels for duty-paid goods bought in the E.U. You can bring in any amount of goods, but beyond these guide limits you will have to be able to show the items are for your own personal use (this includes gifts); if you are receiving any payment in return for these goods (including payment of your travel expenses) you will be liable for duty.

Cigarettes	800
Cigarillos	400
Cigars	200
Tobacco	1 kg
Spirits	10 liters
Beer	110 liters
Intermediate products (sherry, port, etc)	20 liters
Wine (of which not more than 60 liters to be sparkling wine)	90 liters

Breaking down Car rental companies normally provide coverage with one of the major motoring organizations in Britain, the AA (Automobile Association) or the RAC (Royal Automobile Club). On major highways there are emergency telephones every mile along the hard shoulder. Arrows on posts indicate the direction of the nearest telephone.

Car rental Large firms with numerous branches and desks at airports include Avis tel: 0870 606 0100, Budget tel: 0800 626063, and Holiday Autos tel: 0870 400 4453. These may not be the cheapest; telephone around for the best deal. Most cars have a manual gearshift; if you prefer automatics, reserve one well in advance.

Licenses (permits) Australian, Canadian, Irish, New Zealand, and American driving licenses or permits are acceptable. Holders of permits written in a foreign language should obtain an official translation from an embassy or recognized motoring organization, or an international driving license. Car rental firms all require you to have held your license or permit for at least a year.

Motorways These freeways link most major cities; service areas (few and far between) are indicated well in advance. On some motorways, however, there are even fewer stopping places, e.g. the M25 (London's busy orbital route), the M11, and the M20.

Hiking is a national pastime

Parking restrictions Never park on a double yellow line; parking on single yellow lines is generally permitted on Sundays and at other times as displayed. Wheel clamps are now used to combat illegal parking, and the fee/fine to release your car is hefty.

Traffic regulations Traffic drives on the left (it goes clockwise at traffic circles, which are common at intersections). Speed-limit and destination signs use miles. Speed limits are 70 mph for motorways and dual carriageways, 60 mph for other roads, and 30 mph in residential or commercial areas unless otherwise indicated. Front-seat passengers and drivers must wear seatbelts; rear-seat passengers must wear seatbelts if the vehicle has them. Drivers must be at least 17 years of age. Traffic cannot turn left at a red traffic light unless there is a green "filter" arrow.

Electricity
The current in Britain is 240 volts, alternating current. Plugs have three flat pins.

Embassies and consulates in London
Australia Australia House, Strand, WC2, tel: 020-7379 4334
Canada 1 Grosvenor Square, W1, tel: 020-7258 6600
New Zealand New Zealand House, Haymarket, SW1, tel: 020-7930 8422
U.S.A. 24 Grosvenor Square, W1, tel: 020-7499 9000

Health
Accident victims must be admitted through emergency rooms in hospitals. Local doctors (G.P.s) will see visitors; ask at your hotel or at a pharmacy for details. Under the National Health Service, visitors from countries which do not have a reciprocal agreement may find they are charged. If you take medication, make a note of medicines you use. A charge is made for dental treatment.

Free medical advice from a qualified nurse is available over the phone through the government service NHS Direct, tel: 0845 4647.

Pharmacies (usually called chemists) and larger supermarkets have a fair range of medicines you can buy without a doctor's prescription. Opening time rotas of chemists are often maintained: details of locations of the duty chemist are posted in the windows.

Hitchhiking

Hitchhiking is legal in Britain, but the occasional report of violent crime keeps many people from doing it. It is illegal to stand on the hard shoulder of motorways; however, hitchhikers may wait near traffic circles by motorway feeder roads.

Holidays

Schools' summer vacations generally last from late July to early September; you may find many places closed from Christmas Day through to New Year's Day.

January 1 New Year's Day
January 2 New Year's Day (Scotland only)
Late March to early April Good Friday, followed three days later by Easter Monday
First Monday in May May Day Bank Holiday
Last Monday in May Spring Bank Holiday (Whitsun)
First Monday in August Bank Holiday (Scotland only)
Last Monday in August Bank Holiday (England and Wales only)
December 25 Christmas Day
December 26 Boxing Day

Insurance

Travel insurance should cover accident or illness, loss of valuables, injury or death while driving, and trip cancellation. You may be covered for personal items through your homeowner's insurance. Shop around for the best buy: prices and what is covered vary enormously.

Language

Although there is nowhere in Britain where English is not understood, in certain parts it is very much the second language. Welsh is the main tongue in parts of Mid, West, and North Wales, but less so in South Wales and the Welsh borders. Throughout Wales, road signs are in both languages. Gaelic is spoken in parts of Scotland, notably the Hebrides. Britain's cultural diversity is often simplified into the notion of a land of two cultures, separated by a north/south divide. But to simplify accents this way would not be possible. In whatever area of the country you visit, you will come across marked regional accents; from "Scouse" in Liverpool to "Brummie" in Birmingham, from "Geordie" in Newcastle to "Cockney" in London.

The differences between American and British English can be the source of confusion (and amusement). A Briton thinks of a subway not as a mode of transportation but as a pedestrian passageway beneath the street, and "pants" is another word for "briefs." In America the Postal Service delivers the mail, whereas in Britain the Royal Mail delivers the post. Other examples are:

269

American	British
Bill	Bank note
Check (for food or drinks)	Bill
Chips	Crisps
Crosswalk	Pedestrian crossing
Diaper	Nappy
Elevator	Lift
Freeway	Motorway
French fries	Chips
First/second floor	Ground/first floor
Garbage can	Dustbin
Gasoline	Petrol
Hood (of car)	Bonnet
Overpass	Flyover
Pants	Trousers
Panty hose	Tights
Restroom	Toilet/W.C./ loo
Sidewalk	Pavement
Subway	Underground/ Tube
Trunk (of car)	Boot
Two weeks	Fortnight
Windshield	Windscreen
Yard (of house)	Garden

Lost property

Items are often handed into police stations; they pass on information about lost items to other branches. Make sure your address in Britain is shown on all your valuables. For items lost on public transportation, contact the bus station, train station, or airport involved. The London Transport Lost Property Office is at 200 Baker Street, NW1 5RZ, tel: 020-7486 2496 (recorded message).

Maps

The Automobile Association (AA) publishes a comprehensive road atlas of Great Britain with a section on city and town plans. Britain has been mapped accurately by the Ordnance Survey (O.S.). If you intend to spend some time exploring a region, invest in the pink-covered O.S. Landranger maps, 1:50,000 scale (2 cm to the km): contours show relief, and footpaths are marked. For hiking, the O.S. orange-covered Explorer maps, 1:25,000 scale (4 cm to the km), showing field boundaries, are best; for some of the most popular walking areas (including many national parks) the yellow O.S. Outdoor Leisure at 1:25,000 scale, are available instead. Most bookstores have local O.S. maps; the full range is sold at Stanfords Map and Travel Bookshop, 12–14 Long Acre, London WC2, tel: 020-7836 1321.

Media

Newspapers The style contrasts between the "quality" broadsheets (*The Times*, *Independent*, *Guardian*, *Financial Times*, and *Daily Telegraph*) and the more widely selling "popular" tabloids (the *Daily Mail*, *Daily Express*, *Sun*, *Mirror*, *Star*, and *Sport*). For London, the weekly *Time Out* gives the lowdown on eating places and entertainment. There are several regional dailies

Television There are five channels: the government-funded BBC1 and BBC2, and the commercial channels ITV, Channel 4, and Channel 5. Many hotels now have cable and satellite TV, giving access to foreign stations

Radio There are five national B.B.C. radio stations, Radio 1 (pop music), Radio 2 (light music), Radio 3 (classical music), Radio 4 (news, drama and general interest), and Radio 5 Live (sports and news). Classic F.M. broadcasts lighter classical music.

Frequencies can be found in newspapers and the weekly TV listings magazines.

Money matters

Credit cards are accepted at nearly all gas pumps, most restaurants, and many stores. Traveler's checks are a safe way to carry money. Using your bank card or credit card to draw cash from ATM machines can get you more favorable exchange rates, but be sure to check the fees first—both your bank and the bank where you're making the withdrawal may charge you. The pound (£) is divided into 100 pence (or "p," pronounced "pee."). Denominations are 1p, 2p, 5p, 10p, 20p, 50p, £1 and £2 coins, then £5, £10, £20, and £50 notes. Banks in Scotland issue their own banknotes; they are legal currency throughout the U.K.

Nationals of countries outside the E.U. may claim **V.A.T. refunds** for the value-added tax on goods bought within the E.U.; ask the store when you make your purchase for a form.

Tipping Generally, tip 10–15 percent in a restaurant if service has not already been added (ask if it is not clear), or not at all if you think the meal and/or service was not up to par; total payment boxes on credit card slips are often left empty, leaving you to add a tip (remember to fill it in!). Taxi drivers expect 10 percent; with minicabs, which are ordered by phone, you are told a price before you travel, and drivers generally do not expect anything. Porters in luxury hotels will expect a £1 tip. Barbers and hairdressers can be tipped 10 percent.

Opening hours

Standard office hours are Monday to Friday, 9 to 5; stores generally stay open until 5:30 or 6, and operate 9 to 5:30 on Saturdays. In central London and certain other cities many stores are open until late in the evening on Thursdays. Banks are open Monday to Friday; most close at 4:30; some open on Saturday mornings.

Restaurants generally open for lunch from noon–2 PM, and for dinner 6 PM–10 PM, but practice varies; while you may be able to get lunch at 3 PM in one place, another may stop serving evening meals at 9 PM. Cafés usually operate from 9 AM to 5 PM.

Hours and dates when tourist attractions are open vary; many places close from the beginning of November through Easter, and are also closed on Sunday morning, plus one day each week. Typical hours are 10 AM–5 PM, with last admission an hour before closing. Check with the tourist office (phone numbers given for each entry) for opening times.

Pubs may stay open from 11 to 11 seven days a week, but some choose to close for the afternoons; on Sundays, English and Welsh pubs open from noon–10:30 on Sundays.

Organized tours
In London, sightseeing buses run by **London Pride** and the **Big Bus**

A London "bobby" on the beat

Company take a number of routes around the center, with commentary; for the price of a one-day ticket you can get on and off where you like; or you can save money by taking ordinary buses and using a Travelcard. The day tours can be a good way of seeing the sights, particularly for those with a crowded itinerary. Tour buses frequently circuit the sights of Oxford, Stratford-upon-Avon, Windsor, Bath, Cambridge, Edinburgh, and other historic centers. The Original London Sightseeing

Tour makes a 1.5 hour round trip (join it at Piccadilly Circus, Victoria, or Baker Street), while the London Plus tour enables the user to get on and off at will over a two-day period. Tickets for both are available on the buses or at a discount rate from the Piccadilly Circus travel information center. Special-interest **walking tours** are given daily by Original London Walks (020-7624 3978). Themes among the 300–350 walks each week include pubs, ghosts, the Beatles, and royalty, and there are trips to Oxford, Canterbury, Bath, Windsor, Salisbury, and Stonehenge. Walks last about two hours, usually starting from a tube station; reservation is not necessary. From Westminster Pier several operators offer **Thames river cruises**, west to Hampton Court, Richmond and Kew, and east to Greenwich.

Places of worship
Established churches in Britain are Protestant, but there are many Roman Catholic churches. In London, all major religions are represented. Denominational headquarters are **Westminster Abbey** (Church of England), Deans Yard, SW1, tel: 020-7222 5152, **Westminster Cathedral** (Roman Catholic), Victoria Street, SW1, tel: 020-7798 9055, **United Synagogue**, High Road, N12, tel: 020-8343 8989, **London Central Mosque**, 146 Park Road, NW8, tel: 020-7724 3363.

Police and traffic police
Telephone 999 for emergencies only; police stations are listed in the *Yellow Pages* under "Police." Traffic wardens (black and yellow uniforms) deal with everyday parking matters and sometimes direct traffic.

Post offices
Main post offices open from 9 to 5:30, Monday to Friday and 9 to 12:30 on Saturday. Many newsdealers sell stamps. Domestic letters bearing first-class stamps take a day less than those with second-class ones. First-class letter rate is the same as the rate for E.U. countries. Postcards and letters are charged at the same rate.

Mailboxes ("letterboxes") vary in size and shape but are always red

Public transportation

Air travel There are over 30 regional airports in England, Scotland, and Wales. British Airways tel: 0345 222111 and British Midland tel: 0345 554554 have networks of domestic flights, with discounts available; and domestic flights are also offered by Ryan Air tel: 0541 569569, and KLM Direct tel: 0990 074074. There are also bargain-price "no-frills" services run by EasyJet tel: 0870 600000 (internet booking available; website: www.easyjet.com).

Local buses Generally, services in rural areas are infrequent. The exception is the Isle of Wight, where bus services are excellent.

County-wide timetables and/or bus maps are available from the tourist information center for the area in which you wish to travel.

Long-distance buses Known as coaches, these serve the towns the railroads don't; fares are lower than rail, but the trip may not be as comfortable. The major national network is run by National Express reservations tel: 020-7730 3499 (or book online, website: www.gobycoach.com); numerous cards are available giving discount travel for students, families, lone parents, young persons (16–25), and the Tourist Trail Pass gives unlimited travel for a given period. The main London terminal is Victoria Coach Station, Buckingham Palace Road (near Victoria Station), SW1, tel: 020-7730 3499 (reservations). For some trips, tickets are purchased on board.

Rail The national network, formerly run by British Rail, is now in the hands of 26 private operators, each covering a different area. You can buy through tickets from any point in the country, even if it means traveling on services of more than one operator. Staff selling you tickets must sell you the cheapest ticket for that route, but the complexity of ticketing means they sometimes make mistakes. Always check services before you travel, and beware that you may not be quoted for the cheapest possible fare. Beware of weekend engineering works: regional maps showing affected services for each weekend ahead may be posted at stations. Special bus services fill in for the closed sections of line, but they add significantly to the journey time. Train tickets are subject to numerous special deals; day return or saver tickets (return within a given period) are much cheaper than two single tickets for the same journey, but are subject to time restrictions (typically not to be used before 9 AM); Saver tickets are more expensive on Fridays and certain days such as Easter and May bank holidays. Apex tickets give discounts for booking seven days or more in advance on InterCity (long-distance) journeys. A BritRail pass is a good buy if you intend to make more than one train journey. This is only available to non-U.K. residents, and gives unlimited travel over the whole network for a certain number of days. Young Persons' Railcards (for under-26s and students) and Senior Citizens' Rail-cards (for over-60s) give one-third off the full ticket price. Bicycles are carried free of charge on most services. Apart from the London–Scotland and London–Cornwall lines at peak periods, it is seldom necessary to reserve.

Season tickets and memberships

Those intending to visit a number of stately homes and castles should consider taking out a membership for the **National Trust** (N.T.) and **National Trust for Scotland** (N.T.S.) (see panel, page 102; note that membership in the N.T. entitles you to entry to N.T.S. properties, and vice versa) and/or **English Heritage** (E.H.), **Cadw** (for Wales), **Historic Scotland** (H.S.) (see panel, page 124). Membership is available at any staffed property. Many other houses are under the umbrella of the Historic Houses Association (2 Chester Street, London SW1X 7BB, tel: 020-7259 5688).

Senior citizens

Anyone aged 60 or over is entitled to a Senior Citizen's Railcard and can get discounts on admission fees.

Student and youth travel

Youth hostels These offer bargain-basement accommodations. The Youth Hostels Association (Y.H.A.) has an excellent network of hostels ranging from primitive converted primary schools to manor houses and medieval castles. Some have stunning locations, such as in the Lake District, Snowdonia, and the Scottish Highlands. There is no maximum age restriction. Accommodations are simple, usually in dormi- tories, although some hostels have family rooms; food is served at most hostels, at set times, although it is always possible to bring your own. Few establishments allow hostelers to stay in during the day; at peak times and weekends reserve ahead. You must join the Y.H.A. (unless you hold a youth hostel card from another country) in order to stay.

The central London information outlet is the Y.H.A. Shop and Y.H.A. Travel, both at 14 Southampton Street, WC2E 7HY, tel: 020-7379 0597; the head office is at PO Box 11, Matlock, Derbyshire DE4 3YX, tel: 0870 870 8808 (website: www.yha.org.uk). The Scottish Y.H.A. is based at 7 Glebe Crescent, Stirling FK8 2JA, tel: 01786 891400 (website: www.syha.org.uk).

International student cards These useful IDs help you gain reduced admission to tourist sights and places of entertainment. Young Persons' Railcards give a third off the price of under-26s and student rail tickets.

Telephones

In emergencies tel: **999** (police, fire, and ambulance); calls are free. Operator for national calls tel: **100**; for international calls tel: **155** (both free). Directory inquiries (Information) for national calls tel: **192**; for international calls tel: **153** (both free from payphones only). Calls on numbers prefixed **0800** are free.

To make a call from a public telephone, put the money in before dialing (if you put in large-denomination coins, beware: you will not get change), and collect any unspent coins when you hang up. Phone cards are useful, as many booths no longer take coins; cards can be bought from post offices and newsdealers in denominations of £3, £5 and £10. Mobile phones have become hugely popular in recent years, and "pay as you go" phones are sold at electrical shops and supermarkets. Prices vary enormously; very cheap models tend to incur high call charges, but if you are visiting Britain for a week or so this option may be practical.

The dial tone is a continuous purr, the ringing tone is a repeated *brr-brr*, and a repeated single tone tells you the line is busy; a continuous tone means the number dialed is "unobtainable" or else you will get an automated message.

To call abroad, dial 00 followed by the country's code, followed by the local number minus the initial 0.

Australia 61
Canada 1
New Zealand 63
Republic of Ireland 353
U.S. 1

Time

When it is 12 noon in Britain between the last Sunday in October and the last Saturday in March it is 8–10 PM in Australia, 4–8:30 AM in Canada, 12 noon in the Republic of Ireland, midnight in New Zealand and 4–7 AM in the U.S. The rest of the

CONVERSION CHARTS

FROM	TO	MULTIPLY BY
Inches	Centimeters	2.54
Centimeters	Inches	0.3937
Feet	Meters	0.3048
Meters	Feet	3.2810
Yards	Meters	0.9144
Meters	Yards	1.0940
Miles	Kilometers	1.6090
Kilometers	Miles	0.6214
Acres	Hectares	0.4047
Hectares	Acres	2.4710
Gallons	Liters	4.5460
Liters	Gallons	0.2200
Ounces	Grams	28.35
Grams	Ounces	0.0353
Pounds	Grams	453.6
Grams	Pounds	0.0022
Pounds	Kilograms	0.4536
Kilograms	Pounds	2.205
Tons	Tonnes	1.0160
Tonnes	Tons	0.9842

MEN'S SUITS

U.K.	36	38	40	42	44	46	48
Rest of Europe	46	48	50	52	54	56	58
U.S.	36	38	40	42	44	46	48

DRESS SIZES

U.K.	8	10	12	14	16	18
France	36	38	40	42	44	46
Italy	38	40	42	44	46	48
Rest of Europe	34	36	38	40	42	44
U.S.	6	8	10	12	14	16

MEN'S SHIRTS

U.K.	14	14.5	15	15.5	16	16.5 17
Rest of Europe	36	37	38	39/40	41	42 43
U.S.	14	14.5	15	15.5	16	16.5 17

MEN'S SHOES

U.K.	7	7.5	8.5	9.5	10.5	11
Rest of Europe	41	42	43	44	45	46
U.S.	8	8.5	9.5	10.5	11.5	12

WOMEN'S SHOES

U.K.	4.5	5	5.5	6	6.5	7
Rest of Europe	38	38	39	39	40	41
U.S.	6	6.5	7	7.5	8	8.5

year, clocks go forward one hour to British Summer Time.

Toilets
Public toilets are well signposted in town centers, and nearly all filling stations have them. Toilets in pubs and restaurants are reserved for customers.

Tourist offices
There are over 800 tourist information centers in Britain, run by regional tourist boards: most are well-marked (look for the i sign). National park visitor centers also have good local information.

The British Tourist Authority's website is www.visitbritain.com, linking on to attractions, events, and accommodations. Its U.S. office at 7th Floor, 551 Fifth Avenue, Suite 701, New York, NY 10176-0799, tel: 212-986 2266. The English Tourism Council and British Tourist Authority are at Thames Tower, Black's Road, Hammersmith, London W6 9EL, tel: 020-8846 9000, fax 020-8563 0302. English Tourism Council's website: www.TravelEngland.org.uk. The Scottish Tourist Board is at 23 Ravelston Terrace, Edinburgh EH4 3EU, tel: 0131-332 2433, fax: 0131-343 1513. Their website is found at: www.holiday.scotland.net. The Wales Tourist Board is at Brunel House, 2 Fitzalan Road, Cardiff CF2 1UY, tel: 029-2049 9909, fax: 029-2048 5031. Website: www.visitwales.com. For details of any tourist information center in Britain, tel: 0800 192192.

Walking and hiking
England and Wales are served by public rights of way open to walkers; Scotland has an informal rule tolerating access to open land except in the shooting season (see page 266). Footpaths (marked with yellow arrows) are for walkers only; bridle paths (marked in blue) are open to horseback riders and cyclists too.
Long-distance paths are indicated with acorn motifs. Guided walks are offered by numerous bodies (contact information offices for details). If you devise your own walks, you need a good map and appropriate equipment: do not underestimate the perils of the mountains (see page 168).

ACCOMMODATIONS

Tourist information centers hold lists of local accommodations, and many provide a reservation service. Bed-and-breakfast ("B&B") is ubiquitous and great value: typically it consists of a room in a private house (some have separate bathrooms) and use of a living room ("lounge"). Regional tourist boards publish lists of farmhouses, inns, and guesthouses offering B&B (including the English Tourism Council's book *Where to Stay*). Country house hotels give you the chance to stay in period country homes; many are privately run by families. Many pubs have a few rooms for overnight visitors. Generally, supply outstrips demand: provided you are prepared to drive to the next town, you will always find a bed, although be warned that the most popular resort towns and the Scottish Highlands get very busy in season. The following recommended hotels and inns are divided into three price categories, based on bed and breakfast for one person sharing a double- or twin-bedded room:

($) = inexpensive: generally under £35.
($$) = moderate: generally £35–£60.
($$$) = expensive: generally over £60.

The AA Hotel Booking Service is a free, fast and easy way to find a place for a short break, vacation, or business trip; tel: 0870 5 05 05 05. Full listings of British and Irish hotels can be found at the AA's website www.theAA.com/hotels

LONDON

Bayswater, Kensington, and Hyde Park
Delmere Hotel ($$$)
130 Sussex Gardens W2 1UB
tel: 020-7706 3344
Friendly staff, well-equipped rooms, jazz-themed bar and a comfortable lounge.
The Millennium Gloucester Hotel ($$$)
4–18 Harrington Gardens, SW7 4LH
tel: 020-7373 6030
Cosmopolitan, stylish hotel; marble bathrooms, air conditioning.
Parkwood ($$)
4 Stanhope Place, W2 2HB
tel: 020-7402 2241
Pretty hotel overlooking Hyde Park.
Thistle Hyde Park ($$$)
90–92 Lancaster Gate W2 3NR
tel: 020-7262 2711
Elegant well-cared-for "town house" style hotel.

Bloomsbury and West End
Bloomsbury Park ($)
126 Southampton Row, WC1B 5AD
tel: 020-7430 0434
Cozy hotel catering to all markets.
Thistle Trafalgar Square ($$$)
Whitcomb Street WC2H 7HG
tel: 020-7930 4477
Popular hotel adjacent to the National Gallery and convenient for many West End theaters.

Chelsea, Knightsbridge, and Victoria
Basil Street ($$$)
8 Basil Street SW3 1AH tel: 020-7581 3311
Formal, old-fashioned yet stylish.
Quality Eccleston Hotel ($$$)
82–83 Eccleston Square SW1V 1PS
tel: 020-7834 8042
A well-maintained, comfortable hotel.
The Rubens at the Palace ($$$)
Buckingham Palace Road SW1W 0PS
tel: 020-7834 6600
Luxury in an enviable location overlooking the Royal Mews behind Buckingham Palace.

Regent's Park
Hotel Ibis Euston ($$)
3 Cardington Street NW1 2LW
tel: 020-7388 7777
Popular and convenient for Euston Station, this good-value hotel also has a secure parking lot.
Kennedy Hotel ($$$)
Cardington Street NW1 2LP
tel: 020-7387 4400
Modern hotel close to Euston Station. Bar with satellite TV and all-day snacks, Spires Restaurant, meeting rooms.

Beyond the center
The Barbican Clerkenwell ($$)
Central Street EC1V 8DS tel: 020-7251 1565
Large, modern, near the Barbican arts complex and the City.
Justin James Hotel ($)
43 Worple Road SW19 4JZ
tel: 020-8947 4271
Pretty, creeper-clad Victorian house just minutes from Wimbledon station.
Thistle Tower ($$$)
St Katharine's Way E1 9LD
tel: 020-7481 2575
Modern hotel very convenient for City; fine views of Tower Bridge.

THE WEST COUNTRY

Bristol
Berkeley Square Hotel ($$$)
15 Berkeley Square, Clifton BS8 1HB
tel: 0117 925 4000
Smart Georgian hotel with tastefully decorated rooms. Near the university and art gallery.
Rodney Hotel ($$$)
4 Rodney Place, Clifton BS8 4HY
tel: 0117 973 5422
Attractive terraced hotel with brightly decorated rooms. Convenient for the city center and M5.

Cornwall
Carbis Bay Hotel ($$$)
Carbis Bay, St Ives TR26 2NP
tel: 01736 795311
Family-run hotel in fine seaside location.
Island Hotel ($$$)
Tresco, Isles of Scilly TR24 0PU
tel: 01720 422883
Modern hotel; island a refreshing getaway.

Pedn-Olva Hotel ($$)
The Warren, St. Ives TR26 2EA
tel: 01736 796222
Friendly hotel affording glorious views across
the bay.

Port Gaverne ($$)
Port Gaverne, near Port Isaac PL29 3SQ
tel: 01208 880244; freephone 0500 657867
Pleasant inn by a cove on an unspoiled coast.

Skidden House Hotel ($$$)
Skidden Hill, St Ives TR26 2DU
tel: 01736 796899
The oldest hotel in St. Ives. Cosy bedrooms,
modern facilities.

Devon

Halmpstone Manor ($$)
Bishop's Tawton, near Barnstaple EX32 0EA
tel: 01271 830321
Lovely manor house surrounded by farmland.

Holne Chase ($$$)
Two Bridges Road, near Ashburton TQ13 7NS
tel: 01364 631471
Peacefully located by the River Dart; well-
appointed rooms.

Oxenham Arms ($$)
South Zeal, near Okehampton EX20 2JT
tel: 01837 840244
Pleasant 15th-century inn in village street.

Royal Castle ($$$)
11 The Quay, Dartmouth TQ6 9PS
tel: 01803 833033
17th-century coaching inn on the quayside.

St. Olaves Court ($$$)
Mary Arches Street, Exeter EX4 3AZ
tel: 01392 217736
Georgian-style house near cathedral.

Dorset

Plumber Manor ($$$)
*Hazelbury Bryan Road, Sturminster Newton
DT10 2AF tel: 01258 472507*
Jacobean manor with 16 bedrooms.

Priory ($$$)
Church Green, Wareham BH20 4ND
tel: 01929 551666
An 800-year-old priory with riverside gardens.

Somerset

Ashwick House Hotel ($$$)
Dulverton TA22 9QD tel: 01398 323868
Grand turn-of-the-century country house in large
grounds on the edge of Exmoor.

The Oaks Hotel ($$$)
Porlock, near Minehead TA24 8ES
tel: 01643 862265
Enchanting Edwardian country house overlooking Porlock Bay.

Paradise House ($)
86–88 Holloway, Bath BA2 4PX
tel: 01225 317723
Quietly located in an elevated position, minutes
from the center.

Royal Crescent ($$$)
16 Royal Crescent, Bath BA1 2LS
tel: 01225 823333
On Bath's famous street; the interior matches
the setting.

Wiltshire

Bradford Old Windmill ($)
4 Masons Lane, Bradford on Avon BA15 1QN
tel: 01225 866842
Converted windmill with amusing decor.

Milford Hall Hotel ($$)
206 Castle Street, Salisbury SP1 3TE
tel: 01722 417411
A personally managed Georgian mansion house
close to the town center.

SOUTHERN ENGLAND

East Sussex

Adelaide ($$$)
51 Regency Square, Brighton BN1 2FF
tel: 01273 205286
Small hotel in elegant square facing on to the
seafront.

Courtlands ($$)
21–27 The Drive, Brighton BN3 3JE
tel: 01273 731055
Quietly situated, easy walk to town and
seafront; swimming pool.

Jeake's House ($$)
Mermaid Street, Rye TN31 7ET
tel: 01797 222828
Gabled, part tile-hung 17th-century house in
cobbled street.

Isle of Wight

George Hotel ($$)
Quay Street, Yarmouth PO41 0PE
tel: 01983 760331
This historic townhouse between the pier and the
castle has been decorated with great taste and
style; the restaurant is highly rated and the
brasserie is good for less formal meals.

Seaview Hotel ($$)
High Street, Seaview PO34 5EX
tel: 01983 612711
First-class, ideal for families; nautical trappings.

Kent

Ebury Hotel ($$)
65-67 New Dover Road, Canterbury CT1 3DX
tel: 01227 768433
Fine period detailing, a very comfortable lounge
and the restaurant is recommended.

Falstaff ($$)
8–12 St Dunstan's Street, Canterbury CT2 8AF
tel: 01227 462138
Old coaching inn near Westgate Tower.

Hotel du Vin & Bistro ($$)
Crescent Road, Tunbridge Wells TN1 2LY
tel: 01892 526455
Pleasantly old-fashioned hotel offering
spacious, simply decorated bedrooms.

Kennel Holt Hotel ($$$)
Goudhurst Road, Cranbrook TN17 2PT
tel: 01580 712032
Homey yet distinguished country house set in
five acres of lovely gardens.

The Limetree ($$)
The Square, Lenham, near Cranbrook ME17 2PG
Tel: 01622 859509
Fine 14th-century timber-framed house with a
relaxed, peaceful air.

Accommodations and Restaurants

Wallett's Court ($$$)
West Cliffe, St. Margaret's at Cliffe, near Dover CT15 6EW tel: 01304 852424
Old-fashioned rooms in manor house, newer ones in barn annexe.

HEART OF ENGLAND

Cotswolds
Bibury Court ($$)
Bibury, near Cirencester, Gloucestershire GL7 5NT tel: 01285 740337
Old-world Jacobean mansion by River Coln, offering a relaxed retreat.
Buckland Manor ($$$)
Buckland, near Broadway, Worcester WR12 7LY tel: 01386 852626
Top class hotel in a medieval manor.
Collin House ($$)
Collin Lane, Broadway, Worcester WR12 7PB tel: 01386 858354
Exemplary country house hotel.
Cotswold House ($$$)
The Square, Chipping Campden, Gloucestershire GL55 6AN tel: 01386 840330
Formal elegance with murals and antiques.

Herefordshire
Feathers Hotel ($$)
High Street, Ledbury HR8 1DS tel: 01531 635266
Striking, black-and-white timber-framed coaching inn with traditional interior decor.

Oxfordshire
Beetle and Wedge ($$$)
Ferry Lane, Moulsford-on-Thames OX10 9JF tel: 01491 651381
Ideal for exploring the Thames Valley.
Linton Lodge ($$)
13 Linton Road, Oxford OX2 6UJ tel: 01865 553461
Large hotel comprising several houses close to colleges and river.
Randolph ($$$)
Beaumont Street, Oxford OX1 2LN tel: 01865 247481
Large, comfortable hotel in city center.
Stonor Arms ($$–$$$)
Stonor, Henley-on-Thames RG9 6HE tel: 01491 638866
18th-century inn in peaceful village near deer park and walks. Two restaurants.
White Hart Hotel ($$$)
High Street, Dorchester on Thames OX10 7HN tel: 01865 340074
Charming, friendly inn located in historic Thameside village.

Shropshire
Cliffe Hotel ($$)
Dinham, Ludlow SY8 2JE tel: 01584 872063
Friendly hotel with castle views.
Overton Grange ($$)
Hereford Road, Ludlow SY8 4AD tel: 01584 873500
An Edwardian mansion set in attractive gardens and surrounded by the Welsh Marches.

Warwickshire
Billesley Manor Hotel ($$$)
Alcester, Stratford-upon-Avon B49 6NF tel: 01789 279955
Peacefully located 16th-century manor house.
Falcon Hotel ($$$)
Chapel Street, Stratford-upon-Avon CV37 6HA tel: 01789 279953
Traditional inn in the heart of town. Pretty gardens, cozy restaurant.
White Swan ($$$)
Rother Street, Stratford-upon-Avon CV37 6NH tel: 01789 297022
Half-timbered building with modern facilities.

EASTERN ENGLAND

Cambridgeshire
Arundel House ($–$$)
53 Chesterton Road, Cambridge CB4 3AN tel: 01223 367701
Victorian terrace by Jesus Green.
Cambridge Garden House Moat House ($$$)
Granta Place, Mill Lane, Cambridge CB2 1RT tel: 01223 259988
Modern riverside hotel, close to colleges.
George ($$$)
71 St Martins, Stamford PE9 2LB tel: 01780 750750
Splendid coaching inn; elegant public rooms and a good restaurant.
Gonville ($$$)
Gonville Place, Cambridge CB1 1LY tel: 01223 366611
Traditional hotel by Parker's Piece park.

Lincolnshire
D'Isney Place ($$)
Eastgate, Lincoln LN2 4AA tel: 01522 538881
Red-brick house (1735) offering bed and breakfast, near cathedral.

Norfolk
Beaumaris Hotel ($$$)
South Street, Sheringham NR26 8LL tel: 01263 822370
Five minutes from seafront and town.
Morston Hall ($$$ inc. dinner)
Morston, Holt NR25 7AA tel: 01263 741041
By marshes, a 17th-century brick-and-flint house; four bedrooms; great restaurant.
Maid's Head ($$)
Tombland, Norwich NR3 1LB tel: 01603 209955
Dating from 1272, England's oldest hotel in continuous use; the best bet in the city.
Quality Hotel ($$$)
2 Barnard Road, Bowthorpe, Norwich NR5 9JB tel: 01603 741161
Modern hotel on outskirts of the city.

Suffolk
Great House ($$)
Market Place, Lavenham, Suffolk CO10 9QZ tel: 01787 247431
Georgian exterior belies an ancient timber-framed structure. Only four bedrooms.

Swan ($$$)
Market Place, Southwold IP18 6EG
tel: 01502 722186
Traditional hotel; good standards of comfort.

WALES

Brecon Beacons
Gliffaes ($$)
near Crickhowell NP8 1RH tel: 01874 730371
Traditional family-run hotel, overlooking River
Usk and set in parkland; good fishing nearby.
Llangoed Hall ($$$)
Llyswen LD3 0YP tel: 01874 754525
Stylish Edwardian country house with personal
touches; classic cooking.

Monmouthshire
Celtic Manor Hotel ($$$)
Coldra Woods, Newport NP18 2YA
tel: 01633 413000
Magnificently restored 19th-century manor
house with three championship golf courses.
Crown at Whitebrook ($$–$$$)
Whitebrook NP25 4TX tel: 01600 860254
Small with pretty rooms, comfortable lounge; in
densely wooded valley.
Parva Farmhouse ($$)
Tintern, near Chepstow NP6 6SQ
tel: 01291 689411
Cozy without being cute.
Three Salmons ($$–$$$)
Bridge Street, Usk NP15 1RY
tel: 01291 672133
Charming town center coaching inn that has a
stylish appeal.

Pembrokeshire
Penally Abbey ($$$)
Penally, near Tenby SA70 7PY
tel: 01834 843033
Georgian house, close to coast, four-poster
beds; French-influenced cooking.

Powys
Lake Country House ($$$)
Llangammarch LD4 4BS tel: 01591 620202
A graceful retreat near Llandrindod Wells.

Snowdonia
Maes-y-Neuadd ($$$)
*Talsarnau, near Harlech, Caernarfonshire
LL47 6YA tel: 01766 780200*
Ancient building with splendid views.
Old Rectory ($$$)
*Llanwrst Road, Llansanffraid Glan Conwy,
Conwy LL28 5LF tel: 01492 580611*
Fine views of mountains and Conwy Castle;
gourmet dinners.
Portmeirion Hotel ($$$)
Portmeirion, Gwynedd LL48 6ET
tel: 01766 770000
Hotel fronts estuary and has lavish interior.
Princes Arms Hotel ($$)
Trefriw, Conwy, LL27 0JP
tel: 01492 640592
Family-run hotel with splendid views across the
Conwy Valley. A wonderful place to stay.

St. Tudno ($$$)
Promenade, Llandudno, Conwy LL30 2LP
tel: 01492 874411
Oustanding hospitality on the seafront.

Swansea
Fairyhill ($$$)
Reynoldston, Swansea SA3 1BS
tel: 01792 390139
Mansion with own trout stream; local dishes
feature on an ambitious menu.

NORTHWEST ENGLAND

Cheshire
Grosvenor ($$$)
Eastgate Street, Chester CH1 1LT
tel: 01244 324024
Four-star luxury hotel at the heart of the city.

The Lake District, Cumbria
Mill ($$–$$$)
Mungrisdale, near Penrith CA11 0XR
tel: 017687 79659
Cozy, informal former mill cottage.
Old Vicarage ($$$)
*Church Road, Witherslack, near Grange-over-
Sands LA11 6RS tel: 015395 52381*
Fine cooking, very comfortable; beneath
Whitbarrow Scar.
Patterdale Hotel ($$)
Patterdale, near Penrith CA11 0NN
tel: 017684 82231
Fine views of the valley and fells.
Sharrow Bay ($$$)
Lake Ullswater, near Penrith CA10 2LZ
tel: 017684 86301
One of Lakeland's most celebrated hotels,
Sharrow Bay is highly rated for comfort and
its cuisine.
Skiddaw Hotel ($$)
Main Street, Keswick CA12 5BN
tel: 017687 72071
Pleasant hotel in the heart of town. Cheerful
restaurant.
The Trout Hotel ($$$)
Crown Street, Cockermouth CA13 0EJ
tel: 01900 823591
This long established, cozy hotel is by the
banks of the River Derwent. It also has an
attractive restaurant.
Wasdale Head Inn ($$)
Wasdale Head, near Gosforth CA20 1EX
tel: 019467 26229
Long-established haunt of walkers and climbers;
in spectacular isolated position.
White Moss House ($$$ including dinner)
Rydal Water, Grasmere LA22 9SE
tel: 015394 35295
Elegant house (formerly owned by Wordsworth
family); English cuisine.

The Peak District, Derbyshire
Cavendish ($$$)
Baslow, Derbyshire DE45 1SP
tel: 01246 582311
High-class comfort in a civilized retreat in the
Chatsworth estate.

Accommodations and Restaurants

Riber Hall ($$$)
near Matlock, Derbyshire DE4 5JU
tel: 01629 582795
Charming Elizabethan manor house perched
above Derwent Gorge; period character but
modern facilities.

NORTHEAST ENGLAND

County Durham
The Postchaise Hotel ($$)
36 Market Place, Bishop Auckland DL14 7NX
tel: 01388 661296
Old town-center hostelry; lively atmosphere and
good value. Home-cooked meals.
Swallow Royal County ($$$)
Old Elvet, Durham DH1 3JN
tel: 0191-386 6821
Ample, comfortable hotel, on the river bank.
Swallow Three Tuns ($$$)
New Elvet, Durham DH1 3AQ
tel: 0191-386 4326
Old-established, comfortable city center hotel.

North York Moors, North Yorkshire
Lastingham Grange ($$$)
Lastingham YO62 6TH tel: 01751 417345
Old-fashioned, welcoming, in tranquil village.
Mallyan Spout ($$$)
Goathland, near Whitby YO22 5AN
tel: 01947 896486
Located in a village in fine walking country.

Northumberland
White Swan Hotel ($$$)
Bondgate, near Alnwick NE66 1TD
tel: 01665 602109
Elegant 300-year-old hotel in town center.

York
Abbots Mews ($)
6 Marygate Lane, Bootham YO30 7DE
tel: 01904 634866
Just outside city walls, quiet former coachman's
cottage.
Cottage ($$)
3 Clifton Green YO30 6OH tel: 01904 643711
Attractive, friendly, and 10 minutes from center.
Mount Royale ($$$)
The Mount YO24 1GU tel: 01904 628856
Two early 19th-century houses with antiques,
plants, and a welcoming atmosphere.

Yorkshire Dales, North Yorkshire
Amerdale House ($$$)
Arncliffe, near Skipton BD23 5QE
tel: 01756 770250
Manor house in beautiful setting; run with flair.
Ashfield House ($$)
Grassington, near Skipton BD23 5AE
tel: 01756 752584
Small hotel off the Square: rustic décor.
Miller's House ($$$)
Middleham, Wensleydale DL8 4NR
tel: 01969 622630
Off an enchanting village square; elegantly
furnished rooms and accomplished cooking.

SOUTHERN SCOTLAND

Borders (Scottish)
Burts Hotel ($$)
Market Square, Melrose TD6 9PL
tel: 01896 822285
This family-run country town hotel is within
easy driving distance of 16 golf courses.
Welcoming atmosphere.
Cringletie House ($$$)
Duncar Road, Peebles EH45 8PL
tel: 01721 730233
Romantic-looking country house, family-run.

Dumfries and Galloway
Balcary Bay ($$$)
Auchencairn, near Kirkcudbright DG7 1QZ
tel: 01556 640217
Small, lone hotel, pleasantly located on
Balcary Bay.
Knockinaam Lodge ($$$)
Portpatrick, Rhinns of Galloway DG9 9AD
tel: 01776 810471
Looks towards Mountains of Mourne in Ireland.

East Lothian
Greywalls ($$$)
Gullane, Muirfield EH31 2EG
tel: 01620 842144
Designed by Lutyens, overlooks golf links.

Edinburgh
Caledonian ($$$)
Princes Street EH1 2AB tel: 0131-459 9988
90-year-old former railroad hotel; grand foyer,
attractive rooms, friendly service, with castle
views.
Howard ($$$)
32–6 Great King Street EH3 6QH
tel: 0131-557 3500
Georgian terraced house in the city's New Town.
Rothesay ($$)
8 Rothesay Place EH3 7SL
tel: 0131-225 4125
Reasonably priced, family-run hotel.
Roxburghe ($$$)
38 Charlotte Square EH2 4HG
tel: 0131-225 3921
Fine example of Adam architecture minutes from
Princes Street; range of bedrooms.

Fife
Scores ($$$)
76 The Scores, St. Andrews KY16 9BB
tel: 01334 472451
In two 1880s terraces; seafront view.
Convenient for Old Course.
St. Andrews Old Course ($$$)
Old Station Road, St. Andrews KY16 9SP
tel: 01334 474371
By the famous golf course and the sea;
elegant, well-equipped, and comfortable.

Glasgow
Ewington ($$$)
132 Queens Drive, Queens Park G42 8QW
tel: 0141-423 1152
Well-equipped, friendly, overlooks the park.

Malmaison ($$$)
278 West George Street G2 4LL
tel: 0141 5721000
The bedrooms at Malmaison are both striking
and stylish, with state-of-the-art equipment
including ISDN lines and CD players.
One Devonshire Gardens ($$$)
1 Devonshire Gardens G12 0UX
tel: 0141 339 2001
Elegant hotel occupying three town houses.

Stirling
Roman Camp Country House ($$$)
Main Street, Callander FK17 8BG
tel: 01877 330003
Manor house on River Teith.
Terraces Hotel ($$)
4 Melville Terrace FK82 2ND
tel: 01786 472268
Welcoming hotel convenient for the center.

NORTHERN SCOTLAND

Aberdeenshire
Banchory Lodge ($$$)
Banchory AB31 5HS
tel: 01330 822625
Rambling Georgian house in secluded gardens;
antiques, and hearty Scottish fare.
Kildrummy Castle ($$$)
Kildrummy AB33 8RA
tel: 019755 71288
Victorian mansion by castle ruin.

Argyll and Bute
Airds ($$$ including dinner)
Port Appin, Appin PA38 4DF
tel: 01631 730236
Small hotel with views of Loch Linnhe.
Isle of Eriska ($$$)
Eriska, Ledaig by Oban PA37 1SD
tel: 01631 720371
Idyllic island setting (bridge to mainland);
putting green, croquet lawn. Pretty rooms.

Highland
Ardsheal House ($$$)
Kentallan, Glencoe PA38 4BX
tel: 01631 740227
Good base for Loch Linnhe and Glen Coe.
Arisaig House ($$$)
Arisaig PH39 4NR
tel: 01687 450210
Austere exterior, attractive interior. Imaginative
menu.
Ceilidh Place ($$)
14 West Argyll Street, Ullapool IV26 2TY
tel: 01854 612103
Bookstore, gallery, coffee and wine bar as well
as hotel; friendly owners; simple bedrooms.
Columba House ($$)
Manse Road, Kingussie PH21 1JF
tel: 01540 661402
Comfortable 19th-century manse in elevated
grounds; good home cooking.
Dunain Park ($$$)
near Inverness IV3 6JN tel: 01463 230512
Friendly house with good country cooking.

Kilcamb Lodge ($$$)
Strontian, Acharacle PH36 4HY
tel: 01967 402257
Friendly hotel with fine views of Loch Sunart.
Kinloch Lodge ($$$)
Isle Ornsay, Sleat, Isle of Skye IV43 8QY
tel: 01471 833214
Friendly Gaelic hotel; small and peaceful.
Knockie Lodge ($$$)
Whitebridge, Inverness IV1 6UP
tel: 01456 486276
Restful and "lived in" rather than elegant.
Royal Hotel ($$)
Portree, Isle of Skye IV51 9BU
tel: 01478 612525
Hotel with health and leisure facilities.

Perth and Kinross
Guinach House ($$)
By the Birks, Urlar Road, Aberfeldy PH15 2ET
tel: 01887 820251
Edwardian house, off A826, open fire, books;
fine cooking, own produce.
Killiekrankie Hotel ($$)
Killiekrankie PH16 5LG tel: 01796 473220
Delightful hotel in extensive grounds. Bedrooms
are light, and public rooms include a sun lounge
and a bar.

281

Shetland
Busta House Hotel ($$$)
Brae ZE2 9QN tel: 01806 522506
Charming 16th-century former laird's home in
its own grounds.

RESTAURANTS

Meals at the following restaurants are divided
into three price categories:
($) = inexpensive: probably under £15 per head.
($$) = moderate: probably £15–£30 per head.
($$$) = expensive: probably over £30 per head.

LONDON

For further suggestions, see page 59.

Alastair Little Soho ($$–$$$)
49 Frith Street W1V 5TE
tel: 020-7734 5183
Unassuming Soho restaurant, minimalist décor,
but high-quality dishes with Asian and
Mediterranean flavors.
Alfred ($$$)
245 Shaftesbury Avenue WC2 8EH
tel: 020-7240 2566
English, Welsh, and Scottish dishes; range of
traditional beers.
Crivelli's Garden ($$)
The National Gallery, Trafalgar Square
WC2N 5DN tel: 020-7747 2869
Accomplished innovative cooking on the
mezzanine level of the Sainsbury wing.
El Rincon ($$)
2a Pond Place SW3 6QU tel: 020-7584 6655
Inspired modern Spanish food from an up-and-
coming chef.

Accommodations and Restaurants

Le Gavroche ($$$)
43 Upper Brook Street W1Y 1PF
tel: 020-7408 0881
Superlative restaurant; a friendly atmosphere.
The Ivy ($$)
1 West Street WC2H 9NE tel: 020 7836 4751
A fashionable brasserie where regulars return
again and again; classic dishes. Reserve ahead.
J. Sheekey ($$)
28-32 St. Martin's Court WC2N 4AL
tel: 020 7240 2565
One of London's best-known seafood restaurants,
serving traditional English fish dishes.
Lindsay House ($$)
21 Romilly Street W1V 5TG
tel: 020 7439 0450
Irish chef Richard Corrigan's Celtic roots are
very evident in a gutsy, almost robust style.
Mirabelle ($$–$$$)
56 Curzon Street W1Y 8DL
tel: 020 7499 4636
First-rate classic French cooking, especially good-
value at lunch. It is essential to reserve ahead.
St. John ($$)
26 St. John Street EC1M 4AY
tel: 020 7251 0848/7251 4998
Fergus Henderson reworks traditional English
recipes and explores Mediterranean dishes.

THE WEST COUNTRY

Bristol
River Station ($$)
The Grove BS1 4RB tel: 0117 914 4434
A relaxed bistro as well as an upbeat
restaurant. The food has a Mediterranean slant.

Cornwall
The Kitchen ($$)
The Coombes, Polperro PL13 2RQ
tel: 01503 272780
Cozy cottage featuring fresh fish caught locally.
Old Custom House ($$)
South Quay, Padstow PL28 8ED
tel: 01841 532359
This attractive restaurant in the center of the
town has an imaginative fixed-price menu.

Devon
22 Mill Street ($$)
22 Mill Street, Chagford TQ13 8AW
tel: 01647 432244
The restaurant is comfortable, though small,
and the cooking is assured.
Carved Angel ($$$)
2 South Embankment, Dartmouth TQ6 9BH
tel: 01803 832465
French regional and British cuisine, with
personal touches. A national institution.
Chough's Nest ($$)
North Walk, Lynton EX35 6HJ
tel: 01598 753315
Interesting dinners in a bright, airy dining room.
Holne Chase Hotel ($$$)
Ashburton, Newton Abbot TQ13 7NS
tel: 01364 631471
Former hunting lodge; specialities include lamb
and seafood.

Old Rectory Hotel ($$$)
Martinhoe, Barnstaple EX31 4QT
tel: 01598 763368
Stylish décor and delicious home-cooked meals.
Rising Sun ($–$$)
Lynmouth EX35 6EQ tel: 01598 753223
Former smugglers' inn, now a paneled
restaurant and bar; accommodation available.

Dorset
Bistro on the Beach ($$)
*Solent Promenade, Southbourne, Bournemouth
BH6 4BE tel: 01202 431473*
Fresh seafood that draws the crowds. Reserve
some weeks in advance.
Three Horseshoes ($–$$)
Powerstock, near Beaminster DT6 3TF
tel: 01308 485328
Pleasant inn in center of thatched village.

Somerset
The Moody Goose ($$)
7A Kingsmead Square, Bath BA1 2AB
tel: 01225 466688
A stylish restaurant with modern English food.
No. 5 Bistro ($$)
5 Argyle Street,Bath BA2 4BA
tel: 01225 444499
Inventive mix of French and Far Eastern dishes,
with English specialities.

SOUTHERN ENGLAND

Berkshire
Waterside ($$$)
*River Cottage, Ferry Road, Bray, near Windsor
SL6 2AT tel: 01628 620691*
Splendid restaurant serving Mediterranean/
French cuisine; accommodations available.

East Sussex
Black Chapati ($$)
*12 Circus Parade, New England Road, Brighton
BN1 4GW tel: 01273 699011*
Indian, Thai, and Chinese influences inspire the
truly adventurous and creative menu.
Roser's ($$)
64 Eversfield Place, Hastings TN37 6DB
tel: 01424 712218
Intimate restaurant; small French-inspired
menu, excellent wines.
Star ($$)
Alfriston, near Polegate BH26 5TA
tel: 01323 870495
Famous old-world inn in charming village.
Soup, ploughman's lunch, hot dishes;
accommodations available.
Terre à Terre ($$)
71 East Street, Brighton BN1 1HQ
tel: 01273 729051
Innovative vegetarian meals.

Kent
Honours Mill ($$)
87 High Street, Edenbridge TN8 5AU
tel: 01732 866757)
Carefully prepared French-based cooking; dress
up to come here. Pretty river views.

Rankins ($$)
Sissinghurst TN17 2JH tel: 01580 713964
English dishes with a hint of the Mediterranean and Middle Eastern, using local produce.
Soho South ($$)
23 Stone Street, Cranbrook TN17 3HF
tel: 01580 714666
Country-pine chic; French-based menu that ranges from snacks to three-course meals.
Thackeray's House ($$)
85 London Road, Tunbridge Wells TN1 1EA
tel: 01892 511921
Historic house linked with William Thackeray; accomplished, uncomplicated cooking.
Whitstable Oyster Fisher Co ($$)
Horsebridge Beach, Whitstable CT5 1BU
tel: 01227 276856
The best seafood restaurant in the area. Look out for native Whitstable oysters. Reserve a table, especially at weekends.

New Forest, Hampshire
Le Poussin ($$)
The Courtyard, Brookley Road, Brockenhurst SO42 7RB tel: 01590 623063
Delicious, well-presented ingredients.

HEART OF ENGLAND

Cotswolds
Feathers ($$)
Market Street, Woodstock OX20 1SX
tel: 01993 812291
A gracious old hotel with daily menu; close to Blenheim Palace.
Harry Hare's ($–$$)
3 Gosditch Street, Cirencester GL7 2AG
tel: 01285 652375
Popular all-day eatery, from breakfast (brunch at weekends) to supper. There's a Mediterranean bias, but fish and chips, too.
Inn for all Seasons ($$)
The Barringtons, Burford OX18 4TN
tel: 01451 844324
Generous portions of home-cooked food, served in both the bar and stone-walled restaurant.
The Lygon Arms ($$$)
Broadway WR12 7DU tel: 01386 852255
Traditional fare served in the stunning Great Hall of this distinctive hotel.

Herefordshire and Worcestershire
The Evesham Hotel ($$)
Coopers Lane, Evesham WR11 6DA
tel: 01386 765566
Friendly, with acclaimed menu and wine list.
Olde Salutation ($–$$)
Weobley, near Hereford HR4 8SJ
tel: 01544 318443
Medieval inn in picturesque village; good-value Sunday lunch.

Oxfordshire
Le Manoir aux Quatr' Saisons ($$$)
Church Road, Great Milton OX44 7PD
tel: 01844 278881
Some of the finest, most inspired cooking in the land. Splendid bedrooms.

Liason ($$)
29 Castle Street, Oxford OX1 1LJ
tel: 01865 242944
Chinese restaurant; good dim sum.
Munchy Munchy ($)
6 Park End Street, Oxford OX1 1HH
tel: 01865 245710
Idiosyncratic Southeast Asian gem.

Warwickshire
The Boathouse ($)
Swan's Nest Lane, Stratford-upon-Avon CV37 7LS tel: 01789 297733
Robust, flavorful meals for theater crowds.

EASTERN ENGLAND

Cambridgeshire
Cambridge Lodge Hotel ($$)
139 Huntingdon Road, Cambridge CB3 0DQ
tel: 01223 352833
Classic cuisine in comfortable surroundings.
Midsummer House ($$–$$$)
Midsummer Common, Cambridge CB4 1HA
tel: 01223 369299
A short walk from the center; excellent wines and cheeses.
Old Fire Engine House ($$)
25 St. Mary's Street, Ely CB7 4ER
tel: 01353 662582
Eat in the quarry-tiled rear garden in summer.

283

Essex
White Hart Hotel ($$)
Market End, Coggeshall CO6 1NH
tel: 01376 561654
Traditional Italian; home-made pasta speciality.
White Hart ($–$$)
Halstead, Great Yeldham CO9 4HJ
tel: 01787 237250
Old Tudor pub serving good food and a selection of wines.

Lincolnshire
Wig and Mitre ($–$$)
30 Steep Hill, Lincoln LN2 1TL
tel: 01522 535190
Brasserie-style 14th-century inn; on a picturesque street, close to the cathedral.

Norfolk
Adlard's ($$$)
79 Upper St. Giles Street, Norwich NR2 1AB
tel: 01603 633522
Friendly service; fixed-price French menus; good-value lunches.
Brasted's ($$)
8-10 St. Andrews Hill, Norwich NR2 1AD
tel: 01603 625949
Mediterranean influences mixed with classic European, and the wine list is excellent.

Suffolk
Crown ($–$$)
90 High Street, Southwold IP18 6DP
tel: 01502 722275
Elegant posting inn with excellent fish; reservations are recommended.

WALES

Brecon Beacons
Griffin Inn ($$$)
Llyswen LD3 0UR tel: 01874 754241
Local produce features strongly in the dishes of this very popular country inn.

Snowdonia
Castle Cottage Hotel ($)
*Pen Llech, Harlech LL46 2YL
tel: 01766 780479*
Highly acclaimed cooking in delightful 16th-century cottage.
The Hotel Portmeirion ($$$)
*Penrhyndeudraeth, Portmeirion LL48 6ET
tel: 01766 770000*
Menus are in Welsh (with English subtitles).

NORTHWEST ENGLAND

The Lake District
Appleby Manor Country House Hotel ($$$)
Roman Road, Appleby-in-Westmorland CA16 6JB tel: 017683 51571
Imaginative dishes and generous portions.
The Punchbowl ($–$$)
*Crossthwaite, Kendal, LA8 8HR
tel: 015395 68237*
A 17th-century coaching inn. Fine wines and modern British cooking. Must reserve ahead.

Cheshire
Broxton Hall Country House Hotel ($$)
*Whitchurch Road, Broxton CH3 9JS
tel: 01829 782321*
A fine collection of dishes; lovely gardens.

The Peak District
Fischer's Baslow Hall ($$–$$$)
*Baslow Hall, Calver Road, Baslow DE45 1RR
tel: 01246 583259*
Innovative cuisine with Japanese touches.

NORTHEAST ENGLAND

Northumberland
Lord Crewe Arms ($$)
*Blanchland, near Consett DH8 9SP
tel: 01434 675251*
A 13th-century lodging house for monks.

North York Moors
Appleton Hall Country House Hotel ($$)
*Appleton-le-Moors YO62 6TF
tel: 01751 417227*
Reliable English dishes.
Milburn Arms Hotel ($$)
*Rosedale Abbey, Pickering YO18 8RA
tel: 01751 417312*
Imaginative use of local ingredients.

York
Devonshire Arms Country House Hotel ($$$)
*Bolton Abbey, Skipton BD23 6AJ
tel: 01756 710441*
Chef Steven Williams produces quality dishes featuring local produce.

Melton's Restaurant ($$)
*7 Scarcroft Road, YO23 1ND
tel: 01904 634341*
The cooking is Anglo-French and everything is made on the premises, including the bread.

SOUTHERN SCOTLAND

Borders (Scottish)
Burt's Hotel ($–$$)
*The Square, Melrose TD6 9PN
tel: 01896 822285*
Fine 18th-century inn with fixed-price and à la carte menus.

Edinburgh
Iggs ($$)
15 Jeffrey Street EH1 1DR tel: 0131-557 8184
Spanish and Scottish dishes.
Bonars at L'Auberge ($$)
*56 St. Mary's Street EH1 1SX
tel: 0131-556 5888*
Authentic French cuisine.
Martin's ($$)
*70 Rose Street North Lane EH2 3DX
tel: 0131-225 3106*
Unpretentious, accomplished cooking.

Fife
Peat Inn ($$$)
*Cupar, near St. Andrews KY15 5LH
tel: 01334 840206*
One of the best-known restaurants in Scotland. Classical French cuisine.

Glasgow
Buttery Restaurant ($$)
*652 Argyle Street G3 8UF
tel: 0141-221 8188*
Traditional Scottish food in opulent Victorian surroundings.
Ubiquitous Chip ($–$$)
12 Ashton Lane G12 8SJ tel: 0141-334 5007
Ex-warehouse off Byres Road; Scottish dishes (but no chips!).
Yes ($$)
*22 West Nile Street G1 2PN
tel: 0141-221 8044*
Ultra-modern dining, with an emphasis on fresh produce.

NORTHERN SCOTLAND

Perth and Kinross
Killiecrankie ($–$$)
*Pass of Killiecrankie, near Pitlochry PH16 5LG
tel: 01796 473220*
Scottish game, meat, and fish.

Highland
Hotel Eilean Iarmain ($–$$)
Isle Ornsay IV43 8QR tel: 01471 833332
Small inn looking over Sound of Sleat; home cooking; good wines.
Altnaharrie Inn ($$$)
Ullapool IV26 2SS tel: 01854 633230
Exquisite former drovers' inn; world class virtuoso dinners.

A la Ronde 78
Abbey Dore 122
Abbotsbury 77
Abbotsford 36, 219
Aberdeen 239
Aberfeldy 253
Aberystwyth 159
Aboyne 241
Adam, Robert 51
Aira Force 178
Aldeburgh 146
Alfriston 99
Allerford 79
Alloway 216
Alnwick 199–200
Altarnun 67
Althorp 137
Alton Towers 189
Amberley 20, 97
American Museum 65
Anglesey, Isle of 154
Anglesey Abbey 17, 138
Angus 215
Anstruther 230
Antony 71
Arbor Low 186
Arbroath 215
architecture 22, 28–31
Armley Mills 21
Arnside Knott 175
Arran 215
artists 38–39, 149
Arundel 97
Ashburton 73
Ashdown Forest 89, 92
Ashmolean Museum 126
Audley End House 143
Austen, Jane 36, 65, 77, 108
Avebury 65
Aviemore 256
Axbridge 85
Ayr 36, 216
Aysgarth Falls 209

Bakewell 186
Balmoral Castle 241
Bamburgh 199
Bannockburn Heritage Centre 231
Barnard Castle 209
Barnsley House Garden 118
Barra 261
Bateman's 103
Bath 63, 65–66
Battle 99
Beachy Head 98–99
Beamish: North of England Open Air Museum 21, 192, 194
Beaulieu Abbey 101
Beaumaris 154
Bedfordshire 137
Bedruthan Steps 68
Beinn Lora 238
Belvoir Castle 137
Ben Nevis 244
Berkeley Castle 119
Berkshire 89
Berwick-upon-Tweed 199
Betws-y-coed 167
Beverley 192, 194
Bewdley 115
Bewl Water 92
Bibury 119

Big Pit Mining Museum 20, 156
Bignor Roman Villa 97
Birmingham 114, 184–185
Black Country 111–112
Black Country Museum 20
Black isle 242
Blackpool 95, 176
Blaenau Ffestiniog 20, 167
Blair Castle 253
Blenheim Palace 30, 115
Blickling Hall 142
Blists Hill Victorian Town 123
Bluebell Railway 90
Bodiam Castle 99
Bodmin Moor 67
Bodnant Garden 17, 169
Bolderwood 101
Bonawe Iron Furnace 248
Bonnie Prince Charlie 246
Borders, The (Scottish) 217, 218–219
Boscastle 68
Bosham 96
Bothwell 220
Bourton-on-the-Water 120
Bowhill House 218
Bradford 192, 194–195
Bradford Industrial Museum 21
Bradford on Avon 67
Braemar 240
Branklyn 17, 252
Brechin 215
Brecon Beacons National Park 153, 155
Bridgewater Canal 128
Bridgnorth 115
Brighton 88, 90–91, 94, 95
Bristol 63, 72
Broads National Park 141
Broadstairs 91
Broadway 120
Brockick Castle 215
Brontë Parsonage Museum 197
Brontë sisters 36, 198
Buckfastleigh 73–74
Buckie 257
Buckinghamshire 113
Buckland Abbey 74
Bucklers Hard 101
Bude 68
Burford 120
Burghley House 147
Burnham Overy Staithe 142
Burnham Thorpe 142
Burns, Robert 36, 216
Burrell Collection 229
Buscot Park 118
buses and coaches 272
Bute 215
Buttermere 175, 178
Buxton 187
Byland Abbey 202

Cadw (Welsh Historic Monuments Commission) 167
Caerlaverock Castle 221
Caernarfon 167, 169
Caerphilly Castle 157
Calderdale 195
Caldey Island 165
Callander Crags 214
Callanish 260

Cambrian Mountains 159
Cambridge 137, 138–139
camping 264
canals 128–129
Canterbury 93
Cape Wrath 259
Cardiff 157
Carisbrooke Castle 100
Carlisle 176–177
Carreg Cennen Castle 155
Cartmel 179
Castell Coch 157
Castell Henllys 165
Castle Acre 140
Castle Bolton 209
Castle Drogo 73
Castle Howard 30, 195
Castle Kennedy Gardens 222
Castle Museum, York 206
Castle Rising 140
castles and manors 26–27
Castleton 186
Cawdor Castle 242
Centre for Alternative Technology 164
Cerne Abbas 76
Chalfont St. Giles 36, 116
Channel Tunnel 98, 264
Charleston Farmhouse 91
Charlestown 71
Chartwell 102–103
Chastleton House 120
Chatham Royal Naval Base 20, 96
Chatsworth House 17, 187
Chawton 36
Cheddar Gorge 64, 85
Chedworth Roman Villa 119
Chee Dale 175
Cheltenham 117
Chenies 116
Chepstow 171
Cheshire 174
Chesil Beach 77
Chester 177
Cheviot Hills 201
Chichester 96–97
Chiddingstone 107
Chilham 93
Chillingham Castle 201
Chiltern Hills 113, 115
Chipping Campden 120
Chipping Norton 120
churches and monasteries 28–29
Cinque Ports 34, 105
Cirencester 118
clans and tartans 233
Cley 142
climate 265–266
Clovelly 72
Clyde Valley 220
Coalbrookdale Furnace and Museum of Iron 123
Cockermouth 178
Coldharbour Mill 20
Constable, John 38, 148
conversion charts 274
Conwy 167, 169
Cook, Captain James 203
Cookham 39, 109
Corfe Castle 77
Cornwall 62
Corrieshalloch Gorge 258
Cotehele 71
Cotswold Wildlife Park 119
Cotswolds 113, 118–121
Coventry 112
Coxwold 36, 202
Cragside 201

Craignethan Castle 220
Cramond 226
Craster 199
Crathes Castle 17, 241
crime 266
Crinan Canal 248
Croft Castle 122
Cromarty 242
Cromford 21, 40, 186
Cuillins 254
Culloden 242
Culross 226–227
Culzean Castle 216
Cumbria 173
customs 266, 267

D-Day Museum 104
Dalby Forest 203
Dalmeny 226
Dan-yr-ogof Caves 155
Dartmoor 37, 62, 73–74
Dartmouth 74
Deal 98
Dedham 148
Deeside 240–241
Dent 209
Dentdale 209
Derbyshire 174
Derwent Water 178
Devon 62
Dickens, Charles 50, 91, 104
Dinas Island 158
disabilities, visitors with 266
Dolaucothi Gold Mines 159
Dolgellau 167–168
Dorchester 37, 75
Dornoch 258, 259
Dorset 63
Doune 231
Dounreay 259
Dove Cottage 36, 178
Dove Dale 186
Dover 88, 98
Down House 103
Drake, Sir Francis 80
Drewsteignton 73
driving 267–268
Druid's Temple 209
Drum Castle 241
Drumlanrig 222
Dryburgh Abbey 219
Dumfries and Galloway 212, 221–222
Dunblane 231
Duncansby Head 238, 259
Dunfermline Abbey 227
Dungeness 105
Dunkeld 252
Dunkery Beacon 79
Dunrobin Castle 259
Dunstanburgh Castle 199
Dunster 79
Duntisbournes 119
Dunvegan Castle 255
Durham 196
Durham, County 192

Earth Centre 192
East Anglia 136
Eastbourne 98–99
Eastwood 137
economy 14
Eden Project 67

Index

Edinburgh 213, 223–225
Edzell Castle 17, 215
E.H. (English Heritage) 124
Eildon Hills 218
Eilean Donan Castle 258
Elan Valley 159
Elgar, Sir Edward 125
Elgin 257
Ely 140
English Heritage 124
English Marches 112–113
Erddig 159
Eskdale 178
Eton 109
European Union 14
events 18
Exeter 62, 78
Exmoor National Park 78–79

F

Fairford 119
Falkland Palace 227
Felbrigg 142
Fens 136
Finchcocks 103
Finchingfield 148
Fingal's Cave 247
Firth of Forth 226–227
Fishbourne Roman Palace 96, 97
Fishguard 165–166
Fitzwilliam Museum 138
Flag Fen 147
Flamborough Head 192
Flatford Mill 148
Floors Castle 219
Fort William 244
Fortrose 242
Fountains Abbey 29, 197
Fowey 71

G

gardens 16–17
Gardens of the Rose 146
Gatehouse of Fleet 222
Glamis Castle 215
Glasgow 228–229
Glastonbury 80
Glen Coe 244–245
Glen Nevis 238
Glendurgan 16
Glenelg 258
Gloucester 117
Gloucestershire 113
Golf 230
Gordonstoun 256
government 11
Gower 153, 162
Grasmere 175, 179
Grassington 208
Great Coxwell Tithe Barn 118
Great Malvern 125
Grey Cairns of Camster 259
Grey Mare's Tail 214
Grime's Graves 140
Guisborough Priory 202

H

Haddo House 239
Haddon Hall 187
Hadleigh 148

Hadrian's Wall 193, 201
Hailes Abbey 120
Halifax 195
Hampshire 89
Hardknott Pass 178
Hardy, Thomas 37, 63, 75
Harewood House 197
Harlech 167, 169
Harris 260–261
Hartland Quay 72
Hastings 99
Hatfield House 146
Hawes 209
Hawkshead 179
Haworth 36, 197, 198
Hay-on-Wye 155
health 269
Hebden Bridge 195
Helmshore Textile Museums 21
Helmsley 202
Henley-on-Thames 109
Heptonstall 195
Hereford 122
Herefordshire 112–113
Hertfordshire 137
Hesket Newmarket 178
Hever Castle 17, 102
Hexham 201
Hidcote Manor 120
High Force 208
Higher Bockhampton 75
Highland Folk Museum 256–257
Highlands 236–237, 262
Hill House 229
Historic Houses Association 273
Historic Scotland 124
history of Britain
  Industrial Revolution 40–41
  maritime history 34–35
  monarchs 32–33
  prehistoric Britain 24–25
Holkham Hall 142
Holy Island 193, 199
Hop Farm Country Park 107
Hopetoun House 226
hotels 276–281
Houghton Hall 142
H.S. (Historic Scotland) 124
Hughenden Manor 116
Hull 192
Hunterian Art Gallery 228–229
Hutton-le-Hole 202
Hythe 105

I

Ightham Mote 103
Imperial War Museum Duxford 138
industrial museums 20–21
Ingleborough 209
Ingleton Waterfalls 193
Inner Hebrides: see Mull, Skye and islands off Oban
insurance 269
Inveraray 248
Inverewe Garden 258
Inverness 242
Iona 247
Ironbridge Gorge 20, 123
Islay 249
Isle of Man 176
Isle of Wight 89, 92, 100

J

Jamaica Inn 67
Jarlshof 251
Jedburgh 218
Jervaulx Abbey 209
John O'Groats 259
Johnson, Dr 122
Jura 249

K

Kellie Castle 230
Kelso 219
Kenilworth Castle 133
Kenmore 238, 253
Kent 88
Keswick 178
Kiftsgate Court Gardens 120
Kilmartin 249
Kilpeck Church 122
Kingley Vale 97
King's Lynn 140
Kings and queens 32–33
Kingussie 256
Kirkcudbright 222
Knockan Cliff 258
Knole 103

L

Lacock Abbey 67
Lake District 36, 39, 173, 174, 175, 178–181
Lancashire 173–174
Land's End 69
Lanhydrock House 67
Laugharne 36, 160
Launceston 67
Lavenham 148
Ledbury 125
Leeds 197
Leeds Castle 103
Legoland 109
Leicester 137
Leicestershire 137
Lewes 91
Lewis and Harris 260–261
Lichfield 122
Lincoln 141
Lindisfarne Castle 199
Linlithgow Palace 226
Linn o'Dee 240
literary heritage 36–37
Little Moreton Hall 30, 189
Little Walsingham 142
Liverpool 174, 182
Lizard peninsula 64, 70
Llanberis 20, 167
Llandrindod Wells 162–163
Llandudno 94, 167
Llangollen, Vale of 163
Llechwedd Slate Caverns 20, 167
Lochaber 244–245
Lochaline 245
Loch Awe 248
Loch Lomond 232
Loch Morar 245
Loch Ness 242
Loch Tay 253
Logan Botanic Garden 222
London
  accomodations 58, 276
  airports 264
  Apsley House 50
  art exhibitions 48

Bloomsbury 44
British Library 47
British Museum 45, 47
Buckingham Palace 43, 51, 53
Cabinet War Rooms 49
Chancery 45
Chiswick 46
Chiswick House 46, 51
churches 54
Courtauld Gallery 47
Covent Garden 44, 47, 52
day-trips 47
Design Museum 49
Dickens' House 50
Docklands 46
Eltham Palace 51
embassies and consulates 268
Fenton House 51
Gilbert Collection 47
Globe Theatre 49, 53
Greenwich 46, 47
Ham House 46, 51
Hampstead 46
Hampton Court 30, 46, 50, 51
Hermitage Rooms 47
Highgate Cemetery 46
historic houses 50–51
history 45
Horse Guards' Parade 53
HMS Belfast 49, 53
Houses of Parliament 44, 53
Imperial War Museum 49
Kensington Palace 50–51
Kenwood House 51
Kew 16, 46
Leighton House 51
Lloyds Building 45
London Aquarium 49
London Eye 49, 53
London Transport Museum 47
London Zoo 45, 48
Madame Tussaud's 48
Monument 45
Museum of London 46, 49
museums and art galleries 47–49
National Army Museum 49
National Gallery 43, 47, 52
National Maritime Museum 46, 47
National Portrait Gallery 47
Natural History Museum 48
nightlife and entertainment 55
Osterley Park 51
Planetarium 48
Public Record Office 45
pubs 59
Queen's Gallery 49
Regent's Park 45, 48
Richmond 46
Royal Festival Hall 53
Royal Mews 49
Royal Observatory 46
Shakespeare's Globe Theatre 49, 53
St. Bartholomew the Great 46, 54
St. James's Palace 53
St. James's Park 43

St. Katharine's Dock 53
St. Martin-in-the-Fields 43, 52, 54
St. Paul's Cathedral 46, 54
Science Museum 48
shopping 56–57
Sir John Soane's Museum 50
Smithfield 46
Soho 44
Somerset House 47
Southwark Cathedral 54
Spencer House 51
Spirit of London 48
street markets 57
Tate galleries 49
Theatre Museum 47, 53
tours, organized 271
Tower Bridge 45, 53
Tower of London 45, 49, 53
Trafalgar Square 42, 52
Victoria and Albert Museum 48
views 56
Wallace Collection 48
Westminster Abbey 37, 44, 54
Westminster Cathedral 54
Wetland Centre 46
Long Man of Wilmington 99
Long Melford 148
Longleat 80
Lost Gardens of Heligan 71
Lower Broadheath 125
Lower Slaughter 120
Lowry, L S 39, 183
Ludlow 124
Lullingstone 92, 103
Lulworth Cove 64, 77
Lundy Island 78
Lydford Gorge 64, 73
Lyme Hall 187
Lyme Regis 77

Machynlleth 164
Mackintosh, Charles Rennie 229
Maes Howe 250–251
Maiden Castle 75
Malham 208
Mallaig 245
malt whisky 240
Malt Whisky Trail 256, 257
Malvern Hills 125
Manchester, 183, 185
Mapledurham 116
maps 269–270
  see also Contents
Matlock Bath 187
media 270
Mellerstain House 219
Melrose 219
Mevagissey 71
Midland Motor Museum 115
Milford Haven 166
Milton Abbas 76
Milton, John 36, 116
Milton Keynes 137
Minsmere 146
Minster Lovell 120
Minterne Magna 74
Moel Fammau 158
monasteries 28–29
money 270

Monk's House 91
Monmouth 171
Monsal Dale 175, 186
Montgomery 166
Montrose 215
Morecambe Bay 173
Moretonhampstead 73
Morwenstow 68
Mount Edgcumbe 71
Mount Grace Priory 202
Mousehole 69
Mull 247

National Gallery of Scotland 224
National Gardens Scheme 17
national holidays 269
National Lighthouse Centre 70
National Motor Museum 101
National Museum of Photography, Film and Television 194
National Museum of Wales 157
National Parks 145
National Railway Museum 206
National Tramway Museum 187
National Trust 102, 144
National Trust for Scotland 102, 213
National Waterways Museum 117
Near Sawrey 178
Nelson, Lord Horatio 35, 142
Nether Stowey 82
New Forest 101
New Lanark 214, 220
New Lanark Mills 21
Newcastle-upon-Tyne 200
Newquay 69
Nidderdale 208
Norfolk 136, 142
Norfolk Broads 141
North Bovey 73
North of England Open Air Museum 21, 194
North and South Uist 261
North York Moors National Park 202–203
North Yorkshire Moors Railway 202
Northamptonshire 137
Northleach 119
Northumberland 192
  Coast 199–200
  National Park 200–201
Norwich 143, 149
Nottingham 137
Nottinghamshire 137
N.T. (National Trust) 102
N.T.S. (National Trust for Scotland) 102, 213

Oban 248
Offa's Dyke Path 153
Okehampton 74
Old Man of Hoy 251
Old Radnor Church 162
Old Sarum 83

opening hours 270–271
Orkney Islands 250
Osborne House 100
Outer Hebrides 260–261
Owletts 103
Oxford 113, 126–127

Padstow 19, 68
Painswick 17, 118, 119
Paradise Silk Mill and Museum 21
Parham House 97
Parracombe 78
Peak Cavern 187
Peak National Park 174, 186–187
Peebles 218
Pembroke 165
Pembrokeshire 153
Pembrokeshire Coast National Park 165–166
Penjerrick 16, 71
Pennines 191
Penrhyn Castle 169
Penshurst Place 102
Penwith 68, 69
Penzance 70
Perth 252
Perth and Kinross 252–253
Peterborough 147
Petworth House 101
Pevensey Castle 99
pharmacies 271
Pickering 203
Pistyll Rhayader 164
Pitlochry 252–253
Plas Newydd (Anglesey) 154
Plas Newydd (Llangollen) 164
Plockton 258
Pluscarden Abbey 257
Plymouth 80
Polesden Lacey 102
police 271
Polperro 71
Pontcysyllte Aqueduct 129
Port Isaac 68
Port Sunlight 188
Portloe 71
Portmeirion 169
Portsmouth 104
post offices 271
Postbridge 73
Potter, Beatrix 145, 178
Powis Castle 17, 166
Preseli Hills 166
Presteigne 163
Princetown 73
Prinknash Abbey 119
public transport 272
pubs 15

Quantock Hills 62, 82
Quarry Bank Mill 21, 189
Quebec House 103

Raasay 255
rail services 272–273
Ramsey Island 165
Ramsgate 91

Reeth 207, 208
restaurants 281–282
Restormel Castle 67
Ribblesdale 209
Richborough Castle 105
Richmond 208–209
Ridgeway Path 115
Rievaulx Abbey 202
Ring of Brodgar 250
Ripon 197
Rob Roy 232
Robert the Bruce 231
Robin Hood's Bay 203
Rochester 36, 96
Romney Marsh 105
Romsey 108
Rosemarkie 242
Ross-on-Wye 171
Royal Naval Base 20, 96
Royal Yacht Britannia, former 224
Royal Society for the Protection of Birds 144
Rum 255
Runswick Bay 193, 203
Rye 104–105

Saffron Walden 143
St. Abb's Head 214, 219
St. Albans 146
St. Andrews 230
St. David's 165
St. Ives 39, 69
St. Just in Roseland 71
St. Michael's Mount 70
St. Neot 67
Salisbury 63, 82–83
Saltaire 194
Sandringham 142
Sandwich 105
Scarborough 203
Scilly, Isles of 83
Scone Palace 252
Scott, Sir Walter 36, 218–219, 232
Scottish Mining Museum 21
seaside resorts 94–95
season tickets (historic houses) 273
Selborne 36
Selkirk 218
Selworthy 79
senior citizens 273
Seven Sisters 98, 99
Severn Valley Railway 115
Sezincote 120
Shakespeare, William 36, 131, 132
Sheffield 21, 192
Shetland Islands 250, 251
Shobdon 122
Shrewsbury 130
Shropshire 112
Shropshire Hills 130
Sissinghurst Garden 17
Skara Brae 250
Skegness 95
Skokholm 165
Skomer 165
Skye 254–255
Slimbridge 113, 119, 144
Smailholm Tower 219
Snowdon 167, 168
Snowdonia National Park 153, 167–170
Snowshill 120
Solva 166
Somerset 62–63
South Downs 87–88

Index/Acknowledgments

South Uist 261
Southampton 89
Southsea 104
Southwell 146
Southwold 146
Spalding 141
Spey Valley 256–257
Spurn Head 192
Staffordshire 174
Staithes 193, 203
Stamford 147
Standen 102
Stinsford 75
Stirling 231
Stoke-by-Nayland 148
Stoke-on-Trent 21, 189
Stokesay Castle 27, 124
Stonehenge 63, 83, 84
Stonor House 116
Stott Park Bobbin Mill 179
Stourhead 16, 84
Stourport-on-Severn 115
Stratford-upon-Avon 36, 131–132
student/youth travel 273
Studley Royal 17, 197
Sudbury 148
Sudeley Castle 120
Surrey 89
Sussex 88–89
Swaledale 208–209
Sweetheart Abbey 222
Sygun Copper Mine 20, 167
Symonds Yat 158

T

Tarn Hows 179
Tarr Steps 79

Teesdale 208
telephones 273
Tenby 165
Tewkesbury 117
Thames Valley 109
Thaxted 148
Thirlmere 178
Thomas, Dylan 36, 160
Thornton Dale 202
Thorpeness 146
Threave Castle and Gardens 221–222
Three Peaks 209
Tintagel 62, 68
Tintern Abbey 171
tipping 270
Tissington 186
toilets 274
Tolpuddle 76
Torridon 258
Totnes 74
tourist offices 274
Traquair House 218
Trebah 16, 71
Trelissick 16
Trerice 69
Tresco 83
Tretower 155
Trewithen 16
Tring Reservoir National Nature Reserve 115
Trossachs 232
Trooping the Colour 18
Tunbridge Wells 107
Tyne and Wear 192

U

Ullswater 175, 178
Ullapool 258

V

Valle Crucis Abbey 163
Valley of Rocks 64, 78
Verulamium 146
Veryan 71

W

Waddesdon Manor 132
Wakehurst Place 17
Walberswick 146
Walker Art Gallery 182
walking, hiking 145, 274
Walmer 98
Walpole St. Peter 140
Walsoken 140
Warkworth 200
Warwick 133
Warwickshire 113
Wast Water 178
Watercress Line 108
Watersmeet 79
The Weald 87, 103, 107
Weald and Downland Open Air Museum 96–97
Wells 84–85
Wells-next-the-Sea 142
Welsh Folk Museum 157
Welsh language 160–161, 269
Welsh Slate Museum 20, 167
Wensleydale 209
West Highland Line 245
West Highland Way 245
West Somerset Railway 82
West Wycombe 116

Western Isles 260–261
Westonbirt Arboretum 118
Weymouth 77
Wharfedale 208
Wheal Martyn 20
Whipsnade Wild Animal Park 116
Whisky 240, 256, 257
Whitby 37, 202, 203
Whithorn 222
Wicken Fen 140
Widecombe in the Moor 73
Wilton House 83
Wiltshire 63
Wimpole Hall 138
Winchcombe 120
Winchelsea 105
Winchester 89, 107–108
Windermere 179
Windsor 109
Winkworth Arboretum 17
Wisley Garden 16–17
Woburn Abbey 147
Woodstock 114
Wookey Hole 85
Worcester 125
Wordsworth, William 36, 82, 178
Wren, Sir Christopher 54
Wroxeter Roman City 130
Wye Valley 171

Y

Yarmouth, Isle of Wight 100
York 204–206
Yorkshire 191–192
Yorkshire Dales National Park 192, 207, 208–209

Picture credits

The Automobile Association would like to thank the following for their assistance in the preparation of this book.
BRIDGEMAN ART LIBRARY 38a *Fitting Out, Mousehole Harbour, 1919* by Stanhope Alexander Forbes (1857–1947) (Bradford Art Galleries and Museums/Bridgeman Art Library, London), 149a *Wood Scene 1810* by John Crome (1768–1821) (By courtesy of the Board of Trustees of the V & A/Bridgeman Art Library, London), 149b *Fishing Boats off Yarmouth* by John Sell Cotman (1782–1842) (Christie's London/Bridgeman Art Library, London). **BRITISH WATERWAYS BOARD** 128a Buckby Locks. **EYE UBIQUITOUS** Back cover. **LLANGOLLEN INTERNATIONAL MUSICAL EISTEDDFOD** 152 Dancers. **MARY EVANS PICTURE LIBRARY** 32a Charles II, 32b Elizabeth I, 32c Henry VIII, 33 Charles I, 39a J. M. W. Turner, 40a Manchester 1870, 94b bathing machine at Brighton, 94c Hastings. J. MORGAN 160a Royal National Eisteddfod of Wales, 161 Rhymney Valley. **PICTURES COLOUR LIBRARY** Spine. **RITZ HOTEL** 59b tea at the Ritz. **THE MANSELL COLLECTION** 216a Robert Burns, 246b Charles Stuart. **POWERSTOCK/ZEFA** Front cover (b) and (c). **TONY STONE IMAGES** Front cover (a).

All remaining pictures are held in the Association's own picture library (AA PHOTO LIBRARY) with contributions from: **M ADELMAN** 36a, 41, 227a, 238, 261a, 262b. **M ALLWOOD-COPPIN** 26–7, 130a, 130b. **P AITHIE** 151b. **A BAKER** 4, 20b, 64b, 69b, 112, 123c, 179, 198a, 198b, 198c, 208a, 212a, 230a, 230b, 231, 232, 252, 256. **P BAKER** 21b, 23b, 26b, 44, 60, 63, 68, 73, 74, 75b, 77, 106b, 140, 173, 186a, 187, 197a, 203a, 206a. **J BEAZLEY** 16a, 186c, 190, 194a, 194b, 196b, 199, 200, 214, 216b, 217, 221, 222b, 237, 249a, 259. **A W BESLEY** 5b, 70c, 71a. **M BIRKITT** 5c, 28b, 65a, 84, 95a, 111b, 131, 135b. **E A BOWNESS** 18a, 173b, 243. **P & G BOWATER** 229b. **P BROWN** 12b, 86, 88b, 90, 91, 97a, 99, 104a, 105. **D BURCHILL** 37a, 176a. **I. BURGUM** 110a, 123a, 123b, 124b, 150, 155a, 156a, 157a, 162, 164a, 165a, 165b, 167, 168, 169a, 169b, 171b, 269. **J CARNIE** 233a, 245a, 245b, 253c, 258. **T COHEN** 263b. **D CORRANCE** 225, 233b. **D CROUCHER** 159a, 163, 164b, 222a. **P DAVIES** 146, 147. **S DAY** 8a, 176, 236. **P EDEN** 50b. **P ELLIOTT** 224, 226–7. **P ENTICKNAP** 108. **R FLETCHER** 34b. **D. FORSS** 15a, 30b, 50, 81b, 89, 92, 95b, 98, 102b, 103, 109a, 109b, 128b, 142a. **S GIBSON PHOTOGRAPHY** 213, 220, 228, 229a. **J GRAVELL** 166. **V GREAVES** 132. **S GREGORY** 202a. **A GRIERLY** 154b. **J HENDERSON** 211b, 235. **A J HOPKINS** 25, 82–3, 171a, 193. **R JOHNSON** 250, 251. **C. JONES** 115, 117. **P KENWARD** 275b. **A LAWSON** 23, 61b, 69a, 70a, 70b, 116, 126–7, 144b. **S & O MATHEWS** 191b. **J McCRAE** 125b. **E MEACHER** 5a, 65b. **C MOLYNEUX** 209a. **R MORT** 12a, 14a, 54b, 272. **J MORRISON** 192, 209b. **R MOSS** 79. **R NEWTON** 21a, 37, 80a, 85, 143a, 158, 160b, 189, 206b. **D NOBLE** 17, 93, 104b, 106. **K PATERSON** 215, 249b. **A PERKINS** 156. **J PERRIN** 153. **N RAY** 19, 62, 67. **P. SHARPE** 3, 175, 178, 219, 240, 248. **M SHORT** 110b, 118a, 119. **B SMITH** 11a, 45, 56a, 59a. **A SOUTER** 10a, 24a, 72, 81a, 118b, 120, 136. **F STEPHENSON** 18b. **R STRANGE** 11b, 13b, 14b, 43b, 46, 48, 51, 57a, 57b, 185. **R. SURMAN** 28a, 113. **D TARN** 207. **M TAYLOR** 223. **T D TIMMS** 27. **M TRELAWNY** 7a, 47, 54a, 58b, 96, 241, 271. **P. TRENCHARD** 35b. **R VICTOR** 13a. **W. VOYSEY** 9b, 16b, 22b, 34a, 35a, 38–9, 49, 53b, 78, 82b, 87, 88a, 101a, 107b, 156b, 157b. **R. WEIR** 6, 7b, 239, 244a, 254, 257, 260. **J. WELSH** 114, 184. **L WHITWAM** 10b, 30a, 40b, 129, 138a, 138b, 143, 177, 182, 183a, 183b, 184a, 185a, 186b, 188a, 188b, 188c, 195, 201, 204, 206c, 208b, 266, 268, 275. **H WILLIAMS** 24b, 29, 64a, 122a, 122b, 207. **P WILSON** 55, 56b, 58a. **T WOODCOCK** 9.

Contributors

Original copy editor: Sue Gordon
Revision verifier: Tim Locke